MASTER INDEX
An Illustrated Guide

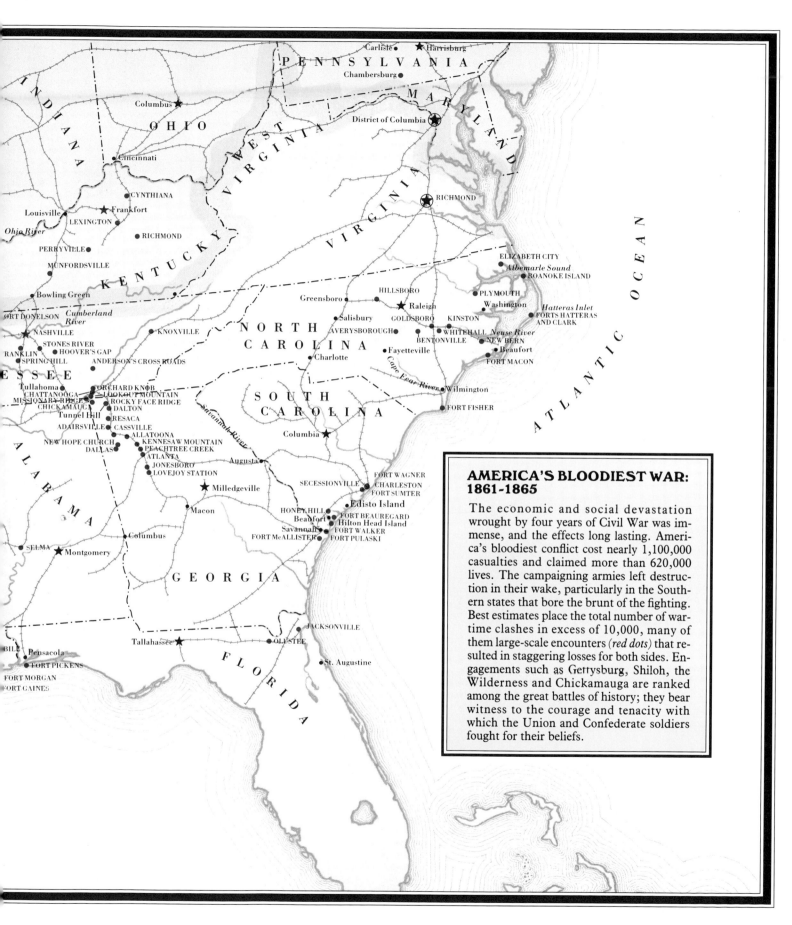

PENNSYLVANIA

Carlisle • ★ Harrisburg
Chambersburg •

MARYLAND

Columbus ★

OHIO

WEST VIRGINIA

District of Columbia ★

INDIANA

Cincinnati •

VIRGINIA

★ RICHMOND

CYNTHIANA •

Louisville •
★ Frankfort
LEXINGTON •

Ohio River

• RICHMOND

PERRYVILLE •

KENTUCKY

ELIZABETH CITY •
Albemarle Sound
• ROANOKE ISLAND

MUNFORDSVILLE •

• PLYMOUTH

Bowling Green •

Cumberland River

HILLSBORO •

Greensboro •

Washington •

Hatteras Inlet
• FORTS HATTERAS AND CLARK

ORT DONELSON

★ Raleigh

• Salisbury

GOLDSBORO
KINSTON •

Neuse River

NASHVILLE ★

KNOXVILLE •

NORTH
CAROLINA

AVERYSBOROUGH •

• WHITEHALL
BENTONVILLE •

• NEW BERN

STONES RIVER •
HOOVER'S GAP •

RANKLIN •
• SPRING HILL

ANDERSON'S CROSS ROADS •

• Charlotte

Fayetteville •

• Beaufort

FORT MACON •

ESSEE

Tullahoma •
CHATTANOOGA
MISSIONARY RIDGE
CHICKAMAUGA
Tunnel Hill •

ORCHARD KNOB
LOOKOUT MOUNTAIN
ROCKY FACE RIDGE
• DALTON
RESACA

Cape Fear River

Wilmington •

SOUTH
CAROLINA

ADAIRSVILLE • • CASSVILLE
ALLATOONA •

Savannah River

• FORT FISHER

NEW HOPE CHURCH
DALLAS •
KENNESAW MOUNTAIN
PEACHTREE CREEK
ATLANTA •

Columbia ★

ALABAMA

JONESBORO •
• LOVEJOY STATION

Augusta •

FORT WAGNER •

★ Milledgeville

SECESSIONVILLE •
• CHARLESTON
FORT SUMTER •

Edisto Island •

• Macon

HONEY HILL •
Beaufort •
FORT BEAUREGARD •
Hilton Head Island •

SELMA •

• Columbus

Savannah •
FORT McALLISTER • • FORT PULASKI

FORT WALKER •

★ Montgomery

GEORGIA

ATLANTIC OCEAN

JACKSONVILLE •

BILE •
Pensacola •
• FORT PICKENS

Tallahassee ★

• OLUSTEE

FLORIDA

FORT MORGAN
FORT GAINES

• St. Augustine

AMERICA'S BLOODIEST WAR: 1861-1865

The economic and social devastation wrought by four years of Civil War was immense, and the effects long lasting. America's bloodiest conflict cost nearly 1,100,000 casualties and claimed more than 620,000 lives. The campaigning armies left destruction in their wake, particularly in the Southern states that bore the brunt of the fighting. Best estimates place the total number of wartime clashes in excess of 10,000, many of them large-scale encounters (*red dots*) that resulted in staggering losses for both sides. Engagements such as Gettysburg, Shiloh, the Wilderness and Chickamauga are ranked among the great battles of history; they bear witness to the courage and tenacity with which the Union and Confederate soldiers fought for their beliefs.

Scale in Miles

0   150   300   450   600

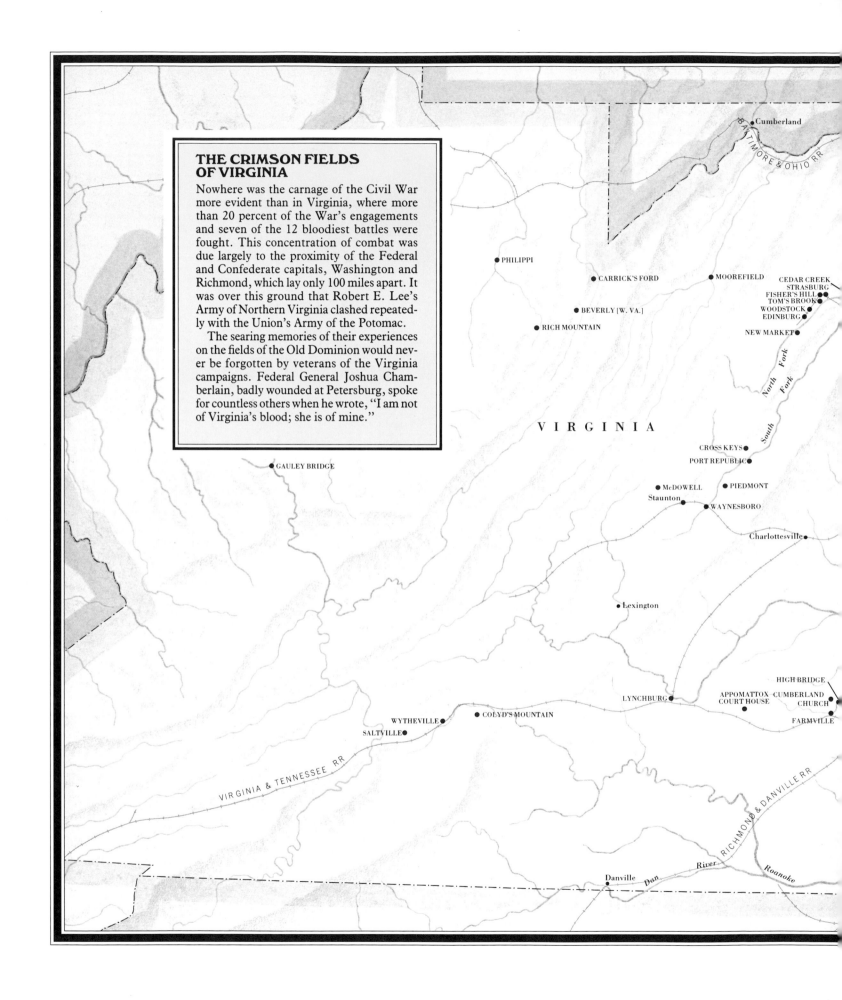

THE CRIMSON FIELDS OF VIRGINIA

Nowhere was the carnage of the Civil War more evident than in Virginia, where more than 20 percent of the War's engagements and seven of the 12 bloodiest battles were fought. This concentration of combat was due largely to the proximity of the Federal and Confederate capitals, Washington and Richmond, which lay only 100 miles apart. It was over this ground that Robert E. Lee's Army of Northern Virginia clashed repeatedly with the Union's Army of the Potomac.

The searing memories of their experiences on the fields of the Old Dominion would never be forgotten by veterans of the Virginia campaigns. Federal General Joshua Chamberlain, badly wounded at Petersburg, spoke for countless others when he wrote, "I am not of Virginia's blood; she is of mine."

VIRGINIA

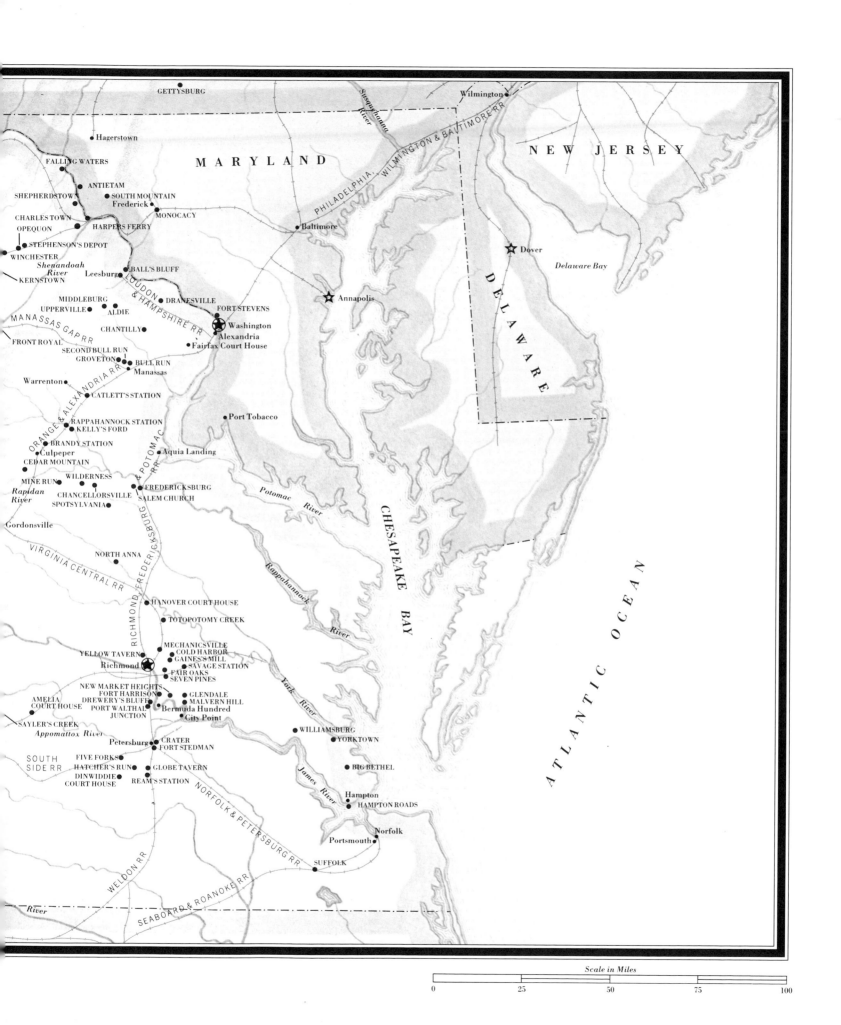

GETTYSBURG

NEW JERSEY

Wilmington

Susquehanna River

MARYLAND

PHILADELPHIA, WILMINGTON & BALTIMORE RR

Hagerstown

FALLING WATERS

ANTIETAM

SHEPHERDSTOWN   SOUTH MOUNTAIN
Frederick

CHARLES TOWN   MONOCACY
OPEQUON   HARPERS FERRY

Baltimore

Dover

STEPHENSON'S DEPOT

WINCHESTER

DELAWARE

Delaware Bay

Shenandoah River   Leesburg   BALL'S BLUFF

KERNSTOWN

MIDDLEBURG   DRANESVILLE

UPPERVILLE   ALDIE   FORT STEVENS

Annapolis

MANASSAS GAP RR   CHANTILLY   Washington
Alexandria
FRONT ROYAL   SECOND BULL RUN   Fairfax Court House
GROVETON   BULL RUN
Manassas

Warrenton   CATLETT'S STATION

Port Tobacco

RAPPAHANNOCK STATION
KELLY'S FORD

BRANDY STATION
Culpeper   Aquia Landing
CEDAR MOUNTAIN

MINE RUN   WILDERNESS

Rapidan River   CHANCELLORSVILLE   FREDERICKSBURG
SALEM CHURCH
SPOTSYLVANIA

CHESAPEAKE BAY

Potomac River

Gordonsville

VIRGINIA CENTRAL RR   NORTH ANNA

Rappahannock River

ATLANTIC OCEAN

HANOVER COURT HOUSE

TOTOPOTOMY CREEK

MECHANICSVILLE
COLD HARBOR
YELLOW TAVERN   GAINES'S MILL
Richmond   SAVAGE STATION
FAIR OAKS
SEVEN PINES
NEW MARKET HEIGHTS
FORT HARRISON   GLENDALE
AMELIA   DREWERY'S BLUFF   MALVERN HILL
COURT HOUSE   PORT WALTHALL   Bermuda Hundred
JUNCTION   City Point
SAYLER'S CREEK
Appomattox River
Petersburg   CRATER
FORT STEDMAN
SOUTH   FIVE FORKS
SIDE RR   HATCHER'S RUN   GLOBE TAVERN
DINWIDDIE   REAM'S STATION
COURT HOUSE

York River

WILLIAMSBURG
YORKTOWN

BIG BETHEL

James River

Hampton
HAMPTON ROADS

NORFOLK & PETERSBURG RR

Norfolk
Portsmouth

WELDON RR

SUFFOLK

River

SEABOARD & ROANOKE RR

Scale in Miles

0   25   50   75   100

Other Publications:

TRUE CRIME
THE AMERICAN INDIANS
THE ART OF WOODWORKING
LOST CIVILIZATIONS
ECHOES OF GLORY
THE NEW FACE OF WAR
HOW THINGS WORK
WINGS OF WAR
CREATIVE EVERYDAY COOKING
COLLECTOR'S LIBRARY OF THE UNKNOWN
CLASSICS OF WORLD WAR II
TIME-LIFE LIBRARY OF CURIOUS AND UNUSUAL FACTS
AMERICAN COUNTRY
VOYAGE THROUGH THE UNIVERSE
THE THIRD REICH
THE TIME-LIFE GARDENER'S GUIDE
MYSTERIES OF THE UNKNOWN
TIME FRAME
FIX IT YOURSELF
FITNESS, HEALTH & NUTRITION
SUCCESSFUL PARENTING
HEALTHY HOME COOKING
UNDERSTANDING COMPUTERS
LIBRARY OF NATIONS
THE ENCHANTED WORLD
THE KODAK LIBRARY OF CREATIVE PHOTOGRAPHY
GREAT MEALS IN MINUTES
PLANET EARTH
COLLECTOR'S LIBRARY OF THE CIVIL WAR
THE EPIC OF FLIGHT
THE GOOD COOK
WORLD WAR II
HOME REPAIR AND IMPROVEMENT
THE OLD WEST

This volume is one of a series that chronicles in full
the events of the American Civil War, 1861-1865.
Other books in the series include:

Brother against Brother: The War Begins
First Blood: Fort Sumter to Bull Run
The Blockade: Runners and Raiders
The Road to Shiloh: Early Battles in the West
Forward to Richmond: McClellan's Peninsular Campaign
Decoying the Yanks: Jackson's Valley Campaign
Confederate Ordeal: The Southern Home Front
Lee Takes Command: From Seven Days to Second Bull Run
The Coastal War: Chesapeake Bay to Rio Grande
Tenting Tonight: The Soldier's Life
The Bloodiest Day: The Battle of Antietam
War on the Mississippi: Grant's Vicksburg Campaign
Rebels Resurgent: Fredericksburg to Chancellorsville
Twenty Million Yankees: The Northern Home Front
Gettysburg: The Confederate High Tide
The Struggle for Tennessee: Tupelo to Stones River
The Fight for Chattanooga: Chickamauga to Missionary Ridge
Spies, Scouts and Raiders: Irregular Operations
The Battles for Atlanta: Sherman Moves East
The Killing Ground: Wilderness to Cold Harbor
Sherman's March: Atlanta to the Sea
Death in the Trenches: Grant at Petersburg
War on the Frontier: The Trans-Mississippi West
The Shenandoah in Flames: The Valley Campaign of 1864
Pursuit to Appomattox: The Last Battles
The Assassination: The Death of the President
The Nation Reunited: War's Aftermath

The Cover: Few episodes in history have inspired as
voluminous a body of writing as has the American
Civil War. The decades following Appomattox
saw the publication of countless diaries, memoirs and
regimental histories by veterans eager to recount
their wartime experiences. Many shared the obliga-
tion felt by former Confederate Colonel William
Oates, who called his history of the War "a duty that
I owe to those who participated, to their children
and to the generations who succeeded them."

For information on and a full description of any of
the Time-Life Books series listed on this page, please call
1-800-621-7026 or write:
Reader Information
Time-Life Customer Service
P.O. Box C-32068
Richmond, Virginia 23261-2068

THE CIVIL WAR

MASTER INDEX

BY THE

EDITORS OF TIME-LIFE BOOKS

An Illustrated Guide

TIME-LIFE BOOKS, ALEXANDRIA, VIRGINIA

TIME-LIFE BOOKS

EDITOR-IN-CHIEF: Thomas H. Flaherty

Director of Editorial Resources: Elise D. Ritter-Clough
Executive Art Director: Ellen Robling
Director of Photography and Research:
John Conrad Weiser
Editorial Board: Dale M. Brown, Janet Cave, Roberta
Conlan, Robert Doyle, Laura Foreman, Jim Hicks,
Rita Thievon Mullin, Henry Woodhead
Assistant Director of Editorial Resources: Norma E. Shaw

PRESIDENT: John D. Hall

Vice President and Director of Marketing: Nancy K.
Jones
Editorial Director: Russell B. Adams, Jr.
Director of Production Services: Robert N. Carr
Production Manager: Prudence G. Harris
Supervisor of Quality Control: James King

Editorial Operations
Production: Celia Beattie
Library: Louise D. Forstall
Computer Composition: Deborah G. Tait (Manager),
Monika D. Thayer, Janet Barnes Syring,
Lillian Daniels
Interactive Media Specialist: Patti H. Cass

Time-Life Books is a division of Time Life
Incorporated

PRESIDENT AND CEO: John M. Fahey, Jr.

The Civil War

Series Director: Thomas H. Flaherty
Designer: Edward Frank
Series Administrator: Judith W. Shanks

Editorial Staff for *Master Index*
Associate Editor: Jane N. Coughran (pictures)
Index Coordinator: Elizabeth Graham
Staff Writers: Margery A. duMond, John Newton,
Brian C. Pohanka
Researchers: Harris Andrews, Kristin Baker
Assistant Designer: William Alan Pitts
Copy Coordinator: Ruth Baja Williams
Picture Coordinator: Betty H. Weatherley
Editorial Assistants: Donna Fountain, Alice T. Pascual

Correspondents: Elisabeth Kraemer-Singh (Bonn);
Maria Vincenza Aloisi (Paris); Ann Natanson (Rome).
The master index for the Civil War series was com-
piled from the indexes of the individual volumes,
which were prepared by Nicholas J. Anthony and Roy
Nanovic. The editors also wish to thank Luke Hodg-
son of the Data Imaging Group of William Byrd Press,
Inc. for his valuable assistance.

The Consultants:

Colonel John R. Elting, USA (Ret.), a former Associate
Professor at West Point, is the author of *Battles for Scandi-
navia* in the Time-Life Books World War II series and of
*The Battle of Bunker's Hill, The Battles of Saratoga, Mili-
tary History and Atlas of the Napoleonic Wars, American
Army Life* and *The Superstrategists.* Co-author of *A Dic-
tionary of Soldier Talk,* he is also editor of the three volumes of *Military Uniforms in America, 1755-1867,* and associate editor of *The West Point Atlas of American Wars.*

William A. Frassanito, a Civil War historian and lecturer
specializing in photograph analysis, is the author of two
award-winning studies, *Gettysburg: A Journey in Time* and
*Antietam: The Photographic Legacy of America's Bloodiest
Day,* and a companion volume, *Grant and Lee, The Virginia Campaigns.* He has also served as chief consultant to the
photographic history series *The Image of War.*

Les Jensen, Director of the Second Armored Division
Museum, Fort Hood, Texas, specializes in Civil War artifacts and is a conservator of historic flags. He is a contribu-
tor to *The Image of War* series, consultant for numerous
Civil War publications and museums, and a member of
the Company of Military Historians. He was formerly Curator of the U.S. Army Transportation Museum at Fort
Eustis, Virginia, and before that Curator of the Museum
of the Confederacy in Richmond, Virginia.

Michael McAfee specializes in military uniforms and has
been Curator of Uniforms and History at the West Point
Museum since 1970. A fellow of the Company of Military
Historians, he coedited with Colonel Elting *Long Endure:
The Civil War Years,* and he collaborated with Frederick
Todd on *American Military Equipage.* He is the author of
Artillery of the American Revolution, 1775-1783, and has
written numerous articles for *Military Images Magazine.*

James P. Shenton, Professor of History at Columbia University, is a specialist in 19th-century American political
and social history, with particular emphasis on the Civil
War period. He is the author of *Robert John Walker* and
Reconstruction South.

Library of Congress Cataloguing in Publication Data
   Master index.
   (The Civil War)
   1. United States — History — Civil War, 1861-1865 —
Indexes. 2. Civil War — Indexes. 3. United States —
History — Civil War, 1861-1865 — Art and the war.
4. United States — History — Civil War, 1861-1865 —
Portraits. 5. United States — History — Civil War, 1861-
1865 — Pictorial works. I. Time-Life Books.
II. Series: Civil War.
Z1242.C57 1987 [E4687]   973.7   87-10171
ISBN 0-8094-4796-7
ISBN 0-8094-4797-5 (lib. bdg.)

CONTENTS

Essay
The Great Conflict Captured on Canvas 10

INDEX 38

Essay
Treasured Images of the Unknown 126

APPENDIX 136

Essay
Artistry with a Camera 146

ACKNOWLEDGMENTS
174

PICTURE CREDITS
174

The Great Conflict Captured on Canvas

Federal artillerymen wrestle a gun and limber down a muddy Virginia road in William Trego's painting *Battery of Light Artillery en Route*. Trego overcame the

Through the Civil War and the decades that followed, many of the nation's most talented artists recreated the drama of the great conflict on canvas. Some, such as Winslow Homer and Edwin Forbes, had followed the armies as newspaper artists. Others, such as Conrad Wise Chapman and Julian Scott, drew on their military experiences for inspiration. William Trego and Gilbert Gaul were among the postwar painters who were too young to have witnessed the War firsthand. They collected period artifacts to authenticate their work.

The artists seldom received the recognition accorded wartime photographers, yet their paintings conveyed the excitement of battle, a feat unmatched by the cameras of the day. *Harper's Weekly* paid tribute to these "skillful and devoted artists," and concluded, "their faithful fingers, depicting the scene, have made us a part also."

handicap of a partially crippled body to become one of the most respected American artists of the late 19th Century.

A water color titled *Equipment* by Confederate veteran William Ludwell Sheppard, depicts a young Southern woman fitting her beau with a havelock — a linen cap cover popular with troops of both sides during the early months of the War.

In a scene (*opposite*) repeated in countless towns throughout the North, civilians bid farewell to a trainload of Federal infantry bound for the front. *The Departure* was painted in 1864 by an obscure artist named G. Grato; it is his only known work.

A Federal brigade commanded by General Winfield Scott Hancock (*on brown horse at left*) repulses a Confederate attack at Williamsburg in 1862. The action, which

earned Hancock the sobriquet "The Superb," was painted by Julian Scott, who had won the Medal of Honor while serving as a drummer boy in the 3rd Vermont.

Federal soldiers huddle around a campfire during a torrential downpour in Winslow Homer's 1871 oil painting *A Rainy Day in Camp*. The most accomplished artist

to emerge from the Civil War, Homer based much of his work on sketches made during a visit to the Army of the Potomac in the spring of 1862.

Artist Julian Scott studied period photographs and drew upon memories of his wartime experiences to portray Colonel

Robert B. Potter leading the 51st New York in a successful assault at the Battle of Antietam.

Confederate gunners fight on amidst the wreck of their battery in a heroic mural inspired by the battle of Fredericksburg in December 1862. The

painting, by the French-born artist Charles Hoffbauer, flanks a doorway in Battle Abbey, a memorial to Confederate troops in Richmond.

On the night of March 14, 1863, a Federal flotilla led by Admiral David Farragut's flagship, the *Hartford*, launches an unsuccessful attack on heavily fortified Port Hudson, Louisiana. The scene was painted a year after the fight by Edward E. Arnold, a New Orleans artist who specialized in maritime subjects.

Carrying the flag of the 1st Pennsylvania Reserves, General Samuel W. Crawford (*on horseback, right center*) leads a charge on the second day of the Battle of

Gettysburg. One of a series of paintings by Peter Frederick Rothermel, it was commissioned by the Pennsylvania legislature to commemorate the Union victory.

Edwin Forbes, a wartime artist for *Frank Leslie's Illustrated Newspaper*, used his field sketches as a basis for this post-war painting of rain-swept Federal soldiers in pursuit of Lee's Confederates after the Battle of Gettysburg.

A semisubmersible Confederate torpedo boat known as a "David" lies moored beside a city wharf during the siege of Charleston.

The scene was painted by Conrad Wise Chapman, a talented young artist serving with the 59th Virginia.

Artist James Walker relied on his wartime sketches to render this 13-by-30-foot painting of the Battle of Lookout Mountain. Completed in 1874, the canvas was purchased by General Joseph Hooker, who is shown at center mounted on a white horse and conferring with artillery Major John Reynolds.

In 1869, Union veteran Edward Lamson Henry
painted this view of Westover, a palatial Georgian mansion on the James River that had been used
as a signal station by Federal troops during Grant's
Richmond campaign. Henry based the work
upon sketches he had made while camped near the
house five years earlier.

A Federal battery gallops into action near Richmond
in 1864, in this oil painting by Swedish-
born artist Thure de Thulstrup. Thulstrup became a
prolific illustrator of military themes
after emigrating to the United States in 1873.

Proudly bearing their tattered colors, survivors of the Irish Brigade stand on the deck of a troopship entering New York Harbor at the end of the War. Thomas Waterman Wood's *Return of the Flags* was one of many works done to commemorate the home-coming of the triumphant Federal armies.

In Gilbert Gaul's *Faithful unto
Death*, a cavalry horse stands guard
over its fallen rider. Although Gaul
was not a veteran of the War, his
renditions of Confederate subjects
made him one of the most popular
illustrators in the postwar South.

INDEX

Beginning here and continuing for the next 87 pages is a comprehensive index to the 27 volumes of the Civil War series. At the bottom of each page is a key that explains the abbreviations used to represent the various volumes. Page numbers in roman type denote text references; those in italic type indicate illustrations.

Homes in Alexandria, Virginia, used as hospitals for Federal troops

Major General Adelbert Ames, division commander in XXIV Corps and Medal of Honor recipient

A

A and A, BL 24
Abatis, DE 144-145, FO 109
Abbeville, South Carolina, NA 18
Abbot, Henry L., TR 65, *138*
Abbott, Albert, TR *62*
Abbott, Henry, RE 53
Abbott, Henry L., KI 78, *171*
Abilene, Kansas, NA 91
Abingdon (Virginia) *Democrat,* FI 28
Abolitionist movement, BR 30-31, 34-35, 38-40, *40, 41,* 44, 46-47, 62-69, 70-76, 89, 108-109
Abolitionists, SP 141, 142, 148
Absence without leave, TT 65
Academy of Music, YA *53, 141*
Ackerman, Richard, TT 101
Ackworth, Georgia, AT 60
Acton, Minnesota, FR 77, 83, *89*
Acushnet River, BR *20-21*
Acworth, Georgia, SM 19
Adairsville, Georgia, AT 48
Adams, Charles Francis, BL *127,* NA 77, 111; and *Trent* Affair, BL 114, 116, 118-119; and warship construction, BL 121, 125-128
Adams, Charles Francis, Jr., KI 22
Adams, Daniel W., TE 129, 130
Adams, Henry, BL 67, 114, 118, 121, 126, NA 77, 83, 88, 108
Adams, John, SM 114, 115, *119;* death of, SM *114,* 115
Adams, John Quincy, BR 34, 101, 108
Adams, Robert N., AT 99
Adams Express Company, AS 26
Adams hand grenade, SP *163*
Adams revolver, FI *75*
Agassiz, Louis, BR 49
Agricultural production: national, BR 9; Northern states, BR *20-21;* Southern states, BR 10, 29, 31-32
Agriculture: exports, YA 63; farm machinery destroyed, OR 3; government program for, OR 29; production expansion, YA 2, 20, 56, 62-63; tax in kind on, OR 83; tools for, OR 26; women in production, YA 62. *See also* Farmers; Planters
Agrippina, BL 149
Aiken, Frederick, AS 148, 157
Aiken's Landing, Virginia, TR 134, 139
Akerman, Amos, NA 97, 99
Akin, Warren, OR 11
Akron, Ohio, NA 79
Alabama: anti-Klan laws, NA 97-98; civil disorders, OR 149; Confederacy proposed by, BR 128; conscription evaded in, OR 80; deserters in, OR 89; education, NA 120; educational system, OR 55; federal property seized by, BR 129; as iron source, OR 29; loan to government, OR 30; Mitchel's operations in, TE 14;

money issues, OR 72; niter production, OR 20; operations in, SH 8, 98-99; readmission to Union, NA 69; refugees in, OR 121, 123; in secessionist movement, BR 3, 24, 128; slave impressments, OR 23; slave uprisings, OR 150; troops withheld by, OR 155; violence in, NA 28; voting fraud in, NA 145; Wilson's campaign in, AP 160-161, *map 161*
Alabama, NA *126;* characteristics and armament, BL *18,* 121, 149, *153,* 155-156; construction and repair, BL 121, *123,* 149, 155-157; itinerary, BL *map 154; Kearsarge,* battle with, BL 155, *156,* 157-160, 162, *map 163, 164-171;* ships captured and destroyed by, BL 131, 142, 146, *148,* 149-155, 160
Alabama River, CO 143
Alabama troops, AP 85, AT 51, 54, *82-83,* BD 51, *52-53,* CH 142, FL 120, FO 141, GE 45, 53, 74, 76, 79, 162, MI *93,* RE 154, TE 118, TR 88, 149, TT 56, 113; at Bull Run, FI 132-135, 138-140; Raccoon Roughs, FO 141
    Infantry: 1st Infantry Battalion, CH 67; 2nd Infantry Battalion, CH 68; 3rd Infantry Regiment, FO 164, LE 70; 4th Infantry Regiment, FI 132-135, 138-140, GE 80; 5th Infantry Regiment, BD 103, KI 71, LE 39-42; 6th Infantry Regiment, BD 95-96, 101-103, FO 141; 8th Infantry Regiment, RE 38; 9th Infantry Regiment, FO 110, RE 154-155; 10th Infantry Regiment, TT 62; 11th Infantry Regiment, LE 59; 12th Infantry Regiment, AP 93; 15th Infantry Regiment, CH 65, DE 164, GE 77, 80, *81,* 83-84, KI 165, 167, LE 42, 131, 141, SM *98;* 16th Infantry Regiment, SM 122; 18th Infantry Regiment, CH 50; 20th Infantry Regiment, CH 133; 22nd Infantry Regiment, SH 141; 23rd Infantry Regiment, MI 102; 25th Infantry Regiment, AT 135; 26th Infantry Regiment, BD 52; 30th Infantry Regiment, MI 130; 33rd Infantry Regiment, SM 122; 38th Infantry Regiment, AT *43;* 42nd Infantry Regiment, MI 41; 44th Infantry Regiment, GE 80; 45th Infantry Regiment, AT 111-112; 47th Infantry Regiment, AT 48; 48th Infantry Regiment, TR *98;* 59th Infantry Regiment, AP 41; 60th Infantry Regiment, CH 52
Albany, Kentucky, SH 54
Albany (New York) *Atlas and Argus,* BR 127
Albatross, BL 28, MI 162
Albemarle, BL 78-85, *CO 95, 96,* 97
Albemarle Battery, TR *46*
Albemarle River, CO 97
Albemarle Sound, CO 17, 31, 33, 37, 97

Albuquerque, New Mexico Territory, FR 20, 23, 26, 28, 33, 34
Alcoholic beverages: consumption of, TT *13,* 58-60; industry, YA 67, 72; production banned, OR 29
Alcoholism, campaigns against, BR *21*
Alcorn, James: cotton profiteering by, OR 83-84; Davis criticized by, OR 77
Alcorn, James L., NA 65
Alcott, Louisa May, TT *94,* 98
Alden, A. J. and J. M., MI *92*
Alden, James, CO 147, 150
Aldie, Virginia, GE 27, 28
Aldrich, Edgar, bugle of, FR *47*
Aldrich, Mrs. Alfred P., AP 56
Aleck Scott, SH *34-35*
Alexander, Edward Porter, AP 88, 129, *139,* 140, 144, BR *142,* 143, CH 109, 110, 111, 112, 113, FI 113, 129, GE *131,* LE 23, 52, RE 50, 52, 73, 142, *146,* SP 44, *46,* TR 67, 149; communications and espionage, SP 45-46; in Lee retreat, GE 150; at Peach Orchard, GE 108; and Pickett's Charge, GE 129-131, 136, 147
Alexander, Frederic W., FL 71, 72, 75
Alexander Nevski, BL 133
Alexander's Battery, FL 75
Alexander's Bridge, CH 44
Alexandria, Louisiana, FR *53,* 54, 67, 70
Alexandria, Virginia, DE *142-143,* FI 57-59, 61, *64-65,* 150, FO 8, *26-27, 72-73, 88-89,* 91-92, 96, LE *10-11,* 126, 151, NA 163, RE *8-13,* 18, 30, SP *102;* hospitals in, TT *108-109;* prostitution in, TT 61; refugees in, OR 126; as Union supply depot, OR *144-145*
Alexandria *Democrat,* NA 63
Alger, Horatio, NA 88
Alison, Joseph, MI 151-152
Allatoona, Battle of, SM *map 2-3,* 15, 21, *22-23,* 24-26
Allatoona Pass, AT 15, 50, 59; SM 20
Allebaugh, William, BD 126
Allegheny Mountains, DE *8-9, 12-13,* 45-46, 95, 99, 101, 129, 146, 150; strategic value of, SH 8-9
Allen, Cornelius T., TR 143-144
Allen, Daniel B., MI 70
Allen, E. J. *See* Pinkerton, Allan
Allen, Henry W., SH 126-127, *133*
Allen, Lawrence, OR 91
Allen, Lieutenant, CO *45*
Allen, Robert, MI 34
Allen, Thomas, RE 154
Allen, William, OR 150
Allison, Andrew B., LE 39
Allison, Charles, TT 119
Allston, Mrs., OR 150
Alpine, Georgia, CH 42
Alsop farm, KI 86, 124, 126
Alton, Illinois, BR 106, 108
Altoona conference, YA 143
Ambrose, Ellsberry, OR 74
Ambrose, Henry, OR 74
Ambrose, Warren, OR 74

AP Pursuit to Appomattox; AS The Assassination; AT Battles for Atlanta; BD The Bloodiest Day; BL The Blockade; BR Brother against Brother; CH The Fight for Chattanooga; CO The Coastal War; DE Decoying the Yanks; FI First Blood; FL The Shenandoah in Flames; FO Forward to Richmond; FR War on the Frontier; GE Gettysburg;

Ambrotype, TE *143*

Ambulances, TT 90, *100-101, 104*

Amelia Court House, Virginia, AP 97, 101, 109-112, 114

America, BL *90*

American Anti-Slavery Society, BR 62, *63*, 67; NA 98

American Bank Note Company, OR 69

American Colonization Society, BR 38

American Panorama Company, AT 88; *The Battle of Atlanta* (cyclorama), AT *82-89*

American Party, BR 101, *102*

American Railroad Journal, YA 66

Ames, Adelbert, CO 165, 167-168, KI *163*, NA 145, 147, 148

Ames, John W., RE 89

Ames, Mary, NA 120, 123

Amissville, Virginia, LE 127

Ammen, Jacob, SH 140-141

Ammunition production and procurement, OR 17-18, *19*, 21-23

Ammunition shortages, SH 51

Ammunition supply, TT 156

Ammunition types, CO *78-83*, 135, 137

Amnesty offers, OR 166

Amphibious assaults, MI 69

Amphibious operations, BL *map 2-3*, 26, 29-31, *32-35*, SH *162-163*. *See also* names *of operations*

Amputations, policy and practice, TT 52

Amusements. *See* Recreational activities

Anaconda Plan, BL 15, FI 44-45, 48, 110, SH 8

Anacostia River, FO *20-21*

Analostan Island, FO *10-11*

Ancient and Honorable Artillery Company, TT 21

Anderson, George, SM 152

Anderson, George B., BD 86, 94, 101, *106*

Anderson, George T. (Tige), BD 86, 88, 89, GE 70, 80, 98-99, 108, TR 149

Anderson, Hiram, CO 87

Anderson, James Patton, AT 144, TE 61, 62, 66, 155

Anderson, John, KI 136-137

Anderson, Josephine, SP 152

Anderson, Joseph M., AP *36*

Anderson, Joseph Reid, OR *20;* and Tredegar Iron Works, OR 17, 21-22

Anderson, Mary, SP 152

Anderson, Mary Jane, AS 70

Anderson, Richard H., AP 18, 80, 82, 85, 88, 95, 110, 117, 128, 133, BD 86, 99-101, BR 120, FL 104, 105, 108, FO 144, GE 69, 104, 109-111, 113, 128, KI 58, 73, *86*, LE 91, RE 33, 36, 122-125, 129, 156-158, TR 44, 95, 147, 149; at Cold Harbor, KI 152-154; at North Anna, KI 132, 133, 135, 136; and Sayler's Creek, AP 120-123, 125, 126; at Spotsylvania, KI 83-84, 86, 89, 103, 104

Anderson, Robert H., AP *162*, 163, BR *124-125*, *136*, *143*, *148*, FI 32, TT 110; capitulation by, BR 159-161; commands Charleston forts, BR 120; in Fort Sumter defense, BR 121-128, 132-141, 147, 149-154, *155*, 156-157, 163; and surrender demand, BR 138-141, 157-159

Anderson, S. J., OR 158

Anderson, Tennessee, CH *96-97*

Anderson, William (Bloody Bill), FR 157, SP *151*, 152, *160;* death, SP 161; and Quantrill, SP 157; raids in Missouri, SP 158-159

Anderson's Crossroads, Tennessee, CH 78, 79, 80, 88

Andersonville, Georgia, AT 80, 138, 139, *141*, NA 37, 169, SM 68

Andersonville prison camp, TT 117-119, 122, 129, *130-133*, 134-135

André, John, SP 10

Andrew, John, BD *160*, FI 21

Andrew, John A., NA 28, YA 39, 143

Andrews, BL 133

Andrews, Eliza, NA 26

Andrews, George L., LE 108

Andrews, James J., SP *111*, TE 8, 11; and Great Railroad Adventure, SP 111-113

Andrews, John W., RE 77

Andrews, Richard Snowden, LE *102*, 103

Angle, the, GE *120-122*, 131, 135, *map 138*, 140-143

Animals, care of, TT 52. *See also* Mascots

Annapolis, Maryland, CO 19, 22, SP 53, TT 82; as troop-staging area, FI 26, 29

Annapolis & Elk River Railroad, FI 29

Annapolis Junction, Maryland, FI *28*

Ann Arbor, Michigan, YA *24-25*

Anthony, Daniel, SP 145

Anthony, Scott, FR 127

Anthony's Bridge, AT 145

Antietam, Battle of, BD *map 2-3*, 4, *map 22*, *map 69*, 77, *map 78*, 80-81, 84-85, *map 98*, 110-119; bridges, role in, BD 63, 65, 120-132, 139-141, BL 125-126, MI 83, OR 77, 129, RE 24, 32, 47, YA 39, 93; casualty totals, BD 150; civilians' behavior during, BD 65, 66-67; road system, BD 60-61; strategic and political results, BD 8, 150, 156-157, 168; terrain features, BD 60, 64, 66-67, 121; weather, effect on operations, BD 65-66. *See also* Sharpsburg, Maryland

Antietam Creek, BD *map 2-3*, 60, *61-63*, 64-65, 68, *map 69*, 87, *map 98*, *116-117*, *123*, *map 130*, 137-139

Anti-Semitism, OR 15

Apache Canyon, FR 28-31

Apache Indians, FR 112-118, 120, 125

Apache Pass, New Mexico Territory, FR 35, 113

Appalachian Mountains, strategic value of, SH 8

Appler, Jesse J., SH 111, 114-116

Appomattox, CO 33

Appomattox, Union celebration after, AS 8, 55-56, *94-95*

Appomattox Court House, AP 18, 135, 144, 145, FI 127; Confederate surrender at, AP *cover*, 134, *152-155;* Union pursuit to, AP *map 114-115*

Appomattox River, TR *14-15*, 27, *30-31*, 33, 39, 48, 70, 110

Aqueduct Bridge, YA *18-19*

Aquia Creek, CH *102-103*, RE 8, 14, *18-19*, 20, 34-36, SP *30*, TT *90*

Aquia Landing, LE 99, 101, 125

Arapaho Indians, FR 122, *124*, 125-130, 160, NA 93

Arbridge, Private, SM 113

Archer, Fletcher H., TR 31, 32

Archer, James J., GE 45, 48-50, LE 34, RE 61, 65-67, 126, 142-143, TR 152

Ariel, LE 95

Arkansas: in Confederate supply system, MI 16; fighting in, FR 3, 136-155; joins Confederacy, FI 18; loyalist government in, NA 30, 32; money issues, OR *72-73;* Quantrill's winter quarters, SP 149; readmission to Union, NA 69; refugees in, OR 121; secession by, BR 3; Union sentiment in, FR 152; violence in, NA 76; warning poster, SP *155*

Arkansas: at Baton Rouge, MI 33, 35; construction, MI 26-28; destroyed, MI *33*, 35; at Vicksburg, MI *30-31*, 32; on Yazoo River, MI 29, 32

Arkansas Post. *See* Fort Hindman, Arkansas

Arkansas River: operations on and near, MI 17, *22*, 69; operations on, SH 101, 107

Arkansas troops, Confederate, AT 35, 54, 104, FR 52, 56, 60, 61, *135*, *161*, GE 86, MI 41-43, 119, SM 115, TE 47, 59, 60; 1st Mounted Riflemen, SH 26-27, SM 142 Artillery: Key's Battery, AT 54 Infantry: 1st Infantry Regiment, CH 59, SH 125, *132*; 1st and 15th Infantry Regiments (consolidated), AT 70, 71; 2nd Infantry Regiment, OR 160; 3rd Infantry Regiment, AP 134, BD 103-104, TT *39;* 4th Infantry Regiment, TT 115; 5th Infantry Regiment, TE 59; 6th Infantry Regiment, SH 121; 6th and 7th Infantry Regiments (combined), AT 133; 7th Infantry Regiment, TE 59; 8th Infantry Regiment, flag of, FI *125;* 15th Infantry Regiment, MI 85, 103; 20th Infantry Regiment, MI 42

Arkansas troops, Union, FR 152

Arlington, Virginia, DE *136-137*, FI 59, *60-61*, *116*, TT *146-147*

Arlington House, LE *14*

Arman, Lucien, BL 128, 131

Armies. *See* names *of commanders*

Armistead, Lewis A., FO 159, 161, 164-165, GE *cover*, *121*, 137-138, *139*, 140-141, *143*, LE 67-69

Armor-plate production, OR 22

Armour, Philip, YA 79

Armour, Philip D., NA 83

Arms, Samuel, drum of, SM *45*

Confederate Brigadier General James J. Archer, captured on the first day of the Battle of Gettysburg

Flag of the 3rd Arkansas, C.S.A., part of the Army of the Tennessee

KI The Killing Ground; LE Lee Takes Command; MI War on the Mississippi; NA The Nation Reunited; OR Confederate Ordeal; RE Rebels Resurgent; SH The Road to Shiloh; SM Sherman's March; SP Spies, Scouts and Raiders; TE The Struggle for Tennessee; TR Death in the Trenches; TT Tenting Tonight; YA Twenty Million Yankees

39

Battery D, 1st New York Light Artillery, drilling near Fredericksburg, Virginia, in April 1863

Artillery rounds stacked near the powder magazine of Battery Rodgers in Alexandria, Virginia

Arms production, YA *57, 66, 67-69;* fraud in, YA 73

Armstrong, Frank C., AT 57, CH *68,* FR *145*

Armstrong, Samuel C., NA *51*

Army and Navy Journal, NA 93

Army of Northern Virginia battle flag, FI *124*

Army of the Valley. *See* Jackson, Thomas Jonathan

Arnold, Benedict, SP 10

Arnold, Richard, SM 160

Arnold, Samuel B., AS 20, 24, *25,* 29, 39, 40; arrest and confinement, AS 109, 139, *143;* imprisonment, AS 160-161; plot to kidnap Lincoln, AS 48-51; quits conspiracy, AS 53, 54; trial of, AS 141-145, 151-154, *156,* 158

Arnold, William, GE *124*

Aroostook, FO 128

Arp, Bill (pseudonym of Charles Henry Smith), OR 51-52, SM 30

Arrests, YA *27, 31,* 32

Arsenal Park, FO *22-23*

Arsenals seized by South, BR 128

Arsenal system, OR 19

Artillery: ammunition for, TE *140-141;* ammunition and guns, FI 51; at Atlanta, AT *118-121;* effectiveness of, TE 134; field howitzer, TE *89;* manufacture of, TE 89; mortars, TR *76-77, 87, 135, 138;* Napoleons, TE *134-135,* 145, TR *164;* at Nashville, TE *72-73;* operation of, TE *136-139;* organization, FI 44; Parrott Rifle, TE *134,* TR *134-135;* personal arms, FI *72-73;* range and effectiveness, FI 51; rifled, TE 135; seacoast guns, FI *60-61;* shell fragment, TR *95;* siege guns in Confederate fortifications, AT 76; siege guns at Petersburg, TR 65; smooth-bore, TE *135;* tactical doctrine, FI 49, 51, 54-55; training program, FI 54; unconventional designs, SP *166-169;* use by guerrillas, SP 99, 119, 122, 130. *See also names of commanders; state troops*

Artillery actions, FO *40-41;* at Ball's Bluff, FO 40, 46; Confederate, AP 30, 36, 37, *68,* 70, 92-93, 96, *136,* AT 32, 42, 46, 52, 54, 68, 69, 74, 149, BD 47, 51, 53, 56, 58-59, 64, 67-68, 88-89, 91, 96-97, *99, 102,* 104-108, *110-111,* 122, 129, 132, 153, CH 24, 50, 54-55, 109, 123, 139, 140, 142, 145, 150, DE 36, 54, 87, 125, 130-131, 135, 156, 161, 164, 170, FL 23, 33, 34, 36, 47, 60, 74-75, 75-78, 81, 112, 114, 118, 140, 150, 153, 156, TR 24, 31, 41, 45-46, 78, 83, 86-87, *106-107,* 108, 142-144, 146; at Cynthiana, TE 24; at Fair Oaks, FO 154-155, 164; Federal, DE 67, *75,* 130-131, 133, 151, 161, 164,

167-168; at Hanover Court House, FO 133; at Hartsville, TE 87; at Murfreesboro, TE 29; at Perryville, TE 62, 64, 65; at Seven Pines, FO 139, 141; at Stones River, TE *109,* 113, 120, 121, 126, 127, 130, 145, 150, 152, 153, 154; at Triune, TE 93; Union, AP 37, 39, 67, 69, 73, 92, 102, 122, 124, *129,* AT 43, 49, 64, *65,* 66, 93, 95, 99-100, 106, 111, 139-140, 145, *150,* BD 47, 51, 64, 67-68, 70-71, 74-75, 78-79, 83, 91-92, *102,* 108, 125, 131, 153, *154-155,* CH 24, 33, 45-46, 48, 54-55, 56, 58, 93, 109, 114, 123, 131, 133, 140, 145, FL 23, 31, 34, 37, 47, 60, 75, 115, 146, 150, 153, KI 29, *51,* 64, 102, 119, 133, MI 35, *36,* 37, 40-41, 68, 71, 94, 102, 113, 121, 130, 134, 136, 139, SM 24, 26, 92, 105, 113, 115, 117, 135, 147, TR 26, 32, 45, 76, 78, 82, 103, *106-107,* 108-109, 136, 152-153; at Williamsburg, FO 108-111; at Wynn's Mill, FO *92;* at Yorktown, FO 93-94, 99, 102, 105, 107, *122-123. See also names of commanders; state troops*

Artillery ammunition: canister and case shot, SH 21, 122, 125

Artillery losses: Confederate, FO 107-108, *132-133,* MI 68, 103-104, 118, 121, *168,* SH 56, *66-67,* 97, 166; Union, FO 110, MI 37, 102-103, SH 27

Artillery pieces, FL *64-65, 66-67,* 75, FR *34, 109*

Artillery regiments, conversion to infantry, TT 48

Artillery units: branch colors, FO 60; expansion of, FO 17; organization, FO 20; training, FO *26-27, 30-31. See also names of commanders, units, or under states*

Artillery weapons, DE *115, 136-137, 139-141,* RE 64, *124-125, 164-165,* YA *10-11;* Armstrong gun, CO 82, *83;* Brooke gun, CO 82; characteristics, CO 80, 92; columbiads, CO *49,* 80, FO 128; Confederate losses, CO 19, 30, *47-49, 83,* 85; Confederate strength, CO 21, 31, 35, 124, 158-159; Dahlgren gun, CO *80-81, 154-155;* development, CO 80, 82; fieldpieces, FO *31,* 46, *88-89, 126-127, 132-133;* fortification pieces, FO *69;* howitzers, FO *25;* James cannon, FO 46; mortars, FO *105;* Napoleon 12-pounder, FO 155; Napoleon cannon, OR 22; naval guns, OR 22; Parrott guns, CO 37, 39, *81-82, 132-133,* FO 105, 154, MI *164-165;* production and procurement, OR 19, 20-22; Rodman gun, CO *78;* salvages, CO 120; seacoast guns, CO *14-15, 48-49, 104-105, 111, 160-161, 166-167;* 24-pounder rifle, MI *168;* Union losses, CO 96, 139

Artillery weapons and assaults: at Belmont, SH 48; at Boonville, SH 20; at Carthage,

SH *24-25;* at Corinth, SH 157; at Fort Donelson, SH 87, 91; at Fort Henry, SH *66-67;* at Island No. 10, SH *158-159, 164-165;* at Shiloh, SH 114-115, 121-122, *124-125, 130, 132,* 136-139, 143-144, *145, 150;* strategic siting, SH 8, 59; 12-pounder James, SH 126; at Wilson's Creek, SH 26-27, 29

Artwork, wartime, BD *110-119,* BL *102-113,* CO 99-109, FO *94-95, 114-123,* MI *21-23, 38-39, 70-71, 128-129, 154-155,* SH *22-23, 28, 130-133,* TT 20, *117, 136-143, 162-169*

Asboth, Alexander, FR 144

Ash, John S., SM 50

Ashby, Turner, DE *cover, 90, 164,* FI 15-16, FL 139, 142, SP 108, 116; at Buckton, DE 123, 126, 130; death of, DE 158, 161, *162-164;* equipment of, DE *90-91;* at Front Royal, DE 122-123, 149; at Harrisonburg, DE 157-158; Jackson, relations with, DE 5, 90, 92, 158; at Kernstown, DE 66-71, 90, 92; at Middletown, DE 130-131; at Newtown, DE 131; in Potomac area, DE 151; at Rude's Hill, DE 87; at Staunton, DE *88-89,* 101; at Stony Creek, DE 83, 86-87; at Strasburg, DE 157; in Valley area, DE 44; at Winchester, DE 135

Ashby's Gap, DE 39

Ashby's Harbor, CO 24, *map* 26

Ashland, Virginia, OR 128

Ashmun, George, AS 79

Ashwood, Tennessee, SM 96, 118

Assiniboin Indians, FR *14-15*

Astor, John Jacob, III, FO 22

Astoria, New York, and drug production, SM 108

Atchafalaya River, MI *110*

Atchison, David R., BR 71, 74

Athens, Alabama, TE 14, 15

Athens, Georgia, BR *14-15,* OR 64

Athens *Southern Watchman,* OR 13, 48, 58, 153

Atkins, Smith D., CH 49, 50

Atkinson, Edmund M., FL 79, 114

Atkinson, Edmund N., RE 71

Atlanta, BL *108-109, 117*

Atlanta, Battle of, AT *82-87,* 97-114, *map* 101, 109; battlefield, AT *114-115;* Hood's command failure at, AT 106

Atlanta, Georgia, CH 18, 33, 36, 84, NA 26, 123, SM *map* 2-3, *18-19,* 20, 29, 35, 44; capture of, YA 158; city hall, AT *156-157;* civil disorders, OR 85; civilian casualties, AT 95, 139; civilian evacuation, AT 78, *162-163,* SM *15, 16;* clothing production, OR 25; Confederate evacuation, AT 152-153, 155; demolition and looting in, SM 45, *48-49;* fortifications, AT *116-131,* 132, *map* 135; industry, OR 21; living conditions, AT *142;* martial law, OR 82; as objective, TE 15; premature celebration, AT 143;

AP Pursuit to Appomattox; AS The Assassination; AT Battles for Atlanta; BD The Bloodiest Day; BL The Blockade; BR Brother against Brother; CH The Fight for Chattanooga; CO The Coastal War; DE Decoying the Yanks; FI First Blood; FL The Shenandoah in Flames; FO Forward to Richmond; FR War on the Frontier; GE Gettysburg;

railroad depot, AT *160-161*, *168;* rebuilding of, SM 46-47; refugees in, OR 123; slave market, AT *163;* strategic value of, AT 3, 21; Union armies at, AT 77, 91; Union artillery bombardment of, AT 95, 139-140; Union drive on, OR 148, 155; as Union objective, AT 3, 8, CH 155, 156; Union occupation of, AT 154, 155, *156-171,* SM 14

Atlanta & West Point Railroad, AT 132, 141, 143

Atlanta Campaign, AT *map* 2-3, 41; trench warfare, AT 62, 65, 66, 140. *See also individual battles*

Atlanta *Constitution,* SM 30

Atlanta prison camp, TT 122

Atlanta *Southern Confederacy,* OR 74

Atlantic, YA *43*

Atlantic & Great Western Railroad, YA 65

Atlantic & North Carolina Railroad, AP *68,* CO 35, 37

Atlee's Station, Virginia, KI 148

Atrocities, SH 80, TE 12, 14, 22; and Anderson, SP 158-159, *159-160,* 161; against black soldiers, TT 35; and Brown, SP 141; and "bummers," SM 70; and Clement, SP 159, 160; and foragers, SM 56; by Indian troops, TT 31; and Jennison, SP 144, 146; and Lane, SP 143; lynchings, SP 140, 144; massacre at Fort Pillow, AT 24, *25,* 47; and prisoners of war, SM 68; and Quantrill, SP 148, 149, 153, 154, 155-157; and Todd, SP 152-153; and Wheeler's cavalry, SM 68, 70

Atwill, Samuel F., FL 159

Atzerodt, George A. (Port Tobacco), AS *25,* 27, 29, 39, 40, 44, 54, 68; arrest and confinement, AS 108, 110, *111, 143;* execution of, AS 159-160, *161, 162-171;* plot to kidnap Lincoln, AS 48-51; plot to murder Johnson and Lincoln, AS 59, 69-70, 71-74, 97-98; trial of, AS 144-145, 151, 154, *156,* 158

Atzerodt, John, AS 110

Augur, Christopher C., AS 96, 108, 110, 114, FL *63,* LE 103, 106, MI 95

August, Thomas P., LE 71

Augusta, Georgia, BR 41, FI 18-19, 44, SM 48, 52, 66, 67, TT *10;* arsenal seized, BR 128; gunpowder production, OR *20, 21;* newspapers, OR 49; as railroad center, OR 27-28

Augusta *Baptist Banner,* OR 59

Augusta *Chronicle,* OR 75

Augusta *Constitutionalist,* OR 155

Austin, Nevada Territory, YA 116

Austro-Prussian War, BL 118

Authors. *See Literature*

Autrey, James L., MI 19

Averell, William Woods, FI 162, FL 20, *21,* 53, 56, 59-60, 89-91, 101, 109, 113, 116, 119, 121, 124, 125, FO 24, LE 18, 73, RE 105-107, *108,* 109-111

Avery, Clark M., KI 74

Avery, Isaac E., GE 60, 116-117

Ayock, George G., RE *106*

Ayres, Romeyn B., AP 30, 85, 87-90, KI 63, 66, NA 14, TR 101, 103

Ayres' battery, FI 118

Azores Islands, BL 121, 149

B

Babcock, John C., SP 81

Babcock, Orville E., AP 145, *146-147, CH 116,* NA 115, 116, SM 156

Babo, Alois, FO *50*

Bache, George M., MI 136-137

Back River, FI 79, *map* 83

Badeau, Adam, KI 60, *128*

Baden, Joseph, AS 132

Bad Wound, FR 125

Bagby, Arthur, FR 71

Bagby, George, OR 46, 48

Baggage trains, TT 47

Bagley, Parker, SH 137

Bahama, BL 149

Bahama Islands, used by blockade-runners, BL *map* 2-3, 21

Bahia, BL 150, 161

Bahnson, Henry T., AP 127, 131

Bailey, George, AT 107

Bailey, Joseph, FR 68, *69,* 70, 71

Bailey, Theodorus, CO 66, 69, *73,* 74

Bailey's Crossroads, Virginia, FO 24

Bailie, George A., AT 68

Bainbridge, Absalom R., AS 115, 117

Baird, Absalom, AT 149, CH 45, 49, 64, 66, 79, 120, 134, 143

Baker, Cullen, AS 114, 132, 136, 137, 139, SP 56-57; and Jefferson Davis, SP *57*

Baker, Edward D., FO 43-46, *47, 52*

Baker, Enoch T., TT 24

Baker, Francis H., BL *8-9*

Baker, Henry, TR *101*

Baker, Lafayette C., AS 114, 132, 136, 137, 139, SP 56-57; and Jefferson Davis, SP *57*

Baker, Laurence S., AP *73*

Baker, Luther B., AS 132, 134, 137, 139

Baker, Page M., RE 107

Baker, T. Otis, CH *41*

Baker, Thomas, BL 28

Baker's Creek, MI 116, 118, 121

Bald Hill, AT *86-87,* 95, 97, 104, 105, 106, 108, 111, 113

Baldwin, Philemon P., CH *63,* TE 117

Balfour, Emma, MI 125, 139

Ball, Dabney, SP 54

Ball, Eustace H., SH 114

Balloons, FO 99, 105, *146-153*

Ballou, Sullivan, FI *119*

Ball's Bluff, Battle of, BD 156, SP 109, TT 60, 71

Ball's Bluff, Virginia, FO 39-43, *map* 44, 45-52

Baltic, BR 152-153, 156, 161

Baltimore, Maryland, AS 10, 15, BD 10, 14, 18, FL 73, 83, 84, FO *69,* 130, OR 49; attacks on Union troops, FI 21-25, *26-27;* Confederate sympathizers' actions, FI 20-21, 29-30; occupation by Union troops, SP 12; Southern sentiment in, SP 14; Union espionage in, SP 34, *36-39;* Union occupation of, FI 31, 77

Baltimore *American,* SP 124

Baltimore & Ohio Railroad, BD *30-33, 36-37,* DE *16-17,* 33-34, *36-37,* 43, 45-46, 61, *64-65,* FL 25, 26, 41, 71, 74, 91, 104, 109, FO 8, 12, 63, 74-75, KI 26, SP 114, 122, 124, 126, 127, 131, YA 65, 73; bridges sabotaged, FI *94-95;* safeguarding, FI 23, 29-31, 85, 87-88

Baltimore Democratic convention, BR 110

Baltimore *Sun,* AS 17

Bancroft, George, RE 92

Bands, BD 17, 56, 151, CH *153,* FO 54-57, 99, KI 105, SH *22, 46,* 48, SM 14, 45, 47, 48, 82, 100, 158, SP *120-121, 158,* TE 50, 99, TR *59, 168-169,* TT *34-35,* 158; Confederate, CO 115, 135; Union, CO *43,* 88. *See also Musicians*

Bankhead, John H., NA 124

Banking industry, YA 78

Banks, OR 16

Banks, Nathaniel P., CH 86, DE *60,* FO 131, FR 47, *50,* 51-57, 59-67, 70-71, LE 99, MI *164,* YA 75-76; background, DE 59-60; at Buckton, DE 121; at Cedar Mountain, LE 99, 100, 103, 107, 109-111; at Culpeper, LE 98, 101, 103; Franklin's evaluation of, DE 60-61; at Front Royal, DE 123, 126, 135; Gordon's evaluation of, DE 59; at Gordonsville, LE 98; Grant, relations with, MI 108; at Harrisonburg, DE 87, 101; ineptness, DE 60-61; at Middletown, DE 131; miscalculations by, DE 87; near the Potomac, DE 146-147, 151; at New Market, DE 87; at New Orleans, MI 73; at Port Hudson, MI 73, 108, 110, 140, 161-162, 164, 166, 168; in Shenandoah Valley, LE 93, 98; at Staunton, DE 95, 98, 103; at Stony Creek, DE 83, 86-87; at Strasburg, DE 65, *88-89,* 114, 120-123, 128-129, *map* 130; troop strength, DE 61, 121, MI 110, 162; in Valley area, DE 44-45, 59, 61, *62-63,* 71, 82-83, 86, 89, 95, 114, 116; at Winchester, DE 64, 121, 129, *map* 130, 133-135

Banks' Ford, RE 118-120, *156-157*

Bannock Indians, FR 106, 112

Banshee, BL 92-95

Banshee No. 2, BL 95

Banta, Daniel, GE *155*

Baptist Alley, AS 70, 71, 79, 86

Baquet, Camille, LE 45

Barber, TT *14*

Barboursville, Kentucky, SH 54, TE 44

Bardstown, Kentucky, TE 54, 57

Barker, James G., FI *102*

Barker, Thomas E., KI 166

Brigadier General Romeyn B. Ayres, V Corps division commander at Petersburg and Appomattox

Jacket of Federal Cavalry trumpeter or bandsman

KI The Killing Ground; LE Lee Takes Command; MI War on the Mississippi; NA The Nation Reunited; OR Confederate Ordeal; RE Rebels Resurgent; SH The Road to Shiloh; SM Sherman's March; SP Spies, Scouts and Raiders; TE The Struggle for Tennessee; TR Death in the Trenches; TT Tenting Tonight; YA Twenty Million Yankees

41

The arsenal at Baton Rouge, Louisiana, photographed after the city was occupied by Federal troops

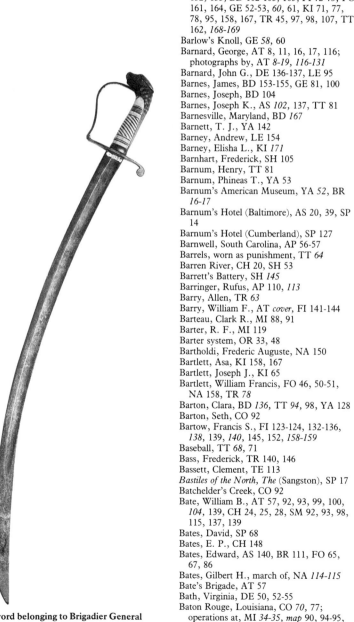

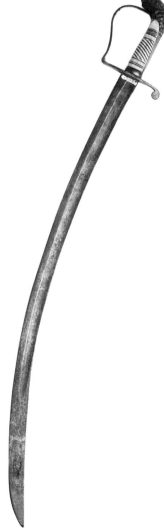

A sword belonging to Brigadier General William Barksdale, C.S.A., mortally wounded at Gettysburg July 2, 1863

Barksdale, William, BD 39, 43, GE 101-102, 104-106, 108-109, RE 51-54, 156, *162-163;* sword of, GE *109*

Barlow, Francis Channing, AP 127, 131, 132, 133, BD 102-103, 105, FI *42-43*, FO 161, 164, GE 52-53, *60*, 61, KI 71, 77, 78, 95, 158, 167, TR 45, 97, 98, 107, TT 162, *168-169*

Barlow's Knoll, GE *58*, 60

Barnard, George, AT 8, 11, 16, 17, 116; photographs by, AT *8-19*, *116-131*

Barnard, John G., DE 136-137, LE 95

Barnes, James, BD 153-155, GE 81, 100

Barnes, Joseph, BD 104

Barnes, Joseph K., AS *102*, 137, TT 81

Barnesville, Maryland, BD *167*

Barnett, T. J., YA 142

Barney, Andrew, LE 154

Barney, Elisha L., KI *171*

Barnhart, Frederick, SH 105

Barnum, Henry, TT 81

Barnum, Phineas T., YA 53

Barnum's American Museum, YA *52*, BR *16-17*

Barnum's Hotel (Baltimore), AS 20, 39, SP 14

Barnum's Hotel (Cumberland), SP 127

Barnwell, South Carolina, AP 56-57

Barrels, worn as punishment, TT *64*

Barren River, CH 20, SH 53

Barrett's Battery, SH *145*

Barringer, Rufus, AP 110, *113*

Barry, Allen, TR *63*

Barry, William F., AT *cover*, FI 141-144

Barteau, Clark R., MI 88, 91

Barter, R. F., MI 119

Barter system, OR 33, 48

Bartholdi, Frederic Auguste, NA 150

Bartlett, Asa, KI 158, 167

Bartlett, Joseph J., KI 65

Bartlett, William Francis, FO 46, 50-51, NA 158, TR *78*

Barton, Clara, BD *136*, TT *94*, 98, YA 128

Barton, Seth, CO 92

Bartow, Francis S., FI 123-124, 132-136, *138*, 139, *140*, 145, 152, *158-159*

Baseball, TT *68*, 71

Bass, Frederick, TR 140, 146

Bassett, Clement, TE 113

Bastiles of the North, The (Sangston), SP 17

Batchelder's Creek, CO 92

Bate, William B., AT 57, 92, 93, 99, 100, *104*, 139, CH 24, 25, 28, SM 92, 93, 98, 115, 137, 139

Bates, David, SP 68

Bates, E. P., CH 148

Bates, Edward, AS 140, BR 111, FO 65, 67, 86

Bates, Gilbert H., march of, NA *114-115*

Bate's Brigade, AT 57

Bath, Virginia, DE 50, 52-55

Baton Rouge, Louisiana, CO *70*, 77; operations at, MI *34-35, map* 90, 94-95, *97, 98-99;* refugees from, OR 121; Republican campaigning in, NA *68;* slave migration to, OR 135; Union capture of, OR *96-109;* Union occupation, MI 18, *28*, 33

Baton Rouge Arsenal, Louisiana, SH 15

Battalions. *See names of commanders, units, or under states*

Batteries. *See names of commanders, units, or under states*

Battery Buchanan, CO 158, 169

Battery Gregg, CO 113, 120-121, 124, 131, 134

Battery Martin Scott, DE *139*

Battery Robinett, MI 40-41, *42-43*, *44-45*

Battery Simkins, CO *100-101*

Battery Stevens, CO *132-133*

Battle, emotions during, TT 144, 156-161

Battle above the Clouds, CH 136. *See also* Chattanooga, Battle of

Battle ax, MI *64-65*

Battle flags, LE *145. See also* Color-bearers; Flags

Battle of Atlanta, The (cyclorama), AT *82-89*

"Battle of Manassas" (song), OR 54

Baumfree, Isabella (Sojourner Truth), BR 65

Baxter, DeWitt C., BD 89

Baxter, Henry, GE 52-55, 59

Baxter's Fire Zouaves, BD *89*

Baxter Springs, Kansas, FR 147, 153, SP 155-157, 158

Bayard, George D., DE 157-158, LE 107, 125

Bayard, George G., RE 64

Bayard, Nicholas, FL *14*

Bayard, Thomas, NA *139*

Baylor, John R., FR 19, 20, 22, *24*, 25

Baylor, Thomas C., BR *145*

Baylor, William, LE 154

Bayonet assaults: DE 40, FI 51, 130, 143, *153*, FO *45*, 50, 164, MI *42-43*, 114, 118, 123, *124-125*, 130, *146-147*, TE *116*, 153; Confederate, LE 41, 45, 150; decline of, FI 50; at Fort Donelson, SH 91; at Mill Springs, SH 56; at Shiloh, SH 116-117, 123-125; Union, LE 39

Bayonet drill, FO *14*, 20

Bayonets, OR *65*

Bayou City, FR *48-49*

Bayou Montecino, MI *165*

Bayou Teche, FR 50, 51, 53, 54, 71, MI 110

Beach, Francis, BR *145*

Beach, John, BD 54

Bear Creek, LE *56-57*

Beard, Richard, AT 101-102

Beardslee, George, RE 48

Beardstown, Illinois, NA 126

Bear Hunter, FR 108, 110, 111

Beatty, John, CH 21, 36, 39, 44, 55, 56, 65, 66, 72, 78, 99, 163, TE 16, 92, 123, 124, 144, TT 152; description of Buell, TE 15; response to guerrilla attack, TE 12

Beatty, Samuel, TE 143, 145, 150, 152, 153, 164-165

Beaty, Powhatan, TR *125*

Beaudrye, Louis, KI 41

Beaufort, BL 53, CO 33

Beaufort, North Carolina, BL 21, 87, CO 37, 159, 162, 164

Beaufort, South Carolina, NA 49; former slaves educated in, OR *142-143;* slavery in, OR *132;* Union occupation of, OR *32-33*, 117, 122

Beauregard, Pierre Gustave Toutant, AP 53, 61, 145, 157, BR *137*, DE 38, 40, FI *126*, *152*, FO 38-39, 75, 78, KI 119, 130, 131, 150, MI 18, NA *58*, 117, *118*, SH *110*, SM 11, *28*, 44, 52, 120, SP 25, 26, 27, 44, 45, TE 17, 20, 82, TR *41*, 69, 101, 150; appointed Army commander, FI 57; and Battle of Bull Run, OR 46; at Bowling Green, SH 81; broadside issued by, AP *66;* on Bull Run campaign, FI 110; at Charleston, CO 99, *112*, 113, 119, 136; and Columbus, SH 101; commander in west, SM 18; commands in West, SH 136; at Corinth, SH 157; criticized, SH 155; Davis, relations with, FI 152; SH 79; at Drewry's Bluff, TR 28; and Fort Sumter, CO 130-133; and Fort Sumter reduction, BR 135-141, 157, 159-161, 163; and Fort Wagner, CO 131; and Hardee, SM 149; and Hood, SM 28-29, 32-33, 82; illness, SH 101; at Jackson, SH 101; Johnston, relations with, FI 152; Johnston yields command to, FI 123, 129, 136; joins Confederacy, FI 27; in Kentucky operations, SH 101; personal leadership, FI 121, 126, 139, 141, 145, 148, *166-167;* at Petersburg, CO 97; and Petersburg's defense, TR 36, 39-45, 48-49, 52-53; in Petersburg siege, OR 148; popularity, FI 152; relations with Davis, TE 17; reprimanded by Davis, OR 15; ruse by, SH 157; and Savannah's evacuation, SM 158; at Shiloh, SH 105, 108-113, 120, 122, 128-129, 136, 144, 147-148, 151, 155; strategic plans, SH 101; surrender demand by, BR 138-141; tactical plans and orders, FI 111-113, 117-118, 123-124, 132, 136, 140-141, 144, 146, 149, 152, 166; in Tennessee operations, SH 61, 79-81, 97; vanity of, FI 111

Beaver Dam Creek, LE 33, *34-35*, 36-37

Beaver Dam Station, Virginia, KI 115

Beckford, William, TR *63*

Beckwith, Dr., YA 89, 92

Bee, Barnard E., DE 40, FI 123-124, 132-138, *139*, 152, *158-159*

Bee, Hamilton, FR 59, 61, 70

Beecher, Henry Ward, BD *160*, BR 89, NA 121, YA 151

Beerly, Nathaniel, RE 118

Behnke, Henry, FR 72, 74, 78, 81

Bel Air, Maryland, AS 14, 15

Belknap, Charles, SM 40, 66

Belknap, William W., AT 104, 112, 136, NA 114, *116*

Bell, Alexander Graham, NA 151
Bell, Henry H., BL 142, CO 66
Bell, John, BR 110-111, 113, 118-119
Bell, John T., SH 121-122
Bell, L. L., FL 152
Bell, Louis, CO 168
Bell, Mary and Mollie, TT 61
Bell, W. B., SH 126
Bell, William, AS 95-96, 97, 110
Bellard, Alfred, FO 18-20
Bellbuckle Gap, CH 22, 23
Belle Grove plantation, FL 41, 140, 147, 148, 157, *159*, 170
Belle Isle, Virginia, OR 38
Belle Isle prison camp, TT 135
Belle Plain, Virginia, AS 132, 136, KI *106-113*, 148
Bellows, Henry, YA 122, 127
Bell tent, TT *50*
Belmont, August, BR 104
Belmont, Battle of, SH 46-49, *53*, 59
Belts, leather, OR *62-63*
Benedict, Lewis, FR 61
Benham, Henry, RE 156-157
Benham, Henry W., CO 110-111
Benjamin, Judah P., BL 15, 123, CO 22, 30, 55, DE 44-45, 58-59, FO 39, *78*, 79-81, 103, KI 39, SP 41, 47, 107; background, OR 14; as Cabinet officer, OR 15; denounced by Thomas Cobb, OR 15; as Secretary of War, OR 13, 15; on slave enlistment, OR 166
Benjamin, Samuel L., CH 114
Bennett, Henry H., SH 132
Bennett, James, home of, AP *158*
Bennett, James Gordon, FI 10, YA 144, 158
Bennett, L. G., SM 90
Benning, Henry L., CH 50-51, GE 78-80, 86, 98
Bent, George, FR 127
Benteen, Frederick W., FR 160
Benton, MI *87*, 100, SH *62*, *72-73*
Benton, Thomas Hart, BR 9
Bentonville, Battle of, AP 70-71, *map 72*, 73-74, 75
Berdan, Hiram, FO *100*, GE 76
Berdan's Sharpshooters, FO *100-101*, 133
Bering Sea, BL 159
Berlin, Maryland, BD 168, *169*
Bermuda, BL 24
Bermuda, as blockade-runners' port, BL *map 2-3*, 21, 86-88, *89*, 90, 95-98, 100-101, OR 18, 22
Bermuda Hundred, Virginia, CO 163, KI 130, SP *65*, *88*, TR 18-19, 27-28, *30-31*, 33, 35, 38-39, 44, 49, 64, 95, 112, 137
Bernard, George S., BD 11, 54, LE 68-69, TR 83
Berrian, John H., LE 39
Berry, Hiram, RE 135, 144-145
Berry, James, CH *119*
Berry, Thomas, CH 46
Berry, Thomas J., BR *143*
Berryville, Virginia, FL 89, 104-105, 108

Bessemer, Henry, NA 82
Best's Grove, Maryland, BD 17
Bethune, "Blind Tom," OR *54*
Beverly, West Virginia, FI 86-87, 91-92
Beverly Ford, GE 16, 18, 20, RE 119
Beyer, Edward: lithographs by, TR *18*, *19*; paintings by, DE *8-17*
Bibb, CO *119*
Bickerdyke, Mary Ann, AT 24-26, YA 128-130
Biddle, James, KI *10-11*
Bidwell, Daniel, FL 150
Bierce, Ambrose, AT 54, 56, *78*, CH 72; artifacts belonging to, AT *78-79*
Bierstadt, Albert, painting by, FR *10-11*
Big Barren River, TE *52-53*
Big Bethel, Virginia, FO 93; battle at, FI *map 3*, 78-82, *map 83*, *84-85*, 86, 110
Big Black River, MI 109-111, 122-123, *127*, 142, 156
Big Eagle, FR 75, 80, 83, 85, 87
Big Kennesaw, AT *19*, 66
Big Mound, Battle of, FR 93
Big Round Top, GE 65, 68, 69, 79, 80-81, *90-91*, 144-145
Big Sewell Mountain, DE 76-77
Big Shanty, Georgia, AT 61, SM 19, SP 111, TE 8
Big Spring, Virginia, DE 38
Billings, John D., TT 45, 47-48, 52, 65, 156
Bills, John, OR 136
Billy Bowlegs, DE 26
Biloxi, Mississippi, CO 54
Bingham, George Caleb, BR 22-23; painting by, SP *156-157*
Bingham, John A., AS 141, *149*, 157, NA 40
Birbeck, C. G., SP 162
Birch Coulee, FR 85, 86, *89*
Birge, Manning D., FL *132*
Birkenhead shipyard, BL *123*, 149
Birney, David B., GE 77, 98, 101, 103-104, KI 70, 71, 76, 78, 95, 133, 158, RE 71, 128, TR 50, 55-56, 95, 97-99, 139-140, 145-148
Birney, James G., BR 39, 62
Birney, William, TR 146-147
Bishop, Edward P., BD *16*
Bishop, Ella, TE *49*
Bishop, John F., FR 79
Bishop, Judson W., CH 4
Bissell, Josiah, SH 160
Bissell, Lewis, FL 157
Black, Edward, TT 26
Black, Jeremiah, BR 123-125
Black abolitionists, BR *63-68*
Black Bayou, MI 80
Blackburn's Ford, DE 38, FI 113, 118, *map 121*, 122, 124, 126, 135, 149
Black Codes, NA 33-34, 40
Blackford, Susan Leigh, OR 112
Blackford, William, LE 127-128, 131, 138-139, 142, 145, 153-154, TT 94
Blackford, William W., AP 110, 111, 151,

BD 17, 27, FI 160
Black Friday, NA *106-108*, 109
Black Hat (Iron) Brigade, BD 51, 73-76, 79. *See also* Gibbon, John
Black Hawk, MI 80
Black Horse Troop (Virginia), FI 153
Black Kettle, FR 125-128, NA 93
Black market, MI 58
Blacknall, Charles C., FL 74, 122, *123*
Black people, CO 24, *40*, *43*, FR 136; children, care of, YA *104*, 105; and Confederate Army, AP 20, *26;* Confederate emancipation proposal, AT 27; as Confederate servants, TT *10*, *16*, 35; Confederate use of labor, SH 57-58; Confederate use of slave labor, AT 62, 76, 116, TR 48; and Congressional Medal of Honor, TR 117, *124-125;* discriminatory laws, NA 33-34, 40, 124; and Ebeneezer Creek, SM 72; education of, NA *48-49*, *50-51*, 120-123; emancipation of, NA 26, 28-29, 33; family life, NA *46*, *47;* 15th Amendment, NA 98, 99; fighting ability of troops, TR 116-117, 119, 124; and foragers, assistance to, SM 54; fraternization with white troops, TR 121; free, number in Confederacy, TT 35; freedmen in labor force, OR 16; Freedmen's Bureau, NA 28, 36-39, 42, *45;* free workers in Petersburg, TR 15; and Fugitive Slave Law, FI 78; fugitive slaves, SP 31; in government, NA 69-70, *71*, 118-119; hostility toward, YA 35, 99-103, 105, *106-107*, 108-110; immigrants, relations with, YA 40; inventions by, NA *107;* labor contracts for, NA *45;* and land redistribution, NA 29, 36-39; liberated in Carolinas, AP 61-64; liberation of, BL *36-37*, 126; SM *cover*, *56-57*, 59, *64-65;* and Lincoln, AS 56, *58;* and Lincoln in Richmond, AP 109; living conditions, YA 102; lynchings, YA 35; massacre of, at Fort Pillow, AT 24, *25*, 47; military emancipation of, FL 40-41; and military intelligence, FL 113; militia in South, NA 98, 143, 147, 150; minstrel shows, TT *15;* murders of, YA 103, *107*, 108, 110; in naval service, BL 24, 28; Northern criticism of, NA 117-119, 127; number enslaved, FI 45; percentage of population, YA 21; public opinion on, YA 35-36; racial relations in South, NA 28-29, 64, 65, *129*, 140; racial violence, NA 34, *35*, 36, 120, 131, 141-142, 145-147, 149-150, *157;* refugees along march, SM 71, *72-73;* Regular Army, NA *100-101;* Republican Party, NA 16-17, 40-41, 66-67, 112; runaway slaves, TR 25, *57;* as scouts, SP 29, *30;* sharecropping, NA *42-44*, 123-124, 158; slaves, value of, FI 144; slaves as contraband, FI 77-78, *81;* slaves freed by Frémont, SH 30-32; and the West, NA *93;* and Union Army, AP *10*, *64*, 108,

Brigadier General Seth Barton, taken prisoner by Federal troops at Sayler's Creek in 1865

Conrad Wise Chapman's portrait of Brigadier General Barnard E. Bee, killed at First Bull Run

KI The Killing Ground; LE Lee Takes Command; MI War on the Mississippi; NA The Nation Reunited; OR Confederate Ordeal; RE Rebels Resurgent; SH The Road to Shiloh; SM Sherman's March; SP Spies, Scouts and Raiders; TE The Struggle for Tennessee; TR Death in the Trenches; TT Tenting Tonight; YA Twenty Million Yankees

43

The U.S.S. *Sabine*, a vessel of the South Atlantic Blockading Squadron

Brigadier General Milledge L. Bonham, Confederate congressman and Governor of South Carolina

Black people (continued)
139; FL 41, FR 55, 64, *147*, 152, OR *144-147*, 166-167, SM 113, 126, 135, 161; Union troops, TR 27, 39, 43, 74, 80, 82-83, 88, *116-125*, 139, 146; Union employment of, MI 50-51, 58, *60-61*, 100; as Union servants, SH *88-89*, TT *8-9, 13;* in Union service, FI *42-43*, 78, *81;* Union use of freedmen as laborers, AT 62; voting rights, NA 31-32, *49*, 52, 61, 63, 65-66, 67, 76, 97, 156, 158. *See also* Black troops; Emancipation; Slavery

Black sailors, TT 32-33

Black troops, CO 164, MI 164, YA *100;* 8th U.S. Colored Troops, CO 139; 20th U.S. Colored Troops, YA 4; 26th U.S. Colored Troops, YA *101;* African Brigade, MI *146-147;* atrocities against, TT 35; casualties, MI 146, TT 35; combat behavior, TT 33-35; commissioning policies, TT 33; Confederate, OR *166*, 167; Confederate attitude toward, TT 35; Confederate recruitment, TT 35; Medal of Honor awards, TT 35; number enlisted, YA 101; number in service, TT 33, 35; pay rates, TT 33; prisoners of war, TT 111; recruitment of, YA 36, 95, *100*, 101; Union, OR *144-147*, 166-167; in Union Army, TT 31, *32-33*, 34-35; Union attitude toward, TT 32-33 Artillery: 2nd Colored Light Artillery, TT *32* Infantry: 1st Kansas Colored Infantry, TT 33-35; 54th and 55th Massachusetts Infantry Regiments, YA 101; 54th Massachusetts Infantry Regiment, CO *125-127*

Black Warrior, CO 31-32

Blackwater River, TR 56, 110-111, 115

Blackwell, Elizabeth, YA 120

Blaine, James G., NA 149, 150-152

Blair, Charles, SP 155

Blair, Francis Preston, AP 20-21, AT 60, 98, 100, 134, 152, BD 168, FL 86, NA *10*, OR 162

Blair, Francis Preston, Jr., AP 54, MI 63, 136, 147, SH *13*, SM 50, *51*, 66, 71; Frémont, relations with, SH 19; Grant, relations with, SH 45; Jackson, relations with, SH 16-17; Lincoln, relations with, SH 12-13; Lyon, relations with, SH 13; and Missouri security, SH 15; Price, relations with, SH 16-17; and St. Louis Arsenal, SH 13; Sherman, relations with, SH 13; troops mobilized by, SH 13

Blair, Henry, SM *40*

Blair, Montgomery, BL 17, BR 133, CO 61, FO 68, SH 12-13, YA 29

Blair, Silas, SM *40*

Blake, Homer C., BL 142

Blake, Lyman, YA 66

Blakeslee, B. F., BD 137

Blanchard, Jonathan, YA 71

Blandford Cemetery, TR *9*

Blemill, Chaplain, TT 152

Blenker, Louis, DE 71, *152-153*, 164-165, FO 87, 92, 97

Bliss, Philip Paul, SM 27

Blockade, CO 16-17, 54, 110, 158; duty routine, BL 90-91; effect on economy, OR 17, 22, 29, 31, 33, 82-83, 148; effectiveness, BL 161; evasion of, MI 16; imports by blockade runners, OR 15, 17, *18-19*, 22, 46, 76; legal aspects, BL 12, 93; monitors in, BL 87; proclaimed, FI 13, 44-45; proclamation and objectives, BL 11, 24; stone-fleet use, BL *26-27;* target areas, BL 21, 24-25, *26-27*, 28-29, *30-31*, *32-33*, 34, *43*, 87, 107. *See also* United States Navy

Blockade-runners: captains, BL 86-87, 92-96; characteristics and types, BL 88-89; construction of, BL *124-125;* cotton cargoes, BL 161; exploits of, BL 24, 33, 86, *92-93*, 100-101, 161; government role in, BL 87, 98-100; home ports, BL *map 2-3*, 21, 86-88, *89*, 90, 93, 95-98, *99*, 100-101, 107, 116, 121, 142, 153, 161; luxury imports, BL 98-99, 161; military cargoes, BL 86, 89, 98, 100-101, 115-116, 161; motivation of, BL 87, 91, 98, 100; pay and profitability, BL 87-88, 95-98; routes, BL *map 2-3*, 88-89; ships lost, BL 8-9, 21, 24, *90-91*, 95, 97, *100*, 101, *106-107;* smoke-screen use, BL 101; tactics and ruses, BL 89-90

Blockade Strategy Board, BL 29, CO 16

Block House Bridge, KI 85, 86

Blood Tubs, SP 14, 15

Bloody Angle, KI *cover*, *100-101*, 102-103, 105, 125

Bloody Hill, SH 25-26, 29

Bloody Lane. *See* Sunken Road

Bloody Pond, SH 147

Bloomery Gap, DE 52

Bloomington, Illinois, BR 102

Blount's Creek, CO 90

Blue Ridge gaps, GE 25, 26, 27, 28

Blue Ridge Mountains, BD 10, 18, 164, 168, DE 8-9, 21, 39, 43, 65-66, 84, 86, 95, 100, 114, 121, 129, 149, 157, 170, FI 44, 57, 76, LE 95, 127

Blue Springs, Missouri, SP 154

Blunt, James G., FR 147, 150-153, 160, SP 155, 158, *159*, TT 33

Boatswain's Creek, LE 36-37, 39-41, *43-45*, 47, 72

Boatwright, B. S., FL 81

Body armor, DE *147*

Boernstein, Henry, SH 15

Bogue Banks, CO *38-39*

Boise, Idaho, NA 92

Bolivar Heights, BD 38-39, *40-41*, 56, 59

Bolling's Dam, TR *14-15*

Bombship venture, CO 158-162

Bonding, BL 147-148, 152, 159

Bond issues, OR 30-31

Bonham, Milledge L., FI 113, 124, 136, 140, 147, 149; and Confederate spy, SP 26-27

"Bonnie Blue Flag" (song), OR 52

Book publishing, OR 46. *See also* Literature

Books. *See* Reading; Recreational activities

Boomer, George, MI 119

Boon, Tracey G., YA 133

Boone, Mr. *See* Booth, John Wilkes

Boonsboro, Maryland, BD 18, *map* 22, 38, 44, 47

Boonsboro Turnpike, BD 95, 132, 139

Boonville, Battle of, SH 17, *20*, 24-25

Booth, Asia, AS 15, 16, 30, *35*, 38

Booth, Edwin, AS 16, 17, 18, 28, *116*, YA 53; open letter by, AS 116; saves Robert Lincoln's life, AS 75; theatrical career, AS 30, *31-33*, 36-37

Booth, Edwina, AS *116*

Booth, John Wilkes, AS 2, *19*, 28, 33, 35, 60, 65, 108-110, BR 97, NA 17, 72, SP 63, 66; assassination of Lincoln, AS 67-71, 83, 85, *86-87;* breaks leg, AS 85, 88; capture and death of, AS *134-135*, *136*, *137; cartes de visite*, AS *60-63*, 138; childhood and family, AS 13-15; and Confederate agents in Canada, AS 20; derringer of, AS *65*, 72; diary of, AS *138-139;* escape from Ford's Theatre, AS 85-86, *88, 89, 90-91;* escape route in Maryland, AS 105-108, 111, *112*, *map* 113, 114; escape route in Virginia, AS *map* 113, 114-117, 132-134; escape route in Washington, AS 104, *106-107*, *map* 113; family home, AS *19;* and fellow conspirators, AS *25;* and Ford's Theatre, AS 44-48, 70, 72, 79, 82, *diagram* 84; and Grants, AS 68, 71; identification of corpse, AS 137; at John Brown's execution, AS 18; letter by, AS 71; at Lincoln's inauguration, AS 41-43, *47;* personal items of, AS *138-139;* and Petersen house, AS 92; plots against Lincoln, AS 19-21, 24, 27-29, 38-41, 43, 44, 48-51, 53, 54, 57-59, 68-74; resolves to murder Lincoln, AS 56; return of corpse to Washington and burial, AS 136-139, *141;* reward and poster for, AS *93*, 111, 114, 117; riding boot of, AS *109;* and Samuel Mudd, AS 21, 24, 105-106, 110, 111; Southern sympathies of, AS 18; temperament, AS 16; theatrical career, AS 16-17, 30, *34*, 36-37

Booth, Joseph, AS 30, *35*

Booth, Junius Brutus, AS 13-15, *16*, 20, *30-31*

Booth, Junius Brutus, Jr., AS 16, 30, *35*, *36-37*

Booth, Mary Ann Holmes, AS 14, 16, *17*, 18, 37, 59

Booth family, in theater, AS *30-37*

Borcke, Johann August Heinrich Heros von, GE *17*

Border Ruffians, BR *74*, 75-77, 105, SP 142

Border ruffians. *See* Guerrilla operations

Border states, BR *map 2-3*

Bosbyshell, Oliver C., TR 75

Bostick, Joseph, SM 95

AP Pursuit to Appomattox; AS The Assassination; AT Battles for Atlanta; BD The Bloodiest Day; BL The Blockade; BR Brother against Brother; CH The Fight for Chattanooga; CO The Coastal War; DE Decoying the Yanks; FI First Blood; FL The Shenandoah in Flames; FO Forward to Richmond; FR War on the Frontier; GE Gettysburg;

The band of the 9th U.S.C.T., a regiment of black troops, in the defenses of Washington, D.C.

Boston, Massachusetts: draft riot, YA 110; and fugitive slaves, BR 46-47; living conditions in, NA 89; patriotic demonstrations, FI 10, 13; prostitution in, TT 61
Boston, Reuben, AP 120, GE 29
Boston & Worcester Railroad, YA 79
Boston *Daily Advertiser*, NA 158
Boston Female Anti-Slavery Society, BR 69
Boston *Herald*, correspondents and artists, SP *53*
Boston *Post*, AS 17
Boston Review, YA 71
Boston *Transcript*, BL 116
Boston Vigilance Committee, BR 64
Boswell, James, RE 119
Boteler, Alexander R., DE 59, 149
Boteler's Ford, BD 61, 129, 135, 151, 153, *154-155*, 156
Bottom's Bridge, FO 133, 136, LE 49
Botts, John Minor, OR 87
Bounty jumpers, TT 37, 153-154
Bounty system, TT 24, YA 87, 89, *94-95*, 98
Boutwell, George S., NA 113
Bouve, Edward T., AP 120
Bovina, Mississippi, MI 122-123
Bowditch, Nathaniel, RE 110
Bowen, James L., AP 29
Bowen, John S., MI *122*, SH 122; at Big Black River, MI 122; at Champion's Hill, MI 116, 118-122; at Grand Gulf, MI 104; at Port Gibson, MI 84, 101-104; Van Dorn, charges against, MI 44; at Vicksburg, MI 152-153, 156
Bowerman, Stephen, SP 168
Bowers, Theodore S., AP *146-147*, 150, TR *17*, 157
Bowie knives, OR *64*
Bowlegs, Billy, FR *139*
Bowles, Pinckney D., TR 147
Bowles, Samuel, NA 85
Bowley, Freeman S., TR 83, 86, 87
Bowling Green, Kentucky, SH 53, 79-81, TE 51
Bowling Green, Virginia, AS *115*, 117, 132, 133, KI 132-133
Bowman, Michael, DE *106*
Bowser, Mary Elizabeth, SP 88
Boxing, TT *69*
Boyce, William, OR 155
Boyd, Belle, DE *122*, SP *48-49; Perils of a Spy* (dramatic reading), SP 48
Boyd, Davy. *See* Herold, David
Boyd, James W. *See* Booth, John Wilkes
Boyd, William H., FL 27, 28, 29, 30
Boyd's Hole, Virginia, SP 57
Boydton Plank Road, TR 150, 155-156
Boyer, Joseph C., SM 143-144
Boyle, Jeremiah T., TE 24
Boys, enlistment of, TT 26. *See also* Drummers
Bradwell, Isaac, FL 68
Brady, Allen, TT 119
Brady, George K., TT *43*

Brady, James, FO 154
Brady, Mathew, BD 142, BL 15, 137, FI 122, FR *107*, KI *162-163*, GE *158-159*, KI 26, NA 94, TR *37;* photographs by, AS *106-107*, NA 57, SP *48;* studio of, photographs by, FR *107*, KI *162-163*
Brady (Confederate chaplain), OR 58-59
Brady's Battery, FO 154-155
Bragg, Braxton, AP 25, 53, 61, 69, AT 27, 80, CH 2, 8, 18, 19, 21, 24, 29, 31, *35*, 36, 40, 42, 43, 44, 61, 67, 69, 99, 105, 110, 112, 113, 117, 121, 134, 146, 154, CO 94, 163-164, FL 19-20, 29, 59, FR 138, KI 117, 119, 123, MI 34, NA 18, SH *108*, *110*, SM 11, 52, SP 75, 78, 79, TE *9*, 21, 31, 32, 39, 40, 41, 44, 49, 55, 80, 81, 85, 88, 91; appearance, CH 22; asks to be relieved of command, CH 155; assumes command, TE 8; and Bentonville, AP 71-73; besieges Chattanooga, CH 73, 87, 95; Buckner's evaluation of, SH 123; cavalry reorganized by, TE 92; at Chattanooga, OR 22; at Chickamauga, CH 45, 47, 48, 53, 54, 55, 62; combat philosophy, SH 108; confused by Grant's maneuvers, CH 118; disciplinarian, CH 22; discipline, TE 20, 148, 149; disposition of troops defending Chattanooga, CH 23; on drunkenness, TT 58; fails to trap Rosecrans' scattered corps, CH 37-38, 39; headquarters on Missionary Ridge, CH 142, 145; health, CH 35; hopes for recruits in Kentucky, TE 41, 55, 148; illness, TE 17; indecisiveness, TE 43, 54, 143-144; installs governor at Frankfort, TE 57; joins Johnston, SH 101; in Kentucky invasion, TT 86; and Kinston, AP 64-67; leadership, TE 112, 148; at Lexington, TE 48; logistical ability, TE 50; loss of confidence in, TE 82, 160; and martial law, OR 82; meeting with Davis, CH 85; in Mexican War, TE *16*, 17; at Missionary Ridge, CH 131; movement into Kentucky, TE 45, 50, 51; opinion of McCown, TE 41, 42, 117; outmaneuvered by Rosecrans, CH 28, 32, 33, 34, 35; at Perryville, TE 2, 59, 61, 62, 67; personal traits, CH 22, 35, SH 106-107, 123, TE 17, 20, 148, 161; relations with Davis, TE 20, 83; relations with Forrest, CH 73, 79; relations with Longstreet, CH 54, 92, 100, 101; relations with Smith, TE 43; relations with subordinates, CH 22, 39, 78, 83, 84, 85; reorganizes army, CH 37, 53, 85; retreats from Tullahoma, CH 30; and rout at Missionary Ridge, CH 147-148, 150; saber and scabbard of, TE *17;* at Shiloh, SH 106-116, 120, 123-128, *133*, 136, 138, 143-148, 150-151; on soldier's qualities, TT 161; at Stones River, TE 2, 94, 96, 99, 118, 123, 127, 129, 133, 143-144, 148, 150, 152, 155, 157, 158, 159; supply difficulties, TE 42, 54;

tactical mistakes, CH 48, 142, 143, 145, 147; unpopularity, CH 22; use of cavalry, CH 19-20, 79; use of ruses, CH 36, 37, 118, 120; at Versailles, TE 61; at Wilmington, OR 167
Bragg, Edward S., TR 101, 103
Branch, Lawrence O'Bryan, BD 137, CO 35, *36*, 37, FO 133, LE 107
Branding, as punishment, TT 153
Brandon, James, SM 115
Brandon, Lane, RE 53
Brandy Station, Virginia, DE 83, GE *map 2-3*, 10, 16-18, 19, *20-21*, 22, KI 8, *16*, 24
Brannan, John M., CH 45, 49, 57, 64, 66, 68, 69, 125
Branson, Mrs., AS 40
Bratton, John, TR 149-150
Bravay & Company, BL 126, 128
Brawner's Farm, Battle of, LE 139, *140-141*, 142, 144, *map 147*, 151-152
Braxton, Carter, FL 114, 118, 119
Brayman, Mason, OR 159
Breathed, James, RE 109
Breckenridge, John C., OR 54
Breckinridge, Cabell, CH 142
Breckinridge, James, AP 90
Breckinridge, John Cabell, AP 25, 33, 95, 158, BR 72, CH 92, 131, DE 18, FL 16, 17, *18*, 23-24, 27-29, 43, 45, 52, 91, 106, 108, 122, 138, KI 130-132, 154, 158, MI 35, NA 18, 19, SH *110*, TE 43, 44, *150;* background, FL 19-20; and Charleston convention, BR 110; at Chickamauga, CH 54, 55, 56; and Early's raid, FL 68, 69, 74, 78, 81, 86; lampooned, BR *105;* at Lynchburg, FL 58-60; at Missionary Ridge, CH 142, 143, 147; at New Market, FL 30-33, 36-39; at Opequon Creek, FL 113, 116, 117, 119; and Orphan Brigade, TE 155; as presidential candidate, BR 110-111, 113, 116, 118-119; relations with Bragg, CH 85; TE 148; and rout at Missionary Ridge, CH 148; at Shiloh, SH 106, 108, 113, 120-121, 128, 136, 138, 141-143; on slavery, BR 113-116; at Stones River, TE 96, 99, 118, 123, 124, 126, 127, 129, 132, 144, 145, 149, 152, 153, 154, 157, 162, 166; as vice presidential candidate, BR 102-103
Breckinridge, Mary, TE 149
Breese, K. R., CO 165
Brennan, T. M., & Co., TE *89*
Brentwood Hills, SM 121
Brewer, Dr. Charles, KI 122
Brewster, Henry, RE 100
Brewster, Henry M., AS *107*
Brickhouse Hospital, TE 143
Bridge construction, BD *30-31, 36-37*, DE 54, 61, MI 84, 123, *127*, 128-129, RE 10, *12, 15-17*, 30, *34*, 36, 50-51, *52-55*, 91, 120, 152, 156-158, *166-167;* and repair, TT 26

Mathew Brady, the most famous photographer of the Civil War

KI The Killing Ground; LE Lee Takes Command; MI War on the Mississippi; NA The Nation Reunited; OR Confederate Ordeal; RE Rebels Resurgent; SH The Road to Shiloh; SM Sherman's March; SP Spies, Scouts and Raiders; TE The Struggle for Tennessee; TR Death in the Trenches; TT Tenting Tonight; YA Twenty Million Yankees

45

The U.S.S. *Brooklyn*, launched in 1858 and a participant in many of the Civil War naval actions

Brigadier General William T. H. Brooks, commanding a brigade of Vermonters in VI Corps

Bridge demolitions: by Confederates, DE *64-65*, 83, *88-89*, 157, *158-159*, 168-169; by Federals, DE 126

Bridgeport, Alabama, CH 78, 79, 83, 88, 89, 95, 97, 117, 118, 136, 164, TE 14

Bridgeport, Connecticut, NA 79, YA *22*

Bridgeport *Farmer*, YA 20, 22

Bridges: construction, FO *20-21*, 74-75, 133; demolition, FO 89; demolition techniques, SP *96-97;* at Nashville, TE *76*, *84, 104;* pontoon, CH *36*, 78, 89, 90, 91, *94*, 111, 117, 118, 121, 123; pontoon repair, TE 52-53; protection of, SP *104-105;* railroad, CH 169, *170-171;* repair of, CH 97, SP 104; wagon, CH *166-167*

Bridge's Battery, TE *134-135*

Brierfield, OR *154*

Brigade organization, FO 20, TT 24; and tactics, FI 55. *See also names of commanders or units*

Bright, Michael, CH 28

Brinton, John H., SH 94

Briscoe, Washington, AS 98

Bristoe Station, Virginia, KI 28, LE 127-129, 133, 143-144

Bristol, England, BL *124-125*

Bristol, Tennessee, OR 91

Bristow, Benjamin Helm, NA 116

British Army & Navy Gazette, SM 48

Broad Run, LE 127-128

Broadside, Confederate recruiting poster, TE *44*

Brobst, John, AT 140

Brock, Sallie, OR 37

Brockenbrough, John M., GE 52, 61, RE 61-62

Brock road, KI 58, 61, 68, 79, 84, 86

Brodhead, Thornton F., LE *168*

Brooke, John, BD 107, BL 48-49

Brooke, John M., CO 82

Brooke, John R., KI 89, 158-159, NA 156

Brooke naval gun, OR 22

Brooklyn, BL 25, 142, 146, BR 126, CO 66, 69, 143, 145-147, 150-151

Brooklyn, New York, YA *48;* civil disorders, YA 102-103; relief work in, YA *138, 140*

Brooklyn Chasseurs, FI 141, *142*, 143, *168-169*

Brooklyn *Daily Eagle*, YA 77

Brooks, Noah, AS 45, 55, DE 136

Brooks, Preston S., BR 76-77, *78*, 84

Brooks, Sanford, FO 164

Brooks, William, KI 164, 165, RE 168, TT 161

Brooks, William T. H., FO 102

Brooks Brothers, YA *107*

Brook Turnpike, KI 119, 122

Brotherton farm, CH 47, 58

Brough, John, YA 95, 150-151

Brown, A. C., TR 50

Brown, Abram, OR 111

Brown, Benjamin G., NA *111*, 134

Brown, Charles, AP 72

Brown, Egbert, SP 158

Brown, George William, FI 26, SP *18*

Brown, Henry, AS *131*

Brown, Isaac Newton, MI 26-29, 31-32

Brown, John, AS 18, BD 30, BR *73*, NA 99, SH 12, SP 108-109, 141, 159; abolitionist activities, BR 70, 85, 89; capture of, LE 20; Harpers Ferry raid, BR 84-85, *86-87*, 88-89, *90-93;* invasion plans, BR 84-85, 87; murders by, BR 70-71, 76-79; revolver of, BR *71;* trial and execution, BR 89, 91, *94-97*, 109

Brown, John C., AT 106, 134, 135, 144-145, SM 92, 95, 98, 103, 105, 112, 116, 119

Brown, Joseph E., NA 66, 124, OR *78*, SM 52, 61; appeal to Macon citizens, AT *140;* conscription opposed by, OR 78; Georgia troops withheld by, OR 155; and habeas corpus suspension, OR 153-154; and peace negotiations, OR 153, 157; and states' rights, OR 76; welfare programs, OR 83

Brown, Joseph R., FR 85

Brown, Oliver, BR 88

Brown, Thomas W., LE 105

Brown, Watson, BR 88

Browne, A. G., SM 159

Browne, John M., BL 169

Browne, Simeon, RE 108

Brownell, Francis E., FI 64, *65*, 68

Browning, Orville, YA 146

Browning, Orville H., NA 40

Browning, William, AS 69-70

Brown's Ferry, CH 89, 90, *91*, 93, *94*, 117, 118; night attack at, CH *92*

Brown's Gap, DE 100, 170

Brownsville, Maryland, BD 39

Brownsville Gap, BD 39

Bruce, Blanche K., NA 69, *70*

Bruinsburg, Mississippi, MI 100-101, 105

Brush Mountain, AT 60, 61

Bryan, E. Pliny, SP 45-46

Bryan, T. B., YA 135

Bryan farm, GE *124*

Bryant, William Cullen, YA 151, 153

Bryantown, Maryland, AS 21, 105, 106, 110, 111, *map* 113

Buchanan, Franklin, BL 49, 53-55, *56*, 57, CO 143, *145*, 146-147, 150-156

Buchanan, James, BR *104*, FI 13, SP 23; administration vilified, BR *127;* elected President, BR 102, 104; and Fort Sumter relief, BR 123-126; and John B. Floyd, BR 123; and Kansas statehood, BR 80-83; lampooned, BR *105;* and secessionist movement, BR 124; and slavery extension, BR 104-105

Buchel, August, FR 61

Buck, Irving A., CH 29, 37, 39, 130, 139, 150, SM 96

Buck, Lucy, DE 125

Buck, Silas C., NA *161*

Buckeystown, Maryland, BD 44

Buckhannon, West Virginia, FI 89

Bucking and gagging, as punishment, TT 65

Buckingham, Catharinus P., BD 168

Buckingham, John E., AS 82

Bucklin, Sophronia, YA 127

Buckner, Simon Bolivar, CH 37, 39, 42, 85, 100, 118, 120, TE 40, 44, 59, 150; at Bowling Green, SH 53-54, 81; Bragg evaluated by, SH 123; at Chickamauga, CH 44, 53; at Fort Donelson, SH 81, 84-85, 90-93; Grant, relations with, SH 94-95; at Knoxville, CH 31, 34; at Perryville, TE 62; relations with Bragg, CH 84; surrender by, SH 93-95; training program, SH 57

Buckner Guards, SH *56-57*

Bucktails (13th Pennsylvania Reserves): BD 64, *65*, 76, DE 158, *160-163*, KI 134

Buckton, Virginia, DE 121, 123

Budd, Enos, KI *104*

Buell, Don Carlos, BR 121, 123, FO 67, *87*, MI 34, 44, 56, SH *146*, TE 8, 12, *14*, 21, 24, 25, 31, 41, 42, 43, 44, 49, 51; advance on Chattanooga, TE 17; at Bowling Green, SH 97-98; commands Department of the Ohio, SH 58-59; discipline, TE 82; in Kentucky operations, SH 79, 97-98; in Mexican War, TE 15; movement on Bragg, TE 50, 54, 55; at Nashville, SH 97-98, 104; operations in Alabama, TE 40; at Perryville, TE 2, 59, 60, 62, 66, 67; relations with Mitchel, TE 8, 10, 15, 16; relieved of command, TE 80; at Shiloh, SH 106, 116, 140-141, 144, 147-148; similarities with Bragg, TE 17; supply problems, TE 15; temperament, TE 15; treatment of civilians, TE 15; unpopularity, TE 14, 17; in Tennessee operations, SH 59, 97-98, 104

Buffalo, New York, YA 103; Lincoln funeral procession, AS *124*

Buford, John, BD 157, GE *46*, LE *171*, RE *29;* at Brandy Station, GE 16, 18, *21*, 22; at Gettysburg, GE 35, 45-46; at Gordonsville, LE 98; in Lee pursuit, GE 150-151, 156-157; at Second Bull Run, LE 134-135, 152; at Seminary Ridge, GE *48;* at Thoroughfare Gap, LE 134-135, 143; at Upperville, GE 28; at Willoughby Run, GE 47

Buglers, FO *4*, 55, *60*, SH *105*, TT *166*. *See also* Musicians

Bugles, FO *61*

Bull, Rice C., AP 54, 55, AT 52, 92, RE 151, SM 47, 62, 68, TT 88-90, 140

Bulloch, James Dunwody, BL 114, *115*, 120-122, 125-126, 128, 131, 143, 149, 161

Bull Pasture Mountain, DE 101

Bull Pasture River, DE 101-103

Bull Run, First Battle of, DE 18, 38, *39*, 40, 137, FI *map* 3, 13, *map* 121, *map* 128, 130, *map* 133, *map* 141, *map* 146, *153*, *156-169*, FO 8, 12, 16-18, 30, 38,

AP Pursuit to Appomattox; AS The Assassination; AT Battles for Atlanta; BD The Bloodiest Day; BL The Blockade; BR Brother against Brother; CH The Fight for Chattanooga; CO The Coastal War; DE Decoying the Yanks; FI First Blood; FL The Shenandoah in Flames; FO Forward to Richmond; FR War on the Frontier; GE Gettysburg;

46, 52, OR 15, 17, 36, 46, 54, 59-60, TT
92-94, 111, 114, 147, YA 87; artifact, FI
149; artillery action, FI 118, 120-121,
127, 129-130, 132-133, 137-139, 141-157,
162-165; bayonet assaults, FI 130, 143,
153; bridges and fords, FI 111-113;
casualties, FI *150-151,* 152; cavalry
action, FI 110, 118, 129, 140-141, 143,
148-159, *153;* civilian spectators, FI 122;
communications in, FI 113, 122, 129,
132; Confederate assaults, FI 121,
130-133, 144-145, 147-148, *160-163,*
166-167; Confederate casualties, FI 122,
131, 133-134; Confederate
reinforcements, FI 122, *123,* 126,
131-133, 135, 137, 141, 166-167;
Confederate withdrawals, FI 135-139,
158-159; discipline breakdowns, FI
116-117, 136, 157, 162-163, *168-169;*
intelligence operations in, FI 113, 122;
Johnston yields command, FI 123, 129,
136; lessons from, FI 155; maps,
deficiencies in, FI 110; medical services,
FI 131; opposing strengths, FI 111;
personal-experience accounts, FI 156;
railroads in, FI 122, *123;* road system in,
FI 112, 122, 129; telegraph use in, FI
122; terrain features, FI 111-113, 116,
118, 120; troop identification, FI 138;
turning point in, FI *map* 141, 144, *map*
146, 152, *162-163;* Union approach
march, FI 116-117; Union assaults, FI
130, 134-135, 137, *164-165;* Union
casualties, FI 122, 152; Union prisoners
taken, FI 149, *154;* Union withdrawals
and rout, FI 121-122, 143-144, 146-147,
148, 149-150, 153, *168-169. See also*
Beauregard, Pierre Gustave Toutant;
Johnston, Joseph E.; McDowell, Irvin
Bull Run, Battles of, BL 17, 121, 125
Bull Run, Second Battle of, BD 8, LE *map*
2-3, 8, 126-146, *map* 147, *148,* 149-153,
154, 155, *156-159, map* 160, 161,
162-163, 164, *165,* 166-167, TE 49, TT
101, 157
Bull Run (Kentucky), TE 59
Bull Run (Virginia), LE *113,* 135, 137-138,
163-164, *165,* 167
Bull Run Mountains, LE 127, *136,* 137
"Bummers," SM 70-*71*
Bunker Hill, West Virginia, DE 64, FL 91,
104, 106, 112
Bunks, construction and repair, TT 9
Burbridge, Stephen, MI 68
Bureau of Freedmen, Refugees and
Abandoned Lands, NA 28, 36-39, 41, 42,
63, 70, 140; and black voters, NA 67;
and labor disputes, NA *45;* and schools,
NA 48, 50, 120; wedding ceremony at,
NA *47*
Burge, Dolly Sumner Lunt, SM 54
Burial services, TT *98,* 158
Burk, Tom, LE 42
Burke's Station, Virginia, TR 53,
55

Burkittsville Road, BD 44, 53
Burks, Jesse, DE 67
Burleigh, Charles Calistus, BR *66*
Burlington County, New Jersey, YA
100
Burnet House, AT 20
Burnett, Henry L., AS 141, *149,* 155
Burnham, Hiram, AP 10, RE 153
"Burning, the," FL 19, 134, 137
Burns, Anthony, BR 46-47
Burns, Francis, AS 82
Burns, John, GE *64*
Burnside, Ambrose E., AP 8, BD *124,*
170-171, CH 32, 34, 42, 79, 99, 100, 103,
105, 116, CO *25,* FI 40, *130,* 131, 133,
134, 135, 137, *156-157,* FO 74, KI 22,
82, 129, 148, LE 99, 101, 133, SP 55, 58,
84, 116, TR 35-37, 38, 45-46, 49-50, 53,
142, YA 26, 30-31; at Antietam, BD 64,
69, 87, *116-117,* 121-122, 124-131, 136,
138-139, 141, RE *25;* appointed army
commander, BD 168-169; RE 24; army
reorganized by, RE 30-31; at Bull Run,
CO 16; captures Cumberland Gap, CH
104; carbine invented by, RE *26,* 27; at
Cold Harbor, KI 154, 165; and
Confederate retreat, BD 169; conference
with Lincoln, RE 39, 94; cooperation
with Rosecrans, CH 43, 104; and Crater,
TR 67, 72, 73-75, 83, 86-88; evaluations
of, RE 29, 91-92, 95-98; at Falmouth,
RE 32, 35, 91; at Frederick, BD 22; at
Fredericksburg, RE 30, 33, 40-41, 50,
54, 56-61, 71-72, 84-85, *87,* 89, 93; at
Goldsboro, CO 38, 84, 97; Halleck,
relations with, RE 24, 30, 35, 94;
Hancock, relations with, RE 29;
headquarters at Falmouth, RE *90;*
Hooker, relations with, RE 24, 32, 87,
96, 98; incompetence, BD 124; intrigue
against, RE 94-98; Knoxville Campaign,
CH 103, 105, 106, 107, 108, 109, 111,
112, 118; Lincoln, relations with, RE
24-27, 93-95; McClellan, relations with,
BD 120, 168, CO 25, RE 27; and Meade,
TR 73-74, 94; modesty, RE 24, *27, 29,*
93; at New Bern, CO 34-37; at North
Anna, KI 133, 135; in northern Virginia,
CO 39; personal traits, RE 27-29; prewar
career, RE 27; pursues Longstreet into
eastern Tennessee, CH 155; and
Rappahannock operations, RE 31-32,
35-36, 39-40, 50, 56-57, 72, 85, 91, 93,
95; reaction to army's defeat, RE 89;
relieved, RE 94-95, 98; relieved of
command, TR 88; and reporters, SP 52;
reputation, CH 101, 104; at Roanoke
Island, CO 16-17, 19-25, 30-31, 35-36,
84; under siege at Knoxville, CH 154;
and Skinker's Neck, RE 39; at South
Mountain, BD 49; at Spotsylvania, KI
87, 93, 103-104; Stanton, relations with,
RE 94; subordinates, relations with, RE
29, 39-40, 89-91; sword presented to, CO
30; tactical plans and orders, RE 2-3,

26-27, 30-32, 35-36, 39-41, 50, 54, 56-61,
71-72, 84-85, 89, 93-95; in the
Wilderness, KI 57, 60, 73-74, 76, 79;
troop strength, CO 19, 22, RE 30, 39;
use of pack mules, CH 106; at
Warrenton, RE *2-3, 28,* 30, 35, 93;
welcome at Knoxville, CH *110*
Burnside Bridge, BD *116-117,* 120-122,
123, 124-127, *128-129,* 131, 141
Burnt Chimneys, Virginia, FO 90, 102-
103
Burnt District, SP 154
Burpee, Thomas, KI *170*
Burrage, Henry, CH 115
Burroughs, Joseph (Peanut John), AS
79-82, 86
Burroughs, Tom, BL 93-94
Burrows, John L., OR 59
Burt, Erasmus R., FO 46
Burton, Henry, TR 42
Buschbeck, Adolphus, RE 132-133
Bush, Asahel, TE 120
Bushnell, Cornelius, BL 51-52
Bushong house, FL 33, 34
Bushrod, Nancy, AS 74
Bush's Battery (4th Indiana), TE 120
Bushwhackers, SP 141, TE 8, 12, 22, 44.
See also Guerrillas; Guerrilla operations
Butler, Andrew J., YA 75
Butler, Andrew P., BR 76
Butler, Benjamin Franklin, BL 26, 29-31,
98, FI *79,* FR 99, KI 26, 60, 114, 119,
123, 130, 150, NA *73, 74-75,* SP 88, TR
19, *26,* 31-32, 35, 44, 48, 53, 64, 94, 124,
YA 75; appointed department
commander, FI 77; and Baltimore
Confederate sympathizers, FI 30;
Baltimore occupied by, FI 31, 77; at
Bermuda Hundred, TR 18, 27-28, 95,
112; at Big Bethel, FI 78-80, 84;
bombship venture, CO 158-162;
Cameron, relations with, FI 77; Chase,
relations with, FI 77; at Drewry's Bluff,
TR 28; at Fort Fisher, CO 157-162; at
Forts St. Philip and Jackson, CO 63,
76-77; at Hatteras Inlet, CO 16, 19;
ineptness, FI 84; in invasion of Virginia,
CO 39; personal traits, RE 27-29;
FI 77; militia service, FI 21; and New
Market Heights, TR 137-139, 142, 145,
149; at New Orleans, CO 58-59, 76-77,
157-158; occupation policies, OR
114-115; and Petersburg, TR 27, 30, 33,
38-39, 41; Porter, relations with, CO
157-158, 162; and railroad security, FI
29-31; relieved of command, TR 158;
repressive measures by, CO 76-77; Scott,
relations with, FI 31, 77; and slaves as
contraband, FI 77-78, 81; troop strength,
CO 61; vilified, FO *76;* and Washington
reinforcements, FI 29; Welles, relations
with, CO 58-59
Butler, Edward K., FI *108*
Butler, Matthew C., AP 53, TR 22
Butler, William, AP 69

Colonel Langhorne Wister of the
150th Pennsylvania "Bucktail" regiment, wounded at Gettysburg

Major General Ambrose E. Burnside, Federal commander at the Battle of Fredericksburg

KI The Killing Ground; LE Lee Takes Command; MI War on the Mississippi; NA The Nation Reunited; OR Confederate Ordeal; RE Rebels
Resurgent; SH The Road to Shiloh; SM Sherman's March; SP Spies, Scouts and Raiders; TE The Struggle for Tennessee; TR Death in the
Trenches; TT Tenting Tonight; YA Twenty Million Yankees

47

Brigadier General William P. Carlin of XIV Corps, distinguished in Sherman's march to the sea

Packet of Confederate Army Merrill Carbine cartridges

Castle Thunder, one of several prisons for Federal troops in Richmond, Virginia

Butte, Montana, NA 92
Butterfield, Daniel, AT 46, 51, 52, GE 25, 119, 134, RE 85, 91
Butternut Guerrillas, MI 89
Buzzard's Roost, AT 32
Byers, Samuel H. M., CH 123, 140, SM 157; at Champion's Hill, MI 119; at Jackson, MI 114-115; at New Carthage, MI 85; at Vicksburg, MI 136; at Yazoo Pass, MI 76-77
Byrnes, Richard, KI 160, 170

C

Cabell, William H., FL 159
Cabell, William L., FR 152, 153, 161
Cabin Creek, FR 152, 156
Cable, George Washington, CO 54-55, 74, SH 155
Caddo Indians, FR 147
Caddo troops, TT 31
Cadwallader, Sylvanus, AP 144, CH 136, 142, MI 78, 115, 143-146
Caffey, Thomas E., TT 147
Cage's Ford, TE 86-87
Cairo, SH 59
Cairo, Illinois, CH 85, 88, MI 16, 18, 20, SH 47, TT 45; as naval station, SH 60; planned attack on, SH 101; strategic value of, SH 11, 40-41, 46; as troop staging area, SH 33, 34-41
Caldwell, Charles, CO 20, NA 148
Caldwell, James F. J., AP 96-97, 110, KI 32, 59, 84, 87, 105, RE 37, 144, TR 48, 99, 159
Caldwell, John C., BD 100, 107, GE 100-101, 103-104, 108, RE 77-79, 87
Calhoun, BL 25
Calhoun, James M., AT 154, SM 15
Calhoun, John, TR 11
Calhoun, John C., BR 35, 39, SP 23, 31; legacy of, BR 47; and morality of slavery, BR 40; presidential aspirations, BR 37; and slavery extension, BR 42, 45; on Southern economic decline, BR 37; and states' rights, BR 33-38; and tariff question, BR 37-38; and war with Mexico, BR 41
Calhoun County, Florida, OR 83
California: disloyalty in, YA 29; economic and strategic value of, FR 16, 109; Indian uprising, FR 107; recruiting in, FR 106; Southern sentiment in, FR 107, 109; statehood application, BR 43
California Battalion, FL 88
California Regiment, FO 40-44, 46, 50
California troops, FR 35, 112, 114, 115, 118
    Cavalry: 1st Cavalry Regiment, FR 115, 116, 117; 2nd Cavalry Regiment, FR 108, 110
    Infantry: 1st Infantry Regiment, FR 113, 117; 2nd Infantry Regiment, FR

107; 3rd Infantry Regiment, FR 108, 111; 5th Infantry Regiment, FR 114, 117; 6th Infantry Regiment, FR 110
Calvert, Charles, AS 157
Camanche, FR 109
Cambria, BL 106-107
Camden & Amboy Railroad, YA 79
Cameron, James, FI 145, FO 16; painting by, TE 18-19
Cameron, Robert A., FR 59
Cameron, Simon, FI 27, FO 70-71; at Bull Run, FI 122; Butler, relations with, FI 77; as presidential candidate, BR 111-113; and railroad reconstruction, FI 29; and relief agencies, YA 120; as Secretary of War, YA 73; as vice presidential candidate, BR 103
Cameron Hill, CH 158-159
Camouflage, DE 48
Camp Anderson, District of Columbia, FI 42-43
Camp Baxter, Vermont, FI 34-35
Campbell, Francis, AT 148
Campbell, Henry, CH 33
Campbell, Jacob M., FL 48
Campbell, John A., AP 21, 109, BR 133-135, OR 162, 165
Campbell Hospital, AS 49-50, 53
Campbell's Battery, BD 74-75
Campbell's Bridge, TR 14
Campbell's Station, CH 107, 108, 109
Camp Chase, Ohio, TT 114, 118
Camp Creek, AT 38, 40, 42, 45
Camp Defiance, Illinois, TT 45
Camp Douglas, Illinois, AT 45, SH 96-97, SP 58-59, TT 111, 116, 118
Camp Douglas, Utah Territory, FR 108
Camp Ford, Louisiana, FR 60
Camp Fry, District of Columbia, FL 76-77
Camp Griffin, Virginia, FO 67
Camp Jester, The, OR 52
Camp Lawton, Georgia, SM 68
Camp Letterman General Hospital, KI 28
Camp life, LE 74-81, 86-89; Confederate, MI 38-39; Union, MI 47, 54-55, 98-99
Camp Morton, Indiana, TT 116, 119
Camp Nelson, Kentucky, CH 106, 107
Camp Pendleton, Virginia, FO 28
Camp Quantico, Virginia, TT 12
Camp Randall, Wisconsin, SH 22
Camp Release, Minnesota, FR 90, 105
Camp Salubrity, Louisiana, MI 106
Campsites, TT 164-165; layout, TT 47, 49; street names, TT 47; terrain, TT 44-45
Camp Smith, Illinois, SH 34
Camp Sumter, Georgia. See Andersonville prison camp
Camp Weld, Colorado Territory, peace conference at, FR 126, 127
Camp William Penn, Pennsylvania, YA 101
Canada, Confederate operations from, SP 58-63
"Canadian Cabinet," AS 145
Canadians in Union Army, TT 30

Canal project, MI 26, 33, 69-71, map 72, 73, 74-75
Canby, Edward R. S., AP 160, 163, CO 156, FR 19, 23-24, 25, 26-28, 33-35, 37, 71, 113
Candler, William, RE 116, 119, 135
Cane Hill, FR 150, 151
Canister ammunition, FO 16
Canonicus, AP 45
Canteens, OR 62
Canterbury, S. M., AT 74
Cantey, James, AT 38, 39
Canyon de Chelly, FR 118-119, 120
Cape Argus, BL 153
Cape Fear River, BL 86, 88, 94, 101, CO 142, 156, map 159, 164, 167
Cape Hatteras, BL 64, 65, 87, CO 20-21, 23
Cape of the Hague, BL 155
Capers, Ellison, SM 82
Caperton's Ferry, CH 36
Cape Town, BL 152-154
Capitol, AS 23, 45-47
Capitol building, YA 15
Capron, Horace, SM 85
Carbines, SM 85, 86-87; Burnside, MI 64-65, SM 85; Gallagher, SM 86-87; Hall's breechloading, SH 50-51; naval, MI 64-65; Sharps, GE 28, 40-41
Cardozo, Francis L., NA 70
Cards and card playing, TT 9, 13, 16, 60
Carleton, James H., FR 35, 37, 112-116, 117-120, 122
Carlin, A. J., painting by, SM cover
Carlin, William P., AP 70, 71, 72, 73, AT 33, TE 66, 120
Carlisle, Pennsylvania, GE 26, 73, NA 160
Carlota (Archduchess), FR 42, 43
Carmen, Isaac, MI 130
Carmody, John, BR 149, 151-152
Carnahan, James, CH 48
Carnegie, Andrew, FI 29, NA 79, 82-83, 86, 88, YA 70-71, 79
Carney, Edward, AP 36
Carney, William H., CO 126, 127
Carnifex Ferry, Virginia, DE 72-73
Carondelet, MI 28-29, SH 59, 61, 64, 76-77, 82-84, 85, 163, 164-167
Carondelet, Missouri, SH 74
Carpetbaggers, NA 63-65; attacks on, NA 140-143
Carpetbags, NA 65
Carr, Eugene A., FR 141, 144, NA 160
Carr, Joseph B., RE 145
Carrick's Ford, FI 92
Carroll, John W., TE 65
Carroll, Samuel Sprigg, DE 161, GE 92-93, 116, 118, 138, KI 80
Carroll Annex, AS 110, 139
Carroll Prison, SP 56
Carroll Row, AS 46
Carson, Christopher (Kit), FR 16, 19, 23-25, 29, 37, 114-115, 118-122
Carter, Charles, SP 85
Carter, Fountain Branch, SM 97, 99
Carter, John C., SM 98, 119

AP Pursuit to Appomattox; AS The Assassination; AT Battles for Atlanta; BD The Bloodiest Day; BL The Blockade; BR Brother against Brother; CH The Fight for Chattanooga; CO The Coastal War; DE Decoying the Yanks; FI First Blood; FL The Shenandoah in Flames; FO Forward to Richmond; FR War on the Frontier; GE Gettysburg;

Carter, Martha, AS 133

Carter, Robert G., KI 43, RE 24, TR 50, 53

Carter, Samuel, AP 65, 67

Carter, Theodore, SM 133

Carter, Theodoric, SM 99

Carter, Thomas H., FO 139, NA 32

Carter, Walter, RE 140

Carter, William Page, KI 98

Carter cotton gin and shed, SM *102*

Carter house, SM 97, *99*, 100, 105, 112

Carter's Battery, FO 139

Cartersville, Georgia, AT 50

Cartes de visite, AP *24*, AS *60-63*, 64, *138*, CH 151, *152-153*

Carthage, Battle of, SH 19, *24-25*

Cartoons, and Edward Ferrero, TR *81*

Cartridge boxes, OR *62-63*

Cartridges, OR *64*

Cary, Hetty, AP *19*, OR 126

Cary, William, painting by, FR *122-123*

Case, Henry, AP 69

Casement, John S., SM 113

Casey, Silas, FO 87, 136, 139-140, 158

Casey's Redoubt, FO 139, 141, 144

Cashier, Albert, TT 27

Cashtown, Pennsylvania, GE 35, 44

Casler, John O., DE 46, 55, 89, 116, KI 83

Cassville, Georgia, AT 48, 49

Castle, Henry A., SM 102

Castle Garden, YA *50*

Castle Pinckney, BR 25, 120-121, *122*, CO *104-105*, 113, FI *154*; prison camp, TT *114*

Castle Thunder, SP 86

Casualties, YA 93; at Ball's Bluff, FO 45, *51*, 52; at Belmont, SH 49; at Big Bethel, FI 80, 82-85, 86; black troops, MI 146, TT 35; at Bull Run, FI 122, 131, 133-134, *150-151*, 152, FO 16; burial services, TT *98*, 158; at Burnt Chimneys, FO 103; at Carthage, SH 20-21; chaplains, TT 152-153; civilians, MI 26, 140; Confederate, BD 4, 51-52, 55, 70, 73, 78-79, 83, 91-92, 104, 108, *118-119*, 126, 135, *143-145*, *147-149*, 150, *152*, DE 38, 55, 71, 103, 128, 165, 170, LE 23, 31, 36, 39, 47, 60, 70, 72-73, *108*, 109, 142, 167, OR 3, 37, 78, 103, TT 78-79, 83-85, 98; Confederate Army, MI 35, 37, 41, *44-45*, 62, 67, 100, 104, 112, 115, 122-123, 127, 132, 149, 162, 166; Confederate Navy, MI 20-21, 29, 31-32; deaths among prisoners, TT 118, 129, 131, *133*, 134-135; at Dranesville, FO 64; evacuation of, YA 124, *125*; evacuation and treatment of, TT 20, 78-79, 81, 88-95, *100-109*; at Fair Oaks, FO 164, 166-167; Federal, DE 69, 71, 103, 128, 135, 165, 170; at Fort Donelson, SH 82, *83*, *88-89*, 97; at Fort Henry, SH 65-67; at Hanover Court House, FO 133; in James River operations, FO 128; at Mill Springs, SH 56; in Peninsular Campaign, FO 102; in St. Louis, SH 15-16; at Seven

Pines, FO 139, 141, *168-169*; at Shiloh, SH 9, 113, 116-119, 125-126, 133-134, 137-138, *140-141*, 144-147, 151-152, *154*, 155; treatment of, YA *17*, 87-89, 116, 120-122, 126-129, *130-131*; Union, BD 47, 49, 51, 55, 64, 73, 76, 79, 83, 87, 89-91, 96, 99-100, 105, 108, *109*, 121-122, 126, 137-138, 150-151, *152*, 156, 159, LE 23, 31, 36, 41-42, 46-47, *54-55*, 60, 72-73, 75, 107, *108*, 109, 142, 149, 158, 167-168, OR 103, *109*, 151, TT 35, 78-79, 81, 83-85, 87-90, *93*, 98; Union Army, MI 20, 35, 37, 40-41, 43-44, 62, 67-68, 94, 96, 104, 112, 114-115, 119, 122-123, 127, 132, 146, 149, 166; Union Navy, MI 26, 32, 100, 139, 162; United States Navy, SH 65-67; war total, FI 54; in western Virginia, FO 12; at Williamsburg, FO 113; at Wilson's Creek, SH 29; wounds, incidence of, TT 88, 92; at Yorktown, FO 92. *See also* Hospitals; Medical Department; Medical Services; Nurses; United States Sanitary Commission

Catharpin road, KI 58-59, 83

Catherine Furnace, RE 126, *map* 127, 133, 140

Catholics, prejudice against, BR 100-101

Catlett's Station, Virginia, LE 125, *126-127*, SP 119

Catoctin Mountain, BD 18, 44

Catonsville, Maryland, AS 18

Catskill, BL *73*, CO *118*, *130*

Caucasian, NA 142

Cavalry, GE 36, 38; armament and equipment, GE *40-43*; arms, FI *72-75*; decline of, FI 39; dismounted tactics, GE 45, *47*; at Gettysburg, GE *132*; organization, FI 55; tactical doctrine, FI 50-51, 55; uniforms, GE *38-40*

Cavalry actions, AP *70*, 82, AT 136-138, 140, 143, FL 27-28, 91, 119, *120-121*, 139, 157, FO 83, 107-108, 110, *119*, FR *57*, *161*, KI 29, 36, 62, 85, 86, 114-119, 149, 151, TE 44, 45, 59, 87, 93, 96, 97, TR 21-23, *24-25*, *54-55*, 56-57, 70, 110-113, *114-115*; at Belmont, SH 53; at Boonville, SH 20; Confederate, CH 18, 79, 80, DE 35-36, 38, 54-55, 66-70, 83, 86-87, *88-89*, 90, 92, 101, 114, 123, 126-129, *131*, 135, 149, 151, 156-158, MI 26, 60-62, 88-96, SM 19, 34, 50, 52, 67, 85, 90-91, 142-143, 144; Federal, DE 87, 130, 157-158, 160; at Fort Donelson, SH 81, 86, *94*; in Kentucky, SH 54; at Mill Springs, SH 55; at Shiloh, SH 105, 111, 140, 148, 152; at Springfield, SH 33; Union, CH 24, *29*, 44, 79, 80, MI 87-89, *map* 90, 91-93, *94*, 95-96, *97*, SM 50, 52, 66, 67, 85, 130, 142-143, 144

Cavalrymen, MI *92-93*

Cavalry units: branch colors, FO 60; organization, FO 20. *See also names of commanders, units, or under states*

Cave Spring, Georgia, SM 28

Cawood, Charles H., SP 51

Cayuga, CO 66-67, 69

Cecile, BL 86

Cedar Creek, DE *14-15*, FL 104, 140, 141

Cedar Creek, Battle of, FL 2, 144-145, *146*, 147, *map* 148, 149, *150*, 151-155, *map* 156, 157-158, *160-171*; Confederate looting at, FL 149, 151; Taylor's narrative, FL *161-171*; Union counterattack, FL 153, *154-155*, 156-157

Cedar Mountain, KI 28, OR *44-45*

Cedar Mountain, Battle of, LE *98-99*, *map* 100, 103, *104-109*, 111, *114-115*, TT 85

Cedar Run, LE 100, 103, 125

Cedarville, Virginia, DE 127-128, *map* 130

Cemeteries, TT 99; military, CH *119*

Cemetery Hill, BD 121, 131-132, GE 52, 62, *map* 63, 64-65, *66*, 67-71, 74-75, 80, *92-93*, 105, 112-114, *115-116*, 117-119, *125*, 131, 133, *136-137*, 138, *160-161*

Cemetery Ridge, GE *map* 63, 68-69, 75-80, 98, 100, 103-106, 109, 110-111, *120-121*, 126, 128, *map* 130, 131-135, *136-137*, *map* 138, *141*, 143, *162*

Censorship, OR 46, 49-51, SH 33; in South, BR 40

Centenary College, OR 54

Centennial Exposition, NA *150-151*

Centralia, Missouri, SP 159-160

Central Pacific Railroad, NA 83, *84-85*, 86

Central Park, YA *54-55*

Centreville, Virginia, FI 111-112, 117-118, *120*, 122, 124-128, 136-137, 148-150, FO 8, 39, 63, *82*, 85, LE 132, 135-138, 143-144, 146, 164, 166-167

Cerro Gordo, Mexico, DE 25

Chaffin, R. B., TT 40

Chaffin's Bluff, TR 69, 95, 97, 138-139, 142, 145-146, 148-150

Chaillé-Long, NA 155

Chain Bridge, DE *138-139*, FO 17, *25*, SP 25, 26

Chalmers, James R., SH 123, 143-144, 148, SM 125, 128, 134, 137, 143, 144, TE 51, 55, 124, 127, 129

Chalmette defense line, CO 55, *map* 62, 74

Chamberlain, Daniel H., NA 149

Chamberlain, Joshua Lawrence, AP 4, 80-81, 85, 86, 88, 91, *152*, 153, 155, GE 76, *81*, 83, RE 88-89, 91, TR *51*, TT 20, 81; letter by, TR *51*

Chamberlain, Thomas, TR 51

Chamberlayne, John H., LE 124

Chambers, Henry, AP 90, 91

Chambersburg, Pennsylvania, BD 166, *167*, FL 91, *92-99*, GE 26, 68, 147, 150

Chambersburg pike, GE 44-45, 48, *56-57*, 58, 72-73

Chambliss, John R., Jr., TR 98, *102*

Chameleon, BL 101

Champion, Sid, MI 123

Champion's Hill, Battle of, SP 75

Champion's Hill, Mississippi, MI *map* 2-3, 108, 116-117, *map* 118, 119, *120-121*, 122, *124-125*, 156

Confederate Brigadier General Francis R. T. Nicholls, a casualty at Winchester and Chancellorsville

The military cemetery in Alexandria, Virginia, containing the graves of more than 3,000 Union soldiers

KI The Killing Ground; LE Lee Takes Command; MI War on the Mississippi; NA The Nation Reunited; OR Confederate Ordeal; RE Rebels Resurgent; SH The Road to Shiloh; SM Sherman's March; SP Spies, Scouts and Raiders; TE The Struggle for Tennessee; TR Death in the Trenches; TT Tenting Tonight; YA Twenty Million Yankees

49

Jacket of John B. Royal, a gunner in the Richmond Howitzers, wounded at the battle of Chancellorsville

The ruins of Secession Hall in war-ravaged Charleston, South Carolina

Chancellor house, KI *49*, 60, RE 120, 124, 133, *136-137*, 142, 148-150
Chancellorsville, Battle of, RE *map 127*, *136-137*, *map* 142, *map* 155, TT 88, 92; casualty total, RE 160; Confederate concentration, RE 123-124; railroads in, RE 8-9, *20-21;* roads in, RE 124, 126-130; Union advance to, RE *162-171;* Union concentration, RE 120-125; Union withdrawal, RE 149-150, 158-160; weather, effect on, RE 118-120, 128, 159
Chandler, Albert, SP 68
Chandler, William E., NA 152
Chandler, Zachariah, FO 68, NA 152, RE 92, YA 146
Chandler's Farm, RE 130, 140
Chantilly, Battle of, BD 8, 54, LE *166*, 167
Chaplains, OR 58-59, SH 117-118; appointment, TT 144, 147; casualties, TT 152-153; in combat, TT 152; Confederate, MI 150-152; as foragers, TT 63; Jews appointed, TT 147; misconduct by, TT 147; number in service, TT 147; services for troops, TT 144-145, *146-147,* 148-152, 154; Union, MI 58. *See also* Dabney, Robert L.
Chaplin, Daniel, TR *61*
Chaplin River, TE 62, 65
Chapman, Alford, KI *171*
Chapman, Conrad Wise, CO 99; paintings by, CO *99-109*, MI *38-39*
Chapman, Horatio, SM 158
Chapman, John Gadsby, CO 99, *108-109*
Chapman, Maria Weston, BR 69
Chapman, William, KI 119, LE *156-157*
Chapultepec, Mexico, DE 25, *26-27*
Charles City Court House, Virginia, TR 26
Charles City Road, LE 55
Charleston, Illinois, BR 106
Charleston, South Carolina, AP 52, 53, 61, 163, BR *151*, CO *map* 113, NA 26, TT *16, 66*, 122; artillery strength, BR 135-137; as blockade-runners' port, BL 87-88, 100-101, 107, 116; as blockade target, BL 21, 24, 25, *26-27*, 28-29, 107; bombardment, CO 110, 135, *136*, 137-139, 161; channel obstructions, CO 113, 118; Democratic convention in, BR 109-110; evacuated, CO 141; fortifications, CO *111*, 112-113; and Fort Sumter reduction, BR 138, 146-147, *153*, 160, *162-163, 166-167;* harbor, BR *map* 150; militia mustered, BR *122;* naval operations, CO 17, 86, 91, 99, *104-105, 108-109*, 110, 112-121, 133-134, 139-141; population, BR 14; refugees in, OR 116, 123; secession convention in, BR 24, *26-29*, *118*, 119-121; as symbol, CO 110; troop strength, BR 137; Union occupation of, OR 133, 166; Union troops in, AP *64*
Charleston, West Virginia, FL 88, NA 120
Charleston *Courier*, BR *118*
Charleston *Daily Courier*, OR 55
Charleston *Mercury*, BR *28*, 45, 116, 126,

161, OR 17, 48, 53, 149, 166
Charles Town, Virginia, AS 18, BR 89, 91, *94-97*, DE 64, 149, SP 108
Charles Town, West Virginia, FL 105, 108, 109
Charlottesville, Virginia, DE 100, FL 41, 52, 53, 134, 140, TR 18-19, 25
Charlottesville-Staunton road, DE *8-9*
Chartres, Duc de, FO 24
Chase, John F., RE 149-150
Chase, Kate, YA *150*
Chase, Salmon P., AS 51, CH 65, DE 147, FO 63, 68, 75, 124-125, NA 20, 34, *74-75*, YA *58, 148;* Butler, relations with, FI 77; and currency supply, YA 58; on emancipation, YA 39, 58; and Kansas-Nebraska Act, BR 72; Lincoln, relations with, YA 146-147, 154; and officer appointments, FI 58; presidential ambitions, YA 150, 152; as presidential candidate, BR 113; resignation, YA 147, 154; Seward, rivalry with, YA 146-147; and slavery extension, BR 42; and war financing, YA 56-58. *See also* Treasury Department
Chatham Artillery, OR 78
Chattahoochee River, AT 50, 60, 76, 78, 141, SM 19, 20; bridges, AT 145, *146-147*
Chattanooga, CH *94*
Chattanooga, Battle of, CH *map* 132, 150, 154, TT 85-86; action at Lookout Mountain, CH 130-136; action at Missionary Ridge, CH 136-150; casualties, CH 154; fortifications at, CH 133, 138, 142-143; lunar eclipse during, CH 134; prisoners, CH 154; rout of Bragg's army, CH 147-148, 150
Chattanooga, Tennessee, AT 22, CH *map* 2, *14-15*, 18, 29, 34, 36, 42, 43, 44, 47, 63, 64, 72, *82-83*, 88, 98, 100, 104, 105, 117, 136, *156-157*, 160, *166-167*, 168, 169, SH 157, SM 14, 17, 28, 32, 34, 83, SP 78, 111, TE *map* 2-3, 41, 43, 50, 85, TT 71; army stables at, CH *162-163;* Bragg at, OR 22; Bragg retreats to, CH 30; civilian flight from, CH 33, 83; conditions in, CH 81, 156; Confederate base, CH 24; as Federal supply base, AT 8, 9, 24; money issue, OR *73;* munitions production, OR 21-22; as objective, TE 8, 17, 80, 161; rail depot, CH 98, *155;* rail junction, TE 8, 10; as railroad center, OR 27; strategic value, CH 8, 18; supply routes for, CH 78, 79, 80-81, 89, 90, 97, 156; topography around, CH 32; Union supply base, SM 44; wharves at, CH *164-165*
Chattanooga *Daily Rebel*, TE 160
Chattooga River Valley, SM 32
Chavez, J. Francisco, FR 118
Cheatham, Benjamin Franklin, AT 71, 75, 90, 92, 106, 111, 134, CH 46, 47, 56, 85, SH 122, SM 88, 89, *93*, TE 59, 60, *62*, 94; background, SM 83; at Franklin, SM 98, 116; at Nashville, SM 125, 126, 133,

134, 137, 139, 142; at Perryville, TE 61, 62, 64, 65; at Spring Hill, SM 91, 92, 93, 95; at Stones River, TE 118, 121, 123, 157, 158
Cheatham Hill, AT 71, 72
Cheat Mountain, Battle of, LE 22
Cheat River, FI 92
Cheeves plantation, SM 150
Cheney, Elnathan S., GE *43*
Cheops, BL 128
Cherbourg, naval battle at, BL 155, *156*, 157-160, 162, *map 163*, *164-171*
Cherokee Indians, FR 136, 138-*139*, 142-143, 146-148, 150, 152, 155
Cherokee troops, TT 31
Chesapeake & Ohio Canal, BD 153, *169*, DE 46, 64, FO 44, 75
Chesapeake Bay, DE 61; strategic value of, FI 76
Chesnut, James: and Fort Sumter surrender, BR 138, 141, 157; in secessionist movement, BR 130
Chesnut, Mary Boykin, AT 155, LE 88, MI 140, NA 28, OR *30*, 42, SP 29, TE 82; on Atlanta loss, OR 148; on casualties, OR 43; on Fort Sumter bombardment, BR 120, 141, 146-147; on morale, OR 150-151; on Nashville loss, OR 160; on politicians, OR 33; on propaganda, OR 58; on Richmond conditions, OR 36-37, 40; on secession, BR 119; on security breaches, OR 49-51; on slave sales, OR 128-129; on social changes, OR 60; on soldier's servants, OR 78; on war atmosphere, BR 138
Chess games, TT *61*
Chester, James, BR 146-147, 151-152, 154
Chester, Samuel Knapp, AS 28-29
Chesterfield Bridge, KI 132, 133, 135, *140*
Chester *Picket Guard*, YA 29
Chevaux-de-frise, FO 105
Chew, Robert P., DE 130
Chewning farm, KI 61
Cheyenne Indians, FR 106, 122-129, *130-131*, 160, NA 93, 96
Chicago, Illinois: BR *106-107*, SH 9, 96, 131-133; civil disorders, YA 99; construction boom, YA 23; Lincoln funeral procession, AS *125, 126-127;* population, BR 16; population growth, YA 22; prostitution in, TT 61; relief work in, YA 133; Republican convention in, BR 111-113
Chicago Daily Times, BR *108*
Chicago Highland Guards, SM 140
Chicago *Journal*, CH 45
Chicago's Irish Brigade, FL *91*
Chicago *Times*, YA 30-31
Chicago Tribune, BR 116, SH 96, YA 30, 79, 133, 146
Chickahominy River, FO 130-133, 136-138, 154-155, *156-157*, 158, 167, TR 19, 34-36, 149; operations around, LE *map* 2-3, 23-25, 27-28, 31, *map* 32, 36-37,

AP Pursuit to Appomattox; AS The Assassination; AT Battles for Atlanta; BD The Bloodiest Day; BL The Blockade; BR Brother against Brother; CH The Fight for Chattanooga; CO The Coastal War; DE Decoying the Yanks; FI First Blood; FL The Shenandoah in Flames; FO Forward to Richmond; FR War on the Frontier; GE Gettysburg;

Officers of the 22nd Michigan at their comfortable quarters near Chattanooga, Tennessee

38-39, 45, 48-49, 53, 86-87
Chickamauga, CO 167-168
Chickamauga, Battle of, CH *map* 49, 57, 58-59, 69, OR 52, TT 122; Bragg's strategy, CH 54; carnage at, CH 46, 47, 52, 73; Cleburne's twilight attack, CH 49, 50, 52, 53; irregular nature of fighting at, CH 58-59; Longstreet attacks gap left by Wood, CH 57, 58; rout of Federal right wing, CH 61; Thomas' stand at Snodgrass Hill, CH 65, 66, 68, 69, 124-125; Thomas' withdrawal, CH 66-67, 68, 69, 72
Chickamauga Creek, CH *map* 2, 43, 44, 45, 46, 47, 49, 50, 52, 55, 59, 138, 142
Chickamauga River, TE 161
Chickamauga Station, CH 117, 121, 150
Chickasaw, CO 143, 156
Chickasaw Bayou, Battle of, TE 160
Chickasaw Bluffs, MI 57, 63-67, 66-67, 70, 80, 96-97, 117, 144
Chickasaw Indians, FR 136, 139, 148-149, 155
Chickasaw troops, TT 31
Chicora, CO 113, 120, 133
Chief of staff, FO 17
Children, military playthings of, YA 112-113
Childs, James H., LE 78
Childs, Thomas, DE 28
Chillicothe, Ohio, TT 34-35
Chilton, Robert H., BD 21
Chimborazo Hospital, OR 167, TT 96-97
Chinault, Sam, AT 146
Chinn Ridge, LE 159, *map* 160, 161, 162-163
Chippewa Indians, FR 72
Chisholm, James A., BR 140
Chisolm, Alexander, SM 158
Chittenden, Lucius E., FI 18-20
Chitwood brothers, AP 67
Chivalry tradition, OR 8, 10-11, 46
Chivington, John M., FR 28-33, 37, 122-123, 125-128, 130
Choctaw Indians, FR 64, 136, 139, 148, 149, 155
Choctaw troops, TT 31
Chowan River, CO 34
Christian, Eli, LE 59
Christian, Robert A., LE 59
Christian, William A., BD 71, 78
Christmas, Charles Thomas, cotton-baling press invented by, NA 107
"Christmas" (Timrod), OR 48
Churcher, Corporal, SH 91
Churches: membership decline, OR 59; propaganda by, OR 42, 58-59. *See also* Clergymen; Religion
Churchill, Thomas J., FR 56, 61, 63, 65, MI 68, TE 44, 47, 48
Churubusco, Mexico, DE 25
Cicero, TT 67
Cilley, Clinton A., NA 64
Cincinnati, MI 136-137, SH 59, 63, 64, 65, 67

Cincinnati, Ohio, CH 32, 101, FI 36-37, NA 111, SH 95, TE 32, 33, 39; business decline, YA 57; civil disorder, YA 35, 103; German influence in, YA 21; panic in, TE 24, 49; prostitution in, TT 61
Cincinnati *Enquirer*, NA 155
Cincinnati *Gazette*, CH 61, TE 32, YA 63
Ciphers: Confederate, SP 24, 26, 66, 67; disks, SP 66; and Mrs. Greenhow, SP 24, 26, 29; Union, SP 70-71, 88
Circassian, BL 21, 112-113
Cities, population shift to, YA 20, 22-23
Citizen-soldier tradition, TT 21
City of Memphis, SH 147
City of New York, CO 23
City of Vicksburg, MI 77, 78
City Point, Virginia, AP 14, 21, 24, 34, 42, 46, 50, 76, 108, 128, 152, AS 43, 53, 54, 56, SM 122, 97, 110, 136, TT 99, 104, YA 100, 132; explosion at, SP 81, 84-85; Union supply base, TR 160-171
City Point Railroad, TR 39, 161, 171
Civil disorders, OR 10, YA 86; in Connecticut, YA 20, 22; in Georgia, OR 85, 149; in Illinois, YA 99; incidence, YA 23; in Kentucky, OR 149; in Maryland, OR 49; in Massachusetts, YA 29, 110; in Michigan, YA 103; in New York City, YA 40, 53, 103-110; in New York State, YA 102-103; in Ohio, YA 27, 35, 103; in Pennsylvania, YA 99; in Virginia, OR 30, 82, 85-86, 88, 168; in Wisconsin, YA 35, 92
Civilian labor volunteers, TE 32-33, 34
Civilians: casualties, MI 26, 140; food shortages, MI 149-151; living conditions, MI 125-126, 139, 140, 141, 149-152; morale, MI 83, 125, 139-140, 151-152; refugees, MI 18, 26, 126
Civil rights, restrictions on, YA 20, 29-34
Civil Rights Act, NA 41
Claflin, Ira W., BR 144
Clalin, Frances, TT 27
Clampitt, John, AS 148, 149, 150, 157, 159
Clarendon County, South Carolina, OR 116
Clark, Charles: Mississippi troops withheld by, OR 155; on slave uprisings, OR 149
Clark, Churchill, FR 144
Clark, Gaylord, FL 14
Clark, Henry T., OR 74
Clark, Hiram, AP 141
Clark, James, TR 63
Clark, John B., BR 109
Clark, Marcellus, SP 143
Clark, Whiting, TR 63
Clark, William H., SM 24
Clark, William S., CO 36-37
Clark, William T., AS 92
Clarke, John Sleeper, AS 28, 35, 37, 38
Clarke, Kate (Kate King), SP 154, 161
Clarke County Journal, OR 79
Clark's Mountain, KI 45, LE 125
Clarkson, J. J., FR 148
Clarvoe, John A. W., AS 108, 109

Clay, Cassius Marcellus, BR 39, FI 26-27
Clay, Clement C., AS 144, 145
Clay, Henry, BR 34, 101; legacy of, BR 47; and Missouri Compromise, BR 36; as sectionalist, BR 33; and slavery extension, BR 44-45
Clay Battalion (District of Columbia), FI 26-27
Clay farm, TR 49
Clayton, Henry D., AT 135, CH 142
Clayton's Store, Virginia, TR 22
Cleary, William C., AS 144
Cleburne, Patrick Ronayne, AT 35, 57, 71, 97, CH 24, 28, 38, 118, 121, 130, 137, 140, 142, SH 114-115, 150-151, SM 119, 120; at Battle of Atlanta, AT 104, 106, 111, 113; at Chickamauga, CH 49, 50, 52, 54, 56, 59; death of, SM 118; emancipation proposal, AT 27; at Franklin, SM 98, 100, 102, 103, 105, 112, 115, TE 43, 44, 45, 48, 57, 96, 99, 108, 117, TT 30; at Jonesboro, AT 144; kepi, sword belt and sash of, SM 120; at Missionary Ridge, CH 141; at Peachtree Creek, AT 95; at Pickett's Mill, AT 54; rear guard, CH 149-150; reputation of, SM 96; at Spring Hill, SM 91-92; at Stones River, TE 113, 114, 117, 121, 123, 157, 164-165; "Stonewall Jackson of the West," TE 117; training of officers, AT 28; at Tunnel Hill, CH 138, 139, 140; wounded, TE 47
Clem, John L. (Drummer Boy of Chickamauga), CH 65
Clemenceau, Georges, NA 70
Clemens, Sherrard, OR 77
Clement, "Little Archie," SP 150, 159, 160
Clendenin, David R., FL 71, 72
Clergymen: propaganda by, OR 42, 58-59; in relief work, YA 17, 131; resistance to Union, OR 159. *See also* Churches; Religion
Cleveland, Grover, AS 124
Cleveland, Henry, OR 155
Cleveland, James, AT 59
Cleveland, Ohio: Lincoln funeral procession, AS 124-125; relief work in, YA 125-126
Cleveland, Tennessee, AT 31
Clifton, MI 26
Climate, effect on economy and society, BR 29
Clinch Rifles, TT 10
Clinedinst, Eliza, FL 36, 37
Clinton, Georgia, AT 138
Clinton, Mississippi, MI 113, 116
Clothing: articles issued, TT 76-77; cleaning and repairing, TT 11-12; costs and shortages, OR 33, 44; production, OR 25, 47, 66-67. *See also* Uniforms
Clothing industry, YA 66, 76
Cloud, William F., FR 153
Cluseret, Gustave Paul, DE 154
Clyne, A. S., TT 110

Chevaux-de-frise, sharpened wooden stakes used as portable obstructions in siege warfare

A Northern child clad in a miniature version of the popular Zouave uniform

KI The Killing Ground; LE Lee Takes Command; MI War on the Mississippi; NA The Nation Reunited; OR Confederate Ordeal; RE Rebels Resurgent; SH The Road to Shiloh; SM Sherman's March; SP Spies, Scouts and Raiders; TE The Struggle for Tennessee; TR Death in the Trenches; TT Tenting Tonight; YA Twenty Million Yankees

51

Confederate Colonel Alfred H. Colquitt of the 6th Georgia, later promoted to Brigadier General

Virginia state buckle

Coal: production, YA 57; resources, BR 18; supplies, OR 19, 22

Coast Survey, United States, CO 16, *119*

Coats, Andrew, LE 155

Cobb, Howell, BD 54-55, BR 130, FO 102, OR 17, RE 78, SM 52, 59

Cobb, Silas T., AS 104

Cobb, Thomas R. R., RE 73, *79*, 80, 84, 86; Benjamin denounced by, OR 15; conscription criticized by, OR 78; Davis criticized by, OR 77

Cobham, George, Jr., sword and scabbard of, AT *91*

Coburn, John, AT 93, 94, 154

Cochise, FR 113

Cochrane, John, RE *29*, 94, 96

Cocke, Philip St. George, FI 112, 124

Cockfighting, TT 69

Cockrell, Francis M., MI 119, SM 21

Cockspur Island, Georgia, LE *map 12*

Coder, Daniel R., RE 67

Codes. *See* Ciphers

Codori farm, GE 104, *122*

Cody, Lieutenant, CO *45*

Cody, William, FR 8

Coehorn mortars, TR *87*

Coey, James, AP 30, 31

Coffey, James, SH 65

Coggins' Point, Virginia, TR 110-111, 114

Cogswell, Milton, FO 45-48, 50, 52

Cogswell, William, AP 73

Coins. *See* Money

Coker, W. J., AT *45*

Cold, protection from, TT 9

Cold Harbor, Battle of, KI *map 2-3*, *54*, 151-167, *map 157*; Confederate trenches at, KI 156; suffering of wounded at, KI 167; Union breastworks at, KI *54*, *160*; Union skeletons at, KI *168-169*

Cold Harbor, Virginia, KI 151, TR 18-19, 21, 36

Coleman, Charles L., KI 98

Coleman, E. C. *See* Shaw, Henry

Coleman's Scouts, SP 79

Colfax, Louisiana, NA 141

Colfax, Schuyler, AS 64, 79, NA *99*, 109

Collamer, Jacob, YA 147

Colleges, OR 42, 54-55

Collie, Alexander, & Company, BL 96

Collier, Robert Porrett, BL 121

Collins, Caspar Wever, sketch by, FR *111*

Collins, Jaspar, OR 93

Collins, John L., RE 133

Collins, Napoleon, BL 150

Collins, William, TT 122

Collins, William O., FR 107, 108, *111*

Collis, Charles, RE *68-69*, 70

Colonna, Benjamin, FL *15*, 32

Colony for slaves proposed, BR 38

Colorado, CO 8, 61, 63; Indian fighting in, FR 122-130; recruiting in, FR 106

Colorado Territory, YA 21-22

Colorado troops: 2nd Cavalry Regiment, FR 152, SP 158; 3rd Cavalry Regiment, FR *126-129*, *130-131*, FR 12, 23-25, 28-29,
34, 123-124, TT 31; 1st Infantry Regiment (Pike's Peakers), FR 17, 27-28, *30-31*, 37, 123, *125*, *126*, 127; militia, NA 93

Color-bearers, CH 45, 148, FL 36, 37, 47, 61, *127*, *133*, 147, *150*, FO *4*, 50, 113, *142-143*, 145, 166, GE *19*, 45, *55-57*, 61-62, 101, KI *33*, *104*, *131*, 160, 161, LE 39, 70, *85*, 107, 145, 154-155, *158*, 167, SH 91, 99, 126-128, TE 115, 126, 146, 154; Confederate, AP 121, AT 112, 116, 148, BD 76-78, 92, FR *165*, MI 41, *42-43*, NA *161*, SM 122, 142, TR 84, 108; Union, AP 28, 37, *40*, 79, 89, 90, 124, 127, AT *39*, 56, 70, *113*, 149, 158, BD 71-73, 100, 133, 170, FR 17, 60, MI 119, 127, 130-131, *132-133*, NA 28, *114*, *115*, SM *63*, 114, 129, TR 24, 51, 103, 124

Colors, FO *125*, GE *36-37*, 45, *150*; Confederate, AP *cover*, 41, 71, 91, 96, 99, 121, *124*, 125, 128, 153, *154-155*, AT *43*, 54, 59, 99, 111, *133*, *148*, BD *10*, 156, *164-165*, CH 25, *58*, 65, 68, 114, *131*, CO *98*, *108-109*, FL *33*, 57, FR 28, 80, 137, *147*, KI 31, 33, 80, 98, 159, MI *85*, *123*, NA *161*, SM 24, 82, 92, 102, *104-105*, 117, *122*, 130, 139, 142, TE *41*, 97, 115, 121, *146-147*, *158*, TR *24-25*, 46, 70, *84-85*, 104, 108; Confederate losses, FO 113; flagstaff ornament, CH *45*; Union, AP *28*, 30, 31, *32*, 37-38, 45, 56, 78, 79, 89, 90, 99, 108, *109*, 120, 122, *162*, 163, *164-165*, AT 70, *86-87*, *94*, 100, 102, *103*, 105, 111, *158-159*, BD *58*, *87*, 100, *101*, *127*, CH 64, 66, 69, 103, 120, 133, 136, 140, 143, 148, CO *85*, *127*, FL *39*, 47, 61, 82, *88*, 91, *120-121*, *126-130*, *132*, *135*, 147, *150*, 153, 157, FR 16, *17*, 28, 35, 60, *110*, KI *90*, *149*, 160-161, *163-164*, NA 28, 68, SM 24, *36-38*, *40*, 42, 58, 62, *63*, 67, 98, *104-105*, *113*, 114, 128, 129, *138*, 150, TE 115, *125*, *146-147*, TR *24-25*, 45, 50-51, *58*, 82, 103, *105*, 110, *116*, *121*, 124, Union losses, FO 16-17, 110

Colors. *See* Color-bearers; Flags

Colquitt, Alfred H., BD 51, 56, *106*, RE *131*

Colquitt, Peyton H., CH *62*, MI 113, *114-115*

Colston, Raleigh E., NA *155*, RE 130, 142, 146-147, TR 31-32, *33*

Colt, Samuel, BR 18, CH 74, 75, LE 18, OR 17, YA 68

Coltart, John G., AT 106, 107

Colt Dragoon revolver, FI *74*

Colt firearms factory, YA 68-69

Colt Navy-model revolver, CO *143*

Colt repeating rifle, FO 101

Colt revolving rifles, CH *74-75*; operation of, CH 76

Columbia, South Carolina, AP 26, 53, 64, BR 24, NA 26, *30-31*, 119, OR 123; civilian sentiment in, AP 52; Confederate
plundering, AP 58-59; destruction in, AP 59-*60*, 61, *62-63*; prison camp at, SM 157; Union torch found at, AP *53*

Columbia, Tennessee, SM 83, 85-88

Columbiad cannon, SM *151*

Columbia Oil Company, YA 70-71

Columbia Pike, SM 84, 85, 92, 93, 96, 100, 116

Columbia prison camp, TT 119-120, 129

Columbus, Georgia, CH 40, OR 23

Columbus, Kentucky, MI 60, OR 58, SH 46, 48, 53-54, 59, 79-81, 101

Columbus, Mississippi, MI 88, NA 158

Columbus (Georgia) *Sun*, OR 29

Columbus *Crisis*, YA 29

Colvill, William, GE 109, *110-111*

Colwell, Wilson, BD 56

Comanche, BL 66-67, *72-73*

Comanche Indians, FR 19, 120, 121, 125, NA 93, 96

Commerce. *See* Economy; Industry

Commerce raiders: captain types, BL 143; characteristics and armament, BL 121, 143, 146, 149, 159; development and construction, BL 20-21, 114-116, 120-121, 145-146; executions threatened, BL 28; privateers, BL *12-13*, 24-25, 28, 31-33; ships captured and destroyed by, BL 25-29, 131, 142, *144-145*, 146, *148*, *150-151*, 154-155, *159*, 160-161; ships lost, BL *13*, 28, *151*, 158-161; whalers as targets, BL 159

Commodore, FO 92

Commodore McDonough, BL *44-45*

Commodore Morris. AP *43*

Commodore Perry, AP 48, CO 32

Communications, combat, FI 113, 122, 129, 132

Communication services, FI 55-56

Communications systems, DE 157, FO 39, RE *42-49*; Confederate, MI 63, 142; Union, MI 62-63, 108, OR *107*

Commutation policies, TT 37

Companies. *See* Artillery; Cavalry; Infantry

Compton, A. H., GE *155*

Compton, James, AT 99

Comstock, Cyrus B., AS 140, KI 84, *128*, RE 59

Comstock Lode, YA 71

Conasauga River, AT 40

Concord, North Carolina, OR 74

Condor, SP 31

Cone, Aurelius F., BR *142*

Conestoga, SH 70

Confederate: 9th Infantry Regiment, CH 55; Orphan Brigade (1st Infantry Brigade), CH 55, 149

Confederate (Federal) Point, CO 158, 164

Confederate Army: abandoned matériel, CH 150; arms supply, FI 46; artillery actions, BD 47, 51, 53, 56, 58-59, 64, 67-68, 88-89, 91, 96-97, *99*, *102*, 104-108, *110-111*, 122, 129, 132, 153, CO 25, 87, 90, *92*, *100-101*, 103, 110, 118, 121, 126, 130, 133, 136, 161, 167, DE 36, 54, 67,

AP Pursuit to Appomattox; AS The Assassination; AT Battles for Atlanta; BD The Bloodiest Day; BL The Blockade; BR Brother against Brother; CH The Fight for Chattanooga; CO The Coastal War; DE Decoying the Yanks; FI First Blood; FL The Shenandoah in Flames; FO Forward to Richmond; FR War on the Frontier; GE Gettysburg;

125, 130-131, 135, 156, 161, 164, 170, FO *92*, 107-108, 139, LE 53, 55, 65-67, 103, 155, 163, MI 4, 24-26, 63, 66, 77-79, 82, 85, 100, 103, 113, 116, 118, 121, 139, *162-163*, RE 54, *62*, 64-65, 67, 72, 74, 76, 77, 80-81, *84-85*, 86, 109, 142-144, 146-149, 153-154, 158, TE 24, 87, *109*, 145, 154-155; artillery losses, BD 136, 153, CO 19, 30, *47-49*, *83*, 85, FO 107-108, LE 67, MI 68, 103-104, 118, 121, *168*, SH 56, *66-67*, 97, 166; artillery lost, AT *47*, 77, 150, CH *147*, 149, 150; artillery salvage, CO 120; artillery strength, CO 21, 31, 35, 124, 158-159, DE 44, 65, 121, MI 18-19, 97-100; artillery units, OR *34-35*; artillery weapons, BD 65, 121, DE *115*; atrocities against blacks, TT 35; atrocities by, FR 64; attacks on foraging parties, SM 55; bands, CO 115, 135, DE *132*; bayonet assaults, DE 40, FO 50, LE 41, 45, 150; bayonet charge, AT 56, CH 113, 114, 140, TE *116*, 140; black laborers, use of, SH 57-58; and blacks, AP 20; black servants in, TT *10*, *16*, 35; black troops, attitude toward, TT 35; and black Union troops, TR 64, 83; booby traps, use by, FO 107-108; breastworks improvised by, SH 33; bridge construction by, DE 54; bridge demolitions by, DE *64-65*, 83, *88-89*, 157, *158-159*, 168-169; bridges, demolished by, FO 89; camouflage use by, DE 48; campaign equipment, TT *73*, *75*; camp life, CH 19, 98-99, CO *12-13*, KI 32-34, MI *38-39*; casualties, AP 31, 39, 67, 69, 99, 102, *103-107*, 110, 128, 161, AT 12, 25, 36, 48, 52, 56, 57, 59, 60, 64, 95, 113, 114, 135, 136, 144, 146, 152, 154, BD 4, 51-52, 55, 70, 73, 78-79, 83, 91-92, 104, 108, *118-119*, 126, 135, *143-145*, *147-149*, 150, *152*, CH 28, 30, 44, 46, 47, 48, 55, 56, 58, 62, 64, 67-68, 73, 80, 109, 114, 115, 136, 139, 149, 150, 154, CO 30, 37, 77, 85, 99, 118, 124, 128, 161, 164, 170, DE 38, 55, 71, 103, 128, 170, FI 122, 131, 133-134, 152, FL 23, 37, 39, 49, 61, 83, 84, 87, 90, 91, 106, 122, *123*, 124, 140, 158, FO 12, 52, 92, 113, 128, 133, 139, 141, 164, FR 25, 26, 30, 37, 59, 62, 65, 70, 71, 146, 151, 155, 161, KI 4, 28, 29, 31, 33, 81, 105, 120, *124*, 130, 165, 169, LE 23, 29, 31, 36, 39, 47, 60, 70, 72-73, *108*, 109, 142, 167, MI 35, 37, 41, 43, *44-45*, 62, 67, 100, 104, 112, 115, 122-123, 127, 132, 149, 162, 166, NA 25, OR 3, 37, 78, 103, RE 71, 87, 111, 129, 160, *170-171*, SM 17, 26, 61, 67, 84, 106, 118, 144, 149, TE 48, 51, 81, TR *cover*, 4, 16, 26, 28, 32, 75, 88, 101, 104, 115, 149-150, 154-*155*, TT 78, 83-85, 88-90, 98; casualties at Perryville, TE 67; casualties at Stones River, TE 123, 126, 130, 132, 150, 158, 159; cavalry, role of, FL 141;

cavalry actions, BD 17, 45, 127, 164, *166-167*, CO 87, DE 35-36, 38, 54-55, 66-70, 83, 86-87, *88-89*, 90, 92, 101, 114, 123, 126-129, *131*, 135, 149, 151, 156-158, FO 83, 108, 110, LE 25-27, *28-29*, 49, 101, 125, MI 36, 60-62, 88-96, RE 33, 39, 50, *map 59*, 61, 105-109, *110*, 111, 121, 126, 130, TE 44, 45, 59, 87, 93, 96, 97; cavalrymen, MI *93*; cavalry raids by, SM 14, 19, 34; cavalry strength, DE 44, 50, 65; cavalry weapons, FL *42-143*; clothing, articles issued, TT *77*; clothing shortages, RE 104; color-bearers, BD 76-78, 92, MI 41, *42-43*; colors, BD *10*, 156, *164-165*, CO *98*, *108-109*, MI *85*, *123*, RE *141*; combat effectiveness, FO 11; commanders, losses in, KI 130, 148; command problems, CH 85; communications systems, BD 134, DE 157, MI 63, 142; conscription program, TT 35-37; consolidated, LE 91-92; corps organization, RE 24; dedication of troops, RE 106; defeats in 1862, RE 24; demolitions by, CO 21, LE 28, *122-123*, 125, 128, 132, MI 76, 85, 123, OR 167-168, RE 14, *16*, *22-23*; demonstrations by, LE 31, 33, 48, 50; deserters, AP 20, 61, 116, AT 27, 28; desertion, BD 11, FR 54, 151, KI 26, OR 10, 16, 78, 86-92, 151, 160, 166-167, SM 18, 19, 70, 121, 125, TE 148-149, TR 158, TT *152*, 153; destruction of, at Nashville, SM 144; discipline, BD 17, TE 20, 24, 80, 91, 148-149; discipline breakdown, FI 157; discipline and morale, DE 46, 55-58, 104, 117, 130-131, LE 23, 41, 72; disease rates, FO 82; diseases in, MI 166; draft animal losses at Chickamauga, CH 73; drill, CH 19, 50, 101; drum, CH *101*; drunkenness, TE 91, 118; enemy disparaged by, FI 96; engineering operations, CO 85, 92, DE 54, LE 29, 55, MI 76, 148; engineer operations, FO 94, 108-109, 128; equipment manufactured for, OR *62-63*; executions, DE 117; executions in, OR 16, 88, 92, 95; fire-direction system, CO 113; first general killed, DE 52; flags of, FI *124-125*, TT *22*; food shortages, MI 149-152, 166, OR 86, 166, RE 104-105, 128; fortifications, LE 24; fortifications, reliance on, TR 64; fortifications construction, FO 94, *98-99*, 108-109, 111, 128, SH 54-58; fraternization with enemy, AT 140, CH 99, 130-131, KI 32, RE *38*, 39, 41, TR 137, 159; fraternization with enemy at Appomattox, AP 150, 152; fraternization with Federals, MI 136; Frenchmen serving in, TT 31; German immigrants in, TT 30-31; graft in, OR 84; guerrilla operations, DE 72; headgear, DE *56*; Hood's evaluation of, SM 95-96; illness

and desertions, CH 34, 36, 37; illness in, DE 46, 55; immigrants in, TT 30-31; impressment program, OR 83; improvisations by, MI 136; Indians in, TT *31*; infantry units, OR *34-35*; intelligence operations, LE 25-29; intelligence reports, RE 33; intelligence services, DE 122, 149; Irish in, TT 30; and Johnston, regard for, AT 90; and Lee at Appomattox, AP *148*; lines of communication, FI 46; looting by, OR 160, SH 119, 141; losses to disease, TE 82, 84; mapmaking, DE 82-83, *84-85*, 158; marches by, DE 21, 38-39, 44, 50, 52, *53*, 54-55, 66, *98*, 99-100, 104, 114, 120-121, 131, 156-157; matériel losses, BL 31, 34, SH 56, 97, 169; medical officers, number in, TT 79; medical services, BD 135, 150, DE 94, LE *115*, TT 78-79; mess facilities, TT *12*, *16*; military heritage, FI 46; mines, use by, FO 107-108; mines used by, CO 35, 113, 115, 118, 152, 158, 161; morale, AP 16, 69, 96-97, 110, 117, 134, 157, AT 27, 28, 29, BD 11, 13, 19, CH 37, 134, 145, 147, CO 76, FI 46, FL 125, FR 35, 56, MI 125-126, 152, OR 78-79, 86, 160, RE 50, 128, SM 33, 82-83, 96, 118-120, 133, 144, TE 50, 82, 159, TR 48; and Mosby, SP 115-116; motivation and morale, TT 22, 26; musicians in, DE *41*, 70, *132*, FO 55, *57*, 99; mutiny in, CO 76; Napoleonic principles' influence on, FI 48-49, 56; Nashville, suffering in lines at, SM 123-124; night attack, CH 93; nurses, TT 78; officers, efficiency of, FI 56-57; officers, election of, FI 96; officer and soldier types, FI *58*, *99-100*, *103-104*, *106*, *109*; officers of Trans-Mississippi Department, NA *19*; panic in, BD 81-82, CH 130, 148, 149, CO 30, 37, FO 165, MI 121; panic in, at Cedar Creek, FL 157, *168-169*; parole pass for, AP *151*; and partisans, SP 109; pay rates, OR 80; personal-experience accounts, FI 156; personal servants in, OR 78, *81*; plundering by, AP 58-59; political appointments in, FI 56; politicians in, OR 11, 78; Polk, regard for, AT 61-62; prisoners captured by, DE 38, 128, 151, 170; prisoners lost, AP 29, 37, 38, 39, *89*, 91, 96, 99, 108, *116-117*, *126*, 127, 134, 161, AT 68, *86-87*, 100, 102, 105, 136, 150, *153*, CH 33, 42, 49, 68, 74, 114, 121, 130, 133, 136, 145, 149, 154, *155*, CO 19, 30, 37, 77, 161, FI 61, 92, FL 46, 49, 73, 85, 90, 105, 116, 122, 124, *154-155*, 157, 158, *159*, FO 113, 133, FR 28, 53, 54, 143, 147, 161, KI *28*, *37*, 54, 91, *94-95*, 98, 103, 105, *112-113*, 153, 159, 160, *166*, OR 60, RE 53, 70-71, 108, 126, 144, SH 56, *96*, 97, 166, *168-169*, SM 26, 67, 116, 118, 129, 130, 139, SP *58-59*, *61*, 86, TE 11, 154, TR 25, 32, 46, 70, 104; prisoners lost to

**A Confederate soldier's shirt, manu-
factured in England**

**A hand-colored ambrotype of a Con-
federate officer from Tennessee**

KI The Killing Ground; LE Lee Takes Command; MI War on the Mississippi; NA The Nation Reunited; OR Confederate Ordeal; RE Rebels Resurgent; SH The Road to Shiloh; SM Sherman's March; SP Spies, Scouts and Raiders; TE The Struggle for Tennessee; TR Death in the Trenches; TT Tenting Tonight; YA Twenty Million Yankees

A Confederate-issued military blanket

Confederate Army (continued)

Federals, BD 47, 103, *116-117*, 135, MI 44, 68, 88, 95, 103-104, 123, TT *111-113*, 135, *168-169;* prisoners taken by Federals, LE *116-117;* prisoners of war, AS 19-20, 43, 71, 109; punishments in, OR 88; and Quantrill, SP 149, 157; railroads, demolished by, FO 63, 74, *118-119;* railroads assaulted by, DE 34-36, 45-46, *64-65*, 123; railroads used by, DE 100-101; railway artillery, LE 50; rations, BD 11, TT 85-87; Rebel yell, AT 57, 99, 107, 110, BD 75, CH 48, 50, 58, 61, 72, 114, FL 28, 47, 60, 78, 115, 145, 149, FO 113, 139, KI 71-73, 78, 84, SH 116, 126, SM 33, 103, 105, TE 29, 64, 114, 116, 119, 121, 153, TR 99, 103; reconnaissances by, BD 21, 44, 164, *166-167*, CO 86, DE 66, 70-71, 114, 129, 133, 149, FO 136, LE 25-29, 49, 65, RE 33, 58, 121, 126; recreation, RE *104;* recruiting by, DE *41;* recruiting campaigns, OR *36,* 74, 78; recruiting programs, SH 11, 21, 54-55, *80,* TT *25,* 35-37, 79-80; regard for Hood, SM 18, 120; religious revival in, OR 59-60; reorganization, CH 37, 53, 85; replacement of losses, TT 48; resentment of Bragg, CH 22; retreat to Appomattox, AP 109-113, *map* 114-115, 116-134, *map* 138, *139;* returning veterans of, NA 26-28, *33;* rockets used by, CO 64; ruses, BD 47, CO 34, FO 39, *85,* 86, 99, 107; scavenging supplies, KI 83; and Shenandoah Valley, reaction to destruction in, FL 68, 69; siege life, TR 65, 136-137, *140-141, 151,* 158-*159;* Signal Corps, SP 46, 50; signalmen, FL 26, 27, 124; slaves enlisted in, OR *166,* 167; snipers, BD 74, CO 129, FO 45-46, *116-117,* 128, 139, MI 136, RE 51-53, *54,* 85, 144, 148; soldiers' civilian vocations, TT 26; soldiers, DE 104, *105-113;* soldiers, portraits of, RE *106-107;* state affiliation of units, FI 54-55; substitutes, policies on, TT 35-37; subversive groups in, OR 152; and supplies, AP 16, 18, 19, 25-27, 31-33, 111-113, 128, KI 115, 132, 149, SM 18, 32, 82, 121; supplies, lack of, FL 53; supply difficulties of, TR 16, 57, 110, 158; supply operations, BD 8-11, 13, CO 35, 84-85, 88, 90-92, 97, 110, 142, 156, DE 83, 94, 146, 151, FI 46, FO 38, 82-83, MI 16-17, 77, 149-150, OR 83, SH 21, 49-52, TE 10, 84, 85, supply problems, CH 18, 98, 101, 111, 117; supply train, FL *70-71;* supply wagons, TE *156-157;* surprise applied by, SH 115; surrender in Alabama, AP 160; surrender at Appomattox, AP *cover,* 134, *152,* 153-155; surrender in North Carolina, AP 160; surrender in Texas, AP 162-163; tactics, SH 33; and Tennessee, SM 82-83; training, FO 39; training and drill, AT 28-29; training programs, CO *13-15,* DE 33, *42-43,* FI 52, 57, 93, SH 19, 21, 57, TT 9, *36-37,* 48, 53, 55; transportation operations, FO 83; troop strength, AP 18, 19, 20, 53, 61, 65, 69, 70, 71, 73, 78, 80, 96, 99, 113, 117, 118, 122, 125, 127, 132, 153, 155, 160-162, AT 22, 25, 27, 30, 35, 38, 39, 40, 49, 54, 60, 64, 68, 69, 76, 136, 140, 144, 148, BD 11-12, 38, 60, 63, 65, 67, CH 19, 20, 21, 34, 37, 39, 42, 44-45, 52, 58, 79, 93, 100, 104, 109, 112, 131, 133, 137, 146, 150, CO 21-22, DE 21, 44, 50, 65, 95, 102, 121, FL 16, 17, 20, 21, 26, 27, 29, 34, 45, 48, 53, 59, 68, 78, 92, 109, 141, 142, 144, 151, 153, FO 17, 28-29, 93, 97-102, 105, FR 17, 19, 22, 23, 24, 25, 31, 35, 37, 46, 50, 52, 56, 59, 63, 65, 70, 136, 137, 140, 149, 150, 151, 152, 153, 154, 156, 160, 161, KI 28, 33, 35, 45, 58, 70, 74, 87, 115, 119, 130, 131, 149, 151, LE 23, 30, 45, 92, 103, MI 17-19, 26, 84, 88, 90, 101, 113, 126, 140-142, NA 18, OR 80, 86, 148, RE 39, 61, 71, 73, 104-105, 118, 125, 128, 140, 154-156, SM 15, 20, 52, 61, 63, 67, 82, 83, 121, 128, 148, 150, SP 26, 33, 72, 73, 75, 106, 142, TE 17, 21, 22, 25, 26, 41, 42, 43, 44, 51, 57, 59, 61, 83, 84, 85, 88, 114, 117, 149, 158, 159, TR 18, 22, 27-28, 31-32, 39, 41-42, 44, 49, 64, 70, 99, 111, 138, 140, 142, 145, 149, 159; troop strength and reinforcements, SH 21, 33, 54, 58, 79, 101; uniforms, CH 43, 64, DE *117,* FI *58, 99-100, 103-104, 106, 109,* FO *59,* OR *19,* 25, 33, 43, *66-67, 81,* TT *53, 73;* uniforms, diversified, SH *106;* unit organization, FI 54-55; use of captured matériel, TE *98,* 144; use of cavalry, CH 18, 19-20, 79, 80; veteran organizations and reunions, NA *159-171;* and VMI cadets, FL 9, 16, 29; water shortage, MI 151; weapons, OR 17-*19,* 21, *22,* 23-25, *64-65;* weapons deficiencies and shortages, SH 21, 25-26, 54, 56; winter quarters at Centreville, FO *82;* woman commissioned in, OR *59;* women in, TT 27, 61; work details, FO *80-81.* *See also* Beauregard, Pierre Gustave Toutant; Johnston, Joseph E.; Lee, Robert E.; Soldiers

Confederate Commissary Department, AP 18, 25, 111-112; broadside from, AP 27

Confederate Navy, AP 42, OR 167; casualties, CO 69, 141, 151, 156, MI 20-21, 29, 31-32; evacuation of Richmond, AP 101; fire rafts, CO 67-68; fleet acquisitions and strength, CO 21-22, 33, 63, 113, 143; at Fort Pillow, MI 20; ironclad construction, BL 33, 46-48, 65, 78, *117, 123,* 125-128, *129, 130;* ironclads, CO 54-55, 61, 63, 67, 69, 72, 74, 76-77, 96-97, *104-105,* 113, 143, *144-145, 148-149,* 150-153, *154-155;* at Memphis, MI 20, *24-25;* mines used by, CO 139, 141-142, 147, *148-149,* 150; Naval Battalion, AP 111, 122, 126; personnel procurement, BL 49; prisoners lost, CO 69; prisoners lost to Federals, MI 20; privateers, BL 11, *12-13,* 24-25, 28, 31-33; prize money, BL 153; rams, CO 69-72, 113, 120, 133, MI 20, 26-32, 80; Savannah River Squadron, SM 145; ship's ensign, BL 159; submarine, CO *138,* 139-141; torpedo boats, CO 139, *140-141;* at Vicksburg, MI 31-32, 77-79; warship construction, BL 10, 17, 33, 46-48, 53, 65, 78, 114-116, *117,* 120-121, *123-125,* 126-128, *129, 130,* 131, 149, 160, MI 26-28, 32; warships, types and armament, BL *13, 18-19,* 28, 48-49, *145, 147, 159;* warships damaged and lost, CO 25, *31,* 32-33, 68-69, 72, 74, 76, 96-97, 141, 151, 156, MI 20, *24-25,* 27, 32, *33,* 77-78; warships lost, BL 60, *63,* 65, *84-85, 108-109,* 117, *151,* 158-160, *164-171;* on Yazoo River, MI 26-29. *See also* Mallory, Stephen R.; Warships

Confederate Regular Army. *See* Regular Army, Confederate

Confederate Signal Bureau, SP 46

Confederate States: agricultural resources, FI 46; arsenals seized by, FI 46; Britain, relations with, BL 14-17, 116, 119, *121,* 125-126; cotton embargo, BL 14-16, 125; fiscal crises, BL 122-125, 161; food shortage, BL 99; foreign intervention sought, FI 46; and foreign recognition, BD 10, 159-160, FO 81, 96; France, relations with, BL 16, 120, 122-123, 125-126, 155; Great Seal of, BL *87;* imports, reliance on, BL 11; inflation in, TT 24, 27; manpower resources, FI 45-48; military and political handicaps, FO 78; mobilization, FI 11, 14, 18, 76; patriotic demonstrations in, FI 13-14, *16,* 18; privateers, BL 11, *12-13,* 24-25, 28, 31-33; propaganda activities, BL 120; railroad systems, FI 46, 57; recognition sought by, BL 16-17, 120, 123, 125-126; Richmond becomes capital of, FO 8; secession movement in, FI 10, 15, 18, 27-28; slaves, number in, FI 45; surrender by, BL 159; transportation facilities, FI 46; and *Trent* Affair, BL 116-120. *See also* Benjamin, Judah P.; Davis, Jefferson; Toombs, Robert

Confederate States Almanac, OR 48

Confederate States Cavalry: 8th, TE 97

Confederate States government: and blacks in Union Army, OR 145; bond issues, OR 30-31; Cabinet, OR 11, 13, *14,* 15, 77, 155, 161; criticized, OR 10, 49; flight from Richmond, OR 167; formation and structure, OR 10-11, 13; hostility and disloyalty to, OR 10, 13, 74-75, *76,* 77, *87,* 88, *92,* 93, *94,* 95-96, 110, 151-152; loans from states, OR 30; money issues, OR *68-71;* newspapers' criticism of, OR 49, 53; recognition sought, OR 29, 148; and states' rights, OR 75-77. *See also*

AP Pursuit to Appomattox; AS The Assassination; AT Battles for Atlanta; BD The Bloodiest Day; BL The Blockade; BR Brother against Brother; CH The Fight for Chattanooga; CO The Coastal War; DE Decoying the Yanks; FI First Blood; FL The Shenandoah in Flames; FO Forward to Richmond; FR War on the Frontier; GE Gettysburg;

Congress, Confederate States; Davis, Jefferson
Confederate States Infantry: 5th Regiment, AT 101, 105; 3rd, SH 121
Confederate States of America: and Fort Sumter, BR 132-141, 160, 163, *168-169;* government instituted, BR 128, 130; peace commission, BR 133; Provisional Constitution of, BR 130; Stars and Bars flag, BR *168-169;* states joining, BR *map 2-3. See also* Southern states
Confederate Torpedo Bureau, SM 152
Confederate Trading Company, BL 96
Confiscation Act (1862), TT 32-33
Conger, Everton J., AS 132, 133, 134, 136
Conglomerates, growth of, YA 78-79
Congress, Confederate States: absenteeism in, OR 11; agriculture program, OR 29; Cabinet, relations with, OR 14, 161; and conscription, OR 13, 22-23, 54, 79; criticized, OR 13, 49; Davis, relations with, OR 13, 15, 160-162; and desertions, OR 78, 88; dissension and disorders in, OR 11-13; and executive branch, OR 11; fiscal programs, OR 33; and habeas corpus suspension, OR 82, 153; leadership vacuum in, OR 11-13; and martial law, OR 80-82; newspapers' criticism of, OR 49; planters in, OR 11; and recruitment of blacks, TT 35; and slave enlistment, OR 166-167; and slave impressment, OR 23; Stephens, relations with, OR 13; and Supreme Court debate, OR 13; tax programs, OR 33, 83, *84;* 20-Negro law, OR 80, 93; and welfare programs, OR 83. *See also* Confederate States government
Congress, United States, BL *18,* 54-57, *58-59,* 60; and Cabinet changes, YA 146-147; Lincoln, relations with, YA 142-147; and reconstruction, YA 154; and recruitment of blacks, TT 32-33; and *Trent* Affair, BL 116-117. *See also* Radical Republicans
Congressional Amnesty Act, NA 145
Congressional Medal of Honor, AP 79, 121, 154, AS 149, FL 48, 82, NA 100, SM 84, TR 117, *124*
Conkling, Roscoe, YA 98
Connecticut, disloyalty in, YA 20
Connecticut troops: TT *43,* 45, 59, 83; militia disbanded, TT 22
  Artillery: 1st Heavy Artillery, TR 65, *134-135;* 1st Heavy Artillery, DE *136-137,* FO *30, 31, 104,* RE *164-165;* 2nd Heavy Artillery, FL 155, 157
  Cavalry: 1st Cavalry Regiment, FL *133*
  Infantry: 5th Infantry Regiment, LE 105, 107; 6th Infantry Regiment, CO 127; 7th Infantry Regiment, CO 111, 124; 8th Infantry Regiment, BD 136-137, CO 37; 9th Infantry Regiment, TT 44; 10th Infantry Regiment, CO 23, 27-28, 36, TT *39;* 11th Infantry Regiment, BD *122,* YA 119; 12th Infantry Regiment,

FL 147, TT 44, 48, 58, 80; 14th Infantry Regiment, BD 93, TT 154; 15th Infantry Regiment, AP 65, 66; 16th Infantry Regiment, BD 136-137; 18th Infantry Regiment, FL 33, 46, 47; 20th Infantry Regiment, RE 146; 20th Infantry Regiment, SM 158; 21st Infantry Regiment, KI 153, 156, 170; 22nd Infantry Regiment, TT *46-47*
Connelly, Henry C., SM 85
Conner, Daniel Ellis, FR 115-116
Conner, Edward J., BR *145*
Conner, James, FL 140
Conner, Zephaniah T., DE 150
Connolly, James Austin, AT 20, 149, 156, CH 23, 25, 26, 33, 35, 134, 136, 148, 149, TE 65, TT 71
Connolly, James H., SM 14, 67; telescope of, SM *15*
Connor, Patrick Edward, FR 108, 110, 111, 112, *113,* 129, 130
Conover, Sanford. *See* Dunham, Charles A.
Conrad, Joseph S., BR *144*
Conrad, Thomas Nelson, AS 12, 20, SP 44, *55;* in Annapolis, SP 58; background, SP 53-54; counterespionage, SP 63; in northern Virginia, SP 57-58; and Peninsular Campaign, SP 55; in Washington, SP 54-57
Conrad's Store, DE 84, 86-87, 89, 117, 167-168
Conscription: exemptions from, OR 22-23, 54, 79-80, 93; instituted and extended, OR 13, 22, 149; opposition to and evasions of, OR 10, 23, 77-80, *81,* 92-93, 148-149, 151, 160; substitute system, OR 79, *82;* and 20-Negro law, OR 80, 93. *See also* Draft; Recruitment
Conscription programs, TT 35-37
Conspirators, AS *25;* trial of, AS 139-151, *152-153,* 154-159; confinement of, AS 139, *142-143, 146-147,* 151; execution of, AS 159-160, *162-171;* shackles and hood for, AS *146*
Constitutional amendments: 15th, NA 98, 99, 111, 157; 14th, NA 2, 52-56, 111, 145, 157
Constitutional Guards, SP 14
Constitutional Union Party, BR 110
Construction programs, YA 23
Construction workers in service, TT 26
Continental Hotel (Philadelphia), SP 16
Continental Iron Works, BL 53
Contrabands, OR 136
Conyngham, David, SM 45
Cook, Benjamin F., BD 71
Cook, George S., CO 135
Cook & Brother, OR 64
Cooke, James W., BL 78, *79,* 80, CO 95-97
Cooke, Jay, NA 83, 125
Cooke, John Esten, AP 112, LE 27, OR 46
Cooke, John R., AP 95-96, BD 103-104, 108, RE 80
Cooke, Philip St. George, LE 29, 46
Cooke and Company, NA 125

Cooking facilities. *See* Mess facilities; Rations
Cooks. *See* Mess facilities
Cooper, A. C., SM 61-62
Cooper, Alonzo, TT 119
Cooper, Douglas H., FR 148, 149, 150, 152
Cooper, Edward, OR 88
Cooper, Samuel, AT 81, FO 79, SH 52-53, TR 136; manual by, FL *12*
Coosa River, SM 28, 33, *35*
Copeland, Charles, SM 75; illustrations by, SM *76-81*
Copp, E. J., TR *28*
Copp, Elbridge, TT 52, 159
Coppens, Gaston, FI 21
Copperheads, SP 58; and draft, YA 149; and emancipation, YA 39, 149; and peace movement, YA 24, 28, *33,* 149, 151
Copper supplies, OR 22
Corbett, Boston, AS 133, *134-135,* 136
Corbett, Thomas H. *See* Corbett, Boston
Corbin, Abel Rathbone, NA 107
Corby, William, BD 100, GE *100,* 101, RE *83*
Corcoran, Michael, FI *60-61*
Corcoran, W. W., YA 16
Corcoran, William, NA *58*
Corinth, Battle of, TE 80, 83
Corinth, Mississippi, MI *46-55,* SH *map 2-3,* SM 82, TE *map 2-3,* 10, 12; artillery assaults, SH 157; Beauregard's role in, SH 157; Confederate evacuation, SH *156-157;* Confederate troop strength, SH 157; Confederate withdrawal to, SH 151-152; fortifications, MI 38-40; Halleck's role in, SH 104, 155-157; operations at, MI 37, *38-39,* 40-41, *42-43, 44-45,* SH 104, 155-157; strategic importance, MI 37, 46; strategic value, SH 101; Union advance on, SH 104; Union occupation, MI 34, 38, SH 157; Union troop strength and reinforcements, SH 104, 157
Corinth Hotel, MI *52-53*
Corliss, Augustus W., BD 57
Corn Creek, SH 20
Corn Exchange (118th Pennsylvania Infantry) Regiment, BD 154
Cornfield, the, BD 67, 70-71, *72-73, map 78, 80-81,* 82-83, 86, 88, 92, *map 98,* 151
Cornish, Virgil, YA 117
Corn Rigs. *See* Summer White House
Corps: activated, FO 84-85, 130; badges, RE *100-101;* organization of, TT 24. *See also names of commanders*
Corps d'Afrique, NA 69
Correspondents. *See* Newspapers
Correspondents captured, MI 86
Corse, John A., CH 137, 138, 139, 140
Corse, John M., AT *137,* SM 22-23, 28, 29; and Allatoona Pass, SM 21-26; and Sherman, SM 20, 24
Corse, Montgomery, AP 90, 127

A typical Confederate infantryman

Sergeant Boston Corbett (*left*), the slayer of John Wilkes Booth, with Lieutenant E. P. Doherty

KI The Killing Ground; LE Lee Takes Command; MI War on the Mississippi; NA The Nation Reunited; OR Confederate Ordeal; RE Rebels Resurgent; SH The Road to Shiloh; SM Sherman's March; SP Spies, Scouts and Raiders; TE The Struggle for Tennessee; TR Death in the Trenches; TT Tenting Tonight; YA Twenty Million Yankees

55

Camp of the Army of the Potomac at Cumberland Landing, Virginia, May 1862

Major General Thomas L. Crittenden of Kentucky, criticized after the Union defeat at Chickamauga

Corse, Montgomery D., LE 159-161, *168*
Cortland, New York, YA 95
Cortland *Democrat*, YA 95
Cory, Eugene, RE 72, 77
Cotton: annual yield, BR 10, 32; destruction of, OR *32-33;* embargo effects, BL 14-16, 125; embargo on, OR *28*, 29; production and marketing of, BR 10, *11*, *29*, *30*, 32, OR *24-25*, 29-31, *136-137;* profiteering in, OR 83-84, *85;* in Southern economy, BR 34; speculation in, YA 73; trade, MI *52-53*, 58
"Cotton Boll" (Timrod), OR 46
Cotton gin invention, BR 29
Couch, Darius N., BD 44, 53, 65, 151, FO 136, 154-155, 158, RE *28;* on artillery efficiency, RE 125; on Burnside, RE 89; at Chancellorsville, RE 125-126, 128, 135, 140-141, 148-149, 151, 158; at Fredericksburg, RE 54-56, 72, 80-81, 85-86, 91; Lincoln's advice to, RE 111
Coulter, S. L., SM 105, 112
Counterfeiting, OR 33, 80
Country Gentleman, YA 22-23
Couronne, BL 157
Coursen, George, BD 97
Courtland, Alabama, SM 33
Courts-martial, TT 153
Coushatta, Louisiana, NA 140-143
Cousins, Robert, FL *14*
Covington, Georgia, AT 98, SM 53, 56
Covington, Kentucky, TE *32-33*, 34
Covode, John, NA 72
Cowan, Andrew, AP 122, GE 135, 140-141, TR 47
Cowan, J. B., CH 79
Cowan house, TE 126
Cowan's Battery, TR *46-47*
Cox, Jacob D., AP 65, 66, 67, 69, AT 42, 53, 102, 147, FO 13, SM 50, 84, 85, 93, 95; at Antietam, BD 120-122, 124, 127, 137, 139; at Bolivar, BD 45; at Franklin, SM 96, 97, 100, 102, 117; at Frederick, BD 27; at South Mountain, BD 45, 47
Cox, Romulus, KI *156*
Cox, Samuel, AS 106
Cox, Samuel S., YA 103
Cox, Theodore, SM 117
Cox, Walter S., AS 145
Coxshall, William, AS *166-167*
Cox's Landing, Virginia, TT 110
Cracker Line, CH 81, 95, 97, 136
Cracker's Neck, Mississippi, OR 95
Craft, William and Ellen, BR 46
Crafts, TT 118, *120-121*
Craig, Samuel A., TT 52, 149
Crampton's Gap, BD 44, *map* 48, 52-54, *55*, 108
Crane, Stephen, NA 159
Crane, William T., CO 115
Craney Island, BL 54, *63*, FO 125
Crater, Battle of, TR 64, 75-78, *map* 79, 80-83, *84-85*, 86-88, *90-93*, *118-119;* relics from, TR *90-93*

Craven, Thomas T., CO 77
Craven, Tunis, CO 147
Cravens, Robert, CH 138
Cravens farm, CH 131, 133
Crawfish Springs, Georgia, CH 47
Crawford, Samuel W., AP 30, 85, 87-88, 90-91, BR 25, 147, *148*, 149-150, 153-156, 160-161, GE *90-91*, 105, KI 68, 150, LE 100, 103, *104-105*, 107-109, TR 101, 103, 155
Crawford Democrat, YA 102
"Crazy Bet." *See* Van Lew, Elizabeth
Crazy Horse, NA 102
Credit Mobilier Affair, NA 109, 110
Creek Indians, FR 136, *139*, 146, 148, 152, 155
Creek troops, TT 31
Crescent Battery, CO 165
Crescent Regiment, Company A, SH 121
Creswell, John A. J., AS 65
Crew House, LE 68, 71
Cribben, Henry, KI 64
Crichton, John, FL *15*
Crime, prevalence of, TT 63, 122
Crimean War, BL 47
Crime rates, YA 23
Crippen, Benjamin, GE *55*
Crittenden, George B., SH 55-56
Crittenden, John J., BR 119
Crittenden, Thomas L., CH 24, 30, 33, 35, 39, 42, KI 136, 141; at Chickamauga, CH 44, 45, 47, 53; criticism of Rosecrans, CH 19; relieved of command by Rosecrans, CH 83
Crittenden, Thomas T., TE 55, 59, 92, 93; at Murfreesboro, TE 26, 29; at Perryville, TE 62, 66; at Stones River, TE 96, 98, 99, 112, 118, 123, 127, 133, 150, 154
Crittenden Compromise, BR 119
Croatan Sound, CO 21, 23-24, 97
Crocker, Frederick, FR 50
Crocker, Marcellus M., MI 114, 118
Crockett, Charles G., FL 159
Croft, Samuel, TT 24
Crook, George, AP 78, 82, 84, 110, 113, 116, 125, 129, 131-132, 138-139, BD 122-126, 131, CH 79, 80, FL 20, *21*, 23-25, 29, 41, 45, 46, 51, 53, 56, 57, 59-61, 89-91, 101, *102*, 108, 109, 113, 124, 126, 158, NA 103, SP 127; at Cedar Creek, FL 140, 141, 145-147, 149, 153, *162;* at Fisher's Hill, FL 125; at Opequon Creek, FL 115-119, 122
Crook, William, AS 64, 76, 82
Crooke, George, MI 130-132
Crooker, Lucien, SH 137
Cross, Charles E., RE 51, 120-121
Cross, Edward E., BD 105, 170, GE 100-101, RE 79-80, TT 157
Cross Keys, Battle of, DE 159-165, *166-167*, 168, *map* 169
Crow Valley, AT 32, 35, 38
Croxton, John T., AP 161, CH 45
Crozet, Claudius, FL 10
Cruft, Charles, CH 130, 142, SH 87,

TE 150
Crummer, Wilbur F., MI 149, SH 82, 144, 154
Crump, Billy, TT *62*, 63
Crump's Landing, Tennessee, SH 105, 116
Crutchfield, Stapleton, AP 123-*125*, DE 125, 131
Cuba, as blockade-runners' port, BL *map* 2-3
Cub Run, FI 127, 149
Culp, Wesley, GE 154, *155*
Culpeper, Virginia, BD 168, GE 14, 16, 18, 25, LE 97-99, 101, 103-105, 108, *116-117*, 124-125, OR *145*, RE 8, 26, 31, 33, 108, TT 154; Union withdrawal from, KI *30*
Culpeper Mine road, KI 62, 73
Culp's farm, GE *160-161*
Culp's Hill, GE *map* 63, 65, 67, 74-75, 80, *94-95*, 98, 109, *112-113*, 114-117, 126-128, *129*, 130, 131, 133
Cumberland, BL 24, 47, *54*, 55-56, 58-59, 60, SH 60
Cumberland, Maryland, SP 127
Cumberland Gap, CH 101, 103, 104, SH 54-57, 59, TE 21, 41, 43, 44, *46-47*
Cumberland Landing, Virginia, FO 130, *134-135*, *137*
Cumberland River, SM 120, TE 70, *86-87;* operations on and about, SH *map* 2-3, 101, *102-103;* strategic value of, SH 9, 54
Cumberland River Bridge, SP *105*
Cumberland Valley Railroad, BD 18
Cumming, Alfred, CH 140
Cumming, Kate, TT 78
Cumming, T. W., CH 114
Cummings, Alexander, YA 73
Cummings, Arthur, FI 143-144
Cummings Point, South Carolina, BR *139*, 147, 152, CO *98-99*, *102-103*, 139
Cunningham, George E., BR *142*
Cunningham, Samuel A., SM 102-103, 116
Curlew, CO 25
Curran, Henry H., RE 72
Currency. *See* Money
Currency supply, YA 45, 57-59, *60-61*
Currier, Charles, KI 164
Curtin, Andrew G., FI *24*, RE 92-93, YA 151
Curtis, Newton M., CO 168
Curtis, Samuel R., FR 124, 138-*140*, 141, 144-146, 150, 160, SH 101, SP 73
Cushing, Alonzo H., GE *121*, 131, 140-141
Cushing, William B., BL 80, *82-83*, 84, CO 97
Cushman, Charlotte, AS 32, 137
Custer, George Armstrong, AP 78, *84*, 85, 91, 110, 121, 125, 135, 136, 138, 139, BD *163*, *FL 102*, 103, 104, 106, 136, FO 113, *137*, *GE 13*, *27*, 38, 132, 157, KI 34, *37*, 115, 118-119, 123, 149, 151-152, NA 92, 93, 96, 102, TR 22-23, *24-25*, TT 158; at Appomattox, AP *142-143*, 144, 146-147, 148; at Cedar Creek, FL 141, 145, 147, 151, 153, 157, 167,

AP Pursuit to Appomattox; AS The Assassination; AT Battles for Atlanta; BD The Bloodiest Day; BL The Blockade; BR Brother against Brother; CH The Fight for Chattanooga; CO The Coastal War; DE Decoying the Yanks; FI First Blood; FL The Shenandoah in Flames; FO Forward to Richmond; FR War on the Frontier; GE Gettysburg;

170-171; and destruction in Valley, FL 135, 137, *138;* at Toms Brook, FL 139
Custer, Thomas W., AP *121*
Cuthbert, George, BR 148
Cutlass, MI *64-65*
Cutler, Lysander, GE 47-51, 53, 58, KI 65, 134, TR 101, 104
Cutting, Francis, BR 72
Cynthiana, Kentucky, TE 24

D

Dabney, Robert Lewis, DE 92, *93,* 94, 115, 135, 160, LE 53, 108
Dabney's Mill, AP 30; action at, AP *28-29,* 31
Daffan, L. A., LE 155
Dahlgren, John A., CO 80, KI 34, SM 155; at Charleston, CO *120,* 121, 133-134; at Fort Sumter, CO 130-133; at Fort Wagner, CO 124, 130
Dahlgren, Ulric, GE *12,* KI 34-36, *39;* gauntlet and sash of, KI *41;* papers of, KI *41*
Dailey, Dennis, TR 104
Daily Loyal Georgian, SM *162-163. See also* Savannah *Daily Morning News*
Dallas, Georgia, AT 50, 59, 60, SM 26, 28
Dalton, Georgia, AT 21, 22, 36, 38, 40, 140, SM 29, TT 71; terrain, AT 27, 30
Dams, assaults on, DE 46, *48-49*
Dana, Charles A., AS 74, CH 47, 60, 61, 63, 81, 83, 88, 89, 121, 142, 147, KI *127,* 137, MI *104,* RE 29, TR 39; Grant, reports on, MI 104-105, 108, 144-145, 147; Lawler evaluated by, MI 122-123
Dana, Napoleon Jackson Tecumseh, BD 90
Dana, Richard Henry, Jr., KI 22
Dandelion, SM *154*
Daniel, Junius, CO 86-87, GE 52-58, 127, KI 65, 100
Daniel Webster, YA 131
Danjou, Jean, FR *41*
Danmark, BL 128
Danville, Virginia, OR 27
Darbytown Road, LE 55-56, TR 97, 139, 145, 153, 155
D'Arcy, John, SP 168
Dare, George, KI *171*
Darnestown, Maryland, DE *62-63*
Darwin, Charles, NA 86
Dauchy, George K., TR 109
Dauphin Island, CO 142
Davenport, Alfred, BD 164, FO 69, LE 39, 155, 158, RE 54, 95, 103, TT 60
Davenport, Edward L., AS *51*
Davenport's Bridge, KI 115
David, CO 139, *140-141*
Davidson's Battery, TR 78
Davies, Harry (alias Joe Howard), SP 14, 15, 16
Davies, Henry E., AP 114, 116, TR *23,* 25
Davies, Thomas A., MI 40

Davis, Andrew, TR *119*
Davis, Benjamin Franklin (Grimes), BD 56-58, GE 16-18, RE 118-119
Davis, Charles Henry, AS *123,* BL 51-52, CO 16-17; at Fort Pillow, MI 20; at Vicksburg, MI 18, 20, 24, 31-32
Davis, David, BR 113, NA 111, YA 153-154
Davis, George E., FL 74, 81-82
Davis, Henry Winter, NA 30, YA 154
Davis, Hugh Wythe, TT *38*
Davis, Jefferson, AP 19-21, 25-26, 77-78, 109, 152, AS 54, 67, 100, 144, 145, AT 27, 90, BD 10-11, BL *11, 121,* BR 74, CH 22, 33, 34, 78, 79, 84, 85, 99, 100, 105, 117, 155, CO 91, 112, DE 58-59, 120, FL 9, 29, 52, FR 20, 137, 138, 149, GE 13-14, KI 26, 39, 43, 150, 166, LE 36, 56, 73, 90, NA 17, *22, 24,* 31, 70, 163, 165, OR *9, 14,* RE 36, 92, 121, SM 18, 19, 33, 144, 152, SP 26, 52, 56, 67, 84, TE 21, 41, 42, 87, 88, 90, TR 45, 64; Alcorn's criticism of, OR 77; appoints Johnston to overall command in West, TE 85; arrival in Richmond, FI 18; and Atlanta defense, OR 148; and Baker, SP 57; Beauregard, relations with, FI 152; FO 38-39, 78, SH 79, TE 17; Beauregard reprimanded by, OR 15; Benjamin, relations with, FO 78; black soldiers, attitude toward, TT 35; and blockade, BL 98-99; and Breckinridge nomination, BR 110; at Bull Run, FI 111, 150; Cabinet, relations with, OR 13-15; call for troops, FI 11; and capital transfer to Richmond, FI 18; capture and imprisonment, AP 162, NA 20, *21-23;* chaplain appointments, TT 144; and civil disorders, OR 86; Cobb's criticism of, OR 77; concedes defeat, NA 18-19; concern for Atlanta, AT 78-80; confidence in Bragg, TE 82, 161; Congress, relations with, OR 13, 15, 160-162; and continued resistance, AP 156-158, 160; and Corinth loss, SH 157; criticized, OR 11, 13, 16, 19, 53, 77, 153, 155; death of son, KI 45; depicted on flag, SH *99;* and desertions, OR 16, 88; TT 153; divine aid invoked by, OR 59, 76; elected President, FO 38, 81; elected provisional Confederate President, BR 130-131; and evacuation of Richmond, AP 95, 97, 100, 112; executive ability, OR 15-16; at Fair Oaks, FO 156, 158; family of, OR *164;* flight from Richmond, OR 167; on food production, OR 29-30; Foote's criticism of, OR 77; and foreign intervention, FI 46; and Fort Pickens reinforcement, FI 17-18; and Fort Sumter reduction, BR 123, 135, 137-138; generals, relations with, FO 38-39, 76, 78-79; at Grenada, MI 59; and habeas corpus suspension, OR 82, 153-154; health of, OR 15, 160-161; and Hood, AT 30; inaugurated, OR 27;

inauguration address, BR 131, *134;* on independence, FI 10-11, 18; Jackson, correspondence with, SH 12; and Johnston, AT 29, 30, 78-80; Johnston, relations with, FI 152, FO 78-79, 81-82, 133, 138, SH 52-53, 98, TE 85; Johnston relieved by, OR 148; jury, NA *24;* leaves Union, BR 128; Lee appointed Army commander by, FO 167; Lincoln compared with, OR 15; and Manassas evacuation, FO 83; and martial law, OR 82; and Mrs. Greenhow, SP 23, 32; newspapers' criticism of, OR 49, 53; and officer appointments, FI 57, 93; optimism and perseverance, OR 8, 151, 157, 165-166; and peace negotiations, OR 151, 157-158, 162-165; and Peninsular Campaign, FO 103; personal traits, OR 15-16; plantation home occupied, OR *154;* on planter class, BR 12; Polk, relations with, SH 19; prewar service, FO 76-78; and privateers, BL *11, 12,* 24, 28; public opinion of, OR 16; on railroad construction, OR 27-28; relations with Bragg, TE 20, 83; removed as commander in chief, OR 162-163; reward poster for, NA *21;* and Richmond security, FO 127; at Seven Pines, FO 145; shawl worn by, NA *22;* and Shiloh, SH 113, 147; and ships seized by Britain, OR 148; and slave enlistment, OR 166; on slavery, OR 75, 151; on slave uprisings, OR 149; spies in household, SP 88; and states' rights, OR 155; Stephens, relations with, OR 13, 90, 165; strategic plans, FI 45-48; FO 78; and subversive elements, OR 151-153; and tallest soldier, TT 28; and *Trent* Affair, BL 116, *119;* and Union mobilization, FI 13-14; and Vicksburg defense, MI 16, 20, 59-60, 109, 116; war aims, OR 151, 157; and warship construction, BL 10, 145; and weapons shortages, SH 54. *See also* Confederate States; Confederate States government
Davis, Jefferson C. (Union general), AP *54,* 72, AT *22-23,* 48, 69, 71, 74, 148, BR 147, *148,* 149, 157, CH 48, 57, 60, 118, FR 143, SM 49, *51,* 60, 70-71, TE 112, 117, 118, 120, 121, 122, 126, 150; and Ebeneezer Creek tragedy, SM 72; shoots Nelson, TE 54, *56;* at Stones River, TE 113
Davis, Joe, KI 45
Davis, John, CO 32-33
Davis, Joseph, MI 61, OR 31
Davis, Joseph R., GE 45, 49-50, 61, 138-139
Davis, Peregrine, AS 112
Davis, Richard B., TR 82
Davis, Sam, SP 79, 80; memorial to, SP 79
Davis, Theodore, AT 89, CH 79, 80, *125,* MI *154;* sketch by, AT *94*
Davis, Varina Howell, AP 19, BR 131, NA 21, 22, OR 116, *164*

Naval Commander William Barker Cushing, celebrated for his attack on the C.S.S. *Albemarle*

Brigadier General Junius Daniel, distinguished at Gettysburg and mortally wounded at Spotsylvania

KI The Killing Ground; LE Lee Takes Command; MI War on the Mississippi; NA The Nation Reunited; OR Confederate Ordeal; RE Rebels Resurgent; SH The Road to Shiloh; SM Sherman's March; SP Spies, Scouts and Raiders; TE The Struggle for Tennessee; TR Death in the Trenches; TT Tenting Tonight; YA Twenty Million Yankees

57

Major General Thomas Devin, one of the Union's best cavalry commanders

The 13-inch siege mortar "Dictator," used to shell Petersburg from a flatcar

Davis' Ford, SM 88
Dawes, Ephraim C., SH 114, 116
Dawes, Henry L., NA 41
Dawes, Rufus R., BD 51, 74-76, GE 44, 50, LE 139-142, 161
Day, William M., AP 35
Dayton, Lewis M., SM 156
Dayton, Ohio, civil disorder in, YA 27
Dayton, Virginia, FL 135
Dayton, William, BL 131
Dayton, William L., BR 103
Dayton *Daily Journal*, YA 27
Dead Angle, AT 72, *73*, 74
Dean, Appolonia, AS 44
Dearing, James, AP 120, CO 93, TR 32, 41, 111, 115
Deas, Zachariah, AP 57
Deavenport, Thomas, AT 43
Debating societies, TT 68
De Baun, James, MI 94
De Bow, James D. B., OR *16*, 17
De Bow's Review, OR 17
Decatur, Alabama, CH 97, SM 33, 83, TE 40
Decatur, Georgia, AT 102
Decatur, Tennessee, SH 157
Decherd, Tennessee, CH 29, 30
DeCourcy, John F., CH 101, 103, 104, MI 63
Deep Bottom, Virginia, TR 64, 69-70, 95, 97, 99, 101-102, 104, 138-139, 145
Deep Gully, North Carolina, CO 86-87
Deep Run, RE 36, 50, 57-58, 61
Deer Creek, MI 80
Deerhound, BL 160, *170*, NA 126
Deery, John, AS 56
Deery's Billiard Saloon, AS 71
De Forest, John, FL 117-118
De Forest, John William, NA 106, TT 44, 48, 58, 63, 71, YA 36
Degas, Edgar, painting by, NA *122-123*
DeGress, Francis, AT *84-85*, 95, 107-108, 111
DeGress' Battery, AT *82-83*, 107, *110*
Deimling, Francis, MI 114
Delafield, Richard, FO *15*
Delamater Iron Works, BL *68-69*
Delaney, Michael, AT 70
Delany, Martin Robison, YA *100*, 101
Delaware: Union control of, SH 9; as Union slave state, BR 3
Delaware, CO 34
Delaware Indians, FR 147
Delaware troops: 1st Infantry Regiment, BD *112-113;* 2nd Infantry Regiment, LE 71; 4th Infantry Regiment, AP *28*
De Leon, Edwin, BL 120
Delia (slave), BR *49*
Democratic Party: Baltimore convention, BR 110-111; and black voters, NA 67; Charleston convention, BR 110; donkey symbol, NA 129, *139;* factionalism in, BR 110-111, YA 24, 142, 155; financial support of, BR 104; and Liberal Republicans, NA 110-111; peace platform

of, SM 14; platform, BR 101-102; reconstruction policy, NA 17; and slavery extension, BR 105, 110
Demolitions: by Confederate Army, MI 76, 85, 123; by Confederates, DE *64-65, 80-81,* 157, *158-159,* 168-169, OR 167, *168-169;* by Federals, DE 126, OR *102-103, 156-157;* by Union Army, MI 63, 78, 88-91, *95,* 115
Denbigh, BL *92-93*
Denison, Frederic, TT 144
Dennison, William, AS 67
Dennison, William N., TR 26
Dent, Stowton, SP 53
Denver, Colorado, FR 122, 124-126, 128-129, NA 92
Denver, James W., SP 146
DePeyster, Johnston L., AP *111*
Derby, William, KI 156, 164
Derby, William P., CO 16
Derrick, Clarence, FL 34, 36
Derrickson, Ann, YA 108
Desertions, TT 31, 37, 48, *152,* 153-156
Deshler, James, CH 56, *62*
De Soto, Louisiana, MI 16, 85
De Trobriand, Regis, RE 95, TT 29
Detroit, Michigan, FI *12-13, 38-39,* YA *96-97*
Detroit Light Guard, TT 21-22
Devens, Charles, Jr., FO 41-44, 51, KI 164-165, RE 56-57, 129
Devil's Den, GE 71, 76, *map* 78, 79-80, 85, *86,* 87, 98, 101, 126, *165*
Devin, Thomas C., AP 78, 81-84, 125, 138-139, FL 104, 120, KI 119, 151, TR 22, 25
Devlin, Mary, AS 30, *35*, 116
DeWees, Thomas R., GE *36-37*
Dewitt, A. H., CH 40
Diaries, TT 20, 71
Dicey, Edward, YA 21, 34-35, 102
Dickens, Charles, BR 22, NA 53, YA 48
Dickert, D. Augustus, BR 137, 160, CH 114, FL 149, KI 152, 167
Dickey, Cyrus, SH 138
Dickey, William H., FR 55
Dickinson, Emily, YA 89
Dickinson, Joseph, GE 12
Dictator, BL *68-69*
"Dictator" (mortar), TR *138, 170-171*
Dikeman, Henry, TT *41*
Dilger, Hubert, AT 61, RE 129-130, *135*
Diligent, MI 144-145
Dillingham, Edwin, FL 79
Dillon, James, RE 83
Dill's Branch, Tennessee, SH 143
Dimmock, Charles H., TR *42*
Dimmock Line, TR 39, 42, *46-47,* 48, *116-117*
Dingle, J. H., BD 76-78
Dinkins, James, LE 63, RE 53-54
Dinwiddie, Hardaway, FL *14*
Dinwiddie Court House, Virginia, AP 27, 79, *80,* 81, 82, 84, 85, TR 15, 55

Discipline, administration of, TT 20, 53-55, 65. See also Morale and motivation
Diseases: FO *66-67,* 82; in Confederate Army, MI 166; control, YA 124-125; incidence of, TT 78, 80, 83, 87-88, 97-98, 117, 129, YA 23; and military casualties, SM 106; in Union Army, MI 18, 35, 40, 47, 166
Dishonorable discharges, TT 65
District of Columbia, slavery in, BR 44
District of Columbia troops: 1st Cavalry Regiment, TR 32, 111, 114-115; Clay Battalion, FI 26-27
Divisions: organization, FO 20, TT 24; organization and tactics, FI 55. See also *names of commanders*
Dix, Dorothea, TT 95, 98, YA 127-128
Dix, Miss, SP 16
Dixon, Jeremiah, BR 37
Dixon, W. Hepworth, NA 92
Doaksville, Indian Territory, FR 161
Dockery, Thomas P., FR 64
Doctors. See Medical officers
Doctor's Creek, TE 59, 61, 62
Doctors' Line, SP 53
Dodd, Theodore H., FR 25
Dodd, W. O., SM 92, 96, 118
Dodge, Grenville M., AT 98, 99, 104, 110, 134, *145,* CH 97, FR 141, NA *82, 84-85,* 90, SP *74;* background, SP 72; at Battle of Atlanta, AT 100, *102-103;* and Henson, SP 75, 76, 78; at Pea Ridge, SP 73; postwar career, SP 89; at Roswell's Ferry, AT *81;* and Sam Davis, SP 79-80; as spymaster, SP *74;* and Vicksburg Campaign, SP 74-75; wounded, AT 140
Dodge City, Kansas, NA 91
Dogs, fate of during march, SM 59, *60*
Dog tent, TT 45-46
Doherty, Edward P., AS 132, 133, 134
Dole, J. S., KI 98
Doles, George, GE 53, 60, 119, KI 91
Dominguez, Manuel, SP 10
Don, BL 86, 96
Donellan, George, SP 26, 29
Donelson, Daniel Smith: SH 56-57; at Perryville, TE 64, 65, 66; at Stones River, TE 124, 126, 127, 129
Donohoe, Michael T., TR 143
Dooley, John, BD 135
Doolittle, Sergeant, SH 91
Dorsey, G. W., KI 122
Dorsey, Sarah, NA 24
Doster, William E., AS 145, 148, 151
Doswell plantation, KI 136
Doty, James D., FR 112
Doubleday, Abner, BD 52, 67, 73-74, BR 146-147, *148,* 149, 156, LE 138, 141-142, RE 63, 65; at Cemetery Hill, GE 63; at Cemetery Ridge, GE 112, 131, 133, 140; at Culp's Hill, GE 65; at Gettysburg, GE 46-49, 51; at Little Round Top, GE 105; at McPherson's Ridge, GE 56-57, 61; relieved by Meade, GE 74; at Seminary

AP Pursuit to Appomattox; AS The Assassination; AT Battles for Atlanta; BD The Bloodiest Day; BL The Blockade; BR Brother against Brother; CH The Fight for Chattanooga; CO The Coastal War; DE Decoying the Yanks; FI First Blood; FL The Shenandoah in Flames; FO Forward to Richmond; FR War on the Frontier; GE Gettysburg;

A view of Confederate batteries at Drewry's Bluff, Virginia, painted by engineer officer John Ross Key

Ridge, GE 62
Dougherty, William, LE 161-163
Douglas, Henry Kyd, AP 17, 31, 34, 155, BD 141, DE *93*, 149, FL 53, 68-69, 87, 109, LE 126, 149, RE 160, TT 117; on Ashby, DE 87, 158; on Ewell, DE 116; on Jackson, DE 18; at Winchester, DE 130
Douglas, James P., TE 47
Douglas, Stephen A., BR *99, 109*, FI 13, FR 108; on blacks' equality, BR 106; concedes Lincoln election, BR 118; debates Lincoln, BR 99, 105-107, *108;* and Dred Scott ruling, BR 108; and house-divided charge, BR 106; and Kansas-Nebraska Act, BR 71-72, 101; and Kansas statehood, BR 83, 105; lampooned, BR 72; and morality of slavery, BR 106; as presidential candidate, BR 72, 100, 110-111, 113, 116, 119; reelected to Senate, BR *106-107*, 108; and slavery extension, BR 45, 71-72, 105-106, 108, 113, 116; on Union preservation, BR 118
Douglas County, Kansas, BR 76
Douglas Hospital, TT *106-107*
Douglass, Frederick, CO 125, NA *99*, 149, TT 32, YA *100;* abolitionist activities, BR *63-64*, 78; on blacks as Americans, YA 35; on blacks as soldiers, YA 101; on emancipation, YA 37; on John Brown, BR 70-71; on race relations, YA 102
Douglass, Marcellus, BD 70-71, 73
Douglas' Texas Battery, TE 47
Douty, Calvin, GE *27*
Dover, Tennessee, SH 81, 93, 95
Dow, Tristram T., SM 118
Dowdall's Tavern, RE 132-133, 142
Dowling, Patrick, SM *138*
Downes, John, BL 102, *103*
Downing, Louis, FR *148*
Doyle, James, BR 70, 78
Draft: commutations, YA 70-71, 88-89, 93, 95, 105, 110; corruption in, YA 89-92, 98-99; evasions and exemptions, YA 86, 89-91, *92-93*, 95, 98-99, 110; instituted, YA 31, 86, 89, 93-95; lottery selection, YA *87;* opposition to, YA 20, 31, 86, 92, 95, 98-105, *106-107*, 108, 110, 149; troop quotas, YA 93, 95, *98*, 110; troops raised, YA 92, 110. *See also* Recruitment; Conscription
Drake, Edwin, YA 67, *70*
Drake, Jeremiah C., KI *171*
Dranesville, Virginia, FO 39, 42, 48, 50, 64
Draper, Alonzo, TR 140
Drayton, Percival, BL 32, 37, CO 147
Drayton, Thomas F., BL 32, 37, CO 20
Drennan, William, MI 151
Dresbach, Michael, TT 71
Drew, John, FR 142, 146, 148
Drewry, Mrs. S. D., OR *111*
Drewry's Bluff, AP 43, *48-49*, 65, 101, FO 128-129, LE 56, TR *28-29*, 95, 134
Drewry's Bluff, Battle of, KI 130

Drill, TT *18-19*
Drill. *See* Training programs
Drips, J. H., FR 94
Drugs: Army medical use, SM 106, 107; patent medicines, SM *111;* plants used for, SM *107*, 108; production equipment, SM *108-109*
Drummer boys, CH 23, *65*, FL *128*, SM 45, 58, 61, 142
Drummers, DE *41*, 70, 170, FI *49*, FO 55, *58-59, 66-67, 76-77*, MI 131, TT *18-19*, 26, *165-167. See also* Musicians
Drumming out of camp, as punishment, TT *64*, 66
Drummond, Thomas, TR *62*
Drunkenness, TT 58-60, 65
Dryer, Hiram, BD 139-141
Dry Tortugas, AS 160
Dry Valley road, CH 47, 48
Duane, James C., TR 67
Dublin, Virginia, FL 17, 20, 21
DuBois, Henry A., FL 103
Dubuque *Herald*, YA 32
Duck River, CH 18, 22, SM 83, 85, 88, 89
Dudley, Thomas H., BL 120-121
Duff, William S., MI 144
Duffié, Alfred Napoleon Alexander, FL 51, 57, *58*, 59, 60, 89, 91, GE 16, 20, 22, 28, RE 109-110, TT 122-124, *125*
Duffield, William W., TE 27
Duffield's, West Virginia, SP 131
Duffner, William, MI 103
Dug Gap, AT 35, CH 38, 42
Duke, Basil W., SH 98, TE 21, *24*, 87, 148
Duke, John K., CH 81
Dumont, Ebenezer, FI 93
Dumont, William W., TE 55
Dunbar, Aaron, MI 132
Duncan, James H., AP 97
Duncan, Johnson K., CO 55, 64, 67, 73, *75*, 76
Duncan, Samuel, TR 139
Dungan, Robert H., FL 83
Dunham, Charles A. (alias Sanford Conover), AS 150-151
Dunker Church, BD 4, 66-68, 74-76, 83, *84-85*, 87, 89, 92-94, *102*, 103, *110-111*, 129, *152*
Dunkers, DE 8-9
Dunn, Alfonso, AS 77
Dunn, Charles, AP 152
Dunn, Oscar J., NA *71*
Dupin, Charles, FR *45*
DuPont, Henry A., FL 37, 39, 41, 42, 46, *47*, 57, 60, 61, 157; at Cedar Creek, FL 141-144, 146; at Opequon Creek, FL 115
Du Pont, Samuel F., CO *114;* and blockade, BL 29, 91; at Charleston, CO 113-120; and monitors, CO 113-114; operations by, BL 31, 34; at Port Royal Sound, CO 20, 113; on warship construction, BL 21
DuPont's Battery, FL 37, 39
Duryée, Abram, BD 70, 73, 78, FI 80
Duryée's Zouaves, FI 80, 82, *84-85*, FO 69

Duryée Zouave Veterans Association, ribbon from, NA *162*
Dushane, Nathan T., TR 101
Dust in camp, TT 45
D'Utassy, Frederic, DE *154*, FI *96-97*
Dutch Gap Canal, TR *112-113*
Duval, Bettie, FI 113
Duval, Isaac H., FL 91, 117, 118, 146
Duvall, Betty, SP 24, 26
Dwight, Henry Otis: sketches by, AT *150*, SM *71*
Dwight, Wilder, BD 92, *96*, DE *82*, LE *144*
Dyer, David P., NA 116
Dyer farm, CH 58

E

Eads, James B., SH 59-60, 69, 72, 74, 76
Eagle Nest, SP 57
Eakle, Martin, BD 108
Early, Jubal A., AP 78, 139, BD 76-78, 89, *90*, 98, FI 113, 121-122, 136, 140, 146, 148-149, FL 2, 40, *52*, 60, 85, 100, 101, 106, 108, 125, 134, FO 113, KI 29, 81, 136, LE 68, 103-106, NA 117, *118*, OR 167, TR 27, 57, 64, 69, 94-95, 136, TT 61; background and temperament, FL 52-53; at Banks' Ford, RE 156; at Barlow's Knoll, GE 60; at Bethesda Church, KI 149-150; at Cedar Creek, FL 140, 141, 144, 145, 148, 149, 151, 156, 158; at Cemetery Hill, GE *map* 63, 65-66, 113, 118; and Chambersburg, FL 93, GE 26; at Cold Harbor, KI 154, 156; at Columbia, GE 31; at Culp's Hill, GE 116; at Fisher's Hill, FL 124; at Fort Stevens, FL 84; at Frederick, FL 74, *75;* at Fredericksburg, RE 58, 61, 67, 70-71, 151-152, 154, 156; at Gettysburg, GE 26-30, 53, 59; at Hamilton's Crossing, RE 121, 124; and Harrisburg, GE 31; and John Meigs's death, FL 135; at Lynchburg, FL 61; at Monocacy, FL 73, 75, 78, 83; at Opequon Creek, FL 112, 113, 116, 117, 122; in Potomac crossing, GE 26; raid on Washington, FL 61, 63, 66, 68, 69, 73, 84-89, *90;* and Ramseur, FL 79; relieved of command, FL 159; replaces Ewell, KI 148; at Salem Church, RE 156-158; and Sheridan, FL 101, 104, 105, 109, 137-139; at Skinker's Neck, RE 39-40, 58, 61; at Spotsylvania, KI 87; and Toms Brook, FL 139; troop strength, RE 152; at Winchester, GE 22-24; at Wrightsville, GE 31; at York, GE 30-31
Early, Robert D., KI 65
East Chatham, New York, BR 114
Eastern theater, FI *map* 2-3, SH 9
Eastlick family, FR *102-103*
Eastman, Albert, TR *62*
Eastman, Arthur, YA 73
East Point, Georgia, AT 140, SM 50

MAJ. HARRY DOUGLAS.

Major Henry Kyd Douglas of Maryland, aide to General Stonewall Jackson

A Federal drummer boy, photographed in the field

KI The Killing Ground; LE Lee Takes Command; MI War on the Mississippi; NA The Nation Reunited; OR Confederate Ordeal; RE Rebels Resurgent; SH The Road to Shiloh; SM Sherman's March; SP Spies, Scouts and Raiders; TE The Struggle for Tennessee; TR Death in the Trenches; TT Tenting Tonight; YA Twenty Million Yankees

59

Brigadier General Arnold Elzey, severely wounded leading a charge at Gaines's Mill, Virginia

Dress hat and insignia worn by soldiers of the U.S. Army Engineers

Eastport, FR 54, 67
East Tennessee & Georgia Railroad, AT 31, 38, CH 18, TE 10, 21
East Woods, BD 64-71, 73, 76, *map* 78, *80-81*, 82, 87-88, 92, *110-113*, *146*
Eaton, John, MI 58
Eaton, Ohio, BR 40
Ebeneezer Creek, tragedy at, SM 72
Ebenezer Church, action at, AP 161
Echols, John, FL 20, 30, 31, 34, 69, 78, KI 159
Eckert, Thomas, AS 76, 132, SP 64
Economy: breakdown of, OR 10; growth of, OR 16; inflation's effect on, OR 22, 30-33, 40, 48, 55, 80, 128, 148, 160
Ector, Matthew D., SM 128, 130, 137
Eddy, Richard, TT 147
Eddy, Samuel, AP 125; identification tag of, AP *109*
Edison, Thomas, patent model, NA *80*
Edisto Island, BL *36-37*, OR 150
Edisto River, Union troops at, AP 57
Edmonds, Sara, TT 27
Edmondston, Catherine Ann, OR 43, 60
Educational system, OR 42, 54-55, 58, *142-143*
Edwards, John N., FR 157
Edwards, Oliver, AP 123, 124
Edwards Depot, Mississippi, MI 111, 113
Edwards Ferry, Maryland, FO 40-42, 44, 47-48
Egan, Thomas, FO 166, TR 45, 156
Eggleston, George Cary, KI 149, TT 53
Egyptian Army, NA 154
Ekin, James A., AS *149*
Elder, William, OR *159*
Eldredge, Daniel, CO 40
Elections: campaign memorabilia, YA *156-157*; national, YA 142-144, 146, 149-155, 158-159, 161; public interest in, BR *22-23*; slave count on ballot, BR 30. *See also* Soldiers; Voters, restrictions on
Elementary Arithmetic (Johnson), OR 58
Elizabeth City, North Carolina, CO *31*, 32-33
Elizabeth River, BL 46, 48
Elkhorn Tavern, FR 145
Elk Ridge, BD 39, *71*
Elk River, CH 30, TE *12-13*
Ellerson's Mill, LE 36
Ellet, Alfred W., FR 52, MI 20, *27*
Ellet, Charles, Jr., MI 20, *27*
Ellet, Charles Rivers, MI 20, 24, *27*, 77-78
Ellet, Edward C., MI *27*
Ellet, John R., MI *27*
Ellet, Richard, MI *27*
Elliot, George, TT 154
Elliott, Fergus, AT *98*
Elliott, J. H., BR 163
Elliott, Robert Brown, NA 70
Elliott, Stephen, OR 58
Elliott, Stephen, Jr., CO 131-132, TR 67, *74-75*, 78, 81, 88
Elliott's Salient, TR 67-68, 70, 73, 75
Ellis, CO 33

Ellis, Augustus Van Horne, GE 85, *87*, RE 143
Ellsworth, Elmer E., FI *62*, *68-69*, YA *139*; first officer killed, FI 63-64, *65*; in invasion of Virginia, FI 61; Lincoln, relations with, FI 63, *66-67*; as national hero, FI *66-69*. *See also* New York Fire Zouaves
Ellsworth, George (Lightning), TE 21, 24
Elmira, New York, AS 109
Elmira prison camp, TT 117-118, 128-129
Ely, William G., FL 47
Ely's Ford, KI 29, 34, 45, 56, 60
Elzey, Arnold, DE 164-165, FI 147, LE 42
Emancipation: opposition to, YA 108-109, 149-150; proclaimed, YA *38*, 39; propaganda for, YA *37*; proposed, BR 38, 62; public opinion on, YA 20, 36-37, 39. *See also* Blacks; Slavery
Emancipation Proclamation, BD 156-161, 168, BL 126, 128, MI 57, OR 111, 136, *140-141*, 146, 149, 158, 163
Emerson, John, BR 79
Emerson, Mark, TR 62
Emerson, Ralph Waldo, BD 159, BR 34, 46, YA 36, 39, 86
Emigrant Aid Company, BR 74
Emigration, YA 23, *64-65*. *See also* Migration; Refugees
Emigration to West, BR 33, 74-75
Emmitsburg road, GE 69, 72-74, 76-78, 81, 98-99, 104, 137, 145
Emmons, James, RE 133
Emory, William H., FL 89, 101, 109, 113, 118, 131, 141, 146, 147, 152, 163, FR 60, 61, 67, MI 110
Empire, Colorado Territory, FR 30
Empty, Colonel. *See* Thompson, Michael
"Empty Sleeve" (Bagby), OR 46
Enchantress, BL 28
Enfield 1853 rifle, FI *70-71*, OR 18, *64-65*
Enforcement Act, NA 98
Engineering operations, DE 54, 61, *64-65*; bridge construction, FO *20-21*, 74-75, 133; Confederate, MI 76, 148; fortifications construction, FO 8, 17-18, 94, 108-109, 128; road construction, FO 105; Union, MI 26, 33, 69-74, 76, 84, 123, *127*, 128-129, 148
Engineer troops: FI 55; and operations, SH *160-161*, 163
England. *See* United Kingdom
Englishmen in Union Army, TT 30
Enlistments. *See* Recruiting programs
Ennis, Thomas Jefferson, AT 137
Ennis, William, AT 137
Enrica, BL 120, 149
Enterprise, Mississippi, MI *map* 90, 91
Eolus, BL 91
Equipment: for campaign, TT *72-77*; maintenance and repair, TT 52
Ericsson, John, BL *47*, 51-53, 65, 67, 73, ·75
Erie Railroad, NA 106, YA 65
Erlanger, Emile, BL 123-125, 128

Erwin, Joseph, AT 132
Escort, CO 90, *92*
Essex, MI 28, 32, *33*, 162, SH 60-61, 63, *64*, 65, 67, 72-73
Etheredge, William H., TR 83
Etheridge, Emerson, NA 29
"Ethnogenesis" (Timrod), OR 46
Etowah River, AT *14*, 50
Europe, arms supplied by, OR 17-18
Evans, Augusta Jane, OR 44
Evans, Clement A., AP 29, 30, 37, FL 78, 79, *81*, 145, 153
Evans, John, FR 106, 122-124, *125-127*, 130
Evans, Nathan G. (Shanks), BD 12, 49, 139, CO 84, 111, FI 112, 127-131, *132*, 133-135, 139-140, 152, *156-159*, FO 42, *43*, 46, 48, LE 159, SP 45
Evansport, Virginia, FO 74
Evarts, William M., NA 73
Evergreen Cemetery, GE *161*
Ewell, Richard Stoddert, AP 19, 110, 117, 133, 139, DE *cover*, *95*, FI 113, 124, 136, FL 52, 53, 124, KI 28, 29, 65, LE 91, *143*, TR 145-146; appointed corps commander, GE 14; at Benner's Hill, GE 114; at Bristoe Station, LE 129, 132; at Carlisle, GE 31, 53; at Cedar Mountain, LE 103; at Cedarville, DE 131; at Cemetery Hill, GE 66-67, 69, 113, 115; at Chambersburg, GE 26; coat of, DE *83*; at Conrad's Store, DE 117; at Cross Keys, DE 159-160, 165; at Culp's Hill, GE 67, 69, 113, 115, 126, 128, 130; at Culpeper, LE 99-101, 103; at Front Royal, DE 123, *124-125*; at Gettysburg, GE 26, 33, 69; at Gordonsville, LE 99; at Harpers Ferry, GE 23; and Harrisburg, GE 31, 33; at Harrisonburg, DE 158; illness of, KI 148; Jackson, relations with, DE 5, 83, 95, 98-99, 114-115; in Lee retreat, GE 151; at Luray, DE 120-121; at Middletown, DE 130; at Mount Jackson, DE 115; at Mount Solon, DE 114-115; at New Market, DE 115-116; at Newtown, DE 129; at North Anna, KI 132, 135-136; at Port Republic, DE 165, 169-170; in Potomac crossings, GE 26, 156; and Sayler's Creek, AP 120-123, 125-127; at Second Bull Run, LE 132, 142; in Seven Days' Battles, LE 42, 65, 72; in Shenandoah Valley, GE *map* 32; at Spotsylvania, KI 84, 87, 91-94, 125-126; at Stanardsville, DE 95; at Stephenson's Depot, GE 25; at Strasburg, DE 151-157; at Swift Run Gap, DE 95, 98, 114-116; Taylor's evaluation of, DE 95-98; in the Wilderness, KI 57-58, 60, 62, 65, 73-74, 80; at Winchester, DE 129, *map* 130, 131, 133, GE 22-25; at York, GE 30-31, 73
Ewing, Charles, MI 127
Ewing, Ellen. *See* Sherman, Ellen Ewing
Ewing, Hugh, CH 137, 138
Ewing, John K., GE *154*

AP Pursuit to Appomattox; AS The Assassination; AT Battles for Atlanta; BD The Bloodiest Day; BL The Blockade; BR Brother against Brother; CH The Fight for Chattanooga; CO The Coastal War; DE Decoying the Yanks; FI First Blood; FL The Shenandoah in Flames; FO Forward to Richmond; FR War on the Frontier; GE Gettysburg;

Ewing, Thomas, SM *8*, 13
Ewing, Thomas F., Jr., AS 145, FR 157, SP 149-152, 153-154, *156-157*
Excelsior Brigade, FO *165*
Executions, OR 16, 88, 92, 95, TT 122, 153-154, *155*, 156, YA 36
Exports, YA 71
Ezekiel, Moses, FL *15*
Ezra Church, Battle of, AT 133-136, *134*

F

Fagan, James F., FR 156, *158*, 160, SH 125, *132*
Fahnstock, Allan, AT 38
Fairchild, Harrison, BD 132-133, 135-137
Fairfax Court House, Virginia, DE *152-153*, FI 110-111, 117, FO 17, 39, 87, GE 12, 28-29, 72, LE 166, SP 26, 117, *123*
Fairfield, Connecticut, YA 92
Fair Oaks, Battle of, DE 21, 151, LE 22-24, 31, 49, OR 36-37
Fair Oaks, Virginia, FO 136, map 140, *142-143*, 144-145, 148, 150, 154-159, map 160, *162-163*; See also Seven Pines, Virginia
Fairview Heights, RE 135, 140-144, 147-148
Fallen Timbers, SH 152
Falling Springs, DE *14*
Falling Waters, West Virginia, DE 36, 18, GE 152, 156
Fall River, Massachusetts, NA 79, 88
Falls, Benjamin F., TT 37
Falls Church, Virginia, TT *8-9*
Falmouth, Virginia, RE 8, 14, *20-21*, 30-32, 34-36, 91, *112-117*, 120-121, *123*, 159
Family groups, TT *38-43*
Fanny, CO 33
Farabee, Harvey, FL *133*
Farley, Henry S., BR 141
Farmers: complaints by, YA 142-143; and conscription, OR 77-80; economic status, OR 8, 42; family connections, OR 43; independence of, OR 8; life style, OR 42-44; livestock taken, OR 3, 149; machinery destroyed, OR 3; number enlisted, YA 62; opposition to war, OR 77; taxation, OR 83, *84*; tool shortages, OR 44, 149. See also Agriculture; Planters
Farm machinery, YA *62-63*, 67
Farms: emigration from, YA 23; numbers expanded, YA 63; typical, YA 22-23
Farm tools: production of, OR 26; shortages of, OR 44, 149
Farmville, Virginia, AP 118, 126-132, 134
Farnsworth, Elon J., GE *144-145*
Farragut, David Glasgow, CO *60*, MI *19*, OR 98, SH 157, YA 158; commands blockading squadron, CO 61; fleet strength of, CO 61, 115, 143, 145; and

Fort Fisher, CO 157; at Forts St. Philip and Jackson, CO 61, 63-73, 77; Fox, relations with, CO 60; at Mobile Bay, CO 142-149, *150*, 151-153, *154-155*, 156; naval career, CO 59-60; at New Orleans, CO 55-59, 61, 72-75, 77, 142, MI 17-18, 24; personal traits, MI 18; Porter, relations with, CO 60-61, 66-67; at Port Hudson, CO 77, MI 161-162; at Vicksburg, CO 142, MI 17-20, 28-29, 31-33, 69; Welles, relations with, CO 59, 61
Farrand, Charles E., BR 145
Farrar plantation, SM 59
Fascines, FO 105, MI *143*
Fashions, YA *48*
Fassena (slave), BR *48*
Fatigue duty. See Work details
Fauquier Sulphur Springs, Virginia, LE *121*
Fayette, Missouri, SP 159
Fearing, Benjamin, AP 72
Featherston, Winfield Scott, FO 50, SM 114
Featherstone, Jane, SP 75
Federal Army. See Union Army
Federal Hill, FO *69*
Fellows, William W., AT 74
Felton, Samuel H., SP 14, 16
Fenner, Charles E., AT 52
Fenner's Battery, AT 52
Fernald, George, TR *63*
Fernandina, as blockade target, BL 21
Ferrandini, Captain, SP 14-16, 21
Ferrero, Edward, BD 124-126, KI 74, RE 28, TR 74, *80-82*, 84, 88, 120
Fessenden, Samuel, LE 168, *170*
Fessenden, William Pitt, NA 40, 75
Field, Charles W., KI 76, 133, TR 49, 97-99, 147, 149, 153-154
Field, George W., TR 83-86
Field glasses, OR *19*
Field-surgeon kits, SM *110*
Fifers, DE *41*, FO 55, *58-59*
"Fighting McCooks," AT 72, 136, TE *94-95*
Fillmore, Millard, AS 124, BR *102*, 103
Financial crisis, YA 57
Finegan, Joseph, CO 139, KI 159, *161*
Fingal, BL 115-117, 120
Finley, Jeremiah, NA 101
Firepower, improved effectiveness of, DE 40
Firewood supply, TT *8-9*, 12, 52
First field hospital, SH *154*
First sergeants, TT 49
First shots fired: Confederate, BR 127, *140-141*, 146; Union, BR 147-148
Fiscal programs, OR 33
Fish, Hamilton, NA 106, 116, 126
Fish, Oliver H., BR *143*

Fisher, Joseph, AP 79
Fisher's Gap, DE 84, 86
Fisher's Hill, Battle of, FL *124-125*
Fisher's Hill, Virginia, FL 104, 122, 124, 140, 157, 158
Fishing, TT *17*
Fisk, Clinton, SP 161
Fisk, James, Jr. (Jubilee Jim), NA 88, 106-108, *109*
Fisk University, NA 50, 121
Fitch, John, TE 81, 143
Fitts, James, FL *130*
Fitzhugh, Norman, LE 125
Fitzpatrick, Honora, AS 44
Five Civilized Tribes, FR 136, 139
Five Forks, Battle of, AP 79-82, map 83, 84, 85-91
Flags, DE *127*, OR 43, *47*; Confederate, FI *124-125*, TT *22*; Crescent Regiment, Company A, SH *121*; 14th Mississippi Infantry, SH *99*; 6th Arkansas Infantry, SH *121*; Union, FI *25*; United States, TT *21*. See also Color-bearers; Colors
Flandrau, Charles E., FR 74, 81-83, *86*
Fleetwood, Christian, TR 117, *125*
Fleetwood Hill, GE 18, 20, *21*, 22
Fleharty, Stephen, SM 62
Flemming, W. W., AP 35
Fletcher, John, AS 108
Fletcher, Thomas Clement, MI 117
Flint, Mortimer, SM 24
Flint River, AT 143, 144, 145
Florence, Alabama, SH 78, SM 82
Florida: Black Codes, NA 34; forts defended by Union, BR 128-129; money issue, OR *72*; newspapers, OR 48; racial violence in, NA 36, 97; readmission to Union, NA 69; in secession movement, BR 3, 24, 128; Union control of, OR 148
Florida, BL 121, 143, *150-151*, 152, 160-161
Florida Independent Blues flag, FI *125*
Florida troops, GE 111, KI 159, SM 115; Marion Light Artillery, Robertson's Battery, TE 149; Independent Blues (3rd Infantry Regiment), FI *125*; 8th Infantry Regiment, RE 51
Flour: costs and shortages, OR 160; production, OR 62
Flournoy, Cabell E., GE 16-18
Flournoy, Thomas, DE 127-128
Floyd, John B., BR 85, SH *86*, TT 63; cartoon, SH *86*; escape from Fort Donelson, SH 93, 95; at Fort Donelson, SH 81, 83-85, 90-91, 93; and Fort Sumter relief, BR 121; ineptness, SH 81; irregularities alleged, BR 123; moves ordnance South, BR 120; resignation, BR 125
Floyd County, Virginia, OR 89
Flusser, Charles W., BL 79, 80, CO 32, 95
Flynn, Tom, AS 16
Folly Island, BL 41, CO 112, 120-121, *122-123*

Brevet Brigadier General Barton Alexander, engineer officer in the defenses of Washington, D.C.

Private Benjamin E. Russell, Company B, 8th Florida, C.S.A.

KI The Killing Ground; LE Lee Takes Command; MI War on the Mississippi; NA The Nation Reunited; OR Confederate Ordeal; RE Rebels Resurgent; SH The Road to Shiloh; SM Sherman's March; SP Spies, Scouts and Raiders; TE The Struggle for Tennessee; TR Death in the Trenches; TT Tenting Tonight; YA Twenty Million Yankees

61

The box at Ford's Theatre in Washington, D.C., where Abraham Lincoln was assassinated

Food: costs, YA 45, 77; costs inflated, OR 30, 84-85, 128, *163;* production expanded, OR 29-30; shortages, BL 99, OR 10, 29, 33, 77, 82-86, 89, 106, 149, 160; shortages, Confederate, MI 149-152, 166. *See also* Mess facilities; Rations

Food production. *See* Agricultural production

Foote, Andrew Hull, SH *63;* at Charleston, CO 120; at Fort Donelson, SH 78, 82-85, 87, 90; at Fort Henry, SH 60-67; at Forts Henry and Donelson, CO 54; Grant, relations with, SH 60, 85, 87, 90; at Island No. 10, CO 77, SH 155, 159-160, 163; in Mississippi operations, CO 55; personal traits, SH 60; Tilghman, relations with, SH 65; Walke's evaluation of, SH 60; wounded, SH 84

Foote, Frank, AP 99

Foote, Henry: Davis criticized by, OR 77; and habeas corpus suspension, OR 82; and peace negotiations, OR 160

Foote, Kate, OR *142*

Foraging, TT *62,* 63-65; during march to the sea, SM 40, 53-54, *64-65,* 68-*70;* and Union strategy, SM 49

Forbes, Charles, AS 82

Forbes, Edwin, BD 169, LE 163; sketches by, KI *46-55,* TR *42-43*

Forbes, Henry C., MI 89-91, 94, *96*

Forbes, Hugh, BR 84

Forbes, Stephen, MI 91, *96*

Forbes, William, SP *128-129*

Forbes, William A., FL *11*

Force, Manning, MI 111

Force, Manning F., AT 84, 95, 105, *108*

Ford, Henry Clay, AS 68, 70, 79, 83

Ford, James H., FR 129

Ford, James R., AS *70*

Ford, John, LE *76-77*

Ford, John T., AS 17, 68, 70, 155

Ford, Thomas H., BD 42-43

Ford's Station, Virginia, TR 55

Ford's Theatre, AS *23, 28-29,* 38, 44-49, 54, 59, 64-65, 76, 77, *diagram* 84, 85, *94-95,* 104; Booth's escape from, AS 88, 89, 90-91; Booth's preparations at, AS 68, 70-72; interior layout, AS 70; Lincoln's assassination, AS 79, *86-87;* Lincoln's seat, AS *83;* presidential box, AS *78,* 83, 85, *86-87*

Foreign-born troops. *See* Immigrants

Foreigners, in Union Army, DE *152-155*

Foreigners. *See* Immigrants

Foreign Legion (French), FR 40, *41*

Forey, Elie Frederic, FR *40,* 41, *42-43*

Forney, John H., MI 126, 152

Forno, Henry, LE 103

Forrest, CO 25

Forrest, Edwin, AS 38, YA 53

Forrest, Nathan Bedford, AP 161, AT 24, 25, 136, CH 20, 23, 24, FI 48, MI 60, 62, NA 36, 76, 146, SM 14, 19, 34, *88,* 123, 137, SP 78, TE 25, 26, *28,* 29, 30, 97, TT 125; at Chickamauga, CH 45, 46;

detached for special service, TE 92; escape from Fort Donelson, SH *94,* 95; at Fort Donelson, SH 83, 86, 93-94; at Franklin, SM 98, 100, 117; and Hood's advance into Tennessee, SM 83, 85, 88; and Hood's retreat from Nashville, SM 144; and Johnsonville raid, SM 82; at Murfreesboro, TE 30; and Murfreesboro raid, SM 125, 134; at Nashville, SH 98; raid on Grant's supply lines, TE 88; raid on Nashville, TE 84; relations with Bragg, CH 73, 79; at Shiloh, SH 148, 152; social scorn for, TE 25-26; at Spring Hill, SM 89, 92, 93; wounded, SH 152

Forsyth, George A., AP 151

Forsyth, James W., FL *102,* 122, 152, 153, 157, FO *137,* TR *23*

Fort Abercrombie, Dakota Territory, FR 84

Fort Anderson, North Carolina, CO 87, 92-94

Fort Barrancas, Florida, BR 128, CO *8, map 9, 10-11*

Fort Bartow, North Carolina, CO 21, 24-25, *map 26*

Fort Beauregard, Mississippi, MI *132-133*

Fort Beauregard, South Carolina, BL 31, 34, CO 20

Fort Bisland, Louisiana, FR 50, MI 110

Fort Blanchard, North Carolina, CO 21, 24-25

Fort Bliss, Texas, FR 19, 22, 35

Fort Bowie, Arizona Territory, FR 113, *114*

Fort Brady, Virginia, TR *134-135*

Fort Breckenridge, FR 20

Fort Bridger, Wyoming Territory, NA *105*

Fort Buchanan, FR 20

Fort Burnham, Virginia, AP *10, 14-15*

Fort Canby, FR 118, 119

Fort Caswell, North Carolina, BL 88, CO 158

Fort Churchill, Nevada, FR 108

Fort Clark, North Carolina, BL 29-31, CO *18-19*

Fort Clark, Texas, FR 21

Fort Cobb, North Carolina, CO 31-32

Fort Corcoran, Virginia, FI *60-61*

Fort Craig, New Mexico Territory, FR 20, 22, 23, 26, 27, 33-35

Fort Darling, Virginia, TR *28-29*

Fort Davidson, Missouri, FR 157

Fort Davis, Texas, NA *100-101*

Fort Defiance, Illinois, SH 34, *40-41*

Fort Delaware prison camp, TT 113, 115, 117-119, *123*

Fort DeRussy, District of Columbia, FL 63

Fort De Russy, Louisiana, FR 53, *59*

Fort Donelson, BL *100. See also R. E. Lee*

Fort Donelson, Battle of, FO 74, 81, YA 87

Fort Donelson, Tennessee, CO 54, MI 33, OR 15, 117, SH *map 82,* TT 113; armament, SH 81, 83; artillery assaults, SH 87, 91; bayonet assault, SH 91; breakout attempt, SH 85-90, 93; Buckner's role at, SH 81, 84-85, 90-93; casualties, SH 82, *83, 88-89,* 97; cavalry

operations, SH 81, 86, *94;* Confederate assaults, SH 93; Confederate command structure, SH 81, 93; Confederate matériel losses, SH 97; construction, SH 54-57, 81; escapes from, SH 93, *94,* 95; Floyd's role at, SH 81, 83-85, 90-91, 93; Foote's role at, SH 78, 82-85, 87, 90; fortifications system, SH 81; Grant's role at, SH 78, 81-82, 84-87, *88-89,* 93-94, 104; gunboats at, SH 78, 82-84, *85,* 87, 90; Johnston and, SH 79-81, 84, 93, 97; Lincoln and, SH 96; medical service, SH *88-89;* panic at, SH 87-90; Pillow's role at, SH 81, 84-86, 90-91, 93; political and military results, SH 95-97; prisoners captured, SH 96, 97; snipers at, SH 82; surrendered, SH 93-95, 99; terrain features, SH 81; troop reinforcements, SH 62, 78-79; Union assaults, SH 9, 81, *92-93;* weather, effect on operations, SH 81-82, 85, 94

Forten, Charlotte, OR 131

Fort Evans, Virginia, FO 42, 48

Fort Fillmore, New Mexico Territory, FR 19, 20, 35

Fort Fisher, North Carolina, AP 2, 18, BL 88, 95, 100-101, TR 158; bombship venture, CO 158-162; fortifications, CO 158; joint operations, CO 17, 83, 142-143, 156-158, *map 159, 160-161,* 162-165, *166-171*

Fort Fisher, Virginia, AP 40, 92

Fort Forrest, North Carolina, CO 21, 24-25

Fort Gaines, Alabama, CO 142-143, *map* 146, 156

Fort Gibson, Oklahoma, FR 152, 153, 155, 156

Fort Gilmer, Virginia, TR *122-123,* 146-147

Fort Granger, Tennessee, SM 97

"Fort Greenhow," SP 31

Fort Gregg, Virginia, AP 78; attack at, AP 96, 97-99

Fort Grey, North Carolina, CO 95

Fort Hamilton, New York, DE 26, FO 70

Fort Harrison, Virginia, TR *map* 96, 123, 139-140, 142, *144-146, 147-150*

Fort Haskell, Virginia, AP 36, 37, 38

Fort Hatteras, North Carolina, BL 29-31, CO *18-19*

Fort Henry, Battle of, FO 74, 81, YA 87

Fort Henry, Tennessee, CO 54, MI 33, OR 15; armament, SH 67; artillery assaults, SH *66-67;* casualties, SH 65-67; construction, SH 54-57, 60; Foote's role at, SH 60-67; Grant's role at, SH 60-63, 67; gunboats at, SH 58, 60-63, *64,* 65-67; surrendered, SH 67, 79; Tilghman's role at, SH 57-58, 62, 67; Union assault, SH 9, 60-67; vulnerability, SH 57

Fort Hill, Mississippi, MI 139

Fort Hindman, Arkansas, MI 68, *69, 71*

Fort Hoke, Virginia, TR 144

Fort Hood, Georgia, AT 153

Fort Huger, North Carolina, CO 21, 24-25

Fortifications, TR 39, *map* 40, 42-43, 60-61,

AP Pursuit to Appomattox; AS The Assassination; AT Battles for Atlanta; BD The Bloodiest Day; BL The Blockade; BR Brother against Brother; CH The Fight for Chattanooga; CO The Coastal War; DE Decoying the Yanks; FI First Blood; FL The Shenandoah in Flames; FO Forward to Richmond; FR War on the Frontier; GE Gettysburg;

65, 67, 73, map 96, 120-121, 126-135, 144, at Allatoona Pass, SM 21, 22-23; at Atlanta, SM 21; at Columbia, SM 85; construction, FO 8, 17-18, 98-99, 105, 108-109, 111, 128, 139, OR 23, 43, SH 30-31, 54-58, 157; field, TE 34; at Franklin, SM 97, 98, 100, 104-105; improvised, SH 33; at Nashville (Confederate), SM 125, 130, 137; at Nashville (Union), SM 120, 124, 143; reliance on by Confederate army, TR 64; at Savannah, SM 146-147, 148, 152; at Spring Hill, SM 90, 91; torpedoes (land mines), use of, SM 148, 152-153
Fort Jackson, Louisiana. See Forts St. Philip and Jackson
Fort Jefferson, Florida, FO 16
Fort Johnson, South Carolina, BR 137, 140-141
Fort Johnson, Virginia, TR 145
Fort Kearney, Nebraska, FR 10
Fort Lafayette, New York, FO 70, SP 17, 20, YA 32
Fort Laramie, Dakota Territory, FR 129
Fort Laramie, Wyoming: Indians at, NA 96-97
Fort Larned, Kansas, FR 122, 124, 129
Fort Leavenworth, Kansas, FR 111, 124, 147, SP 145
Fort Lincoln, District of Columbia, FL 62, 63, 65
Fort Lyon, Colorado Territory, FR 125, 126, 127
Fort McAllister, Georgia, CO 114-115, SM 148-149, 150, 151, 152, 153, 155
Fort McHenry, Maryland, FI 31, SP 37, 39
Fort McLane, FR 116
Fort Macon, North Carolina, BL 87, CO 37, 38-39
Fort McRee, Florida, CO 8, map 9, 13
Fort Magruder, Virginia, FO 109-111, 113
Fort Mahone, Virginia, TR cover, 128; attack at, AP 92-93, 94-95, 99; Confederate casualties at, AP 103-107
Fort Massachusetts, Mississippi, BR 128
Fort Meade, Florida, DE 26
Fort Monroe, Virginia, AS 145, 151, BL 24, 46, 65, BR 126, CO 19-21, 39, DE 61, FI 78, FL 73, 100, FO 89-90, 92, 120-121, LE 23, NA 20, 22, 23, OR 163, SP 54, 88, TR 34, 36, 69; as slave refuge, FI 81; strategic value of, FI 77; as troop-staging area, FI 21-23, 77
Fort Morgan, Alabama, CO 142-145, map 146, 147, 148-149, 150-151, 156, 157
Fort Morris, Maryland, FI 31
Fort Morton, Virginia, TR 130
Fort Moultrie, South Carolina, BR 25, 120-122, 123, 127, 135, 147, 150, 151, 154, 160, CO 113, 118
Fort Pemberton, Mississippi, MI map 72, 76-77
Fort Phil Kearny, Wyoming Territory, NA 93

133, 135, 152, CO 8, map 9, FI 17
Fort Pillow, Tennessee, AT 24, MI 16, 20, 37, TT 35; massacre at, AT 25, 47
Fort Pitt foundry, TE 89
Fort Point, California, FR 109
Fort Powell, Alabama, CO 142, map 146, 156
Fort Pulaski, Georgia, BL 87, BR 128, CO 46-53, 120, LE 12, OR 113
Fort Randall, Dakota Territory, FR 91
Fort Rice, Dakota Territory, FR 99, NA 104-105
Fort Richardson, Virginia, FO 30-31
Fort Ridgely, Minnesota, FR 74, 78-81, 83, 84, 85
Fort Riley, Kansas, SH 13
Fort Ruby, Nevada, FR 108
Fort Sanders, Tennessee: CH 111, 113, 116-117, 119, 154, Confederate attack at, CH 100, 114-115
Fort Sanders, Wyoming, NA 82
Fort Scott, Kansas, FR 155, 160, SP 143
Fort Sedgwick, Virginia, TR 126-127, 130-133
Fort Sherman, Tennessee, CH 160-161
Fort Sill, Oklahoma Territory, NA 114
Fort Slemmer, District of Columbia, DE 144-145
Fort Slocum, District of Columbia, FL 63, 65
Fort Smith, Arkansas, FR 64, 146, 153, 155
Fort Snelling, Minnesota, FR 13, 74, 75, 77, 79, 80, 85, 91, 92, 95
Forts St. Philip and Jackson, Louisiana, CO map 62; casualties, CO 69, 73, 77; fortifications, CO 55; ground operations, CO 63, 76-77; mortar boats at, CO 57-58, 59, 61, 64-67, 70, 73; naval operations, CO 57, 64, 65, 66-73, 77; rams at, CO 69-72; surrender, CO 75, 77
Forts seized by South, BR 128-129
Fort Stanton, New Mexico Territory, FR 20, 114, 115
Fort Stedman, Virginia, attack at, AP 2, 34, map 35, 36-37, 38-39, 41
Fort Stevens, District of Columbia, FL 62, plan 66, 66-67, 84, 86, 87
Fort Sumner, Maryland, FL 62, 63, TR 58
Fort Sumner, New Mexico Territory, FR 115, 116, 118, 120, 121
Fort Sumter, South Carolina, BL 10-11, 15, 17, BR 25, 120, 151, CO 98-99, 104-107, 110, map 113, 115, 118, 119, 120-121, 130-131, 132-133, 135, 136, FI 8-9, 10-11, 17, 57, FO 12, OR 17, 127, TT 110; after-action casualty, BR 161; armament and ammunition supply, BR 147, 150, 152, 154; bombardment by Confederates, BR 146-148, 150-152, 153, 154, 155, 156-157, 158-159, 160; bombardment by United States Navy, BR 163; capitulation and evacuation, BR 159-161, 163, 168-169; ceremony at, AP 162, 163; civilian workers in, BR 147, 152; Confederate government's role in

reduction of, BR 132-141, 160, 163, 168-169; damage to, BR 150, 152-156, 160, 162-167; first Confederate shots, BR 3, 127, 140-141, 146; first Union shots, BR 147-148; garrison flag, BR 162; garrison officers, BR 148; garrison strength, BR 147, 150-151, map 150; morale of garrison, BR 150-151; relief attempts and defense of, BR 121-128, 132-138, 146-150, 151, 152-154, 155, 156-157; surrender demanded, BR 138-141, 157-159; troops moved to, BR 123-125; United States Navy at, BR 133-135, 147, 152-153, 156-157, 160-161. See also Anderson, Robert
Fort Taylor, Florida, BR 129
Fort Thompson, North Carolina, CO 35-36
Fort Thorn, New Mexico Territory, FR 22
Fort Totten, District of Columbia, DE 140-141, FL 63, 64-65
Fort Union, Dakota Territory, FR 14-15
Fort Union, New Mexico Territory, FR 27, 28, 31, 34
Fort Wagner, South Carolina, CO 113, 118, 120-124, 125-126, 127, 128-129, map 130-131, 134
Fort Walker, South Carolina, BL 31, 32-35, CO 20
Fort Warren, Massachusetts, BL 116, YA 32
Fort Wayne, Michigan, FI 38-39
Fort Welles, South Carolina, BL 34-35
Fort Whipple, Arizona Territory, FR 117
Fort Williams, North Carolina, CO 95
Fort Wingate, New Mexico Territory, FR 118
Fort Wise, Colorado Territory, FR 122. See also Fort Lyon
Fort Wool, Virginia, FO 124-125
Fort Yuma, California, FR 35
"Forward to Richmond!" (slogan), FO 11, 62
Foster, Colonel, AS 155
Foster, J. G., BR 148
Foster, James P., MI 77
Foster, John G., CO 32, 87, SM 155, 156; commands department, CO 32; at Goldsboro, CO 84-86; at New Bern, CO 36-37, 84, 88, 90; at Roanoke Island, CO 25-27, 32; troop strength of, CO 84, 86; at Washington, CO 87-88, 90
Foster, John W., SH 137
Foster, Robert S., AS 149, TR 146-147
Foster, Samuel T., AT 56, SM 83, 120, 123
Foster, William, MI 150-152
Foulke, A., KI 15
Fourteen-Mile Creek, MI 111-112
Fowler, Joseph O., NA 75
Fox, Charles B., AP 64
Fox, Cyrus, AT 72
Fox, Gustavus Vasa, BL 17, 20, BR 133-135, 147, 152-157, 160, MI 20; and Charleston, CO 112, 119; Farragut, relations with, CO 60; on monitors, CO 112; and New Orleans, CO 55-58

KI The Killing Ground; LE Lee Takes Command; MI War on the Mississippi; NA The Nation Reunited; OR Confederate Ordeal; RE Rebels Resurgent; SH The Road to Shiloh; SM Sherman's March; SP Spies, Scouts and Raiders; TE The Struggle for Tennessee; TR Death in the Trenches; TT Tenting Tonight; YA Twenty Million Yankees

A caricature of Federal General John C. Frémont by southern artist A. J. Volck.

The U.S.S. *Galena*, an ironclad launched February 14, 1862

Fox's Gap, BD 39, 44, *46-47, map* 48, 49, *50*, 81

France: and blockade, BL 26; Britain, relations with, BL 118; Confederacy, relations with, BL 16, 120, 122-123, 125-126, 128; and cotton embargo, BL 16; influence on uniform design, FI 21, 63; intervention sought by Confederacy, FI 46; Mexico, venture in, BL 128, 155; and privateers, BL 12; warship construction in, BL 47, 53, 126, 128, 130. *See also* Napoleon III

Francine, Louis, RE 145-146

Frank Leslie's Illustrated Newspaper, AS 85, 136, 160, NA 66, 87, TT 67

Franklin, Abraham, YA 110

Franklin, Battle of, SM *map 2-3, map* 101; and Carter cotton gin, SM 102; casualties at, SM 112, 118; close fighting at, SM 112-113, 115; Confederate charge at, SM 82, *104-105;* Confederate colors captured at, SM *122;* Confederate generals killed at, SM *119;* suffering and carnage at, SM 118; terrain unfavorable for attack, SM *96-97*, 100; Union counterattack, SM 112-113; Union line breached, SM 102-105; Union withdrawal, SM 117-118

Franklin, Emlen, RE 144

Franklin, Tennessee, SM 94, 95, 96, 144

Franklin, Virginia, DE 146, 148

Franklin, William B., CH 86, DE 60-61, FI 137, 143, FO 67, *86*, 105, 125, 130, FR 47, 50, 56, 57, 62, 70, LE 27, 29, 95, RE *58;* at Alexandria, LE 126, 151; at Antietam, BD 64-65, 108-109, 122, 127, 139; at Buckeystown, BD 44; at Burkittsville, BD 53; Burnside criticized by, RE 96; commands grand division, RE 30; at Crampton's Gap, BD 48, 52-53, 55, 108; at Frederick, BD 22; at Fredericksburg, RE 50, 56, 58-61, 63-64, 71, 85, 87, 91; personal traits, RE 29; at Pleasant Valley, BD 108, 122; and Rappahannock operations, RE 39, 50-51, 56; relieved, RE 98; at Second Bull Run, LE 132; in Seven Days' Battles, LE 50, 52; at Stafford Court House, RE 30; troop strength, RE 61

Franklin & Columbia Turnpike, SM 83. *See also* Columbia Pike; Franklin Pike

Franklin College, BR *14-15*

Franklin *Herald*, YA 29

Franklin Pike, SM 120, 121, 125, 126, 134, 137, 142-143

Franklin Road, TE 93, 94, 98, 99, 112

Franks, Dora, OR 133

Fraser, Trenholm & Company, BL 24, 98, 114, 120-122

Fraternization, MI 136, RE *38*, 39, 41, TT *158*

Fraudulent practices, YA 72-75, 76, 77

Frayser's Farm, Battle of, LE *map 32*, 52, 55-56, 60, *62*

Frazer, John W., CH 104

Frederick, Maryland, BD 44, FI 29-31, FL 71-74; civilians' behavior, BD 15-18; Confederate ransom demand, FL *75*, 83; operations at, BD 17, *18-20*, 21, *map 22, 26*, 44-45, 151, 166

Fredericksburg, TR 144

Fredericksburg, Battle of, MI 83, RE *map 59, map* 66, *map* 80, *map* 86, TE 160, TT 152, YA 93, 146; balloons at, RE 40; casualty total, RE 111; Confederate concentration at, RE 33-34, 36-39; Union advance to, RE 31, 36; Union withdrawal from, RE 91, 94-96; weather, effect on, RE 31, *32*, 35-37, 88-89, *96-97*. *See also* Marye's Heights; Rappahannock River, operations around

Fredericksburg, Virginia, CO 84, 86, DE 61, 87, 89, 94-95, 114, 121-123, 147, 170, FO 130, 133, 136, LE 25, 93, 99, 101, 133, OR 166, RE *152-153, 162-163, 166-167*, TT 71, *93, 100-102*, 158, *160-161;* civilians' behavior, RE 34-35, 52; hospitals at, KI 111, 120; looting in, RE 54-55, *56*, 88-89; railroad facilities, RE 8, 18; refugees from, RE *37*, 39; strategic value, RE 30; terrain features, RE 36, 61-62, 72-73

Fredericksburg Pike, KI 126

Free, John, FL *83*

Freedmen. *See* Blacks; Refugees; Slaves

Freedmen's Bureau. *See* Bureau of Freedmen, Refugees and Abandoned Lands

Freedmen's Bureaus, MI 58

Freeman, Henry V., SM 126, 135, 136, TE 119, 142

Freeman's Ford, RE 119

Freeport, Illinois, BR 106, 108

Frémont, John C., BR *103*, 104, DE *148, 150*, FO 92, 131, LE 93-94, SP 72, 73, YA *152;* background, DE 147; Blair, relations with, SH 19; candidacy for President, YA 152-153, 158; censorship by, SH 33; commands in West, SH 17-18, 29-30; at Cross Keys, DE 161-165, *166-167*, 168, *map* 169; and emancipation, YA 153; flamboyance of, SH 30; foreigners on staff, DE 153; at Franklin, DE 146, 148; Governors' support of, YA 143; Grant, relations with, SH 33, 46; and gunboat construction, SH 29-30; at Harrisonburg, DE 146-149, 158-160; ineptness, DE 148-149; Lincoln's evaluation of, DE 149, SH 33; martial law proclaimed by, SH 30-32; and Missouri operations, SH 32-33, 48; at Moorefield, DE 148; at Mount Jackson, DE 170; at Port Republic, DE 170; relieved by Scott, SH 33, 58; slaves freed by, SH 30-32; at Staunton, DE 95, 103; at Strasburg, DE 148-157; at Wardensville, DE 151; in Western Department, DE 147-148; in western Virginia, DE 71, 95, 148

French, Samuel, AT 66, 68, 69, SM 20, 21, *22*, 24, 26-28, 112

French, William, NA 127

French, William Henry, BD 87-88, 93-100, 104, *107*, 108, 112-113, 139, DE 26-29, FO 159-161, KI 29, 31, *34, 35, RE 40-41, 72-74, 76-77, 80-81*, 144, *147-148*

Frenchmen: in Confederate Army, TT 31; in Union Army, TT 30

Friars Point, MI *70*

Frick, Henry Clay, Pennsylvania coke works of, NA 79

Friend, C.W.F., RE 129

Frietchie, Barbara, BD *20*

Frontier Guard, YA *8-9*

Front Royal, Virginia, FI 76, FL 17, 104, 109, 136, 140, 141, 144, 153; actions at, DE 86, 121-123, *124-125*, 126-129, *map* 130, 135, 146-147, 149-151, 157

Front Royal-Strasburg road, DE 129

Front Royal-Winchester road, DE 129, 133

Frost, M. O., MI 119

Fry, Birkett D., GE 61, 139

Fry, Hugh, FL *15*

Fry, James B., FI *116*, 118, 148, FL 76, YA 110-111

Fry, Speed S., SH *58*, TE 59

Frying Pan Shoals, BL 88

Fuel costs, YA 45; and shortages, OR 19, 22, 160

Fugitive Slave Law, BR 45-46, 64, 119, FI 78

Fulkerson, Samuel: at Kernstown, DE 67-70; at Port Republic, DE 161; at Romney, DE 55-58; at Winchester, DE 131-132

Fuller, Arthur B., TT 152

Fuller, Charles A., BD 102-103, FO 161-164, LE 71

Fuller, John, AT 99, 100, *103, 105*

Fuller, William A., SP 112

Fullerton, Joseph S., AT 66, CH 65, 66, 69, 120, 121, 134, 149

Fund-raising, OR *58*

Funerals, MI *155*

Funk, John H.S., FL 82, 119, RE 146-147

Funkhauser, R. D., AP *36*, 38

Funsten, Oliver, DE 92

Furloughs, TT 55

Fussell's Mill, Battle of, TR 97, *98*-100

Fyffe, James P., TE 150

G

Gag, Anton, panorama by, FR *88-89*

Gabions, FO 105

Gadberry, James M., LE *170*

Gaddis, John, SH 22-23

Gadsden, Alabama, SM 32-33

Gaines, CO 143, 151

Gaines's Mill, Battle of, LE 22, *map* 32, *map* 40, 41, *42-45*, 46, *47*, 59, TT 104, 157

Gaines's Mill, Virginia, FO 154-155

Gainesville, Virginia, LE 127, 133-134, 136-137, 143, 145-146, 152

Field glass of Brigadier General
Richard B. Garnett, C.S.A., killed at
Gettysburg July 3, 1863

Galbraith, Thomas J., FR 77, 80, 87
Gale, William D., SM 118, 133, 139, 142
Galena, BL 51, CO 145, 150, FO 128, LE 70
Galena, Illinois, SH 42, 44
Galesburg, Illinois, BR 106
Galloway, G. Norton, KI 105
Galt House, CH 88
Galveston, Texas, FR 47, 48, SH 52, as blockade-runners' port, BL 87, 93, 142, 152
Galwey, Thomas, BD 96, RE 54
Gamble, Alice, MI 26
Gamble, William, GE 45, 48
Gamble's Hill, OR 17
Gambling, TT 62-63, 69
Gambo Creek, AS 114
Gano, Richard M., FR 155, *156,* TE 24
Gansevoort, Henry Sanford, SP *120-121*
Gant, C. D., cartridge box of, SM *83*
Garbage disposal, TT 82
Garber, Asher W., RE *107*
Garde Lafayette, TT 30
Garden Key, AS 160
Gardiner, James, TR *125*
Gardner, Alexander, BD 142, LE 75-77, 81; photographs by, AS *142-143, 162-171*
Gardner, Calvin, TR *63*
Gardner, Franklin, MI 90, *160,* 161, 164
Gardner, Joseph W., KI 126
Gardner, W. M., FI 133
Garesche, Julius P., TE 118, 130, *132, 133,* 142
Garfield, James A., CH *43,* 63, 68, NA 56, 108, 153, SH 136; Rosecrans' chief of staff, CH 61
Garibaldi Guards (New York), DE *154,* FI *96-97*
Garland, Samuel, Jr.: evaluated by D. H. Hill, BD 50; at South Mountain, BD 39, 45, *46-47,* 50, *51,* 81
Garner, Margaret, BR *44*
Garnett, Henry H., NA 42
Garnett, James M., BR 36
Garnett, Richard B., DE *54,* GE *122,* 136-137, *139,* 140; Jackson, conflict with, DE 52, 54, 89; at Kernstown, DE 54, 66-70
Garnett, Robert Selden, DE 52, FI *91;* death of, FI 92-93; in western Virginia operations, FI 87-93
Garnett, Thomas S., LE 103-105, RE 147
Garrard, Kenner, AT 59, 76, 77, *80,* 98, 138, 141
Garrett, John M. (Jack), AS 133, 134
Garrett, John W., FL 71
Garrett, Richard, AS 114, 116, 117, 132-134
Garrett farm, AS *map* 113, 132, 133, *134-135,* 136
Garrick, Jacob, BL 28
Garrison, Lindley M., NA 170
Garrison, William Lloyd, BD *160,* BR 38-39, 62, *65,* 66, 68-69, NA 156
Gary, Martin W., AP 101, TR 154
Gaskill, J. W., CH 101

Gaston, Charles, SP 68
Gatch, Charles A., AS 91
Gates, Theodore, LE 153
Gatling, Richard, SP 169
Gatling gun, SP 162, *169,* 171
Gaul, Gilbert, TE 116; paintings by, AP *124,* SP *cover*
Gauley River, DE *72-73, 80-81*
Gautier's (restaurant), AS 27, 48
Gay, Ebenezer, TE 59
Gayle, George Washington, AS 11
Gaylesville, Alabama, SM 32, 34
Geary, Edward, CH 92, 93
Geary, John W., AT 35, 36, 51, 52, 63, 64, 98, BR 79, CH 91, 92, 93, 95, 130, 131, 133, 142
Geddes, James L., SH *134,* 139
Gelston, Mrs. George, SP 20
Gemtypes, TE *131*
General (locomotive), SP *111, 112-113,* TE 8, *10-11*
General Beauregard, MI 20, 24-25
General Lovell, MI 20
General Order No. 28 (Butler), OR *114*
General Price, MI 20
General Quitman, CO 63
General Van Dorn, MI 20
Gentles, Henry, SH 27
Geographical Reader for Dixie Children, OR 58
Geography, effect on economy and society, BR 29
Geography (Moore), OR 58
George, J. Z., NA 145
George Peabody, CO 21
Georgetown, South Carolina, BL 28
Georgetown College, SP 53, YA *18-19*
George Washington Parke Custis, FO *151*
Georgia: Andrews' raid, SP *map* 111, *112-113;* Atlanta, civilian evacuation of, SM 15, *16;* cavalry action, SM 50, 52, 63, 67; charity benefit handbill for Atlanta refugees, SM *17;* civil disorders in, OR 85, 149; conscription evaded in, OR 80; destruction in, SM 45, *48-49,* 159; education, NA 120; educational system, OR 54, 58; foraging in, SM 40, 53-56, 68-*70;* Fort McAllister, fall of, SM 150; Griswoldville, Battle of, SM 60-61, 148; and habeas corpus suspension, OR 153-154; Henson's activities in, SP 78; inflation in, SM 18-19; land redistribution in, NA 29; lowland terrain, SM 144; military operations in, OR 148, *map* 153, 157; Milledgeville, occupation of, SM 62; money issues, OR *72-73;* newspapers and Confederate resistance, SM 68; Northern relief for Savannah, SM *166-167;* readmission to Union, NA 69; recruiting broadside, SM *53;* refugees in, OR *112-113,* 121, 123; Savannah, fall of, SM 159-160; secession by, BR 3, 128; and secession from Confederacy, OR 155; and Sherman's march, AP 52, OR *map* 153, *156-157,* SM 44-73, *58,* 144-159; slave

emigration from, OR 125, 131; state operation of railroads, AT 27; subversion in, OR 155; terrain, AT 8, 60; troops withheld by, OR 148, 157; Union control of, OR 155; Union settlers in, NA 64; Wilson's campaign in, AP *map* 161
Georgia, BL 152
Georgia, University of, BR *14-15*
Georgia Landing, Louisiana, TT 71
Georgia Railroad, AT *82-83, 84-85,* 91, 95, 98, 106, *122-123,* 129, 132, SM 53
Georgia Railway, BR 14
Georgia troops, AP 125, 133, AT 47, BD 51, 70-71, 73-74, 81, *116-117,* 122, 126, CH 113, 139, FL 78, 79, 114, 153, GE 53, 78-80, 86, 98-101, 103, 111, KI 80-81, 91, RE *104,* SM 115, 139, TR 82, 87, 149, TT 26, 31, 63; Benning's brigade, CH *50-51;* at Bull Run, FI 122-123, 132-134, *140,* 145, 156; Lawton's brigade, LE 30, 42; State militia, AP 53, AT 76, 92, 138, 143, SM 52, 60-61, 148-149; Sumter Light Guards (Company), FI *18-19*
  Artillery: 12th Battalion, FL 81; 18th Battalion, AP 16, 124; Chatham Artillery, OR 78; Ross's Battery, TR 45; Van Den Corput's Battery, AT 46
  Cavalry: 1st Cavalry Regiment, TE 29; 2nd Cavalry Regiment, TE 26, 27; 7th Cavalry Regiment, TR 24
  Infantry: 1st Infantry Regiment, AT 68, SP 112, TE 24; 2nd Infantry Battalion, OR *81;* 2nd Infantry Regiment, BD 121, 126; 4th Infantry Regiment, FI *18-19,* KI 65, RE 38; 5th Infantry Regiment, AP 122, TT *10;* 6th Infantry Regiment, TT 159; 7th Infantry Regiment, FI 145; 8th Infantry Regiment, FI 132-133, 156, OR 54; 12th Infantry Regiment, DE 101, 103, TT 158; 15th Infantry Regiment, GE 87; 16th Infantry Regiment, CH 114; 17th Infantry Regiment, TR 142; 18th Infantry Regiment, LE 45; 19th Infantry Regiment, RE 67; 20th Infantry Regiment, TT 157; 21st Infantry Regiment, AT 71, LE 129; 23rd Infantry Regiment, AP, 67, RE 129; 24th Infantry Regiment, RE 77; 26th Infantry Regiment, FL 79; 31st Infantry Regiment, FL 68; 36th Infantry Regiment, CH 140; 44th Infantry Regiment, LE 36, RE *107;* 48th Infantry Regiment, TR 65; 49th Infantry Regiment, LE 166; 50th Infantry Regiment, BD 121; 56th Infantry Regiment, CH 140; 59th Infantry Regiment, GE *155;* 61st Infantry Regiment, FL 81, 145; 63rd Infantry Regiment, AT 68; 66th Infantry Regiment, AT 90, 100, 106
Gere, Thomas P., FR 79, *80,* 82; dispatch from, FR *80*
German Brigade, DE 164

Confederate Brigadier General
Franklin Gardner, who surrendered
Port Hudson, Louisiana, in July 1863

Private Albert Hall, Company D, 1st
Georgia, photographed in April 1861

KI The Killing Ground; LE Lee Takes Command; MI War on the Mississippi; NA The Nation Reunited; OR Confederate Ordeal; RE Rebels Resurgent; SH The Road to Shiloh; SM Sherman's March; SP Spies, Scouts and Raiders; TE The Struggle for Tennessee; TR Death in the Trenches; TT Tenting Tonight; YA Twenty Million Yankees

65

Germanna Ford, KI 45, *49*, 56, *58*, *59*, 60, 62, RE 120, *map* 122, 123
Germanna Plank road, KI 74
German Rangers, BD *101*
Germans: in Confederate Army, TT 30-31; immigrants, BR 16, 33, 100, YA 21; in Union Army, TT 29, *30*
Germantown, Maryland, AS 110
Germantown, Virginia, TT 148
Gerrish, Theodore, AP 117
Getty, George Washington, FL 112, 149, 150, 153, RE 86-87
Getty, Richard, KI 68, 70, 71
Gettysburg, Battle of, BL 131, MI 157, NA 4, OR 51, 110, 128, SP 122, TT 159
Gettysburg, Pennsylvania, GE *map* 63, *map* 70, *map* 130, *160-161;* battlefield debris, GE *148-149, 151;* battle precipitated, GE 44-45; 50th anniversary, NA 4; reunions at, NA *170-171;* road system, GE 45; terrain features, GE 44-45, *48-49*, 65, 76
Gettysburg Address, GE *170-171*
Gholson, Samuel, SP 78
Gibbes, Dr. Robert W., AP 62, 63
Gibbon, John, AP 79, 93, 96, 97, 99, 118, 139, 144, 153, *154-155*, BD *74*, *157*, FO 62, GE 109-111, *121*, 133, 143, KI 71, 77-78, 100-101, 136, 158, 160-161, 170, LE 137-138, *139*, 140-143, 151, 161-162, 164-165, RE 63-64, 67, 70-71, 120, 152-154, 156, TR 44, 97, 105, 107-110; at Antietam, BD 73, 76-79; on McClellan, BD 169; at South Mountain, BD 51
Gibbons, John S., YA 87, 98
Gibbs, Alfred, AP 84
Gibbs, Jonathan, NA 69
Gibbs, Lieutenant, SP 88
Gibbs's Mounted Rifles, FR 19, 23. *See also* U.S. Regular Army, 3rd Cavalry
Gibraltar, BL 12
Gibson, Horatio, LE *64-65*
Gibson, James F., FO 135
Gibson, Randall Lee, SH 122, *123*, 126-128, *132-133*, 134, TE 149
Gibson, William H., AT 56, TE 115
Giddings, Joshua, BR 46
Giesboro Point, Virginia, remount depot at, FL *110-111*
Gifford, Ira W., SP 166
Gifford, James J., AS 68
Gilbert, Charles, TE 55, 59, 60, 62, 66
Gilbert, Nelson, GE *155*
Gilbert, Samuel A., CH 104
Gilham, Mrs. William, FL 57
Gilham, William, DE 52-54
Gill, R. M., AT 107, 111
Gillette, James, LE 90
Gillmore, Quincy Adams: FL *63*, TR 27, 30-31, *32-33*, 39; at Charleston, CO 135-136; and Florida operations, CO 139; at Fort Pulaski, CO 46-47, 120; at Fort Sumter, CO 130-131, 133; at Fort Wagner, CO 120, 124-125, 138-141; on Morris Island, CO 120, *121*, 129, 139; Welles, criticism of, CO 121

Gilmor, Harry, FL 42, 95, 135, 158, SP *108*, 109; and Antietam Campaign, SP 110; background, SP 108; banditry of, SP 124, 126; capture of, SP 127; at Winchester, SP 125
Gilmore, Joseph A., YA 95
Gisiner, John T. D., DE *107*
Gist, George, MI 32
Gist, States Rights, AT 100, CH 45, SM 98, 115, 118, *119*
Gladstone, William, BL 123
Glasgow, Tennessee, TE 51
Gleasman brothers, BD 70
Gleason, Charles W., AP *118*
Glendale, Battle of, LE *map* 32, 52, 55-56, 60, *62*
Glenn, Eliza, CH 47
Glenn, William Wilkins, SP *19*
Glenn house, CH 47, 48, 52, 60
Glenn-Kelly road, CH 47
Globe Tavern, Virginia, TR 55, 101, 103-104, 107, 150, 153
Gloire, BL 47
Glorieta Pass, Battle of, FR 16, 31-32, *map* 33
Gloucester Point, Virginia, FO 93, *96*, 105
Goddard, John, AP *130;* saber and sash of, AP *130*
Godey's Lady's Book, YA *48*
Godfrey, Joseph, FR 101
Godkin, Edwin L., NA 127
Godwin, Archibald, FL 119
Gold: resources, BR 9; speculation in, NA 106-108, YA *47*, 79, 153-154
Golden Rocket, BL 146
Goldman, Thomas Jefferson, RE *107*
Goldsboro, North Carolina, CO 17, 19, 35, 38, 84-86, 97, FI 10
Goldsborough, Louis M., BL 26, CO 19, 23-24, *25*, FO 93
Goldsby, Thomas, FI 133, 139
Gooch, Nat, TE 154
Goode, John T., TR 78
Goodgame, John C., AP 93
Gooding, Michael, TE 66
Goodwyn, Thomas J., AP *60*, 61
Goolsby, J. D., LE 37
Gooney Manor Road, DE 123, 126
"Gopher holes," TT 9
Gordon, George H., BD 92, LE 97, 103, 107-108; Banks evaluated by, DE 59; Jackson evaluated by, DE 64, 89; at Strasburg, DE 121, 128-129
Gordon, George Washington, SM 98, 103, 115, 116
Gordon, Georgia, SM 62
Gordon, J. H., SP *18*
Gordon, James B., KI 115, 117-118, 123
Gordon, John B., AP 16, 18, 29, 31, 110, 113, 117, 128-130, *152*, BD 95-96, 101-102, *106*, DE 18, 40-41, FL 20, 69, 74, 78, 79, 81, 91, 109, *145*, FO 141, GE 23, 30-31, 60, *61*, KI 65, 80-81, 99-100, 126, LE 70, NA *144*, RE 158, TR 16,

97; ability of, FL 68; at Appomattox, AP 135-136, 138-141, 143-144, 153-155; at Cedar Creek, FL 140-141, 144-145, 147-149, 151, 153, 157; and Fort Stedman, AP 33-35, 37-39, 78; at Opequon Creek, FL 112, 113, 115, 119-122; Petersburg, defense of, AP 92, 93, 95; and Sayler's Creek, AP 120, 121, 127
Gordon, Nathaniel, YA 36
Gordonsville, Virginia, FL 140, FO 83, LE 98-99, 109, 124, TR 18, 19, 25
Gorgas, Josiah, MI 157; arms procurement by, OR 17-19, 22-25; on blockade runners, OR 18
Gorman, Willis, BD 89-90
"Gospel of Wealth," NA 88
Gosport Navy Yard, BL 46, 48, *50*, 65, FO 125; evacuated, FI *17*
Goss, Warren Lee, FO 84, RE 160
Gosson, Jack, BD 63
Gould, Charles, AP 93
Gould, Jay, NA 88, 106-108, *109*, YA 78
Gould, John, BD 80
Gould, Joseph, AP 92
Gouldman, Izora, AS 115
Gourley, Jenny, AS 151
Govan, Daniel C., AT 54, 104, *152*, SM 92, 96, 98; and Cleburne, SM 100, 115
Govan's Brigade, AT 149-150, 152
Government, Confederate States. *See* Confederate States government
Governor Moore, CO 63, 66, 69
Governors: relations with Lincoln, YA 143; support of Frémont, YA 143
Gowen, George W., AP *94*
Gracie, Archibald, Jr., CH 67, 112
Grady, Henry W., NA 158
Graft, OR 84. *See also* Profiteering
Grafton, West Virginia, FI 85-86, 88-89
Graham, Charles K., GE 102-104
Graham, Edward, TR 32, 150
Graham, James A., BD 120
Graham, Lawrence P., NA *160*
Graham, Matthew, BD 133
Graham, "Stuttering Dave," SP 32
Graham, William M., BD 108
Graham's Battery, BD 108
Graham's Petersburg Battery, TR 32, 150
Grain production, YA 2, 63
Granbury, Hiram B., AT 54, 56, *57*, 145, 152, CH 139, SM 98, 115, *119*
Granbury's Texas Brigade, SM 83, 98, 115, 119
Grand Army of the Republic, NA 54, 112, *160*, 169; badge, NA *160*
Grand Ecore, Louisiana, FR 54-55, *59*, 62-64, 66-67
Grand Gulf, Mississippi: land operations, MI 86, 101, 104, 108-109; naval operations, MI 97-99, *100-101;* topography, MI 97-100
Grand Review, NA *8-15*

Uniform and personal effects of Lieutenant Robert S. Ellis Jr. of Georgia, killed at Gettysburg

Grand Turk, MI *21*

Grange, NA 90

Granger, Gordon, CH 23, 30, 49, 65, 66, 67, 68, 69, *71*, 83, 134, 142, 143, *144-145*, 146, 149, 154, CO 143

Granger, Henry, TR 108

Granger, Henry W., KI *118*

Granite State Guards, TT 22

Granny White Pike, SM 121, 125, 133, 134, 137

Grant, Fred, KI 22, MI 104-105, *107*, 109, 123

Grant, Hiram P., FR 85

Grant, Jesse, MI 58, TR *169*

Grant, Julia Dent, AS *48*, 55, 65, 67, KI 42-43, NA 107, TR 16, 157, *169;* and Booth, AS 69, 71; and Mrs. Lincoln, AS 54, 55, 57

Grant, Lemuel, AT 116

Grant, Lewis A., AP 92, FL 150, KI 71, 101

Grant, Orvil, NA 115

Grant, Ulysses S., AP 16, 20, 21, 33, 34, 157, 162, AS 19, 43, *48*, 55, 59, 64, 68, 85, 145, AT *22*, 31, 32, 139, 140, 154, CH 2, 19, 30, 31, 43, *84*, 99, 100, 104, 123, 132, 134, 141, 142, 143, 149, 156, FL 17, 20, 23, 52, 71, 112, 122, FO 74, 97, FR 46-47, 51-52, 54, 63, 71, 129, 138, 146, 150, KI 9, *23*, 26, 36-37, 70, 151, MI *106-107*, NA *55*, 56, 70, 72, 77, *99*, *113*, 124, 134, 152, 153, 156, SH *43*, *47*, SM 16, 59, TE 8, 85, TR 16-*17*, 26, 28, 33, 36, 48, 51, 52, 115, *147*, 149, 155, TT 158, YA 75, 124-125, 130, 153; acclaimed, MI 33, 134; Alabama claims, NA 126; allegations of drunkenness, CH 86; anger over unordered advance at Missionary Ridge, CH 145, 146; appearance, CH 84, 88; appointed brigadier, SH 45-46; appointed colonel, SH 44-45; appointed department commander, MI 34, 44, 57; appointed major general, SH 96; at Appomattox, AP 136-137, 140-141, 143-153; Appomattox, pursuit of Lee to, AP 113-114, 117, 121, 128, 133-134; arrives at Chattanooga, CH 89; arrives in Washington, AS 57; assumes command of Military District of the Mississippi, CH 88; Banks, relations with, MI 108; at Belmont, SH 46-49, 59; at Big Black River, MI 123-125; Black Friday, NA 106-107; and black refugees, MI 57-58; Blair, relations with, SH 45; and Booth, AS 71; and Bragg's personal traits, SH 107; at Bruinsburg, MI 105; Buckner, relations with, SH 94-95; and Burnside, CH 105, 155; KI 57; at Cabinet meeting, AS *66;* as cadet, SH 42; campaign against Vicksburg, TE 17, 42; canal project, MI 69-73, *74-75;* and casualties, TR 2, 64; Centennial Exposition, NA *151;* at Champion's Hill, MI 116, 119; and Chickasaw Bluffs, MI 57, 96, 144; at City Point, TR 168, *169;* and City Point explosion, SP 82, 84; and coastal operations, CO 96; at Cold Harbor, KI 153-154, 156, *162*-163, 166-167, 169; at Columbus, SH 46; combat philosophy, SH 42, 45, 49, 90, 104-105; commander-in-chief, KI 22; commands 21st Illinois, SH 45; commands army, MI 68; commands Cairo district, SH 33 34, 46; commission for lieutenant general, KI *27;* communications system, MI 108; at Corinth, MI 34, 38, 40, 43-44, 46; and Corinth, advance on, SH 104-105; corruption in Administration, NA 76-77, 106, 108-109, 112-116, 148; and cotton speculators, MI 58-59; criticism of, TR 94; criticized, MI 33-34, 58-59, 83, SH 155; and Crook, FL 24-25; Dana reports on, MI 104-105, 109, 144-145, 147; and Dodge, SP 73; drinking problem, MI 143, *144*, 145-146; drive on Richmond, OR 59, 151; and Early's raid, FL 73, 84; election campaigns, NA 75-77, 110, 112, 148; entrenchments, attitude toward, SH 105; evaluation of Bragg, TE 20; evaluation of Rosecrans, CH 19, 88; evaluation of Sheridan, CH 150; evaluation of Thomas, CH 88; family, MI *107;* and Five Forks, AP 81, 82, 85, 86, 91; flanking maneuvers, KI 82, 84-85, 130-131, 148-149, 151, 169; Foote, relations with, SH 16, 60, 85, 147, 90; Ford's Theatre invitation, AS 54, 65, 67, *72;* at Fort Donelson, SH 78, 81-82, 84-87, *88-89*, 93-94, 104; and Fort Fisher, CO 157, 162; at Fort Henry, SH 60-63, 67; at Forts Henry and Donelson, CO 54; MI 33; and Fort Stedman, AP 39; Frémont, relations with, SH 33, 46; and Grand Gulf, MI 86, 100-101, 108; at Grand Review, NA *8-9;* Greeley's evaluation of, MI 134; and Greenville, MI 87; and Grierson's Raid, MI 88, 96; Halleck, relations with, MI 34, 134, SH 60, 78, 96, 104; and Haynes' Bluff, MI 74; and Holly Springs, MI 60; and Hunter, FL 39, 41, 43, 53, 89, 90, 101; injured by horse, CH 86, 89; at Iuka, MI 36-37; at Jackson, MI 56, 109, 111, 113, 115; James River, flanking movement across, TR 2, 34-38; and Jews, MI 58-59; Johnston evaluated by, MI 140-142, SH 52, 55; Knox's evaluation of, SH 42; and Lake Providence project, MI 73-74; Lawler evaluated by, MI 122; and Lee at Appomattox, AP 145, *146-147*, 148-151; and Lincoln, meeting with, FL 100; Lincoln, relations with, MI 34, 83, 105, 159, SH 49, 96, 155; and Lincoln at City Point, AS 53, *56;* Lyon, relations with, SH 45; at Massaponax Church, KI 126, *127-129;* McClellan, relations with, SH 45; McClernand, relations with, MI 56-57, 62, 68-69, 132; McClernand relieved by, MI 147-148; and Meade, KI 24-25, 68; meeting with Lincoln and Sherman, AP 76, *77;* meeting with Stanton, CH 88; at Memphis, MI 62, 68; military districts in South, NA 61-62; at Milliken's Bend, MI 69, 83-84; in Missouri operations, SH 45; moves supply base, KI 148; and mystique of Lookout Mountain, CH 136; Nast cartoons, NA *130-131*, *135-137;* as national hero, SH 96; and New Market Heights, TR 145; at North Anna, KI 133, 135, 137; at Orchard Knob, CH 120, 121, *144-145;* at Oxford, MI 57; at Paducah, SH 46, 53; Panic of 1873, NA 125; and peace initiatives, AP 24, 26; on peace negotiations, OR 163; Pemberton, meeting with, MI 153-156; personal traits, MI 106; SH 9, 33, 42, 45; at Petersburg, FL 69, 125, 151, 158, TR 39, 43, 45, 49, 53, 57, 67, 69-70, 74, 86, 88, 99, 136, 139; Petersburg, assault at, AP 92, 97, 108; in Petersburg siege, OR 151; Pillow evaluated by, SH 81, 95; and political constraints, TR 158; Porter, relations with, MI 78, 86; and Port Gibson, MI 101-105; and Port Hudson, MI 73, 108, 140; prewar career, SH 42; pursuit of Bragg, CH 150, 154; railroads, attacks on, TR 19-20, 53, 55, 69, 150, 154, 157; Rawlins as guardian, MI 145-147; and Reams's Station, TR 104, 110; and refugees, OR 112; relieved by Halleck, SH 155; reorganizes army, KI 37-38, 43; and reporters, SP 52; reputation for drinking, SH 42, 45, 155; resignation considered, MI 34; retirement, NA *158;* Rosecrans, relations with, MI 44; at Satartia, MI 144; and Sedgwick, KI 56, 88; and Sharpe, SP 80, 81; and Shenandoah Valley, orders concerning destruction in, FL 42, 90, 101; and Sheridan, FL 103-109, 134, 135, 137, 140, KI 114, TR 95, 111; and Sherman's Carolinas Campaign, AP 52; Sherman's evaluation of, MI 125, 134; and Sherman's plans, SM 34-35, 156, 159; and Sherman, AT 20, 21; Sherman, relations with, CH 117, 122, SH 104, 155-157; Sherman evaluated by, SH 133; at Shiloh, CO 77, MI 144, SH 105, 111, 116-118, 120, 130, 135, 138-139, *140*, 143, 148, 150, 152, 155; and Sigel, FL 24-25; South, civil disorder in, NA 97-99, 142-144, 150; at Spotsylvania, KI *53*, 87, 89, 92-93, 102, 105, 124-125; spying, value of, SP 72; Stanton, relations with, MI 34, 105; at Steele's Bayou, MI 74; and Stonewall Jackson, KI 132; strategic objectives of, TR 16-18, 19; strategic plans, MI *map 2-3*, 4, 44, 56-57, 62-63, 69; strategic success of, KI 169; strategy for war, KI 26, 61; and supplies at Chattanooga, CH 97, 98; and supply lines, AP 42, 45, 50;

Brigadier General States Rights Gist of South Carolina, killed in a charge at the battle of Franklin, Tennessee

1st Lieutenant Henry W. Granger of the 1st New York "Lincoln" Cavalry

KI The Killing Ground; LE Lee Takes Command; MI War on the Mississippi; NA The Nation Reunited; OR Confederate Ordeal; RE Rebels Resurgent; SH The Road to Shiloh; SM Sherman's March; SP Spies, Scouts and Raiders; TE The Struggle for Tennessee; TR Death in the Trenches; TT Tenting Tonight; YA Twenty Million Yankees

67

Brigadier General Benjamin H. Grierson, renowned for his cavalry raid during the Vicksburg Campaign

Two sailors beside a howitzer on the deck of the gunboat U.S.S. *Hunchback*

Grant, Ulysses S. (continued)
  and surrender terms, AP 134, 148-150, 159-160, MI 153-156, SH 94-95; tactical plans, MI 36, *map 72*, 73-76, 79-80, 83-84, 86-87, 96-97, 100-101, 108-109, 115, 123, 126, 134-136, 140-142, 152; temperament, CH 117; in Tennessee, MI 56; in the Wilderness, KI 59-*61*, 62, 68, 73, 79, 81; and Thomas, AT 33; training programs, SH 45; transcontinental railroad, NA *82;* troop strength, MI 34, 84, 101, 113, 126, 134; troop strength and reinforcements, SH 78-79, 82; urges Thomas to attack, SM 122, 123, 125, 134; use of ruse, CH 118; and Van Lew, SP 88-89; at Vicksburg, CH 18, 21, 85, MI 4, 44, 126-132, 134-147, 152, *154,* OR 48; and Wallace, FL 84; in war with Mexico, SH 42, *44;* war strategy, AT 20; and Yazoo Pass project, MI 74-76; and Yazoo River operations, MI 79-80, 144; at Young's Point, MI 68
Grapeshot (locomotive), SP 130
Grapevine Bridge, FO 155, LE *38-39*, 50
Gray, John L., TT *81*
Gray, Thomas, BR 99
Graybeard Regiment, TT 28
Graydon, James (Paddy), FR 23, 115
Great Bahama Bank, BL 121
Great Britain: and Confederacy recognition, OR 29, 148; and cotton embargo, OR *28;* munitions supplied by, OR 18; ships seized by, OR 148
Great Britain. *See* United Kingdom
Great Falls, Maryland, FO *51*
Great Lakes, strategic value of, SH 9, 11
Great Lakes region, population growth in, YA 21
Great Railroad Adventure, SP *111-113*
Great Seal, Confederate, BL 87
Greaves, Robert, FO 166
Greble, John T., FI *86*
Greek fire, CO 135, 137
Greeley, Horace, CO 30, FI 63, FO 11, 25, 62, FR 74, 148, MI 134, NA 63, 78, 107, 111-112, 117, 129, YA *34;* criticism of Scott plans, FI 45; editorial policies, YA 34; election poster, NA *111;* on emancipation, YA 37; and Frémont as presidential candidate, BR 104; on gold trading, YA 77; and Know-Nothings, BR 101; and Lincoln's reelection, YA 155, 158; and Lincoln as presidential candidate, BR 108; Nast cartoons, NA *134-135;* as Oregon delegate, BR 111
Green, Anna Maria, SM 61, 62
Green, Charles, NA 147
Green, Charles J., RE *106*
Green, James, CO 84-85
Green, John, AT 100, CH 55, 98, 149, OR 46
Green, Johnny, AT 149-150
Green, Lucy, pouches of, AP *61*
Green, Martin, MI 101-102, 119, 149
Green, Thomas, FR 25-*26*, 27, 34, 50, 52,

56, 59-61, 66, 70, SP 55
Greenawalt, John G., SH 91, 95
Greene, George Sears, BD 81-83, 88, 92, 97, GE 114-116
Greenhow, Robert, SP 23
Greenhow, Rose (daughter), SP *28*, 29
Greenhow, Rose O'Neal, FI 113, FO 28-29, SP 23-25, *28;* arrest, SP 28-29; background, SP 23; death, SP 31; and First Bull Run Campaign, SP 25-27, 32; mission abroad, SP 31
Greenleaf Point, AS 139
Greenock, Scotland, BL 115
Green River, Kentucky, SH 53
Greensboro, Alabama, OR 26
Greensboro, North Carolina, OR 27
Greenville, Mississippi, MI 87
Greenwich, Virginia, LE 133
Greenwood, Mississippi, MI 26
Gregg, David McMurtrie, GE 16, 20-22, 28, 114, KI 86, 114, 123, 149, TR 21-*23*, 24-26, 95, 97-99, *102*, 104-105, 109, 150, 154, 156
Gregg, Henry, TR 114
Gregg, John Irvin, AP 27, *29*, 30, 84, 125, 131, KI 77, MI 111-112, *113*, 115, TR 24, 140, 142, 154
Gregg, Maxcy, BD 136-137, LE 37, 39, 149-150, RE 62, *63*, 67
Gregory Lode, YA 71
Grenada, Mississippi, MI 59
Grenade assaults, MI *135*, 149
Grenfell, George St. Leger, TE 21, *24*
Grider, Benjamin, TE 150, 153
Gridley, R. C., YA 116, *117*
Grierson, Benjamin H., MI *89*, *97;* Halleck, relations with, MI 87; raid by, MI 87-89, *map* 90, 91-93, *94-95*, 96, 97; Sherman's evaluation of, MI 88
Griffin, Charles, AP 31-*32*, 80-81, 85-88, 90-91, 110, 113-114, 138-139, 153, FI 137, *142*, 143-145, 155, 157, 163, KI 62, 64-68, 73, RE 85-86, TR 101, 150, 152-153
Griffin, Mrs. Charles, AS 53
Griffin, Simon, TR 45
Griffin, William, KI 119
Griffin's battery, FI 137, 139, 141, *142*, 143-144, *160-161*
Griffith, J. E., MI 130
Griffith, Richard, LE 50
Grigsby, J. Warren, AT 35, 36
Grimball, John Berkley, OR 129
Grimes, Bryan, AP 133, 139, KI 136, RE 147
Grimes, James W., NA 52, 75, YA 143
Griswold, Charles E., KI *170*
Griswold, John D., BD 122
Griswoldville, Battle of, SM 60-61, 148
Grose, William, CH 130, TE 150
Ground Squirrel Bridge, KI 115, 118
Grover, Cuvier, FL 114, 115, LE 146, 148-149, MI 110
Grover's Theatre, AS *22*, *52*, 56, 59, 64, 68,

71
Groveton, Battle of, LE 139, *140-141*, 142, 144, *map* 147, 151-152
Guadalupe Hidalgo Treaty, BR 42
Guard duty, TT 49
Guardhouse confinement, TT 65
Guerrilla operations, DE 72; in Kansas, SH 12, 16; in Missouri, SH *map* 2-3, 12, 16, 19, 30-32, 45; in Tennessee, SH 80
Guerrilla operations. *See* Irregulars
Guerrillas, MI 47, 52-53; depredations by, OR 89-91, *92*, 93, *94*, 95, 119-120; in Kansas and Missouri, SP 140-161; nature of fighting, SP *cover*, 106-*107;* organization of partisan units, SP 108; and railroads, SP 122, 124, 126-127, 131, 160; reputation of, SP 126; in Virginia, SP 106-131. *See also names of individual guerrilla leaders*
Guillaume, Louis, painting by, AP *147*
Guinea (Guiney's) Station, Virginia, KI 131, RE 39, 58, 160
Gulf Blockading Squadron, BL 24
Gulf of Mexico, operations, MI 16
Gunboats, SH *diagram* 62, *64*, 68-*77;* armament, SH 62, 69-70, 72-74, 76; at Belmont, SH 70; characteristics, SH 69, 72, 74; construction and repair, SH 29-30, 59, 69-70, *74-75*, 78; conversion from barges, SH 160; crews, SH 60, 73; damage to, SH *64*, 65, 83-84; at Fort Donelson, SH 78, 82-84, *85*, 87, 90; at Fort Henry, SH 58, 60-63, *64*, 65-67; identification system, SH 68; ironclad concept, SH 59, 69, 72; at Island No. 10, SH 155, *158-159*, 160, 163, *164-167;* on Mississippi River, SH 70; at Shiloh, SH *142-143*, 147; ships captured by, SH 70; tactics, SH 84; vulnerability, SH 69. *See also by name*
Gunpowder production and procurement, OR 19-20, *21*, 22
Gunsaullus, Daniel, FR *60*
Gunston Cove, Virginia, SP 51
Guntersville, Alabama, SM 32, 33
Gurley, Phineas Densmore, AS 100
Gurney, Jeremiah, photograph by, AS *123*
Guthrie, R. E., TT 152
Guthrie Grays (Ohio), FI *36-37*
Gutierrez de Estrada, FR *43*
Guy's Gap, CH 22, 23
Guy's Restaurant (Baltimore), SP 14, 15
Gwyn, James, BD 155

H

H. L. Hunley, CO *138*, 139-141
Habana, BL 145
Habeas corpus: suspension of, OR 77, 82, 153-154, YA 31-34, 144
Hacker, J. S., SH 34
Hackett, Wright, TE 126
Hackleman, Pleasant A., MI 40

AP Pursuit to Appomattox; AS The Assassination; AT Battles for Atlanta; BD The Bloodiest Day; BL The Blockade; BR Brother against Brother; CH The Fight for Chattanooga; CO The Coastal War; DE Decoying the Yanks; FI First Blood; FL The Shenandoah in Flames; FO Forward to Richmond; FR War on the Frontier; GE Gettysburg;

Gold medal awarded to General Ulysses S. Grant by act of Congress on December 17, 1863

Hagan, John, TT 26

Hagerstown, Maryland, BD 18, 21-22, 38, 44, 47, 57, FL 69, 104; Confederate ransom demand, FL 72; entrenchments near, GE 152

Hagerstown Turnpike, BD 60-61, 65, 66-67, 68, 70, 73-79, 83, 88-89, 92, 93, 94, 96, 98, 103-104, 108, 114-115, 145

Hagood, Johnson, CO 128, KI 165, TR 104

Haiman, Louis, and Brother, OR 23

Haines, Thomas, SH 119

Hale, James, tombstone of, FR 119

Hale, John P., AS 41, 64-65, BR 42

Hale, Lucy, AS 41, 65; carte de visite, AS 138

Hale, Nathan, SP 10

Haley, John, AP 113, KI 167

Hall, Isaac, BD 70

Hall, J. M., RE 148

Hall, James, TR 63

Hall, James A., RE 65

Hall, Norman, GE 121, 138

Hall, Norman J., BD 151, BR 156, RE 81

Hall, Philip H., MI 63

Hall, Thomas W., SP 18

Halleck, Henry W., BD 38, 161, CH 21, 31, 32, 35, 43, 83, 85, 88, 97, 104, 154, FI 56, FL 39, 41, 63, 84, 86, 90, 100, 101, 103, 108, 140, 151, FO 53, 67, FR 47, 51, 52, 128, 138, 140, GE 23, 34, 153, 156, KI 24, 38, 92, 105, 125, 137, 148, 167, LE 94, RE 24, 30, 32, 35-36, 40, 93, 94, SH 61, SM 10, 35, 122, 123, 134, SP 131, 149, TE 15, 24, 25, 49, 54, 80, 82, TR 26, 39, 57, 88, YA 142; appointed general in chief, MI 34; capabilities, SH 59; command of all Union forces, TE 17; commands Department of Missouri, SH 58-60, 79; commands in West, SH 96, 101; at Corinth, SH 104, 155-157; disabled, MI 47; as general in chief, LE 94-95, 101; and Grant's order on Jews, MI 59; Grant, relations with, MI 34, 134, SH 60, 78, 96, 104; Grant relieved by, SH 155; Grierson, relations with, MI 87; and Jennison, SP 146, 147; Lincoln, relations with, SH 96; McClernand, relations with, MI 56; overall command in West, TE 12; and partisans, SP 107; personal traits, SH 59-60, 104; and Second Bull Run, LE 133; Sherman, relations with, SH 104; Sherman commended by, SH 113; and Shiloh, SH 104-105, 111; and Vicksburg, MI 108; Welles's evaluation of, SH 60; and Tennessee operations, SH 59-61, 67, 78, 84, 95

Halstead, Richard, KI 88-89

Hamblin, Joseph E., AP 125, FI 81, FL 128

Hamburg, South Carolina, NA 149-150

Hames, John E., LE 169

Hamilton, Andrew G., TT 124-128

Hamilton, Daniel H., BD 137

Hamilton, North Carolina, CO 95

Hamilton's Crossing, RE 50, 58, 61, 62, 64-65, 121-123

Hammond, James H., BR 109, on drunkenness in Congress, OR 11; and slave uprisings, OR 23

Hammond, William A., SM 106, 108, YA 128

Hampton, Preston, TR 156, 157

Hampton, Virginia: BL 46, FI 81-82

Hampton, Wade, AP 53, 60, 68, 70, 71, 158, BD 26, FI 123, 137, 144, FL 52, 58, FO 156, GE 18, 26, 28, 132, KI 36, 148-149, LE 91, NA 144, 149, SM 67, TR 21-25, 55-56, 98-99, 105, 109-115, 156

Hampton, Wade (son), TR 156

Hampton Institute, NA 51

Hampton Legion (South Carolina), BD 76-78, FI 109, 123, 137, 139, 144

Hampton Roads, FI 21-23, 78, FO 85, 89, 93, 124; battle at, MI 27; naval actions at, BL 53, 54, 55-65, 58-59, map 60; as naval staging area, BL 31, 65; strategic value, BL 46, 48

Hancock, Maryland, DE 52, 54-55

Hancock, Winfield Scott, AS 159, 160, BD 108-109, FO 111, 112-113, GE 67, 72, 149, KI 56, 82, 130-131, 148, 169, NA 72, RE 28, 151, TR 35-36, 39, 43-45, 49-50, 69-70, 73, 101, 109, 111, appointed corps commander, GE 14; Burnside, relations with, RE 29; at Cemetery Hill, GE 65, 74, 117; at Cemetery Ridge, GE 104-105, 108, 111, 131, 133-134, 137-141, 142-143; at Chancellorsville, RE 124-125, 148, 150-151; at Cold Harbor, KI 154, 160, 163, 165-166; commands at Gettysburg, GE 8-9; at Fredericksburg, RE 77, 80-81, 83, 85; and Fussell's Mill, TR 95, 97-99; and Hatcher's Run, TR 154-157; at North Anna, KI 133, 135-136; and Peach Orchard, GE 77, 100; and Ream's Station, TR 104-110; at Spotsylvania, KI 87-89, 93-95, 102, 125; at Taneytown, GE 65; and the Angle, GE 120-121; in the Wilderness, KI 61, 68, 70-71, 73-74, 76-80

Handy, Isaac, TT 123

Hanes hand grenade, SP 162

Hannas, Stephen, DE 113

Hannibal, Missouri, SH 22-23

Hanover County, Virginia, OR 79

Hanover Court House, Virginia, FO 90, 133, LE 26-27

Hanover Junction, Virginia, FL 39, KI 118, 131, 132, TR 20, 27

Hanovertown, Virginia, KI 148, 150

Hanson, Roger W., TE 148, 149, 153, 154, TT 65

Harbin, Thomas, AS 132

Hardcastle, Aaron B., SH 111-113

Hardee, William J., AP 53, 55, 61, 67-68, AT 29, 35, 49, 90, 92, 113, CH 23, 24, 29, 34, FI 51, SH 110, SM 67, 147, TE 50, 55, 57, 58, 59, 62, 90, 91, 94, 99, TT 52; assumes command of Bragg's routed army, CH 155; author of military tactics text, TE 61; at Averasboro, AP 69; at Battle of Atlanta, AT 97, 105, 106, 111; at Bentonville, AP 71, 72, 75; at Bowling Green, SH 79; Cavalry Tactics, CH 81; concern for troops, TE 50; as corps commander, AT 28; and Hood, SM 18; at Jonesboro, AT 143-144, 146, 147-148, 152; at Macon, SM 52; at Missionary Ridge, CH 131, 136, 140, 149; at Munfordville, TE 51; organizational ability, CH 34; at Peachtree Creek, AT 94; at Perryville, TE 66, 67; and Polk's death, AT 61, 63; relations with Bragg, TE 61, 82, 160-161; and Savannah's defense, SM 148, 149; at Shiloh, SH 106, 108, 111-116, 120, 143, 148, 150-151; at Stones River, TE 113, 118, 123, 124, 126, 127, 132, 157, 159; transfer to Bragg, CH 85; transfer to Mississippi, CH 34; withdrawal from Savannah, SM 158

Hardee, Willie, AP 75

Hardie, James A., RE 61

Hardin, Martin D., FL 63, 65

Harding, John, BL 121

Hardy, Luther, TT 121

Harewood Hospital, TT 107, YA 16-17

Harker, Charles G., AT 70, 71, 75, CH 64, 148

Harker, Charles Garrison, TE 96, 120

Harland, Edward, BD 136

Harland, W. D., SH 81-82, 86-87

Harman, John A., BD 13-14, DE 94

Harman, William, DE 67, 70

Harmon, Oscar F., AT 74, 75

Harney, William Selby, SH 13, 16-17

Harper, George, AS 145

Harper, Kenton, DE 36

Harpers Ferry, FI 94-95, operations at, FI 15-17, 93, 95; strategic value of, FI 29-31, 85

Harpers Ferry, Virginia, BD 30-37, 40-41, FO 18, 63, 74-76, 84, LE 20, TT 18-19; armory, DE 16-17; escape from by Union cavalry, BD 56-58; operations at, BD map 2-3, 18, 22, 30, 32-33, 38-45, 55-60, 86, 151, 156, DE 33-34, 61, 64-65, 149-150, 156; strategic value, BD 30; strategic value of, DE 33-34; surrendered, BD 59-60; terrain features, BD 38-39

Harpers Ferry, West Virginia, FL 17, 53, 69, 88, 89, 90, 101, 104, SP 110

Harpers Ferry raid, BR 84-85, 86-87, 88-89, 90-93. See also Brown, John

Harpers Ferry Road, BD 132, 135-136

Harper's Illustrated Weekly, CH 79, 125

Harper's Magazine, YA 59

Harper's New Monthly Magazine, FL 54, MI 97

Harper's Weekly, AS 119, BD 81, FI 89, FO 52, 92, FR 21, MI 117, 154, NA 129, 132, 157, OR 117, TE 100, TT 67, 162

Major General Winfield Scott Hancock (seated) with II Corps Generals Barlow, Birney and Gibbon

KI The Killing Ground; LE Lee Takes Command; MI War on the Mississippi; NA The Nation Reunited; OR Confederate Ordeal; RE Rebels Resurgent; SH The Road to Shiloh; SM Sherman's March; SP Spies, Scouts and Raiders; TE The Struggle for Tennessee; TR Death in the Trenches; TT Tenting Tonight; YA Twenty Million Yankees

69

Major John G. Hazard, brevetted Brigadier General for service with II Corps's artillery

Federal officer's "Burnside Hat," named after the general of that name

Harpeth River, SM 96, 97, *104-105*, 113, 115, 117, 120
Harries, William, BD 66
Harriet Lane, BR 152, CO 75, *FR 48-49*
Harrington, Fazilo, TE 122
Harris, Clara H., AS 76, 77, 83
Harris, D. B., TR 69
Harris, Elisha, YA 124-125
Harris, George Washington, OR 52
Harris, Ira, AS 76
Harris, Isham G., SH 56-57, 97, 128-129, SM 83
Harris, J. B., MI 119
Harris, James, BR 71, 78-79
Harris, James H., TR *124*
Harris, Joseph E., TE 24
Harris, Nathaniel, AP 97, 99, KI 137
Harris, Samuel J., TE 64
Harris, Thomas, SH 45
Harris, Thomas M., AS 148, *149*, 157
Harrisburg, Pennsylvania, BD 18, FI 21, GE 26, 30-31, 33
Harris farm, KI 126
Harris' Horse Artillery (19th Indiana), TE 24, *64-65*
Harrison, Benjamin, AT 46, 47, 93-94
Harrison, Constance, OR 40
Harrison, Henry Thomas, SP *54*
Harrisonburg, Virginia, FL 17, 42, 125, 134, 135; actions at, DE 84, 86-87, 101, 116, 146-149, 157-159, *160-163*, 170
Harrison's Island, FO 40-41, *map* 44, 46, 48, 51
Harrison's Landing, Virginia, LE 48, 63, 66, *73-81*, 83, 90-91, *94*, 95, 98
Harrisonville, Missouri, SP 146
Harrodsburg, Kentucky, TE 57, 58, 67
Harrow, William, AT *86-87*, 108, 111
Hart, Charley. *See* Quantrill, William Clarke
Hart, David, FI 89-91
Hart, David D., AT 56
Hart, Peter, BR 101
Hart, William, RE 108
Harte, Bret, NA 85
Hartford, CO *4*, *55*, 61, 66-68, *71*, 145, 147-149, *150*, 151-153, *154-155*, MI 19, 24, *29*, 162
Hartford, Connecticut, BR 114, OR 17, YA 87
Hartford *Courant*, YA 95
Hartpence, William R., SM 124, 128, 129, 135, 136
Hartranft, John F., AP 30, *38*, 39, AS 139, 159, *164-165*, BD *126*, CH 107, 109, TR 46
Hartsfield, Alva C., FL 159
Hartsuff, George L., BD 78
Hartsville, Battle of, TE 85, 87
Harvard Regiment, FO 41-42, 46, 51
Harvest of Death (photograph), GE *168-169*
Harvey, Frederick, FO 47
Harvey, Stan C., AT 150
Harvey Birch, BL *144-145*
Hascall, Milo S., AT 63, 64, TE 120, 150

Haskell, Frank, LE 142
Haskell, Frank A., KI 161, *171*
Haskell, John C., KI 78-79, TR *86*
Hassler, Bettie, SP 24
Hatch, Edward, MI 88, 90-91, SM 126, 130
Hatch, John P., BD 51-52, LE 98, 137-138, 141, 146, 151-153, 167
Hatch, Ozias M., BD 161
Hatcher, Clinton, FO 50
Hatcher's Run, Battle of, AP 27-31, *32-33*, TR *map* 96, 154-156
Hatchet Brigade (Wilder's Brigade), CH 21. *See also* Lightning Brigade
Hats, production of, OR 26
Hatteras, BL 142, 152
Hatteras Inlet, CO 16-17, *18-19*, 22-23, 35, 57; as blockade target, BL 26, 29-31
Hatton, Robert, FO 156
Haupt, Herman, RE *8*, 9-10, *14-15*, 20-21, *171*, SP 90, 93, 94, 97, 99, 101, *104*
Hauser's Ridge, BD 76, 88
Havana, as blockade-runners' port, BL *map* 2-3, 88, 93, 116
Havas, Auguste, BL 120
Haverhill, Massachusetts, civil disorder in, YA 29, *30*
Hawes, Richard, TE 57
Hawk, Harry, AS *73*, 85
Hawkins, Eugene, KI *65*
Hawkins, Hiram, AT 59
Hawkins, Rush C., BD 132, CO 27, *28*, 30, 34, RE 41, 87
Hawks, Wells J., DE 94
Hawk's Nest, DE 75
Hawley, William, AP 73
Haw's Shop, Virginia, KI 149
Hawthorne, Nathaniel, YA 87
Haxall's Landing, Virginia, KI 123
Hay, John, BD 15, 164, FO 62, 71, 85, 97, YA 151
Hayden, John, GE *155*
Hayes, Birchard, NA *152*
Hayes, Joseph, TR 101
Hayes, Rutherford Birchard, BD 24, 45, *46-47*, FL 21, *22*, 23, 89, 90, 124, 146, 147, NA 138, 139, 149, *152*, 153-156, TE 25, TT 62-63
Hayes, Thomas, FL *14*
Hayes, Webb, NA *152*
Haymarket, Virginia, LE 145
Hayne, Paul Hamilton, OR 46
Haynes, Luther C., FL 159
Haynes, Martin A., LE 148-149
Haynes' Bluff, MI 67, 74, 80, 109
Haynsworth, George E., BR 127
Hays, Alexander, KI 71, LE 60, MI *106*; at Cemetery Hill, GE 112; and Pickett's Charge, GE 137, 139, 144; at Plum Run, GE 108; at Ziegler's Grove, GE 131
Hays, Harry Thompson, DE 168-169, KI 29, *33*; at Barlow's Knoll, GE 60; at Cemetery Hill, GE 92-93, 116-118; at Winchester, GE 23-24
Hays, John, RE 101
Hays, William, RE 144

Hazard, John G., GE *124*, 134, RE 85
Hazel Grove, RE 128, 133, 135, 140-143, 147
Hazel Run, RE 153-154
Hazen, William B., AP *54*, AT 54, 56, 78, CH 33, 64, 72, *90*, 91, 143, SM *148*, 150, 152, TE 127, 129, 130, 142, 150
Hazlett, Charles E., GE 84-85
Hazlett's battery, LE 153
Head, Truman (California Joe), FO 100, *101*
Headgear, DE *56-57*
Headley, John W., SP 62
Heart of Midlothian (Scott), OR 46
Hébert, Louis, FR 143, MI 148
Hébert, Mr., SP 162
Heckman, Charles A., TR 143-145, 148
Hedley, F. Y., SM 40, 44-45, TT 87
Heg, Hans Christian, CH 48, *50-51*, *63*
Hegeman, George, TT 113, 115, 122
Heiman, Adolphus, TE 84
Heintzelman, Samuel P., BD 15, FI 117, 126-128, 132, 135, 137, 147, 149, FO 84, *86*, 93-94, 130, 136, LE 31, 95; at Alexandria, LE 126; at Bristoe Station, LE 133; at Second Bull Run, LE 133, 148, 162; in Seven Days' Battles, LE 50-52, 72, *74-75*
Helena, Arkansas, TT *134*
Heller, Christian, panorama by, FR *88-89*
Hell Hole, AT *16*, 59
Hell's Half Acre, TE 112, *162-163*
Helm, Benjamin Hardin, CH 55, *62*
Helper, Hinton, BR 108-109
Henagan, John, KI 80, 133
Henderson, David, FR *13*
Henkel, Elon, FL 28
Henry, Benjamin, AT 112
Henry, Edward Lamson, paintings by, TR *160-162*, *165-166*, *169-171*
Henry, Gus A., Jr., SH 93
Henry, Gustavus Adolphus, SH 57, TE 82
Henry, Guy V., KI 153
Henry, Judith, FI 142-143
Henry, M. W., RE 64
Henry, Patrick, FL *14*
Henry, W. F., SM *84*
Henry House Hill, FI 132, 135, *map* 141, 142, 147, *158-165*, LE 159-160, *162-163*
Henry repeating rifles, AT *112-113*, SM 24
Henson, Josiah, BR *46*
Henson, Mr. *See* Herold, David
Henson, Philip, SP 89; background, SP 75; and Black Hawk (horse), SP 76; and Forrest, SP 78; and Polk, SP 78; at Vicksburg, SP 76
Herbert, Arthur, AP *127*
Herndon House, AS 54, 69, 72
Herold, David, AS *25*, 29, 39, 40, 44, 71; and assault on Seward, AS 95, 96; capture and confinement, AS 108, *134-135*, 136, *141*, *142*; escape route with Booth, AS 104-105, *106-107*, 108, 111, *112*, *map* 113, 114-117, 132-134; execution of, AS 159-*160*, *162-171*; plot

AP Pursuit to Appomattox; AS The Assassination; AT Battles for Atlanta; BD The Bloodiest Day; BL The Blockade; BR Brother against Brother; CH The Fight for Chattanooga; CO The Coastal War; DE Decoying the Yanks; FI First Blood; FL The Shenandoah in Flames; FO Forward to Richmond; FR War on the Frontier; GE Gettysburg;

to kidnap Lincoln, AS 48-51; plot to murder Lincoln, AS 72-74; recruited by Booth, AS 20-21; reward and poster for, AS *93;* trial of, AS 145, 151, 154, *156,* 158

Herr, George W., SM 129-130, 135, 136, 142

Herron, Francis J., FR 150, 151

Herr Ridge, GE 44-45, 50, 59, 72

Hescock, Henry, TE 121

Hescock's Battery (Battery G, 1st Missouri, Union), TE 121

Hess, C. Dwight, AS 59

Heth, Henry, AP 29, 30, 95, 96, 110, 117, FR 138, GE 13, *34,* KI 68, 70-71, 73-74, 93, 133-134, 154, OR 91, RE 146, 160, TE 41, 44, 82, TR 94, 101, 103-*104,* 108, 150, 156; at Cashtown, GE 35; at Cemetery Hill, GE *map* 63; at Gettysburg, GE 34-35, 45, 50-51, 53, 68; at Herr Ridge, GE 44-45, 48, 59; at McPherson's Ridge, GE 55, 61; in Pickett's Charge, GE 128; in Potomac crossing, GE 156-157

Heuston, Peter, YA 108

Hewison, James, LE 107

Hewitt, Sylvester, BD 43

Hiawassee River, CH 169

Hickenlooper, Andrew, MI 148

Hickenlooper, Andrew J., SH *125,* 126, 135

Hickenlooper's Battery, SH *124-125,* 126, 135

Hicks, Mr., SP 170

Hicks, Thomas H., FI 21, 24, 29

Higby, Edgar J., AT 42

Higginbotham, Joseph Absalom, RE *107*

Higgins, Jacob, FL 26, 27-28

Higgins, John M., OR 82

Higgins, Thomas H., MI 131

Higginson, Henry Lee, GE *27*

Higginson, Thomas Wentworth, BR 84, TT 68

High Bridge, AP 118-119, 127-128, 130-*132,* TR *19*

Highland County Company (Virginia), FI 86-87

Highlanders (79th New York) Regiment, BD 131, FO 16-17

Hight, John, SM 72

Hildebrand, Jesse, SH 112

Hildebrand, Samuel S., SP 140

Hill, Ambrose Powell, AP 19, 29, 82, 93-94, *98,* 140, BD *131,* FO 136, 159, KI 28, 130-131, *133,* 165, LE *33,* 91, OR 160, TR 44, 53, 56, 103, 105, 107, 150, 156; at Antietam, BD 65, 129-130, 135-137, 141; appointed corps commander, GE 14; at Bolivar Heights, BD 56; cape, hat and sword of, AP *98;* at Cashtown, GE 51, 53; at Cedar Mountain, LE 100, 103, 107-108; at Cemetery Hill, GE 65-69, 71; at Cemetery Ridge, GE 131; at Centreville, LE 132; at Chambersburg, GE 35; at Chancellorsville, RE 129-130, 138-139,

141-142, 160; in Chickahominy operations, LE 30, 33, 37; at Culpeper, LE 99-101; death of, AP 95, 98; dispute with Jackson, BD 12-13; at Emmitsburg road, GE 104; at Fredericksburg, GE 25, RE 58, 61-62; at Gettysburg, GE 35, 59-60, 68-70, 113; at Gordonsville, LE 98; at Hamilton's Crossing, RE 122; at Harpers Ferry, BD 59, 129-130; Jackson succeeded by, RE 139; at North Anna, KI 132-136; at Orange Court House, LE 101; in Potomac crossings, GE 26, 156; in retreat to Virginia, BD 153-154, 156; at Second Bull Run, LE 132, 135, 149-150; in Seven Days' Battles, LE 33-37, 40-42, 45, 49, 55-56, 58-60, 65, 72; in Shenandoah Valley, GE 25; at Spotsylvania, KI 84, 87, 93-94; in the Wilderness, KI 57-59, 62, 68, 70-71, 73; at Yerby House, RE 39, 58

Hill, Benjamin H., OR 13

Hill, Charles W., TT 118

Hill, Daniel Harvey, AP 53, 65, 66, 67, BD *106,* CH 34, 37, 38, 39, 48, 53, 54, 68, 84, 85, CO *91,* DE 25, 29, FI 79-82, FL 59, FO 136-137, *138,* 139-141, 145, 157, 160, 164-166, RE 39-40, 58, 61, TT 55; animosity to North, CO 84, 86; at Antietam, BD 60, 67, 76, 80-81, 86, 94-95, 98-101, 105-106, 114-115; at Boonsboro, BD 38, 44; in Chickahominy operations, LE 30, 33; Garland evaluated by, BD 50; at Goldsboro, CO 88; at Hagerstown, BD 22; and lost order, BD 21; on militia troops, CO 90-91; at New Bern, CO 86-87, 91; in Potomac crossing, BD 13; Reno evaluated by, BD 50; at Richmond, CO 91; in Seven Days' Battles, LE 33, 36-37, 41, 43, 53, 63, 65-67, 69-72; at South Mountain, BD 38, 47-49, 55; troop strength of, CO 86, 88; at Turner's Gap, BD 45; at Washington, CO 87-88, 90

Hill, Dolly, AP 98

Hill, Fred, SM 133

Hill, Herbert E., FL 118, 147, 153, 157

Hill, James J., NA 88

Hill, Lieutenant, SP 14-16

Hill, Sylvester, SM *132-133*

Hillen, J.F.E., sketch by, AT *50-51*

Hillsboro Pike, SM 121, 125, 128, 130, 132, 133

Hill's Point, North Carolina, CO 88, 90

Hilton, Andrew, TR *62*

Hilton Head, South Carolina, SM 48

Hilton Head Island, BL 34, *37-40,* 41, CO 40-41, OR *124-125,* 131, *136-139*

Hindman, Thomas C., AT 42, *49,* 63, 64, CH 38, 39, 57, 60, 61, 65, 66, 69, 84, 85, FR 136, 147-152, SP 149

Hinds, Russell, SP 144

Hines, Tom, SP *59*

Hinks, Edward W., TR 27, 30-*32,* 33, 39, 42-43

Hinman, Wilbur F., TE 60, 112

Hitchcock, Ethan Allen, FO 89

Hitchcock, Frederick L., BD 86, 97-99, RE 75-76, 78-79

Hitchcock, Henry, SM 44, 45, 58, 59, 62, 71, 145, 146, 150

Hoarding, OR 83

Hobart, Harrison C., TT 122, 124

Hobart-Hampden, Augustus Charles, BL 86, 96

Hobson, Edwin L., BD 103

Hodge, Benjamin L., SH 125-126

Hodgers, Jennie, TT 27

Hodgkins, William H., AP 36

Hoffman, Emily, AT 115

Hoffman, William, TT 111-115, *116,* 118, 128

Hoge, Jane, YA 133

Hog Jaw Valley, CH 37

Hoke, Robert F., AP 64-67, *68,* 71, KI 43, 151, 152, 165, RE 71, TR 41, 43-45, 48, 88, 149, 153-154; at New Bern, CO 92, 95-97; at Plymouth, CO 94-95, 97; troop strength of, CO 95; at Washington, CO 96-97; at Wilmington, CO 161, 163-164

Holden, William, OR 154

Holden, William W., NA 64, 98

Holdmann, Friedrich, MI *92*

"Hold the Fort," popularity of Sherman's message in North, SM 27

Holland, Milton M., TR *124*

Holliday, Thomas D., SH 114

Hollister, Ovando J., FR 29, 31, 32, 35

Holly Springs, Mississippi, MI 34-36, 60-62

Holmes, Emma, BR 132, NA 26, 61, OR 150

Holmes, James T., AT 60

Holmes, Mary Ann. *See* Booth, Mary Ann Holmes

Holmes, Oliver Wendell, Jr., BD 91, *92,* FI 16, FL 87, FO 38, 46, KI 104, NA 25; on being wounded, TT 71; on metamorphosis into veteran, TT 44; on tedium of war, TT 20

Holmes, Oliver Wendell, Sr., BD 142, TT 38, 78

Holmes, Samuel A., MI 114, 119

Holmes, Theophilus H., CO 38, FI 123-124, 136, FR 149, 150, 152, LE 56-58, 65, 72, 92

Holmes, William R., BD 126

Holston River, CH 106, 110, 111

Holt, George W., BR *143*

Holt, Joseph, AS 140-141, *149,* 150, 158, 159, BR 123-126

Homan, Conrad, AP 37

Homer, Winslow, BL 148, TT *162;* paintings by, FO *94-95,* TR *159;* sketch by, AS *57;* works by, TT *162-169*

Homespun cloth, OR *66-67*

Homestead Act, NA 78, 90-91, YA 63, 65

Homesteading, YA 63, *64-65*

Honey Springs, Battle of, FR TT 33

Honey Springs, fighting at, FR 153, *154*

Hood, Arthur, TE 26, 29

Captain Andrew Hickenlooper, who served at Shiloh as commander of the 5th Ohio Light Artillery

Brigadier General Edward W. Hincks, severely wounded at the battles of Glendale and Antietam

KI The Killing Ground; LE Lee Takes Command; MI War on the Mississippi; NA The Nation Reunited; OR Confederate Ordeal; RE Rebels Resurgent; SH The Road to Shiloh; SM Sherman's March; SP Spies, Scouts and Raiders; TE The Struggle for Tennessee; TR Death in the Trenches; TT Tenting Tonight; YA Twenty Million Yankees

71

Mill near Fredericksburg, Virginia, used as a Federal hospital after the battle of Spotsylvania

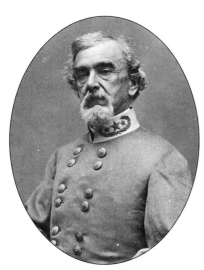

Brigadier General Benjamin Huger, relieved of his command for incompetence in the Seven Days' battles

Brigadier General Henry J. Hunt, capable Chief of Artillery of the Army of the Potomac

Hood, John Bell, AP 8, 52, 53, 61, AT 29, 47, 49, 52, 63, *93*, 95, 139, 143, 154, CH 49, 92, LE *46*, 91, RE 33, 36, 104-105, SM *20*, 34, 52, 97; aggressive tactics, AT 3, 91-92, 95-97, 134; ambition of, AT 30; at Antietam, BD 64, 67, 75-78, *79*, 82, 87; and Atlanta's evacuation, SM 15; at Atlanta, OR 148; baptism by Polk, AT 39; at Battle of Atlanta, AT 105-106, 114; and Bragg's officers, CH 53-54; at Cemetery Ridge, GE 78-79; at Chickamauga, CH 44, 48, 57, 58; as corps commander, AT 28; at Devil's Den, GE 79, 86; dispute with Evans, BD 12, 49; at Emmitsburg road, GE 73, 98-99; evacuates Atlanta, AT 152; and Forrest's raid on Murfreesboro, SM 125; at Franklin, SM 98, 100, 116, 120; at Gettysburg, GE 68; and Hardee, SM 18; health of, SM 18; and Johnston, AT 64, 80; and Jonesboro, AT 146-147; at Nashville, OR 158-160; and Nashville, advance on, SM 120, 121, 122; and Nashville, Battle of, SM 125, 126, 129, 133, 134, 136-137, 142; offensive plans, SM 2, 17, 19, 28-29, 32, 35, 82, 88; at Peach Orchard, GE 78; physical condition, AT 90-91; popularity of, CH 44; and President Davis, AT 30; recovering from wound at Gettysburg, CH 42; relinquishes command, SM 144; replaces Johnston, AT 90; at Resaca, AT 38, 39, 43, 44; at Round Tops, GE 78-79; at Second Bull Run, LE 136, 145, 151-152; in Seven Days' Battles, LE 40, 45; at South Mountain, BD 49-50; and Spring Hill, SM 89, 91, 92-93, 94; and subordinates, anger at, SM 18, 32, 95; and tactics, SM 83, 98, 113, 120; use of cavalry, AT 140; wounded at Chickamauga, CH *60*
Hood, William S., BD 127
Hooker, Joseph (Fighting Joe), AT 45, 49, *93*, CH 89, 91, 93, 117, 118, 132, *137*, 148, *152*, FO 74, 109-110, 136, 158, 160, 166, KI 22, LE 31, NA 162, RE *99*, SM 49, SP 63, 80, 81; at Antietam, BD *61*, 64-67, *68*, 70, 78-80, 83, *84-85*, 87, 108, 120, 122; appointed army commander, RE 98, 101; approach to Gettysburg, GE *map* 32, 33; attacks Bragg's rear guard, CH 150, 154; boasts by, RE 99, 111, 121, 125; at Bristoe Station, LE 133; Burnside, relations with, RE 24, 87, 96, 98; on cavalry, RE 105, 160; at Chancellorsville, GE 13-14, RE 121, 124, 128, 130, 133-135, *136-137*, 140-141, 144, 148-149, 152, 155, 158; commands grand division, RE 30; conference with Lincoln, RE 111; on dictatorship, RE 96, 98, 101; at Frederick, GE *map* 32, 34; at Fredericksburg, RE 50, 85-86, *87*, 91, 118; and Harpers Ferry, GE 34; headquarters, reputation of, RE 98, 126; headquarters on Lookout Mountain, CH

157; indecisiveness, GE 33-34; Lincoln's letter to, RE 101; Lincoln, relations with, GE 16; RE 118-119; at Lookout Mountain, CH *126-127*, 130, 131, 133, 134; at Manassas, GE *map* 32; and Maryland Heights, GE 34; at Missionary Ridge, CH 142; at New Hope Church, AT 51, 52; passed over for promotion, CH 137; at Peachtree Creek, AT *94;* personal traits, RE 29, 126; in Potomac crossing, GE 34; and Rappahannock operations, RE 32, 39, 50, 85, 118-121, *map* 122, 158; reasons for failure, RE 156, 159-160; reforms by, RE 100-102; reinforces Rosecrans, CH 83; relieved by Lincoln, GE 33, 35; reputation, CH 130, 136; at Resaca, AT 45, 46, 47; resigns command, AT 133; Scott, relations with, RE 98-99; at Second Bull Run, LE 133, 148-149; in Seven Days' Battles, LE 48, 59-60, 73; and Sherman, AT 64-65, 132; at South Mountain, BD 48, 50-51, 73; Stanton, relations with, RE 32; strategic plans, GE 2, 10, 16; subordinates, relations with, GE 14; tactical plans, RE 118-121, 123, 125, 128-129, 135, 140-142, 144, 149, 151-152, 158; troop strength, RE 118, 125, 140, 155-156; and Winchester, GE 23
Hoover's Gap, CH 22, 23, 24, 28, *30-31*
Hope, BL 91
Hope, James, BD 110-119, FI 164-165
Hopewell, Eliza, DE 122
Hopkins, Archibald, AP 123
Hopkins, William, AP 99
Hopkinsville, Kentucky, SH 54
Horner family, OR 111
Hornet's Nest, SH 121, *map* 122, 123, *124-125*, 128, *130-131*, 133, 135-137, *map* 138, 139, 141
Horses, OR 26, 29, 43
Horseshoe Ridge, CH 45, 64, 65, 69
Hoskinson, Stuart F., SM 113
Hospitals, TE 67, *74-75*, *111*, 143, 155, 161, YA 8, *16-17;* in Alexandria, TT *106-109;* in Annapolis, TT 88; Chimborazo, TT *96-97;* field, YA *130-132;* in Fredericksburg, TT *93;* Harewood, TT *107;* military, CH *156-157;* for prisoners, TT 118; in Washington, TT 95, *106-107. See also* Casualties; Medical Department; Medical Services
Hospital ships, SH 147, TT *105*, YA 124, 131
Hospital steward, SM *111*
Hospital trains, YA 124, *125*
Hotchkiss, Jedediah, BD 13, DE *84,* FL 141, 144, *145*, RE 60, 126-127; equipment of, DE *84-85;* at Harpers Ferry, DE 150, 156; Jackson's dependence on, DE 82-84; as mapmaker and engineer, DE 82-84, 101, 158; at Port Republic, DE 168
Hotze, Henry, BL 120

Hough, Daniel, BR 161
Houghtaling, Charles, TE 121, 122
Houghtaling's Battery (Battery C, 1st Illinois), TE 121
Housatonic, CO 141
House, Charles, TR 62
House, Colonel, SM 142
House, Edward H., FI 64
House of Lords (saloon), AS 29
House of Representatives speakership, BR 108-109
Houston, Texas, OR 121
Houston (Dodge's servant), SP 79
Houston *Tri-Weekly Telegraph,* OR 48
Hovey, Alvin P., AT 42, MI 103, 108, 116-119, 122
Howard, Charles, FO 161, SP *19*
Howard, Francis Key, SP 17, *19*
Howard, Joe. *See* Davies, Harry
Howard, John C., livery stable of, AS *68-69*
Howard, McHenry, AP 115-116, 125, FI 156, KI 34, 73, 84, 94, TT 119
Howard, Oliver O., AP 53, *54*, 70, 74-75, AT 42, 45, 70, 141, 142, BD 90-91, 150, CH 83, 91, 117, 118, 120, 123, FI 117, 126, 146-149, *164-165*, FO 160-161, *166*, NA 36, 50, RE *133*, SM 29, 32, *51;* as army commander, AT 133; background, SM 49-50; at Cemetery Hill, GE *map* 63, 67, 74, 114, 117; at Chancellorsville, RE 124, 128-130, *131-132*, 140, 158; commands at Gettysburg, GE 51-52, 65; at Emmitsburg, GE 35; at Ezra Church, AT 134; and Fort McAllister, SM 150; at Fredericksburg, RE 79, 81; at Jonesboro, AT 144, 146, 148; and looters, SM 71; and march to the sea, SM 48, 49, 53, 62, 66; at Pickett's Mill, AT 53-54, 56; in Rappahannock operations, RE 120, *map* 122, 123; at Savannah, SM 155; tribute to Jackson, RE 133
Howard, S. E., FL 119, 134, 147
Howard, Uncle Wiley, SM 118
Howard School, TE *74*
Howard University, NA *51*
Howe, Albion, RE 153
Howe, Albion P., AS *149*, FL 88
Howe, Elias, YA 66
Howe, Elias, Jr., YA 87
Howe, Julia Ward, FO 24, TT 68
Howe, Orion, MI 131
Howe, Samuel Gridley, BR 85
Howes, Frederic, TR *62*
Howland, Eliza Woolsey, YA 130-133
Howland, Joseph, LE 41
Hubbard, A. P., FI 149, Bible of, FI *149*
Hubbard, L. F., MI 114
Hubbell, W. S., KI 153, 156
Hudson, Roland, GE *155*
Hudson *Star,* NA 78
Huey, Pennock, RE 133
Huff, John A., KI 122, 149
Huger, Benjamin, CO 22, 30, FO 125, 136, 138-139, 141, 159, 167, LE 31, 49, 55-56, 65-66, 68, 70-71, 92

AP Pursuit to Appomattox; AS The Assassination; AT Battles for Atlanta; BD The Bloodiest Day; BL The Blockade; BR Brother against Brother; CH The Fight for Chattanooga; CO The Coastal War; DE Decoying the Yanks; FI First Blood; FL The Shenandoah in Flames; FO Forward to Richmond; FR War on the Frontier; GE Gettysburg;

Huger, Frank, RE *146*
Huger, Thomas B., CO 72-73
Hughes, John J., AS 112
Hugo, Victor, OR 46, TT 67
Humorists, OR 51-52
Humphreys, Andrew A., AP 27, 41, 79, 81, 82, 97, 113, 117, *122*, 127, 131-133, 140-143, BD 151, GE 77, 103-105, KI 57, RE 86
Humphreys, Benjamin, CH *113*
Humphreys, Henry H., RE 86
Hunchback, CO *94*
Hundley's Corner, Virginia, LE 34-35
Hungate, Nathan, FR 124
Hunkpapa Indians, FR 93
Hunt, Frances, AP 108
Hunt, Henry J., LE 71, RE *28*, 52-53, TR 73; artillery concentration by, GE 105, 133; at Cemetery Ridge, GE 133-135, 140, 145; and Peach Orchard, GE 76
Hunt, Thomas H., TE 87
Hunter, Alexander, BD 11, 133, 135, FI 121, FO 144, LE 161, TT 98
Hunter, Andrew, FL 88
Hunter, David, AS 140, 148, *149*, CO 110-111, FI 117, 126-127, 129-130, 135, 149, FL 2, 39, *43*, 45-53, 74, 88, 89, 100, 101, SH 58, TR 18, 20, 25-27; background and temperament, FL 40-41; at Lynchburg, FL 58-61; retreats from Valley, FL 61, 68; and Shenandoah Valley, destruction in, FL 41-42, 50, 56-57, 69, 93; and VMI, FL 56-57
Hunter, Robert M. T., AP 21, 24-25; as Cabinet officer, OR 11; and peace negotiations, OR 162, 165; and slave enlistment, OR 166
Hunter, Shrod, FR 22, 23
Hunter, Thomas, CO 25
Hunting Creek, DE *142-143*
Huntington, Collis P., NA 86
Hunton, Eppa, FO 43
Huntsville, Alabama, BR *14*, NA *36*, TE *11, 16*
Huntsville, Missouri, SP 158-159
Hurd, Anson, BD *138*
Hurlbut, Stephen A., MI 68, 115, SH 105, 113, 116, 119-123, 138, SP 74
Huron, BL 8-9, 102, *103-107*
Hurst, "Colonel," SP 73
Huske, Benjamin, FI 80, 84
Hustings Court House, TR *8*
Hutcheson, James A., FL 83
Huts, TT *8-9*, *12*, 46, *50-51*
Hyde, James, SM *42*
Hyde, Thomas W., BD 53, KI *12*, *88-89*
Hyneman, Jacob E., TT 62

I

Ida, SM *145*
Illinois: blacks, statutes concerning, YA 35; disloyalty in, YA 23, 29-32; immigrants in, YA 62; and monopolies, YA 79; and recruits for Union Army, SM 47; troops enlisted, YA 62
Illinois Central Railroad, SH *36-37*, YA 64
Illinois River: strategic value of, SH 9, 11; as trade route, YA 24
Illinois troops, CH 147, FO 12, MI *98-99*, SM 112, TE 122, *156-157*, 161, TT 56, 62, 85, 118; Zouave unit, TE *143*
  Artillery: Battery A, 1st Artillery, AT *82-83*, 106; 1st Light Artillery (Waterhouse), SH 115; Battery H, 1st Light Artillery, AT 95; 2nd Light Artillery, Battery B (Barrett), SH *145*; Bridge's Battery, TE *134-135*; DeGress' Battery, AT *82-83*, 107, *110*; Houghtaling's Battery, TE 121; Light Artillery, TE 122, *134-135*
  Cavalry: 2nd Cavalry Regiment, MI 62, SH 114; 6th Cavalry Regiment, MI 87-96; 7th Cavalry Regiment, MI 88-95, *96*; 8th Cavalry Regiment, FL 71, 72, 75, GE 44; 13th Cavalry Regiment, MI *92*; 14th Cavalry Regiment, SM 85; 16th Cavalry Regiment, SM 68
  Infantry: 7th Infantry Regiment, AT *113*, CH *152*, SM 24; 8th Infantry Regiment, TT 33; 9th Mounted Infantry, AT 36, 38; 11th Infantry Regiment, SH *117*; 12th Infantry Regiment, BD 56-58, SM 24; 14th Infantry Regiment, SH 119; 18th Infantry Regiment, SH 81, 86-87; 19th Infantry Regiment, TE 14, *143*; 21st Infantry Regiment, SH 45, *46*; 22nd Infantry Regiment, SH 48, TE 122; 23rd Infantry Regiment, FL *91*; 27th Infantry Regiment, AT 70, TE 122; 32nd Infantry Regiment, SM 40, 44; 33rd Infantry Regiment, MI 102, 130; 34th Infantry Regiment, AT 66, 72, TE 115; 36th Infantry Regiment, FR 143, SM 90, TE 114, *131*; 38th Infantry Regiment, AT *33*; 39th Infantry Regiment, AP 99, CO *129*; 41st Infantry Regiment, SH 104; 42nd Infantry Regiment, AT 71, SH 163, TE 122; 45th Infantry Regiment, MI *109*, *138*, *148-149*, SH 82, SM *41*; 50th Infantry Regiment, SM 24; 52nd Infantry Regiment, AT 99, 145, MI *48-49*, *54-55*; 55th Infantry Regiment, AT *82-83*, *86-87*, 135, MI 131, SH 137, SM 63; 58th Infantry Regiment, SH 138; 59th Infantry Regiment, SM 129, 135, *136*; 61st Infantry Regiment, NA 25, SH 117, TT 79; 64th Infantry Regiment, AT 102; 65th Infantry Regiment, SM 114; 66th Infantry Regiment, AT 45; 72nd Infantry Regiment, SM 94, 97, 103, 113; 73rd Infantry Regiment, SM 113, TE 113; 77th Infantry Regiment, MI *70*, 130; 78th Infantry Regiment, AT 149; 82nd Infantry Regiment, SM *42*; 86th Infantry Regiment, AT 72, 74, SM *37*; 89th Infantry Regiment, CH 47; 92nd Infantry Regiment, CH 49; 93rd Infantry Regiment, CH 140, MI 132, SM 24; 94th Infantry Regiment, TT 152; 95th Infantry Regiment, TT 27; 98th Infantry Regiment, CH 21; 99th Infantry Regiment, MI 131; 102nd Infantry Regiment, SM 62; 104th Infantry Regiment, AT 60; 105th Infantry Regiment, AP 58, AT 47, SM *43*; 110th Infantry Regiment, TE 127; 111th Infantry Regiment, AT *86-87*; 112th Infantry Regiment, SM 118; 116th Infantry Regiment, MI 127; 123rd Infantry Regiment, AT 20, 156, CH 21, TT 71; 125th Infantry Regiment, AT 74; 137th Infantry Regiment, SM 102
Imboden, Frank, FL 46
Imboden, George, FL 46
Imboden, James, FL 46
Imboden, John D., DE 33-35, 165, FI 132, 138, FL 17, 19, 26-30, *31*, 33, 34, 39, 45, 46, 48, 49, 58-60, GE 146-151
"I'm Going to Fight mit Sigel" (ballad), FL *25*
Immigrants, YA *50*; blacks, relations with, YA 40; in Confederate Army, TT 30; number and origin, YA 21, 62; as political force, BR 16, 33, 101; prejudice against, BR 100; problems among, YA 20; in Union Army, TT 24, 28-29, *30*
Immigration, BR 16
Impeachment proceedings, NA 55, 72-73, *74-75*; ticket and tally sheets for, NA *74*
Impending Crisis of the South (Helper), BR 108-109
Imperial, MI 159
Import duties, OR 30-31
Impressment program, OR 29, 43, 83, 160
Income taxes, OR 10, 13, 33, 83
Independence, Missouri, SP 141, 145-146
Index (publication), BL 120
Indiana: blacks, statutes concerning, YA 35; disloyalty in, YA 23, 29; elections, BR 118; and recruits for Union Army, SM 47; volunteer response in, TE 25
Indianapolis, Indiana, CH 88
Indiana troops, CH 143, FO 12, GE 85, TE 66, *164-165*, TT 59-61; in western Virginia operations, FI 87-93; Wilder's Lightning Brigade, NA 64
  Artillery: 1st Battery, Light Artillery, MI 102; 1st Heavy Artillery Regiment, MI *164-165*; 5th Battery, AT *43*; 15th Battery, BD 59; 18th Light Artillery (Lilly), CH 19, 24, 33, 52; 19th Light Artillery (Harris' Horse Artillery), TE 24, *64-65*; Bush's Battery, TE 120
  Cavalry: 3rd Cavalry Regiment, SP *82-83*
  Infantry: 6th Infantry Regiment, CH 45; 7th Infantry Regiment, FI 93; 9th Infantry Regiment, AT 78, TE 127; 10th Infantry Regiment, TE 59, 60; 11th Infantry Regiment, MI 103, 118; 14th Infantry Regiment, BD *138*; 15th Infantry Regiment, SH 105; 16th

Eppa Hunton, Colonel of the 8th Virginia, who was promoted to Brigadier General after Gettysburg

Two officers of the 45th Illinois Infantry, the "Washburn Lead Mine Regiment"

KI The Killing Ground; LE Lee Takes Command; MI War on the Mississippi; NA The Nation Reunited; OR Confederate Ordeal; RE Rebels Resurgent; SH The Road to Shiloh; SM Sherman's March; SP Spies, Scouts and Raiders; TE The Struggle for Tennessee; TR Death in the Trenches; TT Tenting Tonight; YA Twenty Million Yankees

73

Company H, 44th Indiana Infantry, typical of Federal western troops

A soldier of the 88th New York, part of the Irish Brigade, with a green camp color

Infantry Regiment, MI 68; 17th Infantry Regiment, CH 21, TE 51; 18th Infantry Regiment, MI 85; 19th Infantry Regiment, BD 74, GE 49, LE 137, 139, 142; 21st Infantry Regiment, OR *100-101*, TT 26; 23rd Infantry Regiment, MI 111; 24th Infantry Regiment, MI 103, 119, 122; 25th Infantry Regiment, SH 137; 27th Infantry Regiment, BD 81, TT 28, 79; 29th Infantry Regiment, TE 117; 31st Infantry Regiment, ST 123; 33rd Infantry Regiment, AT 154; 34th Infantry Regiment, MI 103, 119, *120-121*; 35th Infantry Regiment, AT 43, TE 153; 37th Infantry Regiment, SM 15; 42nd Infantry Regiment, TE 124; 44th Infantry Regiment, SH 118, *126*; 51st Infantry Regiment, SM 124, 128, 129, 135; 55th Infantry Regiment, TE 47; 58th Infantry Regiment, SM 72; 59th Infantry Regiment, MI 114; 66th Infantry Regiment, AT 145; 70th Infantry Regiment, AT 46, 62, SM 71; 72nd Infantry Regiment, CH 21, 24; 80th Infantry Regiment, TE *64-65*; 86th Infantry Regiment, CH 48; 88th Infantry Regiment, CH 55, TE 124; 97th Infantry Regiment, AT 109; 100th Infantry Regiment, AP 60, SM *39*, 44, 147; 140th Infantry Regiment, AS 53
Indian Bend, MI *110*
Indianola, MI 78-79, *80-81*
Indians: atrocities by, FR 64, 142, 146; and captives, FR *104-105;* casualties, FR 79, 82, 83, 87, 94, 99, 111, 119; and Civil War, FR 74-75, 99; as Confederate allies, FR *cover*, 64, 136, *142;* conflict with whites, FR *map 2-3*, 14, 17, 106; conflict with, NA 92-97; killing and mutilation of, FR 87, 93, 111-112, 116, 117, 123; and Lincoln, FR 72, 90; loyalties of, FR 4, 137, 148; peace talks with, NA *96-97;* punishment of, FR 90-91, *92-93, 95*, 119-120; Sand Creek Massacre of, FR 106, 127-128, 129, *130-131;* victimized by whites, FR 14, 15, 75, 77, 107; weapons of, FR *96-97*
Indian Territory, FR 3, 136, 146, 151-152, TT 31, 33
Indian troops, TT *31*
Indian troops, Confederate: FR 138, 156; 1st Cherokee Mounted Rifles, FR 149; Pike's Brigade, FR 148
Indian troops, Union: FR *137*, 146, 147, 155; 1st Home Guard, FR 148; 2nd Home Guard, FR 148; 3rd Home Guard, FR 150,
Industrial Revolution effect, BR 29
Industry: decline, YA 57; development of, OR 10, 16-17; expansion of, OR 19, 26, 62-67, YA *map 2-3*, 20, 45, 47, 56-57, 66-67; in Northern states, BR *18-19*, 29; patents for, NA *80-81*, 82; in penitentiaries, OR 62; in Southern states,

BR 32-33; taxation of, OR 83; trends in, BR 9, 29; working conditions, NA 88-89
Infantry: arms, FI *70-71;* defensive power, FI 51-54; regimental organization, FI 54; tactical doctrine, FI 49-52, 55; training programs, FI 24-25, *34-35*, 49, 52, 57, 87; weapons' effect on tactics, FI 48-50
Infantry companies, organization of, TT 48
Infantry regiments: organization and strength, TT 22, 47-48; replacement of losses, TT 48
Infantry units: firepower of, DE 40; organization, FO 20; tactics, FO 20, 31, 35; training, FO *32-37*. *See also names of commanders, or under states*
Inflation, OR 10, 22, 30-33, 40, 48, 55, 80, 128, 148, 160, YA 45, 59, 64, 77, 103; in Confederacy, TT 24, 37; and Confederate paper currency, SM 18-19; in South, AP 17-18
Ingalls, Rufus, AP 148, TR *168*
Inge, William, FR *134*
Ingersoll, Robert G., NA 150
Ink, shortage of, OR 48, 51
Inkpaduta, FR 93, 94, 96
Ino, BL 148
Insects: infestation, TT 9, 82-83, 85-87, 116, 118, 133; pests, FO 107
Insignia, U.S. Navy, MI *17*
Inspections, TT 53-55
Inspectors general, TT 53-55
Intelligence operations, BL 114-116, 131, FI 113, 122; Confederate counterespionage, SP 56; mapping, SP 74; and Mexican War, SP 10; payments for, SP 63, 73-74, 78, 89; and Revolutionary War, SP 10; Secret Service Bureau, SP 46-47; Union counterespionage, SP 56; "spy's career," SP 76-77. *See also names of individual espionage agents*
Intelligence reports, FO 28, 131, 151-153
Intelligence services, DE 101, 122, OR 152
Interchangeable parts introduced, BR 18
Invalid Corps. *See* Veteran Reserve Corps
Iowa: disloyalty in, YA 29; immigrants in, YA 62; troops enlisted, YA 62
Iowa troops, FR 142, 147, MI 123, TT 53, 56
    Artillery: 1st Battery, AT 57, *86-87*
    Cavalry: 2nd Cavalry Regiment, MI 88; 4th Cavalry Regiment, FR 161
    Infantry: 1st Infantry Regiment, SH 27, *28;* 2nd Infantry Regiment, SH 81, 91, *92-93*, 95, 121-122, 136; 4th Infantry Regiment, FR 141, MI 66-67, SP 72; 5th Infantry Regiment, CH 123, MI 76-77, 114-115, 119, 136, SM 157; 6th Infantry Regiment, CH 139, FR 94; 7th Infantry Regiment, SH 48; 8th Infantry Regiment, SH 125-126, *134*, 135, 139; 11th Infantry Regiment, SH 119; 12th Infantry Regiment, SM 130, 133, 139; 14th Infantry Regiment, SH 122, *130-131*, 139, TT 80, 161; 15th Infantry

Regiment, AT 102, 112, 136; 16th Infantry Regiment, AT 104; 17th Infantry Regiment, MI *114-115*, SM 29; 20th Infantry Regiment, FR *132*; 21st Infantry Regiment, MI 130-132; 22nd Infantry Regiment, MI 130, *132-133*; 23rd Infantry Regiment, MI 123; 24th Infantry Regiment, FL *131*, MI 119; 37th Infantry Regiment, TT 28; 38th Infantry Regiment, TT 85; 39th Infantry Regiment, SM 24
Irish Bend, MI 110
Irish Brigade, BD 63, 99-100, 170, FO *162-163*, 165, KI 160, RE 77, *82-83, 149*, TR 45
Irish immigrants, BR 16, 100, YA 21, 23, 50. *See also* Draft
Irishmen: in Confederate Army, TT 30; in Union Army, TT *28-30, 146-147*
"Irish 9th," FO 133
Irish Rifles, FO *125*
Iron: industry, YA *57;* shortages, OR 29; supply, OR 19
Iron (Black Hat) Brigade, BD 51, 73-76, 79
Iron Brigade, GE 47-51, 62, 65, 158-159, KI 65, 134, TR 101, 103, 137
Ironclads: characteristics and armament, BL *18-19*, 65, 67, 70-71, *72-73*, 76-77, 125; Confederate, CO 54-55, 61, 63, 67, 69, 72, 74, 76-77, 95-97, *104-105*, 113-114, 143, *144-145, 148-149*, 150-153, *154-155;* evolution of, BL 33, 46-53, 65; Union, CO 112-115, *116-117*, 118, *119*, 124-125, 130-131, 133-135, 143-145, 147, *148-149*, 150-156, 159, 164, 169. *See also* Gunboats
Iroquois, BL 100-101, CO 72-73
Irregulars: attacks on bridges and trains, TE 11, *91;* attacks on Mitchel, TE 12; Buell's policy against, TE 16, 17; bushwhackers harrassment of Smith, TE 44; damage by Confederate guerrillas, TE 15, *90;* pro-Union bushwhackers, TE 8, 22, 44; Squirrel Hunters, TE 32; steamboats burned by, TE *90;* Union reprisals, TE 14, 91
Irregular troops. *See* Guerrilla operations
Irwinsville, Georgia, NA 20, 21
Irwinville, Georgia, AS 145
Isaac Smith, CO 113
Isabel, BR 161
Island No. 8, SH 160
Island No. 9, SH 160
Island No. 10, CO 77, LE 93, SH *map* 160; amphibious operations, SH *162-163;* armament, SH 158; artillery assaults, SH *158-159, 164-165;* Confederate materiel losses, SH 169; Confederate troop strength, SH 158; engineer operations, SH *160-161*, 163; Foote's role at, SH 155, 159-160, 163; gunboats at, SH 155, *158-159*, 160, 163, *164-167;* mortar boats at, SH *158-159;* operations at, SH 101, 155, *158-169;* Pope's role at, SH 155, 159-160, 166; prisoners captured, SH 166, *168-169;* surrendered, SH 166;

AP Pursuit to Appomattox; AS The Assassination; AT Battles for Atlanta; BD The Bloodiest Day; BL The Blockade; BR Brother against Brother; CH The Fight for Chattanooga; CO The Coastal War; DE Decoying the Yanks; FI First Blood; FL The Shenandoah in Flames; FO Forward to Richmond; FR War on the Frontier; GE Gettysburg;

Union troop strength, SH 159; weather, effect on operations, SH 163-164
Isle au Breton Sound, CO 61, 63
Italian immigrants, YA 21
Itasca, CO 64-65, 145
Iuka, Battle of, TE 80, 83
Iuka, Mississippi, MI 34-35, *36*, 37
Iverson, Alfred, Jr., GE 53-55, RE 148
Ives, Joseph, LE 23
Iwonski, Carl G. von, FR *21*, artwork by, FR *21*, *22*

J

J. B. Williams, FR 156
Jack (slave), BR *48*
Jackman, Sidney D., FR 159
Jackson, Andrew, AS 10, BR 39, TT 21; on American government, BR 22; and nullification doctrine, BR 38
Jackson, Claiborne Fox, SH 12-13, 16-19, *20*, 21
Jackson, Conrad F., RE 67
Jackson, Elinor Junkin, DE 29, *34*
Jackson, James S., TE *62*, 65
Jackson, James W., FI *64-65*
Jackson, John H., CO *40*
Jackson, John K., AT *44*, CH 131, 133, SH 143-144, TE 129, 130
Jackson, Laura, DE 22
Jackson, Mary, OR 85-86
Jackson, Mary Anna Morrison, DE 32-33, *34*, 35, 46, 59, 67
Jackson, Mississippi, MI *map* 2-3, 56, 90, 109, 111-113, *114-115*, 121, 140-142, 156, NA 147; matches produced in, OR 26; as railroad center, OR 28
Jackson, Oscar, MI 40-41
Jackson, Tennessee, MI 60, 62, SH 101
Jackson, Thomas J. (Stonewall), BR 97, DE *cover*, *19*, *26-27*, *47*, *96-97*, *134-135*, *171*, FL *12*, 16, 17, 39, 57, 68, 124, FO 79-81, 83, 97, 130-131, KI 79, 81, 132, LE *99*, OR 52-54, RE *139*, SP 108, 109, 110, 112, TT 85; accident to, BD 17; at Antietam, BD 61, 63, 67, 69, 75-76, 78, 86, 92, 121, 127-129; artillery strength, DE 44, 65, 121; Ashby, relations with, DE 5, 90, 92, 158; assigned command by Lee, LE 91; and Barbara Frietchie, BD *20;* at Bath, DE 50, 52-54; on bayonet assaults, DE 40, 70; Benjamin's interference with, DE 58-59; and Boyd, SP 49; boyhood home of, DE *20-21;* at Bristoe Station, LE 127-129, 133; at Brown's Gap, DE 100, 170; at Bull Run, DE 18, 38, *39*, 40, 43, FI 122, 124, 136-138, 140-141, 152, *158-159;* as cadet, DE *24*, 25, 40, 149; caricatured, DE *32;* cavalry strength, DE 44, 65; at Cedar Mountain, LE 100, 103-109; at Chancellorsville, RE 124-130, *131*, 132-133, 138; at Chantilly, LE 166; at

Charles Town, DE 149; at Charlottesville, DE 100; conference with Lee, RE *cover*, *126*, 127; at Conrad's Store, DE 86-87, 89, 167; at Cross Keys, DE 159-165, *map* 169; at Culpeper, LE 99-101, 103; dam assaulted by, DE 46-48; as disciplinarian, DE 21-22, 29, 33, 52, 55, 90, 92, 121, 133, 157; early life, DE 20, 22; Ewell, relations with, DE 5, 83, 95, 98-99, 114-115; flank march by, RE *map* 127, 128-130; at Frederick, BD 17; at Fredericksburg, RE 37-39, 50, 58, 61, 63, 65, 71, 84-85, 88, 120, 122, 124; French, dispute with, DE 26-29; at Front Royal, DE 121-123, *124-125*, 126-129, *map* 130, 146, 150; Garnett, dispute with, DE 52, 54, 89; at Gordonsville, LE 98-99, 109, 124; at Hancock, DE 54; at Harpers Ferry, BD 18, 22, 30, 43-45, 56, 58-60, DE 33-35; at Harrisonburg, DE 87, 116, 157; A.P. Hill, dispute with, BD 12-13; D.H. Hill, relations with, DE 29; Hotchkiss, dependence on, DE 82-84; as hypochondriac, DE 22-24, 32; Imboden, relations with, DE 165; and invasion of North, LE 90-91; at Kernstown, DE 44, 54, *map* 66, 67-71, 82, 133, 167-168; leaves U.S. Army, DE 29; leaves Valley, DE 170; lethargy of, LE 34-36, 41, 43, 50, 52-55, 62; and Little Sorrel, DE 35; Loring, conflict with, DE 50, 58-59; and lost order, BD 21; at Luray, DE 120; at Manassas, LE 129; marriages and family life, DE 29, 32, 34; at Martinsburg, BD 18, 38; at McDowell, DE *map* 101, *102*-103, 114, 148; at Mechum's River Station, DE 100; in Mexican War, DE 25, *26-27*, 40; at Middletown, DE *map* 130, 131; mission in Valley, DE 21; at Mount Jackson, DE 65, 82-83, 157; at Mount Solon, DE 114-115; and musicians, DE 132; near Martinsburg, DE 46-48; at New Market, DE 86, 116, 120; at Newtown, DE 71, 131; nicknames bestowed on, DE 39-40, FI 139; at Orange Court House, LE 99; personal leadership, DE 22, 38-39, 55, 99-100, 114, 135, LE 106-107; personal traits, DE 21-22, 32; physical appearance, DE 18; piety of, DE 22, *23*, 24-25; at Port Republic, DE 99-100, 157-161, 165-168, *map* 169, 170; at Potomac crossing, BD 13-14, DE 149; promotions, DE 38; at Pughtown, DE 50; railroads assaulted by, DE 34-36, 45-46, 64; reconnaissance by, DE 66; recruiting campaign, DE *41;* resignation threatened, DE 58-59; in retreat to Virginia, BD 153; at Romney, DE 2, 45-46, 50, 52, 55, 99; at Rude's Hill, DE 83, 86-87, 157; ruses by, BD 21, DE 45, 48, 100-101, 120, 128; at Second Bull Run, LE 126-132, 134-138, 142-155, 158-163, 167; security measures, DE 33, 65, 101; in Seminole War, DE 26; in Seven Days' Battles, LE

30-35, 37, 40-43, 49-55, 59-62, 72; in Shenandoah Valley, BD 168, LE 23-24, 30, 34, 97-98, RE 26, 31, 33, 37; staff of, DE 82-84, 92, *93*, 94; at Staunton, DE 95, 99, 101; at Strasburg, DE 151, 156; succeeded by A. P. Hill, RE 139; succeeded by Stuart, RE 139, 141; superiors, relations with, DE 26-29, 58-59; at Swift Run Gap, DE 86-87, 99; sword of, DE *45;* tactical plans, LE 99-101, 138; tactics of, DE 40-41, 44-45, 50, 71, 86-87, 95, 100-101, 123, 129, 165, 167-168, 170; Taliaferro, relations with, DE 103; Taylor's evaluation of, DE 22, 114, 117-120, 146, 170; training program, DE 33, *42-43*, FI 93; troops, relations with, DE 18; troop strength, DE 21, 44, 50, 65, 95, 102, 121, RE 61, 71, 128; uniform, RE *60;* on Valley's importance, DE 21; at Virginia Military Institute, DE 18, *19*, 29-33; at Weyer's Cave, DE 170; at Winchester, DE 43-44, 46, 48, 55, 64-65, 131, 133, *134-135*, 149-151; Winder, relations with, DE 89-90, 92; wounding and death, RE 138-139, 141, *160-161*
Jackson, Warren, DE 22
Jackson, William L., FL 51, 57
Jackson Mine, YA *74-75*
Jackson's Mill, West Virginia, DE *20-21*
Jacksonville, Alabama, SM 29, 33
Jacksonville, Florida, CO 139
Jacksonville, Illinois, NA 126
Jacob Bell, BL 150
James, Fleming, FL *14*
James, Frank, SP *151*, 159
James, Frank B., AT 72
James, Garth W., CO 125-126
James, George S., BR 141
James, Henry, NA 127
James, Jesse, SP *150*, 159, 161
James, Jesse (mill owner), SP 140
James, John, FL *15*
James cannon, FO 46
James Island, BR 137, 147, 149, CO *100-101*, 110-111, *map* 113, 133, 136
James River (Missouri), SH 25
James River (Virginia), AP *42-49*, *map* 43, 101, BL 46, 49, *70-71*, 160, CO 97, 163, DE *14*, 61, FO 89, 124-125, 127-128, *129*, *151*, TR 18-19, 26-27, *28-29*, 36, 48, 56, 70, 110, *112-113*, 144; Confederate obstructions on, AP *42-43;* operations, OR 17, 38, *40-41*, 166-167; operations around, LE 29, 48-49, 52, 58, 60, 63, 66, *70*, 73, *74-81*, *88-89*, 91, *94;* strategic value of, FI 76-78; Union army crossing, TR 34-36, *38;* Union monitors on, AP 45
James River Canal, TR *18*, 21
James target rifle, FO *100-101*
Jamison, David F., BR 24, 27
Jamison, Robert D., CH 131
Jaquith, Andrew, TR *62*
Jarrette, John, SP *150*
Jay, John, YA 154

The Confederate ironclad *Chicora* in Charleston Harbor

Major General Thomas J. "Stonewall" Jackson, a sketch made near Ball's Bluff on the Potomac

KI The Killing Ground; LE Lee Takes Command; MI War on the Mississippi; NA The Nation Reunited; OR Confederate Ordeal; RE Rebels Resurgent; SH The Road to Shiloh; SM Sherman's March; SP Spies, Scouts and Raiders; TE The Struggle for Tennessee; TR Death in the Trenches; TT Tenting Tonight; YA Twenty Million Yankees

The U.S.S. *Kearsarge* (foreground), which sank the Confederate raider *Alabama* on June 19, 1864

Major General Edward Johnson, known as "Old Allegheny," captured at Spotsylvania May 12, 1864

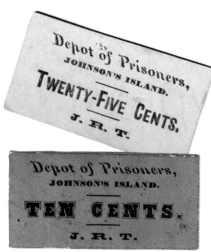

Two types of script used as currency by Confederate prisoners at Johnson's Island, Ohio

Jayhawkers, 141. *See also* Guerrillas; Guerrilla operations
Jefferson, Thomas, BR 34, 101, OR 11, 168
Jefferson, Thomas G., FL *36*, 159
Jefferson City, Louisiana, CO 54, 63
Jefferson City, Missouri, FR 156, 157, NA 50, SH 16-17, *18-19*, 29
Jefferson Davis, BL 28
Jeffries, Lemuel, TT 154
Jenkins, Albert Gallatin, FL 21, *23*, GE 31, 33
Jenkins, David T., KI *170*
Jenkins, Micah, CH 93, 100, 107, 109, 112, 113, FO 140, *144*, 145, 159, KI 78-*79*, LE *169*
Jenkins' Ferry, Battle of, FR 65
Jenney, William, MI 96
Jennings, R. P., BD 75
Jennison, Dr. Charles Rainsford, SP 141, 145, *147;* background, SP 143-144; at Independence, SP 145-146; at Pleasant Hill, SP 146
Jennison's Jayhawkers, SP 145. *See also* Kansas troops, 7th Cavalry Regiment
Jericho Ford, KI 133
Jericho Mill, KI 133, *138-139*
Jersey City, New Jersey, AS 121
Jerseyville *Democratic Union*, YA 29
Jerusalem Plank Road, TR 32, 39, 48, 55-56, 67, 81-83, 111, 115
Jett, William S., AS *114*, 115, 116, 117, 132, 133
Jewish chaplains, TT 147
Jews, Grant's order on, MI 58-59
John, Enoch C., SM 55
John S. Ide, AS 132, 136
Johnsey, Jesse, SP 76
Johnson, Abda, AT 87
Johnson, Andrew, AS *48*, 59, 74, 104, 108, 117, 145, 161, BL 160, FR 129, NA 2, *8-9*, 26, *53*, *55*, 76, SM 123, TE 72, YA 153; cane of, NA *17*; clemency for Mrs. Surratt, AS 159, 160; Confederate leaders, attitude toward, NA 20; election poster, AS *39;* Freedmen's Bureau, NA 36-39; impeachment, NA 55, 72-73, *74-75;* at Lincoln's deathbed, AS 98; at Lincoln's inauguration, AS 45; murder plot against, AS 69-70, 72, 97; Nast cartoons, NA 129, *130-131;* opposition to Congress, NA 39-41, 52-54, 56; political background of, NA 30-31; reconstruction policy, NA 16-18, 31-33, 36, 61-62, 70; and trial of conspirators, AS 140, 158-159; and Wirz, execution of, NA 38
Johnson, Bradley T., DE 123, *126*, 158, *162-163*, FL 72, 73, *85*, 86, 91, LE 42, *43*
Johnson, Bushrod, AP 80, 85, 125, CH *47*, 112, TE 59, 102, 117, TR 44-45, 48-49, 67, *74*, 81-82; at Chickamauga, CH 44, 48, 57, 58, 61, 65, 66, 69; at Hoover's Gap, CH 24, 25, 28; reputation, CH 47
Johnson, Charles, CO 27
Johnson, Curtis, FR 161

Johnson, Daniel D., FL 23
Johnson, Edward, AS 149-150, DE 46, 95, 101-103, KI 29, 31, 62, 94, 98, 102, SM 95; at Chambersburg, GE 26; at Culp's Hill, GE 113-116, 118, 126-128; at Gettysburg, GE 26; in Potomac crossing, GE 26; at Stephenson's Depot, GE 24; at Winchester, GE 22-24
Johnson, Herschel V., OR 11
Johnson, J. Stoddard, FL 39
Johnson, Reverdy, AS 145-148
Johnson, Richard W., AT 54, 56, CH 46, 47, 49, 64, 143, TE 112, 113, 115, 117, 119, 126
Johnson's (Abda) Brigade, AT 86-87
Johnson's Island prison camp, TT 113, 115-116, *117*, 118
Johnson's ranch, FR 31, 32
Johnsonville, Tennessee, SM 34, 82
Johnston, A.V.E., SP 160-161
Johnston, Albert Sidney, FO 39, 81, FR 18, 137, SH *55*, TE 17; appointed general, SH 52-53; brevetted U.S. brigadier, SH 52; commands U.S. cavalry regiment, SH 52; commands in West, SH 52-53; at Corinth, SH 101; Davis, relations with, SH 52-53, 98; and Fort Donelson, SH 79-81, 84, 93, 97; and fortifications construction, SH 54-58; Grant's evaluation of, SH 55; and Houston, SH 52; in Kentucky operations, SH 53-58; and Nashville evacuation, SH 97-98; personal leadership, SH 128-129; popularity decline, SH 98; prestige, SH 52; prewar career, SH 52; recruiting campaign, SH 54-55; Scott's evaluation of, SH 52; Sherman's evaluation of, SH 52; at Shiloh, SH 105-111, 113, 116-121, 128, 136-137, 141-143; strategic and tactical plans, SH 101, 136-137; troop strength and reinforcements, SH 101; and weapons shortages, SH 54; wounding and death of, SH *129*, 136; and Zachary Taylor, SH 52; in Tennessee operations, SH 58-59, 62, 67, 78-81, 84, 93, 97, 99
Johnston, James D., CO 156
Johnston, Joseph E., AP 26, 33, 34, 68, 76, 78, 79, 110, 113, 128, 129, 162, AS 66, AT 8, 20, *30*, 60, 63, CH 18, 31, 34, 42, 85, FI *129*, FO 79, KI 26, LE 22-23, NA 18, 19, *59*, SM 20, 25, 28, 95, SP 26, 27, 33, 45, 75, 109, TE 82, 88, 161; appointed Army commander, FI 57, 93; appointed general, FI 93; appointed Western commander, MI 59, 113; at Atlanta, OR 148; Beauregard, conflict with, FI 152; Benjamin, relations with, FO 79-81; and Bentonville, AP 69, 71, 73, 74, 75; at Big Black River, MI 156; and Bragg, AT 80; at Bull Run, DE 38; FI 122-124, 136, 139, *140*, 141, 147, 149-150, 152, 166-167, FO 38; in Carolinas, OR 167; at Cassville, AT 48-49; at Champion's Hill, MI 156; and Chickahominy operations, FO 133-136,

154; command failure, FO 167; commands Army of the Shenandoah, FI 93; criticized, MI 142-143; at Dallas, AT 56-57; Davis, conflict with, FI 152; Davis, relations with, FO 78-79, 81-82; defensive skill, AT 3, 30; at Fairfax Court House, FO 59; at Fair Oaks, FO 154-156; Grant's evaluation of, MI 140-142; at Grenada, MI 59; and Hanover Court House, FO 133; and Harpers Ferry evacuation, FI 93, 95; and Hood, AT 30, 64, 90; indecisiveness of, FO 133; and Jackson's resignation threat, DE 58; at Jackson, MI 109, 112-113, 121, 126, 140-142, 156; joins Confederacy, FI 27, 93; at Kennesaw Mountain, AT 19, 63; and Kinston, AP 64-65; Lee, relations with, FO 79, 105; Manassas, withdrawal from, DE 64, 83; and Manassas operations, FO 3, 78, 81-83, 89; McClellan appraised by, FO 107; and Mechanicsville, FO 136; at New Hope Church, AT 50; overall command in West, TE 85; in Peninsular Campaign, DE 151, FO 102-103, 105, 107-110, 113, 127, 133-136, 138, 145, 154-155, 167; physical appearance, DE 18; physical characteristics, FO 78-79; political support for, OR 161, 162; and Polk's death, AT 61, *63;* and Port Hudson, MI 164; and President Davis, AT 29, 30, 80; and Quaker guns, FO 39, *85*, 86; rank, dispute over, FO 79; and Rappahannock operations, FO 89; reappointed to command, AP 61; rebuilds defeated army, AT 27-29; relations with Davis, TE 85; relieved of command, AT 81; relieved by Davis, OR 148; at Resaca, AT 43-44, 45; and Richmond security, FO 103, 133, 138; and Rocky Face Ridge, AT 38-39; at Seven Pines, FO 90, 145, 154; in Shenandoah Valley operations, FI 93, 111; on slave enlistment, OR 166; at Smyrna, AT 76; strategic plans, FO 136-139, 145; supplies destroyed by, FO 83; and supply problems, FO 83; and surrender negotiations, AP 155-160; sword of, FO *155;* training programs, FO 39; troop strength, FO 17, 105, MI 113, 126, 140-142; and Urbanna operations, FO 89; and Valley operations, DE 35, 38, 45, 59, 65, 83, 114-116, *120;* and Vicksburg defense, MI 59-60, 109, 115-116, 126, 134, 140-143, 152; Washington threatened by, FO 17, 78; at Williamsburg, FO 109-110, 113; withdrawals, AT 40, 48, 50, 76, 78; wounded, FO 156-157; yields command to Beauregard, FI 123, 129, 136; at Yorktown, FO 105. *See also* Bull Run, Battle of; Confederate Army
Johnston, Lydia, AT 90
Johnston, Robert D., FL 74, KI 81
Johnston, Samuel R., GE 68-69, 75

AP Pursuit to Appomattox; AS The Assassination; AT Battles for Atlanta; BD The Bloodiest Day; BL The Blockade; BR Brother against Brother; CH The Fight for Chattanooga; CO The Coastal War; DE Decoying the Yanks; FI First Blood; FL The Shenandoah in Flames; FO Forward to Richmond; FR War on the Frontier; GE Gettysburg;

John Warner, FR 58
Joint Committee on Reconstruction, NA 36, 40, 52
Joint Committee on the Conduct of the War, FO 65, 67-68, 73, 76
Joinville, Prince de, FO 24, *114-123*
Joke books, OR 52
Jonas, Edward, AT *82-83*
Jones, A. C., AP 134
Jones, A. K., AP 78
Jones, B. F., ΛP 123
Jones, Bushrod, AT 109, 144
Jones, Catesby, BL *56*, 58, 62-64
Jones, Charles C., FI 14
Jones, Charles Colcock, Jr., OR 42, 78
Jones, David R. (Neighbor), BD 121, 129, 133, 135, FI 113, 136, LE 91
Jones, Edward F., FI 23-24
Jones, Hamilton C., AP 35
Jones, Henry J., FL 159
Jones, J. B., FI 134
Jones, Jenkin, CH 140
Jones, John, FR 80-82, *85*
Jones, John Beauchamp, AP 17, FI 18, FO 138; Davis evaluated by, OR 16; on food costs, OR 30; and McClellan's peace platform, OR 158
Jones, John Marshall, GE 115-116, 127, KI *64*, 65
Jones, John R., BD 67, 74-75, 78, 80
Jones, Joseph, OR 43, TT 116-117
Jones, Mary Cadwalader, AP 163
Jones, Patrick Henry, AT *34*
Jones, Samuel, BR 76
Jones, Thomas, TE 65
Jones, Thomas A., AS 106-108, 111-112, SP 51-53
Jones, Wells, AT *86-87*
Jones, William, YA 108
Jones, William E. (Grumble), FL 43-45, *46*, 47, 48, 49-50, GE 14, 20-21, 26, 28, TR 20
Jonesboro, Battle of, AT 3, 132, 144-149, *map* 151, TT 152; artillery action, AT *150*; Confederate exhaustion at, AT 144
Jonesboro, Georgia, AT 142, 143, 144, 148, 150, OR 156-157, SM 50
Jonesboro, Illinois, BR 106
Jonesboro, Tennessee, CH 43
Jones Bridge, TR 35-36
Jones County, Mississippi, OR 92-95
Jones House (Harrisburg), SP 8
Jones's (Bushrod) Brigade, AT 109
Jordan, Thomas, SH 108, 120, 122, 151, SP 24-27, 29
Jordan, Thomas Jefferson, TE 22, 24
Jordan's Point road, TR 30, 31
Joskins, Joe, LE 158
Jouett, James E., CO 151
Joyce, John A., AT 42
Juarez, Benito, BL 128, FR *38*, *42*, *43*, 44
Jubilee Singers, NA *121*
Judah, CO 8
Judah, Henry M., AT 42
Judiciary Committee, NA 55, 61

Julesburg, Colorado Territory, FR 128-129
Julian, George W., NA 110
Jumper, John, FR *139*
Justice, Department of. *See* Benjamin, Judah P.

K

Kanawha, state of, OR 75
Kanawha Canal. *See* James River Canal
Kanawha Valley, DE *74*
Kane, George P., FI 26, 29, SP 15, *18*, 21
Kansas, SP *map* 2-3; black voting rights, NA 72; Border Ruffians' depredations, BR *74*, 75-76, 82; emigration to, BR 74-75; guerrilla operations in, SH 12, 16; John Brown and Pottawatomie Creek, SP 141; political and strategic value, BR 71; Quantrill's raids, SP 149, 153-157; statehood application, BR 80-83; violence in, BR 47, 70-71, 74, *75*, 76, 77, 79, 80-82, *83*, SP 140-141
Kansas City, Missouri, SH 33, SP 145
Kansas City *Journal of Commerce*, SP 149
Kansas-Nebraska Act, BR 71-74, 101, SP 140, 141
Kansas troops, FR 107, *133*, 147, 153; state militia, FR 160, *162-171*; at Wilson's Creek, SH 29
  Artillery: 2nd Battery, FR 152; Topeka Battery, FR *158-159*
  Cavalry: 2nd Cavalry Regiment (Dismounted), FR 150; 6th Cavalry Regiment, FR 148, 150, *154*; 7th Cavalry Regiment (Jennison's Jayhawkers), FR *133*, 146, MI *92*, SP 145-147; 14th Cavalry Regiment, SP 155; 15th Cavalry Regiment, FR *161*, *171*
  Infantry: 1st Colored Infantry Regiment, FR 152, TT 33-35; 1st Infantry Regiment, FR 64; 3rd Infantry Regiment, SP 142; 4th Infantry Regiment, SP 142; 5th Infantry Regiment, SP 142; 8th Infantry Regiment, CH 145, 149; 9th Infantry Regiment, FR 148; 11th Infantry Regiment, FR 150
Kappesser, Peter, CH 131
Kaskel, Cesar, MI 58-59
Kaufman, Joe, DE 100
Kautz, Albert, CO 75, 77
Kautz, August V., AS 140, 148, *149*, TR 27, 30-*32*, 33, 39, 41-42, 53, 55-57, 115, 145, 148-149, 153
Kean, Otto, RE *107*
Kean, Robert, OR 26
Kearny, Philip, BD 54, FO 21-22, *108*, 161, LE *166*; at Chantilly, LE 167; at Fair Oaks, FO 158, 160, 164; McClellan appraised by, FO 129; personal leadership, FO 110, 141; at Second Bull Run, LE 133-134, 149, 164; in Seven Days' Battles, LE 48, 59-60; at Seven

Pines, FO 140-141, 145; at White Oak Swamp, FO 136; at Williamsburg, FO *108*, 110-111
Kearsarge, BL *19*, 148, *162*, NA *126*; *Alabama*, battle with, BL 155, *156*, 157-160, 162, *map 163*, *164-171*; characteristics and armament, BL 155-156
Keebler mansion, TE *93*
Keeler, Charles A., GE *154*
Keeler, William, BL 60-62, 65
Keenan, Peter, RE 133
Keene, Laura, AS 59, *73*, 83, 86
Keifer, J. Warren, AP 126, FL *129*
Keily, Daniel, DE 122
Keith, James, OR 91-92
Keitt, Lawrence M., CO 131, KI 152
Kell, John McIntosh, BL 149, *153*, 155-156, 158, 160, 170
Kellenberger, T. B., CH 45
Kelley, Benjamin, FI 85-87
Kelley, Benjamin F., DE 44, SP 114, 127
Kelley, William D., NA 25
Kelley's Ferry, CH 89, 97
Kellogg, Elisha S., KI *170*
Kellogg, J. J., MI 127
Kellogg, Sanford, CH 56, 57
Kellogg, William P., NA 117, 143, 144
Kelly, Alexander, TR *124*
Kelly, John P., AT 54
Kelly, Patrick, TR 45
Kelly house, CH 66
Kelly's Ford, GE 16, 20, RE 93, 105-109, *110*, 111, 120, *map* 122, 123
Kemper, Delaware, LE *171*
Kemper, James L., FO 141, 144, GE 134, 136, *139*, 140, LE 91, 159, TR 145
Kemper's battery (Virginia), FI 149
Kenansville, North Carolina, OR 23
Kendrick, J. Mills, TE 45
Kenly, John R., DE *127*; at Front Royal, DE 123, 125-128; in Valley area, DE 121
Kennebec, CO 145
Kennedy, John, YA 103-105
Kennedy, John A., SP 16
Kennesaw Mountain, AT 60, 62, 76, SM 20, 24, *25*, 26
Kennesaw Mountain, Battle of, AT 60, 66-75, AT *map* 67; bombardment, AT *65*; at the Dead Angle, AT 72, *73*, 74; truce at, AT *70*, 71, 75
Kennon, Beverly, CO 69
Kensel, George A., BR *145*
Kentucky, TE *map* 2-3; Beauregard's operations in, SH 101; Bragg's disappointment in, TE 82-83, 148; Buell's operations in, SH 79, 97-98; cavalry operations, SH 54; civil disorders in, OR 149; Confederate governor installed, TE 57; Confederate guerrillas in, SP 143; Confederate hopes for recruits in, TE 21, 25, 26, 41, 44; and Confederate sympathizers, SM 32; divided sympathies, TE 150; educational system, OR 55; Johnston's operations in, SH

Colonel Lawrence M. Keitt, a former congressman, killed leading a brigade at Cold Harbor in 1864

Colonel Frederick Bartleson of the 100th Illinois, who lost an arm at Shiloh and was killed at Kennesaw Mountain

KI The Killing Ground; LE Lee Takes Command; MI War on the Mississippi; NA The Nation Reunited; OR Confederate Ordeal; RE Rebels Resurgent; SH The Road to Shiloh; SM Sherman's March; SP Spies, Scouts and Raiders; TE The Struggle for Tennessee; TR Death in the Trenches; TT Tenting Tonight; YA Twenty Million Yankees

77

George M. Sheary, who rode with Morgan's Kentucky Cavalry on daring raids into Union territory

Kentucky (continued)
53-58; Lincoln on neutrality, SH 12; lost to Confederacy, SH 157; neutrality policy, SH 11-12, 53; operations in, MI 34, SH *map 2-3*; population, SH 9-11; restrictions on voters, YA 144; Sherman's operations in, SH 141; strategic and political value of, FI 76, SH 9; as Union adherent, OR 75; Union control retained, TE 80, 159; Union recruits, TE 25; Union troops quota, FI 14; welcome for Bragg, TE 41, 50

Kentucky Central Railroad, TE 24

Kentucky Resolution, BR 37-38

Kentucky troops, Confederate, AT 35, 36-37, MI *93*, TE 26, 30, 87, 149, TT 31, 124, 149; Buckner Guards, SH *56-57*

    Cavalry: 2nd Cavalry Regiment, TE 24, 148

    Infantry: 1st Infantry Brigade (Orphan Brigade), AT 57, 59, 146, 149, 150, 152, TE 148, 149, 150, 153, 154; 2nd Infantry Regiment, TE 87, 154, TT 65; 3rd Infantry Regiment, MI *38-39*, 113-114; 4th Infantry Regiment, TE 154, TT 53, 152; 5th Infantry Regiment, AT 59; 6th Infantry Regiment, AT 100, TE 148, 153, 154; 9th Infantry Regiment, TE 87, TT 67-68; 16th Infantry Regiment, AT 149

Kentucky troops, Union, AT 40-42, SM 112, TE 25, *164-165*, TT 122, 124; Home Guards, TE 24; at Springfield, SH 33

    Artillery: Light Battery, TE 29

    Cavalry: 7th Cavalry Regiment, TE 44

    Infantry: 6th Infantry Regiment, TE 127; 8th Infantry Regiment, CH 136, *153*, TE 153; 10th Infantry Regiment, AT 133, 149; 12th Infantry Regiment, SM 105, 122; 15th Infantry Regiment, CH 56, TE *102*; 24th Infantry Regiment, AT 42; 25th Infantry Regiment, SH 87

Keogh, Myles Walter, DE *155*, GE *46*

Keokuk, CO 115, *116-117*, 118-120

Kepis, DE *56-57*

Kerns's battery, LE 158

Kernstown, Virginia, FL 90, 158; operations at, DE 44, 54, *map 66, 67, 68-69*, 70, 82, 90, 92, 133, 167-168

Kerr, Charles D., SM 68

Kerr revolver, OR *19*

Kershaw, Joseph B., AP 122, 124, 125, BD 39-42, CH 58, 64, 66, 69, FI 147, FL 104, 105, 108, 109, 113, 125, 146, 158, GE 72, 99, 108, KI 76, 78, 133, 152, RE 34, 84, 86, 91, TR 49, 70, 95; at Cedar Creek, FL 140, 144, 145, 147, 149, 151, 157

Ketcham, J. L., AT 62

Key, John, BD 160-161

Key, Thomas J., AT 54

Key, Thomas M., BD 129

Keyes, Erasmus D., FI 133, 135, 137, 145, 149, 169, FO 85, 93-94, 130, 136, 140, LE 52, 95, SP 25

Key's Battery, AT 54

Key West, Florida, BR 129; naval base, BL 29

Khedive of Egypt, NA 154

Kickapoo Indians, FR 147

Kidd, James H., FL 135, 153, 156

Killdeer Mountain, FR *98*

Killibrew, Joseph, OR 75

Killingsworth, John T., TE *81*

Kilpatrick, Judson, AP 56, 69, *70*, 157-158, AT 140, 145, GE *27*, 28, *38*, 132, 145, 156-157, KI *42*, SM *51*, 66, 144; and Alexander Shannon, escape from, SM 55; as cavalry commander, SM 50; at Fort McAllister, SM 150; at Macon, SM 52; raid on Richmond, KI 34-36; at Waynesboro, SM 66, 67

Kimball, Edgar A., BD 132-133, 138

Kimball, Nathan, BD 96-97, DE 66, 70, RE 74, 76-77, SM 95, 115

Kimberly, Robert L., CH 64

Kimmel, Manning M., BR *143*

Kinchloe, W. James, LE *170*

King, Albert F. A., AS 91, 100

King, Clarence, NA 94

King, Curtis, TT 28

King, Edward A., CH *63*

King, J. Floyd, FL 81

King, Kate. *See* Clarke, Kate

King, Preston, AS 159, NA 17

King, Rufus, LE 137-138, 140-143, 146

King Linkum, The First (play), OR 54

Kingsbury, Henry W., BD *122*

King's Schoolhouse, Virginia, LE 31

Kingston, Georgia, AT *50-51*, SM 44

Kingston, CH *164*

Kinman, Seth, FR *107*

Kinsman, William, MI 123

Kinston, Battle of, AP 65-67, *68*, 73

Kinston, North Carolina, CO 37, 84, 86, 91, OR 8

Kiowa Indians, FR 120-121, 125, 128, 129, NA 93, 96

Kirby, Edmund, FO 27, 155, RE 148-150. *See also* Kirby Smith, Edmund; Smith, Edmund Kirby

Kirby's Battery, FO 155

Kirby Smith, Edmund, AP 160-163, FR 52, *55*, 56, 62, 63, 64, 65, 153, 161, NA 19. *See also* Kirby, Edmund; Smith, Edmund Kirby

Kirk, Edward N., TE 113, 114, 115, 118, *120*

Kirkland, Richard, RE *89*, 91

Kirkwood House, AS *22*, 59, 69, 97, 98, 108, NA 16

Kitchens, TT 47. *See also* Mess facilities

Kitching, J. Howard, FL *127*, 146, 147

Kittoe, Edward, CH 88

Klein, Robert, SP *82-83*

Klinger, Frederick, SH 113

Knap, Joseph M., BD 94

Knap's Independent Light Artillery, BD 94-95, NA *168*

Kniffen, G. C., TE 97

Knight, Ben, OR 95

Knight, Newton, OR 92-95, 120

Knights of Liberty, SP 37

Knights of the Golden Circle, YA *28*, 29

Knights of the White Camelia, NA 36, 97

Know-Nothings, BR 101, *102*

Knox, George, FL *130*

Knox, Thomas W., SH 42

Knoxville, Tennessee, CH 31, 42, 99, 100, 101, 104, *110-111*, 113, 118, 119, 169, NA 64, SH *80*, TE 22, 40, 81; Burnside's objective, CH 32, 34; fortifications, CH 106, 109, *110-111*, 112; supply problems, CH 111; welcome for Burnside, CH 103, *110*

Koch, Andrew, and wife, FR *100*

Kolb's Farm, Battle of, AT 63-65

Koltes, John A., LE *168*

Kozlowski's ranch, FR 28, 31, 32

Krzyzanowski, Wladimir, DE 155

Ku Klux Klan, NA 36, 76, 97-99, 120, 142; banners and symbols of, NA *146-147*

Kurtz, George W., DE *109*

Kurtz, Peter L., DE *108*

Kutz, Peter W., YA 99

L

Labor force, YA 2, 64; development of, OR 16; shortages among, OR 22-23, 48; women in, OR 10, 25, 60, 67, 128

Labor union activities, YA 78

Labuzan, Charles, MI 41-42

Lackawanna, CO 145, 151-154

La Coste, Adolphus W., CO 119

La Crosse *Democrat*, YA 29

Ladd, James, SM 37

Ladd, Luther, FI *26*

"Lady Breckinridge" (cannon), CH *147*

Lady Sterling, BL 91

La Fayette, Georgia, CH 36, 38, 39, 42, SM 32

La Grange, Georgia, OR 82

La Grange, O. H., CH 80

La Grange, Tennessee, MI 87-88, *map 90*, 91

Laird, John, and Sons, BL 121, *123*, 125-126, 129, 145

Lake Providence: canal project, MI *map 73*, *74-75;* operations at, MI 87

Lamar, J. H., FL 81

Lamar, Lucius Quintus Cincinnatus, NA *144*, 145, 153

Lamar, T. G., CO 111

Lamb, William, CO 156, *162*, 163-164, 167, 169, 171

Lamb, William W., FO 125

Lambert's Ford, CH 44

Lamey, Michael, RE 141

Lamon, Ward Hill, AS 8, 11, 12-13, *15*, 43, *52*, SP 8

AP Pursuit to Appomattox; AS The Assassination; AT Battles for Atlanta; BD The Bloodiest Day; BL The Blockade; BR Brother against Brother; CH The Fight for Chattanooga; CO The Coastal War; DE Decoying the Yanks; FI First Blood; FL The Shenandoah in Flames; FO Forward to Richmond; FR War on the Frontier; GE Gettysburg;

Lampley, Harris D., AT 111-113
Lampton, James J., hat of, AT *61*
Lampton, Josephine, AT 61
Lancy, John, TR *63*
Lander, Frederick W., FO 84
Land grants, YA 63
Land mines. *See* Torpedoes
Landram, William J., FR 57, 59
Landrum, John J., TE 24
Lane, James H. (The Grim Chieftain), AS 159, BR 76, FR 146, 147, GE 62, 150, RE 33, 61-62, 65-67, 70, 144-145, SP 144, *145*, 152, 155; background, SP 141-142; at Osceola, SP 142-143; and Quantrill, SP 153; suicide of, SP 161
Lane, Joseph, SP 23
Lane's Brigade (Kansas), SP 142
Lang, David, GE 104, 111
Lang, Theodore, LE 163
Langdon, Henry K., FL *133*
Langdon, Loomis L., AP *111*
Langhorne, James H., DE 44
Langhorne, Moses, NA 141
Langley, Virginia, FO 39
Langston, John Mercer, YA *100*, 101
Language barrier, TT 29, 31
Lanier, Sidney, OR 8, 44, 58
Laning, James, SH 63, 65, 67
Lansing, Henry S., FO *132-133*
Latane, John, LE 26
Latane, William, LE 26, 27, 29; burial of, LE *26*
Latham, Edward, TT 154
Latham, Milton S., YA 93
Latrines, TT 47, 52, 80, 82
Lauman, Jacob G., SH 122-123
Laurel Brigade, FL 139, 142, *143*
Laurel Mountain, FI 87-92
Laurel Valley, North Carolina, OR 91-92
Lavergne, Tennessee, TE 97
Law, Evander M., BD 76, CH 48, 93, 109, GE 71, *74*, 78-80, 86, KI 135, 158, LE 45, 136
Lawler, Michael, MI 122-123, 130
Lawlessness, YA 71-72
Lawley, Francis, TR 68
Lawrence, Amos, BR 84
Lawrence, Kansas, BR 75-76, *77*, SP 142, 148, 152, 153, *154*
Lawrenceburg, Tennessee, SM 85
Laws, Thomas, FL *113*
Lawton, Alexander, BD 67, 75-76, 78, 80, 90, LE 30, 42
Lawton, Hattie, SP 29, *43*
Lawton, William J., TE 26, 27, *29*
Lay's Ferry, AT *44*, 45, 48
Lazear, Bazel, SP 154
Leach, Albert, AP 99
Leach, James, OR 151
Leadbetter, Danville, CH 112
Lead supply, OR *19*
Leaf River, OR 93, 95
Leake, James, FR *132*
Leale, Charles A., AS 86, 91, 92, 98, 99, *100*

Lean Bear, FR 123
Leather, OR 26, *62-63*, *66-67*
Leaves of absence, TT 55
Lebanon, Kentucky, TE *22*
Lebanon Pike, TE 59, 62, 66
Lecompton, Kansas, SP 141
Lecompton (Kansas) Constitution, BR 82
LeConte, Emma, AP 59, 61
Le Conte, Joseph, OR 119-120
Ledbetter, M. T., LE 39-41
Ledlie, James H., KI 136, 137, TR 46, 74-76, 78, *80*, 88
Le Duc, William G., CH 95, 97
Lee, Albert, FR 55, 56, *57*, 58, 59
Lee, Ann Hill Carter, LE *10*
Lee, Curtis, FO 128
Lee, Edmund I., FL 89
Lee, Edwin G., FL *50*
Lee, Fitzhugh, AP 80-82, *86*, 87, 88, 91, 110, 136, 139, FL 104, 112, 114, 116, 117, 122, 139, GE 26, *39*, 132, 151, KI 86, 115, 117-119, 122, 123, 151, 152, LE 27, 29, 91, RE 105-108, *109*, 110-111, 126, SP 115-116, TR 21-25, 56, 95, 98
Lee, George Washington Custis, AP 111, 116, 122, 124, 125, *126*, LE 15, NA 57
Lee, Henry (Light-Horse Harry), LE *10*, 11
Lee, John, AS 108
Lee, John C., RE 129
Lee, Mary, TR 64
Lee, Mary Custis, LE *14*, NA 57, OR 110
Lee, Matilda, LE 11
Lee, Mildred, LE 14
Lee, Robert E., AP 16, 38, 53, 113, 133, 155, 157, 158, 160, 162, 163, AS 8, 54, 55, 64, AT 20, 27, 29, 97, BD 9, BL 125, 159, BR 87, *88*, CH 30, 34, 42, FL 8, 20, 39, 73, 104, 106, 108, 122, 125, 134, GE *99*, KI 2, 26, 28, 43-*44*, 82, 114, 130, 149, LE *4*, 9, *13*, *15*, *17*, *19*, *21*, *156*, MI 157, NA 17-19, *57-59*, *128*, SM 17, 32, 122, 156, SP 33, 68, 109, 110, TR 18, 110-111, 145; accident to, BD 13; on amnesty to deserters, OR 166; at Antietam, BD 2, 60-61, 65, 69, 86, 109, 120-122, 127-129, 135-136, 151; appointed Army commander, FO 167; appointed commander in chief, OR 162; appointed general in chief, AP 25; appointed presidential adviser, FO 103; at Appomattox, AP 143-145, *146-148*, 149-151; approach to Gettysburg, GE *map 32*; army reorganized by, GE 14, LE 24, 91-92; at Brandy Station, GE 10; and Breckinridge, FL 29; and Bull Run, FI 111; at Catherine Furnace, RE 126-127, 130, 133, 140; cavalry reviewed by, GE 10; at Cemetery Hill, GE 66; and Cemetery Ridge, GE 128; at Chancellorsville, RE 124, 126, *map 127*, 130, 133, 140, 142, 150, 154-155, 156-160; at Chantilly, BD 8; and Chickahominy operations, LE 25-33, 49; and coastal operations, CO 38, 86, 91; at Cold Harbor, KI 152, 154, 165-167;

commands Virginia forces, DE 34, LE 22, OR 110; conference with Jackson, RE *cover*, *126*, 127; on cost of victory, RE 160; and Crater, TR 81, 88; criticized, LE 22; at Culpeper Court House, BD 168; and Dahlgren raid, KI 39; and Darbytown road, TR 153-154; Davis, conference with, GE 13; Davis, relations with, RE 92, 121; dedication of, LE 8, 10; defeatism dispelled by, LE 24; on desertions, OR 88; dictatorship offered to, OR 161-162; disciplinary measures by, BD 86; drawings and maps by, LE *12*; and Early, FL 138, 151, 158, 159; as engineer, LE 12, *13*, 22-23; at Fair Oaks, FO 156, 159; family, LE 8, *10*, *14-15*; farewell to troops, AP 153; and Five Forks, AP 79-82, 86-87; on food shortages, OR 86, 165-166, RE 104-105; and Fort Fisher, CO 156, 164; and fortifications, LE 24; at Fort Pulaski, CO 46, 50-51; and Fort Stedman, AP 39, 41; at Frederick, BD 15-18; at Fredericksburg, RE 33, 36-41, 50, 57-58, *81*, 84, 92, 121-122; funeral and memorial, NA *60*, *163*; and Fussell's Mill, TR 98; at Gettysburg, OR 51; and Gettysburg Campaign, SP 119, 122; and Gordonsville, LE 98; and Grant, TR 33, 36, 39, 44, 45; and Grant at Appomattox, AP 145, *146-147*, 148-151; at Hagerstown, BD 38, 44; and Harpers Ferry, BD 18, 22, 30, 38, 44-45, 59-60, 151; and Harrisburg, GE 26; and Hatcher's Run, AP 27, 29-31; at Herr Ridge, GE 59; home occupied by Union troops, FI 61; and Hood, AT 90; illness of, GE 69-71, 99, KI 135-136, 148; and initiative, loss of, TR 2, 16, 57, 64; Ives's evaluation of, LE 23; and John Brown's capture, LE *20*; Johnston's evaluation of, LE 23; and Johnston, AP 61, 69, 76, 79, 110; Johnston, relations with, FO 78, 105, 133, 138; joins Confederacy, FI 27-28; and Jones, FL 45, 46; and Kearny, LE 166; letter by, TR *157*; Longstreet, relations with, GE 71; and lost order, BD 21, 38, 81, 156; and Martinsburg, BD 153; McClellan's evaluation of, LE 22; and McClellan's retreat, LE 49, 62-63, 68, 124; McClellan evaluated by, BD 21, 60-61, RE 33; Mexican War service, LE *16-17*; military acumen, LE 8; as military adviser, DE 94; on military bands, FO 55; at Mine Run, KI 29, 31; and Mosby, SP 116, 119, 128; on munitions production, OR 22; names Army of Northern Virginia, LE 24; and New Market Heights, TR 146-147, 149-150; newspapers, use of, SP 52; at North Anna, KI 131-133, 135; offensive plans of, AP 33-34, 82; officer appointments, FI 57; pardon, request for, NA 32-33; partisans, criticism of, SP 126; and peace initiatives,

2nd Lieutenant Fitzhugh Lee, 2nd U.S. Cavalry, who joined the Confederacy and rose to Major General

Robert E. Lee, the peerless Confederate commander, portrayed as a Colonel of U.S. Cavalry in 1860

KI The Killing Ground; LE Lee Takes Command; MI War on the Mississippi; NA The Nation Reunited; OR Confederate Ordeal; RE Rebels Resurgent; SH The Road to Shiloh; SM Sherman's March; SP Spies, Scouts and Raiders; TE The Struggle for Tennessee; TR Death in the Trenches; TT Tenting Tonight; YA Twenty Million Yankees

79

Lee, Robert E. (continued)
AP 26; in Peninsular Campaign, DE 151, 170, FO 105, LE 23-24; personal arms, LE *18;* personal articles of, KI *44;* personal traits, LE 8; and Petersburg, TR 48, 52-53, 68, 70; Petersburg, attack at, AP 93-95; Petersburg, evacuation of, AP 78, 97, 99, 101; physical appearance, DE 18; and Pickett's Charge, GE 128-129, 144, 146, *147;* political outlook, BD 10; on Pope's conduct, LE 98; as presidential adviser, LE 22-23, OR *14;* prewar life and service, LE 8, 10, *12-20;* proclamation by, BD 17-18; on railroads' deficiencies, OR 26; and railroads, SP 84; and Rapidan operations, LE 124-125; and Rappahannock operations, LE 125-126; and Rappahannock Station, KI 33; and reinforcements, KI 43, 45, 150-151; resigns from U.S. Army, LE *20,* 22; retreat to Appomattox, AP 114-115, 117, 121, 127-130, 134, 136; retreat to Virginia, BD 151-153, 156, 168; and Richmond defense, LE 24-25, 31, 91, 124; and Richmond security, CO 38-39, 86, 97, FO 127-128; and Round Tops, GE 68; Scott's commendation of, LE 16; Scott, relations with, FI 27-28; and Second Bull Run, LE 8, 126, 132, 134-136, 144-146, 151, 154, 165-167; at Seminary Ridge, GE 65, 128; in Seven Days' Battles, BD 15, LE 25, 33, 35-37, 41-43, 47, 56-72; at Seven Pines, FO 145; and Shenandoah operations, LE 23, 30; and Shenandoah Valley, FL 16-19, 52; TR 27, 95; on slave enlistment, OR 166; at South Mountain, BD 49, 55; at Spotsylvania, KI 83, 86-87, 89, 92-94, 98-100, 102-103, 125; spying, opinion of, SP 46, 63; and spy report, GE 33; strategic plans, BD 8-11, 18-22, 38, 55-56, GE 2, 12-13, 22, 25-26, *map 32,* 33, 147; and Stuart, KI 116, 123-124; Stuart, directive to, GE 25-26; on Stuart showmanship, GE 10; and Stuart tardiness, GE 71; and subordinates' failures, LE 62, 73, 91; succeeds Johnston, LE 22; and supplies, KI 32; supplies, appeals for, AP 25-26, 31-33, 111-112; on supply shortages, GE 12-13; and surrender negotiations, AP 134-135, 137, 140, 141, 152; tactical plans, BD 60-61, 65, 86, 109, 120-122, 127-129, 151, 156, 168, LE 24-25, 30-31, 36-37, 49, 52, 60, 62, 65-68, 90-91, 98-99, 109, 124-126, 136, 165-167, RE 33, 35-41, 50, 57-58, 121, 124, 126, 142, 154, 156; tactical plans and dispositions, GE 33, 44, 53, 59-60, 65-66, 68-71, 79, 98, 113, 126, 128, 144, 146, 151-152; tactical successes, KI 169; in the Wilderness, KI 57-60, 62, 68, 70-71, 73-77, 79-81; and Thoroughfare Gap, LE 132, 143; and Traveller, DE 35, TR *66;* and Trevilian Station raid, TR 21; tribute to Jackson,

RE 142, 150-151, 160-161; tribute to Pelham, RE 111; tribute to Stuart, RE 143; and troop discipline, BD 17; and troop losses, TR 110; troops' devotion to, RE 150; and troop shortages, AP 20, OR 80, 148-149; troop strength, BD 11-12, 38, 60, 63, 65, 67, 164, GE 14, 44, RE 39, 105, 118, 125, 140, 155-156; and Turner's Gap, BD 45; Union Army command offered to, LE 20; as United States Military Academy superintendent, LE *18-19;* and Valley operations, DE 34, 94-95, 114-116, 120, 149; Washington, affinity with, LE 8, 11, 14; at Washington College, NA 57, *58-59,* 60; and Weldon Railroad, TR 103-105, 138; in western Virginia, DE 44-45, 82; in western Virginia operations, LE 22; and Williamsport, BD 156; at Winchester, BD 156, 164, GE 22-23; withdrawal to Virginia, GE 146-152, 156-157. *See also* Confederate Army
Lee, Mrs. Robert E., AP 108
Lee, Robert E., Jr., BD 86, LE *14,* 19, NA 32
Lee, Samuel Phillips, BL 80, 91, MI 18-19
Lee, Stephen Dill, AT 147, 148, 152, BD 4, 68, 83, 110-111, 129, BR 140, 159, LE 155, MI 63, *67,* 130, SM 83, 88, 89, 93, 95, 98, 116, *136;* at Ezra Church, AT 134, 135, 136; at Jonesboro, AT 144, 146; at Nashville, SM 125, 126, 133-135, 137, 142; rallies line at Nashville, SM 142
Lee, Thomas J., BR *145*
Lee, William Henry Fitzhugh (Rooney), AP 80, 84, 117, GE 20-21, 22, LE *15,* 27, 51, RE 33, TR 48, 55, 98, 103, 105, 111, 115; home of, LE *51, 82-83*
Lee, William R., FO 41-42, 44
Lee and Gordon's Mills, CH *12-13,* 39, 42, 44, 45, 47, 50
Leesburg, Virginia, BD 10-11, 13, 22, FL 88, 89, FO 39-44, 48, 50
Lee's Mill, Virginia, FO 102, *106-107,* 108
Lee's Mill Dam, Virginia, FO 94
Leet, George K., TR 94
Leetown, West Virginia, FL 106
Lefferts, Marshall, FI *59*
Left Hand, FR 124, 126, 127, 128
Leggett, Mortimer D., AT 95, 105, 106, 113, MI 149
Leggett's Hill. *See* Bald Hill
Lehigh, BL 75-77
Lehman, Albert, SH 29
Leigh, Benjamin W., GE 127, *154*
Leister farm, GE *166-167*
Lenoir's Station, CH 107
Leppien's battery, LE 161
Leslie's Illustrated Newspaper, BD 169, BR *81,* 139, FL 160, FO 52, KI 46, LE 99, YA 96
Les Miserables (Hugo), OR 46
Lester, Henry C., TE 29, 30, 31

Letcher, John, DE 58-59, FI 15, 28, 85, OR 86
Letterman, Jonathan, BD *157*
Letter writing, TT 9, *11,* 20, *70,* 71
Leutze, Emanuel, YA 139
Levy, William M., NA 156
Lewis, Asa, TE 148-149
Lewis, Francis, FI 141
Lewis, Henry, MI 21-23
Lewis, Joseph H., AT 57, 146, 149, 150, 152, TE 154
Lewis, Pryce, SP *42,* 43
Lewis, William G., AP 131-132
Lexington, FR 68, *70-71,* SH 60, *70-71, 143*
Lexington, Kentucky, CH 103, TE *48*
Lexington, Missouri, SH *30-31,* 32-33
Lexington, Virginia, FL *8-9,* 16, 17, 53, *56,* 57, 58, 59, 68, 159, NA 59, TR 25
Lexington (Kentucky) *Western Monitor,* BR 35
Libaire, Adolph, BD 133
Libby, Thomas, TR 58
Libby Prison, AT 42, SP 86, 87, TT 116, 119, 124-125, *126-127,* 128
Liberal Republicans, NA 110, 111, 149
Liberator, The, BR 39, 62, 69
Liberia, emigration to, BR 38
Liberty, Virginia, DE *12-13*
Liberty Gap, CH 22, 23, 24, 28
Liberty Party, BR 62
Lice infestation, TT 9, 83
Lick Creek, Tennessee, SH 105
Licksville, Maryland, BD 44
Liddell, St. John, CH 45, 68, TE 59, 60, 61, 117
Life of Stonewall Jackson (Cooke), OR 46
Life styles: among farmers, OR 42-44; among planters, OR 42
Lightburn, Joseph, AT 85, CH 141, 142
Lightfoot, James N., BD 103
Lighthouse Inlet, CO 120-121
Lightning Brigade (Wilder's Brigade), CH 28, 33, 44, 48, 99
Lilian, BL 95
Lilly, Eli, CH 24, 33, 48
Lilly's Battery, CH 19, 24, 33, 48, 52
Lincoln, Abraham, AP 128, 137, AS *cover,* 9, 83, 104, 114, *123,* 141, 145, 161, AT 24, BL *15,* BR *99, 116,* CH 18, 31, 43, 55, 83, 104, 105, 154, FL 19, 24, 25, 40, 69, 71, 84, 104, FR 10, 17, 38, 46, 47, 51, 71, 86, 99, 107, 112, 138, KI 34, NA 2, 16-18, 20, 29-31, 38, 77, *99,* SM 14, 34, 35, 122, 123, 134, 156, SP 68, 119, TE 10, 17, 24, 49, 80, 82, 142, 160, TR 94, 158-159, YA *148, 162-171;* and Andrew Johnson, AS 45, 74; and antiwar movement, BD 10; arrests ordered by, FI 31; assassination of, AP 44, 113, 158, 159, AS 85, *86-87;* assassination plots, SP 14-16; on Atlanta capture, OR 148; Baker, relations with, FO 43, 52; and Ball's Bluff, FO 52; and balloons, FO 147; and Banks's appointment, DE 59; and black enlistment, YA 101; on blacks'

Arlington House, the palatial residence of Robert E. Lee, which overlooks Washington, D.C.

AP Pursuit to Appomattox; AS The Assassination; AT Battles for Atlanta; BD The Bloodiest Day; BL The Blockade; BR Brother against Brother; CH The Fight for Chattanooga; CO The Coastal War; DE Decoying the Yanks; FI First Blood; FL The Shenandoah in Flames; FO Forward to Richmond; FR War on the Frontier; GE Gettysburg;

Sailors crowding the deck of the U.S.S. *Lehigh*, an iron-plated monitor serving on the James River

equality, BR 106; and blacks, recruitment of, TT 32-33; Blair, relations with, SH 12-13; and blockade, BL 11-12, 14, 24; blockade policy, CO 16; blockade proclaimed by, FI 13, 44; and Bull Run, FI 110, 152, 155, FO 38; Burnside, relations with, RE 27, 93-95; Burnside relieved by, RE 98; Butler, relations with, CO 58, FI 77; Cabinet meeting, final, AS 65-66; Cabinet members, BL 15, YA 147, 148-149; calls for troops, FO 16, 18, TT 21; call for troops, FI 13-14, 21, 24, 32, SH 11-12; Campbell Hospital, AS 49-51; and canal project, MI 72-73; and Capitol construction, YA 14; caricatured, YA 143; caricatures of, AS 10; carried to Petersen house, AS 92, 94-95; on Chancellorsville defeat, RE 160; and Charleston, CO 115, 119; Chase, relations with, YA 146-147, 154; at City Point, AS 53, 57; clothing and personal items, AS 80-81; commends troops, RE 93; and commerce raiders, BL 152; and Confederacy, recognition of, TT 111; conference with Burnside, RE 39, 94; conference with Hooker, RE 111; Congress, relations with, YA 142-147; Cooper Union speech, BR 98-99; corps activated by, FO 84-85; criticized, RE 92, 93; Davis compared with, OR 15; deathbed vigil at Petersen house, AS 92-95, 98-100, 102; death of, AS 100; death threat, AS 11; debates Douglas, BR 99, 105-107, 108; and desertions, TT 153; dismay over Buell, TE 54; and draft riots, YA 108; dreams, AS 8-10, 66-67; elected President, BR 98, 118-119, 142, SH 12; and Ellsworth, FI 63, 66-67; and emancipation, YA 35, 37, 38, 39, 142-143, 148-149; and Emancipation Proclamation, BD 156-159, 160, 161, BL 126, OR 111, 136, 140, 146, 149, 158, 163; emergency measures by, FI 11, 13; and enemy troop strength estimates, FO 99-102; evaluated by Welles, YA 142; at Falmouth, RE 111; fatalism of, AS 10, 76; and flag, YA 21; and Florida operations, CO 139; Ford's Theatre, attendance at, AS 57, 65, 68, 72, 79; foreigners commissioned by, TT 29; and Fort Donelson, SH 96; Fort Pickens reinforced by, FI 17-18; and Fort Pickens relief, BR 133; and Fort Stedman, AP 39, 41; at Fort Stevens, FL 86, 87; and Fort Sumter relief, BR 132-135, 137; and Frémont's ineptness, SH 33; Frémont, relations with, YA 153; Frémont appointed by, FO 92; Frémont evaluated by, DE 149; on Fredericksburg defeat, RE 92-93; funeral services and processions, AS 118-131, 141; on generals' inertia, FO 67; generals appointed by, FO 21; Gettysburg Address, GE 170-171; Governors, relations with, YA 143; and Grant's order

on Jews, MI 58-59; and Grant, KI 22, 24, 25; and Grant, meeting with, FL 100; Grant, relations with, MI 34, 83, 105, SH 49, 96, 155; Grant, tribute to, MI 159; and guerrilla warfare, SP 106, 122; habeas corpus suspension, FI 31, YA 31-32, 33, 34, 144; Halleck, relations with, SH 96; and Harpers Ferry, GE 23; and Harpers Ferry operations, FO 76, 84; Hooker, relations with, GE 16, RE 101, 118-119; Hooker relieved by, GE 33, 35; horse, AS 131; house-divided speech, BR 105; and Hunter, FL 40-41, 89, 90; inauguration address, BR 131-132, 135, 161; at Independence Hall, SP 11; interest in Tennessee Union sympathizers, TE 10; and ironclad construction, BL 51; and Joint Committee, FO 65, 67, 76; journey to Washington, SP 8, 10, 14-15, 21; and *Kearsarge* victory, BL 160; and Kentucky neutrality, SH 12; kidnapping plots against, AS 12, 20, 24, 27-29, 38-39, 44, 49-50, 53; and Know-Nothings, BR 101; and Lane, SP 142; and Lee as Union commander, FI 27-28; Maryland, measures against, FI 31; McClellan, relations with, BD 15, 61, 161, 162-165, 166-169, FO 14, 29, 52, 62-64, 67-68, 73-75, 84-85, 91, 102, 124, 131, LE 23, 47, 91, 92-93, 95, 133, 167, RE 24; McClellan appointed army commander by, FO 8; McClellan relieved by, BD 168-169, FO 87, RE 26; McClernand, relations with, MI 56, 59, 62; and Meade, GE 146, 152-153, 157, KI 26; medical assistance, AS 86-91, 98-99; meeting with commanders, AP 76-77; and *Merrimac* threat, BL 57; military science, interest in, FO 62; on Mississippi River's strategic value, FI 45; and Missouri operations, SH 16, 33; and New Orleans, CO 58; news of death, AS 101, 105, 106, 118; in newspaper cartoons, SP 14-15; newspaper pressure on, FI 110; newspapers, relations with, YA 29-31; on New York *Tribune*, YA 34; and Norfolk capture, FO 124-125; and North Carolina operations, CO 16-17, 38; officer appointments by, FI 57-58; office-seekers and public at White House, AS 14, 64-65; order for execution of Sioux, FR 94; and peace movement, YA 27; and peace negotiations, AP 21, 24-26, OR 149, 151, 157-158, 162-165; and peace overtures, FO 11; and Peninsular Campaign, CO 38, DE 61, 147, FO 63, 84, 91, 97, 130; Philadelphia speech, BR 132; and Pinkerton, SP 9; political skill, BR 99; political skills, YA 21, 142, 147; popularity demonstrated, YA 153, 158; postwar policy toward South, AS 2, 55-56, 67; on Potomac Creek bridge, RE 15; as presidential candidate, BR 98-99, 111, 113-114, 116-117, 118; and property

seizures, YA 143; and Radical Republicans, FO 65, YA 143, 151-154; and railroads, YA 64; and Rappahannock operations, GE 16; reconstruction policy, YA 154; and reelection, FL 158, YA 151-155, 156-157, 158-161; reelection campaign, AT 140-141, 154, OR 157-158, 161, SM 50; reelection poster, AS 39; and Republican affiliation, BR 101-102; resentment against, YA 142-143; and Revere's dismissal, RE 145; reviews troops, RE 102-103; in Richmond, AP 108-109, AS 54, 58; and Russian fleet visit, BL 140; and sanitary fair, YA 135; and Savannah, SM 134, 135, 159; and Scott's retirement, FO 29, 53; Scott, meetings with, FO 62; on secession, FI 10; and secessionist movement, BR 118; second inauguration, AS 41-43, 45-47, YA 160-161; security for, AS 10, 11-13, 64; as Senate candidate, BR 105, 108; Seward, relations with, YA 146-147; and Shenandoah Valley operations, FO 130-131; Sherman, concern for, SM 147-148; Shields, relations with, DE 65-66, 70; slaveowners' loyalty, SH 32; on slavery, BR 98-99, 105, 113, 116, 118, YA 34-36; and slaves as contraband, FI 78; and soldiers' vote, YA 151, 158-161; as speaker, BR 116; Springfield home, AS 130; Stanton, relations with, FO 71; and Stone's arrest, FO 71-72; and strategic plans, FI 45, 110, LE 92-93, RE 24-27, 30, 93-94, 118; strategic plans and orders, FO 63-64, 67, 72-73, 84, 124-125, 130; and Stuart's reconnaissance, BD 164; tactical concept, BD 164; and Tennessee operations, SH 59; and theater, AS 27, 30, 38, 49, 52, 59; and *Trent* Affair, BL 117, 119, FO 64-65; troop requisitions by, LE 93, 95; troops, calls for, YA 87, 89, 153; troops detached from McClellan by, FO 92-93, 96-97, 130-131; on Union preservation, FI 11; and Urbanna plan, FO 76, 84; and Vallandigham, YA 24-28, 30; and Valley operations, DE 71, 87, 89, 121, 135, 146-148, 150-151; and Vicksburg's importance, MI 17, 20, 56, 72, 108, 159; at victory celebration in Washington, AS 55-56; vilified, BR 116-117, 118, OR 54, 74, 161, YA 158; and *Virginia* threat, FO 124; visits to Army, FO 24, 124; voting franchise for blacks, AS 56; war aims, YA 142-143, 151; and warship construction, BL 10, 33; war strategy, AT 20; and Washington's security, DE 61, 64, 77, 146, FI 24-27, 29, 31, FO 73, 84, 96-97, 130-131; and welfare agencies, YA 120; and western Virginia loyalists, FI 85, 87; White House reception, AS 48; and Winchester, GE 23; wound recorded, TT 81. *See also* United States

Lincoln, Mary Todd, AS 8, 10, 27, 45, 48, 55, 57, CH 55, FL 86, 87, NA 17, SP 88;

Songsheet cover to one of numerous funeral marches composed after the assassination of Abraham Lincoln

KI The Killing Ground; LE Lee Takes Command; MI War on the Mississippi; NA The Nation Reunited; OR Confederate Ordeal; RE Rebels Resurgent; SH The Road to Shiloh; SM Sherman's March; SP Spies, Scouts and Raiders; TE The Struggle for Tennessee; TR Death in the Trenches; TT Tenting Tonight; YA Twenty Million Yankees

Major General John A. Logan, nicknamed Black Jack by his troops, commander of the Federal XV Corps

Two Confederate prisoners of war photographed on Lookout Mountain near Chattanooga, Tennessee

Lincoln, Mary Todd (continued)
apprehensions of, AS 75-76; and
assassination, AS 85, *86-87*, 91; and
Ford's Theatre, AS 64-65, 67-68, 72,
74, 76, 79; and funeral services, AS
118-119, 123; jealous behavior of, AS
53-54; at Lincoln's deathbed, AS 98, 100;
and Mrs. Grant, AS 55; and Parker, AS
77
Lincoln, Mrs. Abraham. *See* Lincoln, Mary
Todd
Lincoln, Robert Todd, AP 41, 148, AS 53,
64, *75*, 76, 119, 123; at Lincoln's
deathbed, AS 99, *102*
Lincoln, Tad, AP 109, AS *57*, *58*, YA *113*,
169
Lincoln, William S., FL 26, 30, *38*, 48, 56,
58
Lincoln, Willie, AS 27, 118
Lincoln Institute, NA 50
Lind, Jenny, SP 87
Linda, AP 48-49
Linn, Royan M., CH *151*
Liquor industry, YA 67, 72
Lisovski, Stephan S., BL *132*, 133
Literature, OR 42, 44-48
Little, Henry, MI 37
Little Bethel, Virginia, FI 78, 80
Little Big Horn, Battle of, NA 96
Little Crow, FR *73*, 76-78, 80-83, 86-87,
91, 93
Littlefield, Milton S., NA 64
Little Kanawha River, DE 45
Little Kennesaw, AT *18*, 66, *68-69*
Littler, Bob, SH 121-122
Little Raven, FR *124*, 127
Little Rebel, MI 24
Little River Turnpike, LE 166
Little Rock, Arkansas, FR 51, 52, 63, 64,
65, 152, 153, 155
Little Round Top, GE 75, *map 78*, *80-85*,
86-87, *90-91*, 98, 105, 133, 137, *162*
Livermore, Arthur, BR 35
Livermore, Mary: on nurses, YA 127; in
relief work, YA 116, 119-120, 122-124,
133
Livermore, Thomas, BD 23-24, 100, TT
55
Liverpool, England, BL 159
Livestock losses, OR 3, 149
Living conditions, TT 20, 44-46. *See also*
Campsites
Living quarters. *See by type*
Llewellyn, David Herbert, BL 149, 158
Lloyd, John M., AS 26, 50, 69, 74, 105,
155, 157
Lloyd's Political Chart, BR *112*
Loans by government, OR 30
Locke, William, LE 125, RE 52
Lockett, Samuel H., MI 157, NA 154, SH
126-128, 144; coat and helmet of, NA
154
Lockridge, Samuel A., FR 25, 26
Locust Grove, Battle of, FR 148
Locust Grove, Virginia, KI 29, 60

Logan, John A. (Black Jack), AP *54*, 59,
AT 66, 106, 134, 144, NA 164, SM 125,
134; at Battle of Atlanta, AT 83, *84-85*,
104, 110, 111; at Champion's Hill, MI
116, 118-119, *120-121;* at Dallas, AT 57,
58-59; at Fourteen-Mile Creek, MI
111-112; at Kennesaw Mountain, AT
68-69, BR 109, FI 122, MI *149;* and
Thomas, AT 133; at Vicksburg, MI
148-149, 153
Logan, Thomas M., FI *109*
Logan's Cross Roads. *See* Mill Springs
Log cabins, TT 46, *50*
Loggy Bayou, FR 55
Lohman, Frederick W. E., SP 85, 86
Lomax, Lunsford Lindsay, FL 112, 122,
124, 139, *141*, 144, 151, FR *145*, KI 115,
119
Lomax, Tennent, FO 164
London *Chronicle*, BL 115
London *Daily News*, YA 158
London *Herald*, SM 48
London *Morning Post*, BL 117
London *Times*, BL 117-118, TR 68
Long, Alexander, YA 24
Long, Armistead L., FL 74, KI 94
Long Bridge, FI 59, 61, 150
Long Bridge Road, LE 56, 58, 62
Longley, Charles, MI 119
Longstreet, Augustus B., OR 78
Longstreet, James, AP 18, 20, 26, 33, 79,
80, 94, 97, 99, CH 44, 49, 53, 83, 85, 90,
95, 99, *112*, 117, 118, 120, 125, 130, CO
86, 90, FI 113, 121-122, 124, 136-137,
149, FL 140, 141, 153, FO 110-113, 136,
138-139, 141, 144-145, 155, 157-159, 165,
167, FR 18, GE *71*, KI 28, 43, 73, 83,
LE *153*, *156*, NA 65-66, 143, SP 47, 63;
at Antietam, BD 60, 66-67, 69, 94,
104-105, 108, 119, 135, 139; appointed
corps commander, GE 14; at
Appomattox, AP 136, 140-141, 143-145,
153; Appomattox, retreat to, AP 110,
117-118, 120, 121, 127-134; arrives
during battle at Chickamauga, CH 54;
assigned command by Lee, LE 91; at
Brown's Ferry, CH 92; at Cemetery
Ridge, GE 126, 131; at Chambersburg,
GE 35; in Chickahominy operations, LE
30, 33, 37; at Chickamauga, CH 57, 58,
60, 61, 64, 67, 69, 72; commands corps,
RE 24; at Culpeper, GE 25, RE 26, 31,
33; at Devil's Den, GE 126; at
Emmitsburg road, GE 79, 98-99, 102; on
food shortages, OR 86; at
Fredericksburg, RE 33-36, 39, 50, 53,
58, 61, 63, 73, 78, *81*, 84-85, 87; at
Hagerstown, BD 21-22, 38, 47; and
Harrison, SP 54; incapacitated, BD 17;
Knoxville Campaign, CH 101, 105, 106,
107, 109, 110, 111, 112, 113, 114, 115,
154; Lee, relations with, GE 71; in Lee
retreat, GE 151; and lost order, BD 21;
march to Pennsylvania, BD 18; at Peach
Orchard, GE 126, 145; on Pennsylvania

invasion, GE 14; and Pickett's Charge,
GE 128-131, 136; Pickett evaluated by,
GE 126; in Potomac crossings, GE 26,
156; and Rappahannock operations, LE
126; at Second Bull Run, LE 126,
134-135, 143-146, 151-155, 158, 160, 165;
at Seminary Ridge, GE 128; in Seven
Days' Battles, LE 33, 37, 40-43, 49,
55-67, 72, 92; in Shenandoah Valley, GE
25; on slave enlistment, OR 166; in
southern Virginia, RE 104-105, 118; at
South Mountain, BD 49, 51-52, 55; spy
report to, GE 33; tactical plans, GE
68-69, 71-73, 78-79, 128; in the
Wilderness, KI 57-58, 74, 76-78; at
Thoroughfare Gap, LE 132, 135-136,
143, 145; transfer from east, CH 42, 43;
at Turner's Gap, BD 45; and Wheat
Field, GE 102, 104; at Williamsport, GE
151; wounded, KI 79
Lookout Creek, CH 130
Lookout Mountain, CH *map 2*, *8-9*, 10, 32,
33, 35, 37, 42, 73, *86-87*, 89, 92, 93, 95,
117, 118, 121, 125, *126-127*, *128-129*,
132, 137, *138*, 150, *151*, *156-157*, *162;*
assault on, CH 130, 131, 133, *134-135;*
strategic value, CH 78; U.S. flag raised
at, CH 136, *162*
Loomis, J. Q., TE 118
Loomis, John M., CH 138, 139, 140
Looting, RE 54-55, *56*, 88-89; by civilians,
OR 168; by Confederate troops, OR 160;
by Union troops, OR *104*, 111-112, *116*,
147. *See also* Civil disorders
Looting, prevalence of, TT 63
Lord, William W., MI *140*
"Lorena" (song), OR 54
Loring, William Wing, AT 39, 136, DE *50*,
FR 18, MI 76-77, 116, 118-122, NA 154,
SM 113, 114-115; Jackson, conflict with,
DE 50, 58-59; in Valley area, DE 52,
54-55, 58; in western Virginia, DE 45-46,
48; at Winchester, DE 50
Lost Mountain, AT 60, 61
Lost order, BD 21, 38, 81, 156
Loudoun Heights, BD 39, 43, 56, DE
156
Loudoun Rangers, SP 131
Loudoun Valley, GE 2-3, 25, 27-28
Loughborough, Mary, MI 125-126, 139-
140
Loughborough, Mary Webster, OR 117-
119
Loughbridge, James B., GE *154*
Louisa Court House, TR 22, 24-25
Louisiana: Black Codes, NA 34; black
legislators, NA *71;* carpetbaggers, attacks
on, NA 140-143; corruption in, NA 69,
117; devastation in, FR 46; educational
system, OR 54; guerrillas in, OR 103;
and habeas corpus suspension, OR 54;
loan to government, OR 30; loyalist
government in, NA 30, 32; newspapers,
OR 51; racial violence in, NA 97, 120,
141-142; readmission to Union, NA 69;

82

AP Pursuit to Appomattox; AS The Assassination; AT Battles for Atlanta; BD The Bloodiest Day; BL The Blockade; BR Brother against
Brother; CH The Fight for Chattanooga; CO The Coastal War; DE Decoying the Yanks; FI First Blood; FL The Shenandoah in Flames;
FO Forward to Richmond; FR War on the Frontier; GE Gettysburg;

refugees in, OR 121; secession by, BR 3, 128; slave emigration from, OR 151; state lottery, NA *118, 119. See also* Baton Rouge

Louisiana, C.S.S., CO 55, 63, 67, 76-77

Louisiana (U.S. bombship), CO 159-161

Louisiana Institute for the Deaf, Dumb and Blind, OR *108-109*

Louisiana Seminary of Learning, SM *11*

Louisiana State Navy, CO 63-73

Louisiana Tigers, KI 33

Louisiana troops, Confederate, AT 51, BD 71, 73, *148,* FL 78, 81, FR 52, 56, 57, GE 23-24, *92-93,* 116-117, KI 98, MI 18, TT 31, 67, 71, 86; 9th Partisan Rangers, MI 94; at Bull Run, FI 112, 129-132; Crescent Regiment, Company A, SH 121; Louisiana Brigade, DE 117, 123, 126, 129-130, 133-135, 156, 168, LE 128, *154;* Pelican Rifles, SH 27; Seymour's brigade, LE 42; Tiger Brigade, BD 71, GE *114, 116,* 160-161

    Artillery: Fenner's Battery, AT 52; Washington Artillery of New Orleans, AP 97, 113, 131, BD 104-105, RE 76, *84-85,* 154, *171,* TE *144-145,* TR 29, 137

    Cavalry: 2nd Cavalry Regiment, FR 54

    Infantry: 1st Infantry Battalion (Coppens' Zouaves), FI *20-21,* TT *36-37;* 1st Special Infantry Battalion (Wheat's Tigers), DE 116, *117,* 123, 130-131, FI *125,* 129-132, 143, KI 33, LE 42, RE *107;* 3rd Infantry Regiment, FR 142, MI 148, 151, SH 27, TT 44, 55, 157; 4th Infantry Regiment, SH 125-126, *133;* 7th Infantry Regiment, DE 168-169; 8th Infantry Regiment, KI 33; 9th Infantry Regiment, GE *115;* 10th Infantry Regiment, LE 72; 12th Infantry Regiment, SM *33;* 13th Infantry Regiment, AT 148, SH 125, TE 130; 14th Infantry Regiment, GE *112-113;* 15th Infantry Regiment, GE *112-113;* 19th Infantry Regiment, SH 125; 20th Infantry Regiment, TE 130

Louisiana troops, Union, FR 55; black units, MI 164

Louisville, SH 59, 82-84

Louisville, Kentucky, BR *12,* CH 88, TE 32, 54; civilian panic and flight, TE 24, *36-37,* 54; as objective, TE 51; strategic value of, SH 54

Louisville & Nashville Railroad, CH 20, 25, TE 50, 51, 91

Louisville *Courier,* SP 143

Louisville *Courier-Journal,* NA 112

Louisville Fair Grounds, SH *56-57*

Love, Nat, NA *93*

Lovejoy, Owen, YA 153

Lovejoy's Station, Georgia, AT 132, 136, 152, 153, 154, SM 15, 50

Lovell, Mansfield, CO *61;* at New Orleans, CO 55, 61, 63, 73-74; at Ship Island, CO 55; troop strength of, CO 73

Lovell, Thomas, painting by, AP *146-147*

Lovie, Henri, SH *28*

Lovingood, Sut, OR 52

Low, Abiel A., YA 78

Low, John, BL 121

Lowe, Enoch L., BD 18

Lowe, George, TE 154

Lowe, Thaddeus, FO 99, 105, *146-155,* RE *123*

Lowell, Charles Russell, FL 120, 145, 149, 156, *158, 166,* SP 120, 121

Lowell, James Russell, BL 127, NA 56, 110, SP 33

Lower Agency, Minnesota, FR 77, 78, 85, *88, 92*

Lowrey, Mark P., AT 54, 145, SM 98

Lucas, Charlie, AS 115

Lucas, William, AS 115

Ludlow, William, SM 26

Luhn, Gerhard, KI 114

Lula Lake, CH *10-11*

Lumber industry, YA 67

Lumley, Arthur, BD 104

Lumsden, Charles L., SM 130-132

Lunenburg Heavy Artillery, TR 143-144

Luray, Virginia, DE 84, 120-121, 168, 170

Luray Valley, DE 84, 86-87, 157-158, FL 17

Lusk, James, NA 145

Lutheran Theological Seminary, GE 44, *48, 160*

Lyman, Jonas W., CO *165,* 168

Lyman, Theodore, AP 136, KI *10,* 56, 74, 92, 95, 133, TR 50, 52, TT 30, YA 159

Lynch, William F., CO 22, 24, 31-32

Lynchburg, Virginia, FL 2, 19, 23, 41, 50-53, 58, 59-61, TR 18-19, 25, 27, 53; newspapers, OR 49; refugees in, OR 121-123

Lynchburg Rifles, TT 22

Lynchings, SP 140, 144, YA 35

Lynde, Isaac, FR 19, 20

Lyon, James Arthur, Lord Fremantle: CH 22, MI 149; on press freedom, OR 49; on railroad travel, OR 28

Lyon, Nathaniel, FO 12; Blair, relations with, SH 13; at Boonville, SH *20;* death of, SH 27, *28,* 29; Grant, relations with, SH 45; Jackson, relations with, SH 16-17; in Missouri operations, SH 17-24; and Missouri security, SH 15-21, 29; Price, relations with, SH 16-17; and St. Louis Arsenal, SH 13-15; troops mobilized by, SH 13, 15; at Wilson's Creek, SH 24-29

Lyons, Richard, BL *126;* and blockade, BL 14; and *Trent* Affair, BL 118-119

Lytle, William H., CH 60, *63*

M

McAllister, Robert, KI 78, TR 50, 156

Macaria (Evans), OR 44-46

MacArthur, Arthur, Jr., CH *148,* SM 117

McArthur, John, SM 128, 138, 139, *140*

McArthur, John A., SH 122

McBride, George W., SH 137

McBride, Joseph T., TE 117

McCall, George A., FO 39, 42, 48-50, 87, LE 31, 35-36, 59

McCarthy, Carlton, AP 112-113, 127, TT 20

McCauley, Charles S., FI 17

McCausland, John, AP *120,* FL 23, 56, 59, 60, 69, *72,* 73, 75, 78, 96, 105, 113, at Chambersburg, FL 91, 92; at Hagerstown, FL *72,* 74; sword of, FL *61*

McCleave, William, FR 115, *116*

McClellan, Arthur, KI *12*

McClellan, George Brinton, BD *14,* BL 125, FI *88,* FO 9, *15, 70, 86,* KI 22, LE *23, 94,* MI 56, RE 24, 26-27, 33, SH 45, SP 32, 33, 70, 71, 146, TR 2, 94, 157, YA *154;* accomplishments, FO 14; aggressiveness questioned, FO 12-13; at Alexandria, LE 133, 151; and amphibious operations, FO 89, 93, 105; at Antietam, BD 2, 61, 63-65, 69-70, 86-87, 92-93, 99, 108-109, *112-113,* 120, 122, 124-129, 139, 141, 151, 156; appointed general in chief, FO 53, 65; appointed major general, FO 12; army rehabilitated by, FO 14; army reorganized by, BD 15; arrival in Washington, FO 8; artillery strength, FO 89; on Baker's death, FO 52; and Ball's Bluff, BD 156, FO 39-41, 48-50, 52-53, 75; balloons, use by, FO 99; and bayonet drill, FO *14;* bayonet-drill manual, TT 54; becomes national hero, FI 93; and Boonsboro, BD 44; bridge construction by, FO 133; Burnside, relations with, BD 120, 168, CO 25; Butler, relations with, CO 58; candidacy for President, YA 154-155, *156-157,* 159-161; caricatured, YA *155;* caution of, FO 8, 29, 64, 67, 72, 74-75, 102, 124, 129, 131, 167; cautiousness of, LE 33; on cavalry efficiency, LE 81; and Centreville operations, FO 85-86; and Chickahominy operations, LE 23-33; chief of staff appointed by, FO 17; on combat behavior, TT 144; command failure, FO 167; commands Army of the Potomac, FO 8; commands Department of the Ohio, FO 12; command structure, BD 64; commands Union armies, FI 155; complaints by, LE 46-47; and Confederate retreat, BD 152-153, 156, 161-164; Congress, relations with, FO 53, 65-67; and corps organization, FO 84-85, 130; credit claimed by, FI 93; Crimean War experience, CO 16; demands for removal as general, YA 143; discipline restored by, FO 14, 16-18, 30; drive on Richmond, CO 38-39, LE 24, 31, 48, *49,* 90-91, 95, 124; on drunkenness, TT 58; and Emancipation Proclamation, BD 161, 168; enemies

Major General William W. Loring, who had lost an arm in the Mexican War

Brevet Brigadier General William Ludlow, a sketch by artist Alfred Waud

KI The Killing Ground; LE Lee Takes Command; MI War on the Mississippi; NA The Nation Reunited; OR Confederate Ordeal; RE Rebels Resurgent; SH The Road to Shiloh; SM Sherman's March; SP Spies, Scouts and Raiders; TE The Struggle for Tennessee; TR Death in the Trenches; TT Tenting Tonight; YA Twenty Million Yankees

83

Major General George B. McClellan, portrayed in Napoleonic fashion astride his horse, Dan Webster

Brigadier General Samuel McGowan, who served with Lee's Army until Appomattox

McClellan, George Brinton (continued) acquired, FO 13-14; enemy troop strength estimates, FO 17, 28-29, 97-99, 102, 131; evaluated by Lee, BD 21, 60-61; and Fairfax Court House operations, FO 39; farewell to troops, BD 169, *170-171;* foreign armies, report on, FO 12, 14; and fortifications, LE 24; and Fort Monroe capture, FO 91; and Frémont appointment, FO 92; at Frederick, BD *28-29,* 38, 48-49; and Harpers Ferry, BD 18, 38, 44, 55-56, 61, 156; and Harpers Ferry operations, FO 84; hostilities foreseen by, FO 12; illnesses, FO 64, 155; intelligence estimates by, BD 44; intelligence reports, LE 48; intelligence reports to, FO 28-29; Johnston's appraisal of, FO 107; and Joint Committee, FO 65-68, 73, 76; and joint operations, FO 93; kidnapping of, planned, FO 28; Lee evaluated by, LE 22; and Leesburg, FO 39-41; Lincoln, relations with, BD 15, 61, 161, *162-165,* 166-168, FO 8, 14, 29, 52, 62-64, 67-68, 74, 84-85, 91, LE 23, 47, *91,* 92-93, 95, 133, 167; and lost order, BD 38, 44, 156; and Manassas operations, FO 84-86, 89; marriage, FO 12; at Middletown, BD 47; on mine use, FO 108; mutiny suppressed by, BD 131, FO 16; and New Orleans, CO 58; newspaper criticism of, FO 14, 29, 52, 73-74, *75,* 86-87; and North Carolina operations, CO 16-17, 58; and officers' standards, FO 20; overcautiousness, BD 63, 109, 139, 151-152, 156, 164; parades and reviews by, FO 24-25; and peace movement, YA *155;* and peace negotiations, OR 158, *161;* in Peninsular Campaign, BD 15, CO 35, 38-39, 58, DE 21, 45, 61, 83, 89, 114, 135, 146, 151, 170, FO 14, 63-64, 67, 73, 75, 84, 89-91, 93-97, 107, 109, 113, *114-115,* 124-129, 167, LE 23-31; personal staff, FO 17, 22-23; physical characteristics, FO 11; and Pinkerton, SP *22,* 33; political views, BD 168; politicians, disdain for, FO 62-63; and Pope, LE 93-95, 124-126, 133, 151; and Potomac River operations, FO 74-75, 83; as presidential candidate, OR 157-158, *161;* prewar career, FO 11-12; proclamations to troops, FO 12-13, 53; promoted in Regular Army, FI 58; and Radical Republicans, FO 87-89; and railroad use, FO 130, 133; reconnaissances by, FO 94, 99; and regular officer assignments, FO 28; reinforcements for, FO 29, 130; relieved of command, BD 168-169; relieved as general in chief, FO 27; retreat to the James, LE 48-72, 75, 83, 124; Richmond, advance on, FO 14, 63-64, 73, 84, 89-91, 93, 102, 124-127, 130, 167; Richmond threatened by, OR 13; saddle designed by, FI 89; Scott, relations with, FI 93, FO 28-29, 53; self-confidence of, FO 9, 14-16, 53, 93; Sevastopol siege, effect on, FO 102; in Seven Days' Battles, LE 24, 36, 45-52, 68, 72, 84; at Seven Pines, FO 155, LE 23-24; and Shenandoah Valley operations, FO 74-75, 83-84, 97; soldiers' confidence in, LE 75; soldiers' devotion to, BD 29, 49, 109, 169; and South Mountain, BD 48-51, 61, 156; Stanton, relations with, FO 71, 74, 84, 85, 87-89, LE 47, 92-93; and Stone's arrest, FO 72; strategic plans, BD 15, 44, FI 44, FO *map* 2-3, 58, 63-64, 67-68, 73-84, 89-93, 96-99, 130, 155; Sumner evaluated by, LE 58; supply operations, FO 130; tactical plans, BD 63-65, 69, 86-87, 92-93, 99, 108-109, 120, 122, 124-129, 141, 151, FI 88-90, 93, LE 31-33, 36, 48-49, 63, 93, 95; tent proposed by, FO 14; training program, FI 87; training programs, FO 18-20, 63; and troop demoralization, FO 8-11; troop requisitions, LE 24-25, 93, 95; troops' affection for, FO 12, 17, 24-25, 28, 65, 167; troops detached from, FO 92-93, 96-97, 130-131; troop strength, BD 8, 15, 44, 53, 63, 65, 67, 108, 151, 164, FO 8, 24, 53, 64, 127; Urbanna plan, FO 63, 67, 74-75, 84-85, 89; and Valley operations, DE 61-64, 66, 71; at Warrenton, BD 47; and Washington's security, DE 61, 146; and Washington fortifications, FO 8-11, 17-18; and Washington security, FO 17, 74, 84, 91, 96-97; western Virginia, operations in, FI 85-93, FO 12-13; at West Point, FO 125, 129; at White House, FO 130; at Williamsburg, FO 109-113; and woman soldier, TT 27; work habits, FO 22; at Yorktown, FO 93-102, 107, 109. *See also* Union Army

McClellan, Henry, GE 20-22, 71, KI 122
McClendon, William A., LE 42, 131, 141
McClennan, Matthew R., FL 73, 75
McClensville Pike, TE 91
McClernand, John A., MI *59,* SH *47, 119,* SP *9;* ambition, MI 56, 62, 147; at Big Black River, MI 122; at Bruinsburg, MI 100-101; at Champion's Hill, MI 115-116, 119; exaggerated reports by, SH 119; at Fort Donelson, SH 81-83, 85-90; at Fort Henry, MI 63; at Fort Hindman, MI 68, *69,* 71; at Grand Gulf, MI 100; Grant, relations with, MI 56-57, 62, 68-69, 147-148; Halleck, relations with, MI 56-57; Lincoln, relations with, MI 56, 59, 62; McPherson, relations with, MI 147; plans for Vicksburg, MI 56-57; at Port Gibson, MI 101-102, 104-105; relieved by Grant, MI 147-148; Sherman's evaluation of, MI *59,* 132, 147; Sherman superseded by, MI 58, 68; at Shiloh, SH 105, 113, 116, 119-120, 136, 138-139, 143, 145; Stanton, relations with, MI 56-57, 62; troop strength, MI 68, 116; at Vicksburg,

MI 84, 126, 130, 132, 136, 147; Wilson, relations with, MI 147-148; Yates, relations with, MI 105; at Young's Point, MI 68
McConhie, John, KI *171*
McCook, Alexander McDowell, CH 24, 30, 33, 35, 42, 46, 53, 56, 60, 61, 83, FL *62,* 63, TE 55, 59, 60, 62, 93, *94-95,* 97, 98, 99, *110;* at Perryville, TE 62, 64, 66; at Stones River, TE 112, 113, 114, 118, 119, 120, 130, 133
McCook, Anson, TE *94-95*
McCook, Charles Morris, TE *94-95*
McCook, Daniel, TE 60, *94-95*
McCook, Daniel, Jr., AT 72, 74, *75,* 136, CH 45, 66, TE *94-95,* 155
McCook, Edward Moody, AP 161, AT 136, 138, TE *94-95*
McCook, Howard M., CH 79, 80
McCook, John, TE 95
McCook, John James, TE *94-95*
McCook, Robert Latimer, TE *94-95*
McCook family (Fighting McCooks), TE *94-95*
McCord, A. P., TR 142
M'Cormick, T. B., BR 40
McCown, John P., TE 41, 42, 91, 99, 108, *117;* Bragg's opinion of, TE 41, 42, 117; at Stones River, TE 113, 114, 124, 157
McCrady, Edward, LE 127, 149-150
McCray, T. H., TE 47, 48
McCulloch, Ben, BR *131,* FR 17, *19,* 21, 137, 138, 140-146, SH *26;* in Arkansas operations, SH 26, 54; in Missouri operations, SH 17, 21-24, 26, 32; at Wilson's Creek, SH 24-29
McCulloch, Henry, MI 146, SP 157
McCullough, John, AS 41
McDonald, Angus, DE 44
McDonald, John A., NA 115, 116
McDowell, Irvin, FI *116,* FO 67, 84, *86,* 96, 105, 130-131, 133, 136, FR 112, LE *146,* SP 26, 44; appointed Army commander, FI 58; at Bull Run, DE 38; on discipline breakdown, FI 148; at Fredericksburg, DE 87, 89, 94-95, 114, 121-123, 135, 147, 170; at Front Royal, DE 147, 150; and invasion of Virginia, FI 61; at Manassas Junction, DE 71; personal leadership, FI 144-145; personal traits, FI 110; in Rappahannock operations, LE 24-25, 93, 101; relieved of command, FI 155; at Second Bull Run, LE 101, 134-137, 143-146, 151, 153, 164; tactical plans and orders, FI 110, 112-113, 116-117, 121-122, 124-129, 135, 137, 141-142, 145, 150, 155; victory presumed, FI 135. *See also* Bull Run, Battle of
McDowell, Virginia, actions at, DE *map* 101, *102*-103, 114, 148
McDowell, William H., FL 159
McElhenny, Frank, TT 154
McElroy, John, TT 118
McEnery, John, NA 143

AP Pursuit to Appomattox; AS The Assassination; AT Battles for Atlanta; BD The Bloodiest Day; BL The Blockade; BR Brother against Brother; CH The Fight for Chattanooga; CO The Coastal War; DE Decoying the Yanks; FI First Blood; FL The Shenandoah in Flames; FO Forward to Richmond; FR War on the Frontier; GE Gettysburg;

McFadden's Ford, TE 152
McFarland's Gap, CH 61, 64, 68, 72
McGarry, Edward, FR 108, 110, 111
McGee, James, BD 100
McGehee defense line, CO *map* 62, 74
McGehee House, LE 41
McGhee, James, FR 161
McGilvery, Freeman, GE 106-109, 134, 137
McGinnis, George F., MI 118
McGlashan, Peter A. S., AP 122
McGowan, Samuel, KI 71, 76, LE *168*, RE 143-144, 146-147
McGowan, Theodore, AS 82
McGuire, Hunter, DE *93-94*, LE 35, RE 139, 160
McGuire, Judith, OR 110-112, 126-128
Machinery production, OR 21
McIlvaine, William, Jr., LE *83*, 86, 88
MacIntosh, Daniel, FR *39*
McIntosh, James, FR 141, 142, 143, TT 157
Mackall, Lily, SP 24
McKay, Gordon, NA 82
McKay, William, TE 154
McKee, William, NA 115
McKeen, Henry B., KI 161, *170*
McKenny, T. I., FR 124
Mackenzie, Ranald Slidell, AP 79, 91, *137*, 138, 139, FL 115, 157
Mack family, MI 58
Mackie, Mary, NA *51*
McKie, Thomas Fondren, RE *106*
McKim, Randolph, GE *24*
McKinstry, J. A., MI 41
McKissick's farm, FR 140
Mackville Pike, TE 59, 61, 62, 66
McLaughlen, Napoleon B., AP 36
McLaughlin, William, FL 81
McLaughlin's Battery, DE 46, *115*, 130, 135, 161
McLaws, Lafayette, CH 100, 108, 109, 112, 113, RE *40;* at Antietam, BD 65, 86, 88-89, 91, 98, 103; at Brownsville, BD 39; at Cemetery Ridge, GE 78; at Chancellorsville, RE 124-125; at Crampton's Gap, BD 55-56, 64; at Emmitsburg road, GE 72-73, 78, 98; at Fredericksburg, RE 33, 36, 40-41, 73; at Gettysburg, GE 68-70; at Harpers Ferry, BD 18, 22, 39, 44-45, 55-56, 86; at Peach Orchard, GE 101-102; at Salem Church, RE 154, *map* 155, 156, 158; troop strength, GE 73, 155; at Wheat Field, GE 108
McLean, John, BR 113
McLean, Joseph A., LE 168, *169*
McLean, Nathaniel C., LE 159-160
McLean, Wilmer, AP 145, FI 113, 127
McLean house, AP *146-147*, 153
McLean's Ford, FI 113
McLemore's Cove, CH 32, 35, 36, 37, 38, 39, 44, 54, 61, 84
McMahon, James P., KI 161, *164, 171*, TT *61*

McMahon, Martin T., KI 156, 158, 165, RE 156
McMaster, Charles, FL 136
McMaster, Fitz William, TR 75, 81-82, 88
McMaster, John B., SP *19*
McMillan, James, FR 61
McMillan, Robert, RE 77
McMillen, Francis M., AP *40;* diary, watch and belt buckle of, AP *40*
McMinnville, Tennessee, CH 23, 79, 80, TE 49
McMurray, William J., TE 153
McNair, Evander, CH 58
McNeil, Hugh W., BD 64, 65
McNeill, Henry C., BR *142*
McNeill, Jesse, SP 114, 127
McNeill, John H. (Hanse), FL 26-28, 42, 136, 158, SP 106, *114*, 155; background, SP 114; death, SP 127; and Gettysburg Campaign, SP 122; at Piedmont, SP 126; psychological tactics, SP 115
McNeilly, James, SM 118
Macon, George, FL *15*
Macon, Georgia, AP 161, AT 138, NA *22*, OR 65, SM 48, 50, 52, 53, 82
Macon, Mississippi, MI 89, *map* 90
Macon & Western Central Railroad, AT 95-97, 132, 133, 136, 138, 139, 140, 141, 142, 143, 147, 152, OR *156-157*
Macon *Daily Telegraph*, OR 19, 29
McPhail, Samuel, FR 85
McPherson, James B., AT 84, 97, 104, 113, 114-115, 132, MI *112*, SM 49; as army commander, AT 31; at Battle of Atlanta, AT 99, 100; at Champion's Hill, MI 116; at Clinton, MI 113; at Dallas, AT 59; death of, AT 101-102, 105, *107;* at Fourteen-Mile Creek, MI 111; and Hood, AT 91; at Jackson, MI 111, 113-115; at Kennesaw Mountain, AT 66; and Lake Providence project, MI 73-74, 87; McClernand, relations with, MI 147; at Port Hudson, MI 103; at Resaca, AT 44; shells Atlanta, AT 95; and Sherman, AT 33, 98; at Smyrna, AT 76; at Snake Creek Gap, AT 32, 36-39; troop strength, MI 116; at Vicksburg, MI 68, 84, 126, 132, 147, 153; at Young's Point, MI 87
McPherson's Ridge, GE 44-45, 47-48, 51, *56-57*, 61
McPherson's Woods, GE 44-45, 47-48, 51, *52*, 61, *158-159*
McQuaide, John, SM 118
McRae, CO 63, 72-73
McRae, Alexander, FR 25-26, 37
McRae, Duncan, BD 81-82
MacRae, John Burgwyn, uniform of, AP *75*
McRae, Lucy, MI 9, *140*
McRae, William, TR 108
McRae's Battery, FR *26-27*
Macy, George N., KI 78
Maddox, George, SP *151*
Madeira Island, BL 159
Madison, Georgia, SM 59
Madison, James, OR 11, TR 9

Madison, William, BD 155
Madison, Wisconsin, SH 22
Madison County, North Carolina, OR 91
Madison Court House, Virginia, LE 101
Madison road, SM 54
Madrid Bend, SH *map* 160, *162-163*
Maffitt, John Newland, BL 86-87, 100-101, 143, *150*, 160-161
Magee, Horter & George, OR 63
Magoffin, Beriah, SH 11-12
Magruder, James, RE 51, 56
Magruder, John Bankhead, AP 163, DE 25, FI 78-79, *82*, FO 99, 108-109, 111, 136, 159, FR *48*, LE 24, 31, 33, 36, 45, 48, 50, 55, 65-72, 92, SP 33, 50; proclamation by, FR *48*
Magruder, John T., BR 142
Mahan, Dennis Hart, FI 48
Mahaska, LE 70
Mahone, William, AP 110, 128, 131-133, 140, FO 159, 161, 164, KI 88, 89, 103, 154, LE 55, 68, TR 81-*82*, 83, 86-88, 98, 103, 137, 156
Mahony, Dennis, YA 24, 32, 34
Mail service, OR 5, 48. *See also* Reagan, John H.
Maine: admitted into Union, BR 36; voting rights of blacks in, YA 15
Maine troops, GE 85, TT 157; at Bull Run, FI 145-147, *164-165*
    Artillery: 1st Heavy Artillery, KI 126, TR 52, *58-59*, 60, *61, 62-63*, TT 48; 1st Light Battery (Fessenden), LE 170; 2nd Battery (Hall), GE 48, RE 65; 5th Battery (Kirby), RE 148, *149*, 150; 5th Battery (Leppien), LE 161; 5th Battery (Stevens), GE *92-93*, 117
    Cavalry: 1st Cavalry Regiment, DE 130, GE *27-28*, TR 26
    Infantry: 2nd Infantry Regiment, FO 16; 3rd Infantry Regiment, FI 145-147, *164-165*, GE 76; 5th Infantry Regiment, KI 91; 6th Infantry Regiment, KI 33; 7th Infantry Regiment, BD 53, *114-115*; 9th Infantry Regiment, CO 124; 10th Infantry Regiment, BD 80, LE *109*, TT *82, 150*; 16th Infantry Regiment, GE 59, KI 56, 73, 86, TT *38*; 17th Infantry Regiment, AP 113, GE 98, KI *20-21*, 101, 167; 18th Infantry Regiment, TR 58; 19th Infantry Regiment, AP 131, GE 143, KI 57; 20th Infantry Regiment, AP 31, 81, 117, 152, GE 76, *81*, 83-84, RE 88, TR 51, TT 159; 28th Infantry Regiment, YA 126; 29th Infantry Regiment, FL *130*, TT *150*
Maisch, John M., SM *108*
Malingering, TT 52
Mallard, Mary Jones, SM 68
Mallory, Mary, OR 112
Mallory, Stephen R., BL *20*, BR 9, CO 94, OR 14; and commerce raiders, BL 21, 142-143, 145; and ironclad construction, BL 46-48, 65, 125-126; personnel management by, BL 20, 49, 143; and

Colonel George N. Macy, 20th Massachusetts, who survived the loss of a hand to become a Brevet Major General

A group of cavalry officers, including men of the 1st Maine and 1st Massachusetts

KI The Killing Ground; LE Lee Takes Command; MI War on the Mississippi; NA The Nation Reunited; OR Confederate Ordeal; RE Rebels Resurgent; SH The Road to Shiloh; SM Sherman's March; SP Spies, Scouts and Raiders; TE The Struggle for Tennessee; TR Death in the Trenches; TT Tenting Tonight; YA Twenty Million Yankees

85

A Sharps Pepperbox, carried by Private Marcus Shepard of the 1st Massachusetts Cavalry

A recruiting poster for the 12th Massachusetts Battery, promising service under General Nathaniel Banks

Mallory, Stephen R. (continued) warship construction, BL 20. *See also* Navy, Confederate States
Malmborg, Oscar, MI 131
Malone, Mary, SP 75
Malvern Hill, Battle of, LE *map 32*, 49, 52, 56-65, *map 66*, 67-68, *69-70*, 71-73, *88*
Manasco, Jeremiah, SH 141
Manassas, CO *4*, 55, 63, 69-72
Manassas, Battle of. *See* Bull Run, Battle of
Manassas, Second Battle of. *See* Bull Run, Second Battle of
Manassas, Virginia, FO 3, 63, 73-75, 78, 81-85, 89, LE 93, *112-113, 122-123,* 124-125, *129*, 130-131, *134-135*, 136-138, 143, OR 28, TT 45
Manassas Gap, DE 43
Manassas Gap Railroad, DE 39, 86, 114, 121, FI 57, 95, 122, *123*, 126, 135, LE 127, 145, RE *map 8*, SP 109, 128, 130
Manassas Junction, Virginia, DE 38-39, 43, 61, 64, 66, 71, 83, FI *map 3*, 57, 111-113, 119, 122-123, *127*, 135, FO 39, 72, *118-119*, RE 8, 16, SP 110
"Manassas Quickstep" (music), OR 52
Manchester, Tennessee, CH 24, 28-29, 30, TT 68
Manet, Edouard, BL 167
Maney, George Earl, AT *73*, 93, 94, 104, 111, 145, TE 60, 65, 93, 121, 123
Mangas Coloradas, FR 115, 116, 117
Manhattan, CO 143
Manhattan, Kansas, YA *64-65*
Manifest Destiny doctrine, BR 41
Manigault, Arthur M., AT 82, 106, 107, 109, 110, 111, 144, CH 54, 143, 145, 148, TE 118
Manigault, Louis, OR 128-129
Mankato, Minnesota, FR 80, 82, 83, 85, 90, *95*
Mann, Ambrose Dudley, BL 16, 116
Manning, Vannoy H., TT *39*
Mansfield, Joseph K. F., BD 65, 69, 79, *80-82*, 122, FI 58-59
Mansfield, Louisiana, FR 55, 56, 57, 63
Mansfield, Massachusetts, YA 93
Manson, Mahlon D., TE 45
Manuelito (Mescalero Apache), FR 115
Manuelito (Navajo), FR *120*
Manufactures. *See* Industry
Mapmaking, DE 82, *84-85*, 158
Marchbanks, Burton, uniform of, FR *155*
Marches, TT 9, 156, 162-163, by Confederates, DE 21, 38-39, 44, 50, 52, *53*, 54-55, 66, *98*, 99-100, 104, 114, 120-121, 131, 156-157; by Federals, DE *150*. *See also* Training programs
"Marching through Georgia," song sheet and lyrics, SM *74-81*
March to the sea, SM 44-73, 144-159; cavalry action during, SM 50, 52, 63, 67; Cobb plantation and Sherman, SM 59-60; Ebeneezer Creek tragedy, SM 72; Fort McAllister, fall of, SM 150; Griswoldville, Battle of, SM 60-61, 148;

holiday atmosphere on, SM 144; Milledgeville, occupation of, SM 62; Northern concern, SM 75; opposition in Savannah, SM 145-146; and Savannah, fall of, SM 159-160; Sherman cuts his lines of communication, SM 44; Southern press and, SM 62, 68; U.S. Navy, contact with, SM 155; Union troops, increased bitterness of during, SM 68
Marcy, Ellen, LE 33
Marcy, Randolph B., FO 12, 17, 76
Mare Island, FR *14*
Maret, George, TT 83
Margedant, W. C., TR 102
Maricopa Indians, FR 118
Marietta, Georgia, AT 60, SM 20
Marines, United States, CO 143, 165, *166-167*
Marion, Francis (Swamp Fox), SP 106, 116
Marion Artillery (South Carolina), flag of, FI *125*
Marion Light Artillery (Florida), TE 47
Markland, A. H., SM 147-148, 155-156
Marks, James J., LE 52
Marks' Mills, Arkansas, FR 65
Marmaduke, John S., BR *143*, FR 64, 65, 150, 152, 156, *158*, 160, 161, SH 121
Marquis de Gallifet, FR *40*
Marriages, OR 43
Marsh, John S., FR 78, 79, 80
Marshall, Charles, AP 140, 141, 145, *146-147*, 150, RE 150
Marshall, Elisha G., TR 76
Marshall, Humphrey, TE 45
Marshall, James Foster B., LE *171*, NA *51*
Marshall, John, BD 141, SP 87
Marshall, Louis, LE 103, 109
Marshall, North Carolina, OR 91
Marshall, Texas, OR 121
Marshall House, FI *64*
Marston, John, BL 58
Marthasville, Georgia, AT 21
Martial law: instituted, OR 80-82, 162; opposition to, OR 77, 82; proclaimed, SH 30-32
Martin, Gustavus, MI *109*
Martin, James, AT *86-87*
Martin, John, CH 145
Martin, Luther, GE *155*
Martin, William, CH 79, KI 74
Martin, William H., AT *70*, 71
Martindale, James H., KI 164, 165
Martinsburg, Virginia, BD *map 2-3*, 18, 38, 153, DE 35, *36-37*, 45-48, 55, FL 19, 25, 69, 91, 104, 109, 112, 151, SP 49
Mary A. Boardman, FR *49*
Marye's Heights, RE 50-54, *map 59*, 61, 71-73, *74-76*, 77, *78*, 79, *map 80*, 83, *84-85*, *map 86*, 87-91, 152-154, 168, *170-171*
Maryland: anti-Union sentiment, SP *12-13*,14, *17;* bridges sabotaged in, FI 24-26, *28;* Confederate intelligence operations in, SP 51-53, 58; Confederate sympathizers in, BD 10-11, 15, DE 34,

FI 20-21, 24-26, 29-31; disloyalty in, YA 31-33; Lincoln's measures against, FI 31; railroads sabotaged in, FI 29; refugees from, OR 123; suspension of habeas corpus, SP 17; telegraph sabotaged in, FI 29; terrain features, BD 44, 60, 64, 66-67, 121; threat to Virginia, FI 76; threat to Washington, FI 20-26, 29; Union control of, SH 9; Union intelligence operations in, SP 34, *36-39;* as Union slave state, BR 3; Union troops quota, FI 14
"Maryland! My Maryland" (song), OR 49
Maryland Heights, BD 39, *40-41*, 42-43, 56, 65
Maryland-Pennsylvania boundary, BR *36-37*
Maryland troops, Confederate: enlistments of, BD 18
   Artillery: 1st Battery (Dement), GE 24; 3rd Battery, SM 135; Baltimore Light Artillery, KI 119
   Cavalry: 1st Cavalry Regiment, GE 37; 2nd Cavalry Regiment, FL 95
   Infantry: 1st Infantry Battalion, GE *94-95*, 127, *129*, *154-155;* 1st Infantry Regiment, BD 10, DE 123-126, 158, *162-163*, FI 147, 156, LE 42, *43*, TT 119; 2nd Infantry Regiment, KI 159
Maryland troops, Union, BD 42, 56, TR 101; 1st Potomac Home Brigade, FL 74; 3rd Battalion, TR 76; militia, FL 71-73, 81, 83
   Artillery: Baltimore Battery, FL 71
   Cavalry: 1st Cavalry Regiment, BD 43-44
   Infantry: 1st Infantry Regiment, DE 121, 123, 126; 2nd Infantry Regiment, BD 124; 3rd Infantry Regiment, LE 90, RE 144
Mascots, SH *23*, TT *150-151*
Mason, Charles, BR 37
Mason, Frank D., MI 63
Mason, Herbert C., GE *154*
Mason, James M., BL 116, *119*, 148
Mason, W. Roy, LE 131
Mason-Dixon line, BR *36-37*
Masonic lodges, TT 68
Mason's Hill, SP 45
Mason's Island, YA *18-19*
Massachusetts: antislavery campaign, BR 62, 74; blacks, voting rights of, YA 35; civil disorders, YA 29, *30;* industrial production, YA 2; and mergers, YA 79
Massachusetts troops, BD 131, CH *153*, CO 84, KI 43, NA *28*, TR 119, TT 45, 47-48, 52, 60, 65, 132, 144, 156; at Big Bethel, FI 80-82; at Bull Run, FI 118, 121, 157; in invasion of Virginia, FI 77; militia disbanded, TT 22
   Artillery: 1st Artillery Regiment, FO 25; 1st Heavy Artillery, KI 108, *124*, 126, TT *38*; 3rd Heavy Artillery, FL *64-65*, 66-67; 9th Battery (Bigelow), GE 106-107; 10th Battery, TR 108; Ancient and Honorable Artillery Company, TT

AP Pursuit to Appomattox; AS The Assassination; AT Battles for Atlanta; BD The Bloodiest Day; BL The Blockade; BR Brother against Brother; CH The Fight for Chattanooga; CO The Coastal War; DE Decoying the Yanks; FI First Blood; FL The Shenandoah in Flames; FO Forward to Richmond; FR War on the Frontier; GE Gettysburg;

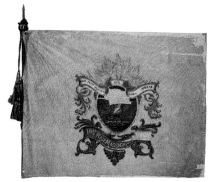

The regimental colors of the 19th Massachusetts Volunteer Infantry, a unit in the Federal II Corps

21; field artillery battery, OR *106-107*

Cavalry: 1st Cavalry Regiment, GE *27*, 28, KI 22, RE 110, TT 63; 2nd Cavalry Regiment, FL *88*, SP 120, *121*; 3rd Cavalry Regiment, FL *133*; 4th Cavalry Regiment, AP 118, 120, *130*

Infantry: 1st Infantry Regiment, FI 118, 121; 2nd Infantry Regiment, AT *156-157*, *158*, BD 92, *93*, *96*, DE 59, 82, GE *154*, LE 108, 144, SM 44; 4th Infantry Regiment, FI 80-82, YA 126; 5th Infantry Regiment, TT 79; 6th Infantry Regiment, FI 21-25, *26-27*, 29, 31, SP *13*, TT 119; 7th Infantry Regiment, RE 154; 8th Infantry Regiment, FI 23, *28*, 29; 9th Infantry (Irish) Regiment, FO 133; 10th Infantry Regiment, FO 140; 11th Infantry Regiment, FI 157; 12th Infantry Regiment, BD 71, 73, LE 170, TT *40*; 13th Infantry Regiment, DE *48-49*, TT 67, 71; 15th Infantry Regiment, BD 90, FO 40-41, 42, *45*, 47-48, 51, 158; 16th Infantry Regiment, TT 152; 17th Infantry Regiment, CO 84; 18th Infantry Regiment, FO *63*; 19th Infantry Regiment, BD 16, 169, GE *121*, *141*, *142*, *155*, KI 160, RE 53, 54-55, 81, TT 37; 20th Infantry Regiment, BD 91, *92*, GE 154-155, KI 78, 171, RE 29, 51, 53, *54-55*, TT 20; 20th Infantry (Harvard) Regiment, FO 41-42, 46, *50*, 51; 21st Infantry Regiment, CO 28, 30, 34, 36-37, LE 135, 163-164, 166, RE 73; 22nd Infantry Regiment, GE 103, KI 43, RE 24, 140, TR 50, 53; 23rd Infantry Regiment, CO 27-28, KI 165, TR *29*; 24th Infantry Regiment, TT 154; 25th Infantry Regiment, CO 25-27, KI 165; 26th Infantry Regiment, FL *131*, TT 44; 27th Infantry Regiment, AP 65, CO 16, 27, *85*, KI 156, 164; 28th Infantry Regiment, CO 111, KI 170, RE 82, TR 45; 29th Infantry Regiment, AP 36, 37, BD *104*; 30th Infantry Regiment, TT 65; 33rd Infantry Regiment, CH 95, SM 45; 34th Infantry Regiment, FL 25-26, 36, 37, *38-39*, 42, 48, 51, 56, 61, *126*; 36th Infantry Regiment, CH 115; 37th Infantry Regiment, AP 29, 109, *121*, 124, 125; 39th Infantry Regiment, KI 92; 40th Infantry Regiment, KI 164, TT 54-55; 44th Infantry Regiment, CO 88; 47th Infantry Regiment, YA 126; 52nd Infantry Regiment, OR 109; 54th Infantry Regiment, CO *125-127*; 54th and 55th Infantry Regiments, YA 101; 55th Infantry Regiment, AP *64*; 56th Infantry Regiment, KI 170, TR 34; 57th Infantry Regiment, AP 36, 39, KI 136, TR *89*

Massanutten Mountain, DE 43, 84, 86-87, 117, 120, 157, FL 17, *27*, 28, 30, 104, 122, 124, 137, 140, 144

Massaponax Baptist Church, KI *126*

Massaponax Creek, RE 50, 61

Massie's Battery, FL 75-78

Matches, production of, OR 26

Mather, John, YA *80*

Mathews, Alfred E., TE 162-171

Matlock, Emmery, BD 59

Matthews, John, AS 29, 71

Matthews Hill, FI 130-137, *156-157*

Matthies, Charles L., CH 140

Mattingly, Henry, AT 133

Mauk, John, AP 95

Maury, Betty Herndon, OR 110

Maury, Henry, OR 95

Maxey, Samuel B., FR 64

Maximilian, Emperor of Mexico, FR 38, 42, *43*, 44, 45, OR 162

Maxwell, James R., SM 132

Maxwell, John, SP 82

Maxwell House Hotel, TE *71*

May, John Frederick, AS 137

Mayfield, Kentucky, OR 149

Maynard carbine, SM *86-87*

Mayo, Joseph, AP 90

Mayo, Robert, GE 137-139

Meade, George, Jr., KI *10*

Meade, George Gordon, AP 8, 39, 110, 113, 136, 137, BD 52, 67, 70, 76-78, FO 20-21, GE *11*, *96-97*, KI *10*, 22, 26, 34, 57, 82, 122, 149, 169, NA *8-9*, 106, RE *65*, SP 80, 81, TR 31, 35, 43, 45, 49, 52-53, YA 110; appointed army commander, GE 33-35; at Appomattox, AP 143, 144, 151; and black troops, TR 74; and Burnside, TR 73-74, 94; and campaign objectives, TR 16; at Cemetery Hill, GE 67, 74; at Cemetery Ridge, GE 119, 131, 133; at Chancellorsville, RE 120-121, 125, 128, 135, 140, 149, 158; at Cold Harbor, KI 152-154, 156, 166, 167; councils of war by, GE 77, *118*, 119, 156; and Crater, TR 73-75, 80, 86-88; and Culp's Hill, GE 127; and Dahlgren raid, KI 39; Doubleday relieved by, GE 74; at Emmitsburg, GE 35; and Five Forks, AP 85, 86; and Fort Stedman, AP 41; at Frederick, GE 152-153; at Fredericksburg, GE 34, RE 63-67, 68-69, 71, and Grant, KI 24-25, 68; Hancock evaluated by, GE 65; and Hatcher's Run, AP 27, 30; at Massaponax Church, KI 126, *127-128*; at Mine Run, KI 28-32, *35*; at North Anna, KI 133; and Petersburg, TR 65, 67, 69-70, 72, 95, 99-101, 104, 107, 155; Petersburg, assault at, AP 92; and Pipe Creek line, GE 44, 67; pursuit of Confederates, AP 114, 117, 121, 132; in Rappahannock operations, RE *120-121*, map 122; and Sheridan, KI 114; at Spotsylvania, KI 85-87, 89, 92-93, 124-125; strategic plans, GE 35, 156; tactical plans and dispositions, GE 46, 65, 67, 74-78, 98, 105, 119, 127, 131, 144, 146, 152; at Taneytown, GE 46, 51; troop strength, GE 44, 74, 145; at Wilderness, KI 60-62, 68, 70, 73, 77, 81, RE 120; withdrawal from Gettysburg, GE 152

Meade, Richard K., BR *142*, 143, *148*

Meadow Bluff, West Virginia, FL 24, 45

Meadow Bridge, KI 123, LE 33

Meagher, Thomas Francis, BD 63, 100, *107*, FO 163, 165, RE 77, *82*, 87, TT 29. *See also* Irish Brigade

Means, John W., LE 168, *171*

Means, Samuel C., SP 110

Meat-packing industry, YA 63, 79

Mechanicsville, Battle of, LE 24-25, *map* 32, 33, *34-35*, 36

Mechanicsville, Virginia, FO 130, 133, 136, 167

Mechum's River Station, Virginia, DE 100

Medal of Honor awards, BD 73, CO 33, *127*, 161, RE 69, 73, 135, TT 35

Medary, Samuel, YA 24, 29

Medical Department: casualties, treatment of, YA *16-17*, 87-89, 116, 120-122, 126-129, *130-131;* deficiencies in, YA 119-120, 122; reorganization, YA 122; women as nurses, attitude toward, YA 127-129, 131. *See also* Hospitals

Medical equipment and supplies, SM *106*, *108-111*. *See also* Drugs

Medical officers, TT *88-89;* number in service, TT 79, 81; qualifications, TT 78-79

Medical services, DE 94, FI 54, 131, FO 17, 55, 91, MI *46-47*, OR *38*, SH *88-89*, 119, *131*, 144, 147-148, *154;* antisepsis, absence of, TT 79, 94, 97-98; casualties, evacuation and treatment of, TT 20, 78-79, 81, 88-95, *100-105;* Confederate, BD 135, 150; in Confederate Army, TT 78; doctors' qualifications, TT 78-79; doctors, shortage of, OR 43-44; hospitals, TT 88, *93*, 95, *96-97*, *106-109*, 118; hospital ship, TT *105;* medical supplies, TT *79;* medication, TT 78, 83, 85; nurses in, TT 78, *93-94*, 98, *106;* photographic records, TT 81; for prisoners of war, TT 118, 133; surgical instruments, OR *19*, TT *91*, 92; surgical techniques, TT 78-79, 90-95, 98, *102-103;* Union, BD *109*, 136, *138-139*, 150; in Union Army, TT 78; Union Army hospital, OR *108-109;* for venereal diseases, TT 62; women in, OR 30, *36-37*, *59*, *60*

Medill, Joseph, RE 92, YA 146

Mediterranean, British influence in, BL 119

Meigs, John Roger, FL 135, *136*

Meigs, Montgomery C., CH 149, FL *63*, FO 67-68, TT 115-116

Mellon, Thomas, NA 86

Melville, Herman, BR 16, YA 109

Memminger, Christopher, BR 130

Memminger, Christopher G.: background, OR 13-14; fiscal programs, OR 30-33

Memorial Day, NA 158, *164-165*

Memphis, Tennessee, CH 83, 97, CO 63, 77, MI 20, *24-25*, 27, 34; racial violence in, NA 34, *35;* strategic value of, SH 8-9, 155; Union garrison, NA *62;* Union

Major General George Meade and Admiral David Porter, two of the Union's highest ranking officers

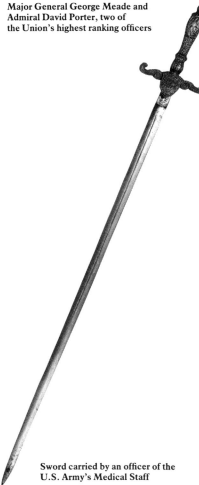

Sword carried by an officer of the U.S. Army's Medical Staff

KI The Killing Ground; LE Lee Takes Command; MI War on the Mississippi; NA The Nation Reunited; OR Confederate Ordeal; RE Rebels Resurgent; SH The Road to Shiloh; SM Sherman's March; SP Spies, Scouts and Raiders; TE The Struggle for Tennessee; TR Death in the Trenches; TT Tenting Tonight; YA Twenty Million Yankees

87

threat to, SH 101, 157
Memphis & Charleston Railroad, CH 18, 33, 83, 97, MI 40, SH 157, SM 82, TE 10
Memphis *Appeal*, AT 40, OR 48
Memphis *Evening Bulletin*, MI 147
Memphis Packet Company, SH 16
Mendell, George H., TR 36
Mendenhall, John, TE 150, 152, 153, 154
Mendota, AP *46-47*, *50*, CO *80*
Mennonites, DE 8-9
Mercer, Hugh, AT 99
Merchant marine, United States: insurance rates, BL 148; ransom bonding, BL 147-148, 152, 159; ship losses, BL *144-145*, 146, *148*, 149, *150-151*, 152-154, *159*, 160-161; size, BL 10. *See also* Commerce raiders; Privateers
Merchant's Cotton Mill, OR *24-25*
Mercie, Antonin, NA 163
Meredith, Solomon, GE 47-48
Meredith, William M., AT 46
Mergers, YA 78-79
Meridian, Mississippi, AT 22, MI 90, OR 28
Meridian *Mercury*, NA 148
Meriwether, Elizabeth Avery, NA 36, 61
Merrell, William, OR 38
Merrick & Sons, BL 51
Merrill, Lewis, NA 143
Merrimac, U.S.S., BL *50*, FO 85
Merrimack salvaged, FI 17
Merrimac-Virginia, C.S.S., BL *18*, *50*, FO 89, 93, 124-125, MI 27; characteristics and armament, BL 48-49, 54, 62; construction, BL 46, 48-49; destroyed, BL 60, *63*, 65; *Monitor*, battle with, BL *58-59*, 60, *61*, 62-65, *74-75*; ships attacked by, BL 46-47, 53, *54*, 55-57, *58-59*, map 60
Merritt, James B., AS 150
Merritt, Wesley, AP 78, 81-82, 86-87, 90-91, 125, 138-139, 148, 153, FL *102*, 103-105, 109, 113, 116, 119, 120, 137, 159, KI 86, 114, 115, 119, 123, 151, TR 22, *23*, 25; at Cedar Creek, FL 141, 145, 147, 153, 156, 157, 162; at Toms Brook, FL 139
Mersy, August, AT *82-83*, 110, 111
Mesilla, New Mexico Territory, FR 19, 20, 22, 35
Mess facilities, TT *8-9*, *12*, *16*, 47, *84*, 86, 156, TT *84*; prostitution in, TT 60-61. *See also* Rations
Metacomet, CO 145, 150-151
Metals industry production, BR 9
Metcalf, Richard, KI 102
Metcalfe, Leonidas, TE 44, 45
Mexican-Americans in Union Army, TT 31
Mexican War: tactics in, FI 89; troop strength in, FI 111
Mexico: arms traffic from, FR 46-47, 51; and Confederate arms supply, MI 16; French adventurism in, FR 38-45; French venture in, BL 128, 155; invasion

proposed, OR 162; *Juaristas*, FR *44*; mercury supply from, OR 22; war with, BR 41, TT 21
Mexico City, Mexico, DE 25, *26-27*; occupation by French, FR *42-43*
Miami, BL *78-79*, 80, CO *70*, 95
Michigan, disloyalty in, YA 29
Michigan Soldiers' Relief Association, YA *129*
Michigan troops, FL 103, 106, 136, *137*, 153, KI 115, 122, 149, MI *92*, TT 45; at Bull Run, FI 118, 121-122; in invasion of Virginia, FI 61; Iron Brigade, KI 65, 134, TR 101, 103, 137; mobilization, FI 32; prisoners lost, FI *154*; training program, FI *38-39*; 19th Regimental Drum Corps, CH *23*
    Artillery: 1st Battery, CH 45
    Cavalry: 1st Cavalry Regiment, KI 119, 151-152, LE 168; 2nd Cavalry Regiment, TE 59; 4th Cavalry Regiment, NA 20, *22;* 5th Cavalry Regiment, KI 149, TR 23-24; 6th Cavalry Regiment, AP *121*, FL *132*, GE 157, TR 24; 7th Cavalry Regiment, GE 132, KI 118; 8th Cavalry Regiment, TT 134; 9th Cavalry Regiment, SM 67 Engineers: 1st Engineers and Mechanics, TE *12-13*
    Infantry: 1st Infantry Regiment, FI 61, YA *96-97;* 2nd Infantry Regiment, FI 118, TT 27; 3rd Infantry Regiment, FI 118; 4th Infantry Regiment, GE 101; 7th Infantry Regiment, AP 131, BD 151, GE *120-121*, RE 53, *54-55;* 8th Infantry Regiment, CO 111, TT 28-29; 9th Infantry Regiment, TE 27, 29; 15th Infantry Regiment, SH 137; 16th Infantry Regiment, GE 84, TR *152-153;* 17th Infantry Regiment, BD 49; 21st Infantry Regiment, CH *26-27;* 22nd Infantry Regiment, CH 65, 68; 24th Infantry Regiment, GE 45, 49, 61-62
Mickey's (crossroads), SH 108
Middle bridge, BD 108, 132, 139
Middleburg, Virginia, GE 26, 28
Middlesex Anti-Slavery Society, BR 66
Middletown, Maryland, BD 44, 47
Middletown, Virginia, FL 140, 149, 157, 158, LE 93; actions at, DE 129, map 130, 131, 156
Migration, OR 75, *118-119*, 121. *See also* Refugees
Miles, Dixon S., BD 38-39, 42, 43-44, 56-57, 59, FI 117, 126
Miles, Nelson A., AP 85, 96, 127, 128, 131, 132, FO 161, KI 159, NA 22, *102-103*, RE 78, 148, *150*, TR 107-*110*
Miles, William Porcher, BR 159, OR 59
Military Road, RE 62, 67
Militia enlistments, OR 79
Militia troops. *See under states*
Militia units: amateur soldiers in, TT 21; ethnic rivalry among, TT 22; ineptness in, FI 37; laws governing, TT 21; political appointments in, FI 21; social

aspects of, TT 21-22. *See also under states*
Mill Creek Gap, AT *11*, 32, 35, *36*
Milledgeville, Georgia, SM 48, 59, 68; and legislature, SM 61; Union occupation of, SM 62, *63*
Millen, Georgia, SM 68
Miller, Dora, MI 126, 152
Miller, George K., TE 97
Miller, James, FO 160-161
Miller, James Cooper, LE 71
Miller, John D., RE *106*
Miller, John F., TE 154, 166, 167
Miller, Lovick P., TR 114
Miller, Solomon, TR *101*
Miller (David R.) farm, BD 67, 70, 73-75, 78, 80. *See also* Cornfield, the
Miller's Ferry, Virginia, DE *78-79*
Milliken Repeater, SP 68
Milliken's Bend, MI 63, 67, 69, 83-84, 86, 109, *146-147*
Millinery production and procurement, OR *19*, 26
Millionaires, YA 77
Mills, Charles J., TR 46
Mills, J. Harrison, LE 142, 154
Mill Springs, Battle of, FO 74, SH 55-56, *58*
Millwood, Virginia, DE 39
Milroy, Robert H., DE 95, 100-103, GE *23*, 24, KI 81, LE 160, 162-163, OR 141
Milwaukee, Wisconsin, civil disorder in, YA 35
Milwaukee *Morning Sentinel*, BL 116
Minerals: production and procurement, OR 22; resources, BR 9, 18; shortages, OR 29; supply of, OR 19, 22
Miner's Hill, Virginia, TT *46-47*, *54-55*
Mine Run, KI 28-31
Mines: Confederate, CO 35, 113, 115, 118, 139, 141-142, 147, 150, 153, 128, 161, FO 107-108; types, CO *152-153;* Union, CO 96-97
Mine warfare, MI 136, *148-149*, *150*, 168
Minié, Claude E., FI 50
Minié balls, AP *135*
Mining: industry, YA 67, 71-73, *74-75*, 77, 79; operations, BL *82-83*
Minks, Charles E., TR 152-153
Minnegerode, Charles, RE *109*
Minnesota, BL 46, 54-58, *59*, 60, 62, 64; black voting rights, NA 72; immigrants in, YA 62; refugee settlers, FR *83;* Sioux uprising in, FR 72-75, map 76, 77-87, *88-89*, 90-99, *100-105*, 122
Minnesota, FO 124
Minnesota Territory, emigration to, BR *32*
Minnesota troops, FR 72, *75*, 78, 84, SM *140-141;* state militia, FR 85
    Artillery: 1st Light Battery (Munch), SH *130*
    Infantry: 1st Infantry Regiment, GE 109, *110-111;* 2nd Infantry Regiment, CH *cover*, SM 54, 72; 3rd Infantry Regiment, FR 87, *153*, TE 29; 4th Infantry Regiment, SM *38-39;* 5th

Rough and ready Michigan cavalry-men on campaign in the field

Private Thomas Gooch, a soldier of the 20th Mississippi Infantry

AP Pursuit to Appomattox; AS The Assassination; AT Battles for Atlanta; BD The Bloodiest Day; BL The Blockade; BR Brother against Brother; CH The Fight for Chattanooga; CO The Coastal War; DE Decoying the Yanks; FI First Blood; FL The Shenandoah in Flames; FO Forward to Richmond; FR War on the Frontier; GE Gettysburg;

Infantry Regiment, FR 81, 83, MI 114; 6th Infantry Regiment, FR 85, 87; 7th Infantry Regiment, FR 87, SM 133
Minstrel shows, OR 54, TT *15*
Minton, Thomas, TR 108
Minty, Robert H. G., CH 44, 46
Mishet, James, RE 71
Missionary Ridge, CH *map 2, 14-15,* 32, 37, 61, 64, 73, 78, 97, 117, 120, 121, 123, 129, 130, 131, 132, 136, 140, 141, 142, 150; Thomas' attack, CH 143, 144; Union troops assault summit without orders, CH 4, 145, 146, 147, 148, 149
Missionary Ridge, Battle of, OR 153
Mississippi: corruption in, NA 119; disloyalty to Confederacy in, OR 92-93; Dodge's operations in, SP 75; education, NA 120; federal property seized by, BR 128; Grierson's Raid in, MI 87-89, *map* 90, 91-93, *94-95,* 96, *97;* guerrillas in, OR 89-91, 93-95; and habeas corpus suspension, OR 154; Henson's operations in, SP 78; money issue, OR *73;* racial violence in, NA 145-147; readmission to Union, NA 69; refugees in, OR 117-119, 121; in secessionist movement, BR 3, 84, 128; slave emigration from, OR 131; troops withheld by, OR 155; Union control of, OR *98,* 145, *map 152-153;* Union settlers in, NA 64-65; University of, OR 54; voting fraud in, NA 145, 147-148
Mississippi, C.S.S., CO 54-55, 63, 74
Mississippi, U.S.S., BL *18,* CO 61, 66, 69, 72, MI *162-163*
Mississippi Central Railroad, MI 56, 83, 88
Mississippi rifle, SH *50-51*
Mississippi River, FR *13,* 46, 138, OR 29, 51, 96, *98,* 148; control of, MI *map 2-3,* 16, 20, 56, 72, 159, SH 155, 157; Lewis' paintings of, MI 21-23; operations on, SH *map 2-3;* steamboats on, FR *11;* strategic value of, FI 44-45, SH 8-9, 11, 29-30, *40-41,* 46; as trade artery, BR 8-9; Union crossing, MI 83-84, 100-101
Mississippi troops, BD 42-43, 151, CH 40, 113, 131, FI *126,* FO 141, GE 101, 105-106, 138, KI 103, 137, MI 56, RE 152, *162-163,* SM 21, 24, 113, 133, TE 51, *55,* 65, 124, TT 44, 52, 56, 59, 62; at Bull Run, FI *126,* 132; Shubuta Rifles (company), SH 99
   Artillery: Ridley's Battery, MI 56, 118; Shannon's Battery, CH 139; Swett's Battery, AT 132
   Cavalry: 1st Cavalry Regiment, MI *93;* 10th Cavalry Regiment, NA *161;* 28th Cavalry Regiment, MI *123*
   Infantry: 2nd Infantry Regiment, FI 132, GE 50; 3rd Infantry Battalion, SH 111-113; 6th Infantry Regiment, MI 102, SH 114-116, SM 114; 7th Infantry Regiment, OR 93; 8th Infantry Regiment, TE 130; 9th Infantry Regiment, FI *15,* SH *108-109,* 139; 11th

Infantry Regiment, FI 132, KI 83, RE *106;* 12th Infantry Regiment, AP 97-99; 13th Infantry Regiment, AT 61, FO 48, GE 102, RE 51-53; 14th Infantry Regiment, SH 99; 16th Infantry Regiment, AP 97-99; 17th Infantry Regiment, FO 46, 50, RE 51-53, *54;* 18th Infantry Regiment, BD 17, 151, FO 46, LE 63, RE 51-53, *54,* 56, 141, *170-171,* TT 147; 19th Infantry Regiment, FO 110; 21st Infantry Regiment, GE 106-107, RE 51-53; 41st Infantry Regiment, AT 107, 111; 42nd Infantry Regiment, TT 80, 147; 43rd Infantry Regiment, MI 148; 46th Infantry Regiment, SM 24; 48th Infantry Regiment, AP 99
Mississippi Valley, YA 21, 56, 75
Missouri, SP *map 2-3;* Anderson's raids, SP 158-160; divided loyalties in, SH 12-13, 19; fighting in, FR 3, 137-161; Frémont's operations in, SH 32-33, 48; German immigrants in, SH 12, 15; Grant's operations in, SH 45; guerrilla bands, FR 145, 157; guerrilla operations in, SH *map 2-3,* 12, 16, 19, 30-32, 45; Jackson's operations in, SH 17-21; Jennison's raids, SP 144, *146-147;* Lane's raids, SP 142-143; Lincoln on operations in, SH 16, 33; lost to Confederacy, SH 157; Lyon's operations in, SH 15-24, 29; operations in, SH 15, 17-24, 32; population, SH 9-11; Price's operations in, SH 17-24, 26, 32, 48; refugees in, OR 121, SH *32;* restrictions on voters, YA 144; Scott and, SH 33; secessionist movement in, SH 16; Sigel's operations in, SH 19-20, *24-25;* Southern sentiment, SP 146-147; strategic and political value of, SH 9; terrain, SH 25; as Union adherent, OR 75-76; Union Army reprisals, SP 153-154, *156-157;* Union control of, SH 29; Union informants, SP 73; Union reinforcements from, SM 83, 121; as Union slave state, BR 3; Union troops quota, FI 14; violence in, SP 140, 141
Missouri Compromise, BR 34-37, 71-72, 79-80, 119, SP 140
Missouri River: gunboat construction on, SH 74; operations on, SH 17; strategic value of, SH 8-9
Missouri troops, Confederate, FR 52, 56, 60-61, 140, 144-145, 148-150, MI 28, 119, SM 21, TT 31; 1st State Guard Regiment, SH *10-11*
   Infantry: 1st Infantry Regiment, FR *134;* 2nd Infantry Regiment, MI 149; 2nd and 6th Infantry Regiments, SM 122; 3rd Infantry Regiment, MI 103; 3rd and 5th Infantry Regiments, SM 83; 5th Infantry Regiment, MI 103; 6th Infantry Regiment, MI 149
Missouri troops, Union, AT 113, 134, FR 142, SP 72; Home Guard, SH 13-16,

19-21, *24-25;* state militia, FR 134; 2nd Mounted Volunteer Regiment, SH 16
   Artillery: Battery H, 1st Artillery, AT 99; Hescock's Battery, TE 121
   Cavalry: 1st Cavalry Regiment, FR *133;* 4th Cavalry Regiment, SP 159; 9th Cavalry Regiment, SP 159
   Infantry: 6th Infantry Regiment, AT 107; 7th Infantry Regiment, TT 58; 8th Infantry Regiment, TT 24; 10th Infantry Regiment, MI *114-115,* 119; 11th Infantry Regiment, MI 41, *42-43;* 18th Infantry Regiment, SH 117; 19th Infantry Regiment, MI 114; 21st Infantry Regiment, SH *106;* 25th Infantry Regiment, SH 111, 113; 31st Infantry Regiment (Zouaves), MI 117; 39th Infantry Regiment, SP 160-161
Mitchel, Ormsby M., TE 8, 10, 12, 14, 15, 17, 21; at Huntsville, TE 10, 11; promotion, TE 11; relations with Buell, TE 8, 10, 15, 16
Mitchell, Barton, BD 81
Mitchell, Ella, SM 50-52
Mitchell, John, AT 72
Mitchell, John K., CO 63-64, 67, 76
Mitchell, Robert B., FR 124, 125
Mitchell's Ford, FI 112-113, 118, 121, 124, 128, 132, 136, 138, 149
Mobile, Alabama, CH 86, CO 54, 142-156, NA 26, 123; as blockade-runners' port, BL 87; refugees in, OR 123; slave impressments in, OR 23; Union capture of, OR 148; Union threat to, SH 101
Mobile & Ohio Railroad, MI 88, 96, OR 95
Mobile Bay: obstructions in, CO 142; operations in, CO 17, 142-145, *map 146,* 147, *148-149,* 150-153, *154-155,* 156, *157*
Mobile Bay, Battle of, YA 158
Mobile Point, CO 142
Mobile *Register,* MI 143
Moccasin Bend, CH 131, 138
Moccasin Point, CH 89
Model 1822 musket, SH *50-51*
Model 1842 Mississippi rifle, SH *50-51*
Model 1842 musket, FI *70-71*
Model 1855 pistol carbine, FI 75
Model 1855 rifle musket, FI *70-71*
Modoc, BL 69
Mohawk, New York, BR 115
Molly Maguires, NA 89
Monaghan, William, KI 98
Monarch, MI *24-25*
Monde Illustré, Le, BR 151
Money: devaluation and shortages of, OR 10, 30-33, 148; variety of, OR 68-73
Monitor, BL *18,* FO 85, 124-125, 128, *129;* characteristics and armament, BL *52-53,* 62, 108; construction, BL 46, 49, 52-53; *Merrimac,* battle with, BL *58-59,* 60, *61,* 62-65, *74-75;* seaworthiness, BL 57-58; sinking, BL *64,* 65
Monitors, AP *44-45,* 48; in blockade service, BL 87. *See also* Ironclads
Monks, Walter G., SP 140

Captain Obediah Taylor of the 3rd Missouri Confederate Regiment

KI The Killing Ground; LE Lee Takes Command; MI War on the Mississippi; NA The Nation Reunited; OR Confederate Ordeal; RE Rebels Resurgent; SH The Road to Shiloh; SM Sherman's March; SP Spies, Scouts and Raiders; TE The Struggle for Tennessee; TR Death in the Trenches; TT Tenting Tonight; YA Twenty Million Yankees

89

The daring Confederate raider Colonel John Singleton Mosby, leading a nighttime scout behind enemy lines

Monocacy, Battle of, FL *map* 80, *82*
Monocacy Junction, FL 73, 101
Monocacy River, FL 71, 73, 74
Monongahela, CO 145, 151-154
Monopolies, growth of, YA 78-79
Monroe, John T., CO 68, *69*, 73-75
Monroe, Louisiana, MI 16
Monroe Doctrine defied, OR 162
Monroe's Crossroads, Georgia, SM 55
Montague, Samuel, NA *84-85*
Montauk, AS 136, 137, 139, 141, CO 114, 118
Monterey, Mexico, DE 25
Montfort, E. R., RE 131
Montgomery, Alabama, BR 130, *134,* FO 8, OR 27; capital moved from, FI 18; patriotic demonstrations in, FI 10
Montgomery, J. R., letter of, KI *83*
Montgomery, James, SP 144
Montgomery, James E., MI 20
Montgomery, L. M., MI 153
Montgomery, Richard. *See* Thompson, James
Montgomery, William, AP *141*
Montgomery Hill, SM 129, 135
Montreal, Canada, AS 20, 27, 109
Mooney, Thomas H., TT *146-147*
Moon Lake, MI 75
Moor, Augustus, BD 26-27, 45, FL 30, 31, 33, 39, 46-48, 51
Moore, Absalom B., TE 87
Moore, Alexander, RE *116*
Moore, Henry, photographs by, CO *40-45*
Moore, J. H., RE 63-65
Moore, John C., CH 133, MI 40-41
Moore, John W., CO 168
Moore, Marinda B., OR 58
Moore, Sally, OR 91
Moore, Samuel P., SM *106*, 108
Moore, Thomas Overton, CO 54
Moore, W. H., MI 42
Moore, William, FR 17
Moorefield, West Virginia, DE 148, FL 91, SP 126
Morale: civilian, MI 83, 125, 139-140, 151, OR 10, 51-52, 59-60, 74-75, 77, 80, 86-89, 95, 110, 148, 150-151; Confederate, DE 46, 55-58, RE 50, 128; Confederate Army, MI 125-126, 152; military, OR 77, 79, 86, 160; national, YA 20-21, 87-89, 95, 135, 142-143, 146-149, 153, 158; survey of, SH 8; of troops, SH 34, 49; Union, RE 92, 95, 100, 102, 112, 140; Union Army, MI 17, 40, 76-77, 129. *See also* Morale and Motivation
Morale and motivation: in Confederate Army, TT 22, 26; in Union Army, TT 20, 24, 37, 68, 150. *See also* Discipline; Morale; Punishments
Moran, Benjamin, BL 114-118, 127
Mordecai, Alfred, FO *15*
Morehead City, North Carolina, CO 37, 87
Morell, George, BD 129, LE 36, 43, 146, 151

Morell, George W., FO 133
Morgan, CO 143, 151
Morgan, Albert T., NA 64-65
Morgan, Charles, RE 85
Morgan, Charles D., BL 21
Morgan, Charles H., BR *144*
Morgan, George W., TE 21, 41, 43, 44, 47
Morgan, George Washington, MI 63, 66
Morgan, J. P., NA 88
Morgan, James, BL 98
Morgan, James D., AP 71, 72, 73
Morgan, John Hunt, CH 20, 25, TE 21, *22-23*, 26, *27*, 91, *92*, TT 67, 124; detached for special service, TE 92; at Gallatin, TE 49; at Hartsville, TE 85, 87; marriage, TE 90; promotion, TE 90; raid on Nashville, TE 84; at Tompkinsville, TE 24
Morgan, John Pierpont, YA *79*
Morgan, Samuel Dodd, TE *88*
Morgan, Sarah, OR 43, 60, *96*, 98, 103-104, 106, 109
Morgan, William, FI 120
Morgantown, West Virginia, FI *92*
Mormons, FR 107, 108, 111, 112, 113
Morphine, SM 106
Morrill, Justin Smith, YA 58
Morrill, Lot M., NA 92-93
Morris, Charles, BL 150
Morris, Clara, AS 60
Morris, Dwight, BD 96
Morris, George, BL *54*, 55-56
Morris, Lewis O., KI *170*
Morris, O. D., MI 130
Morris, Orlando H., KI 160
Morris, Thomas, FI 85-86, 88-89, 92
Morris Island, BL 88, 111, BR 127, 137, *139-141*, 146, 151-152, CO *98-103*, *map* 113, 118-129, *map* 130-131, *132-133*, 134-135, *136-137*, 138-139
Morrison, James T., TE 27, 29
Morrison, Joseph, RE 138
Morristown, Missouri, SP 144
Morristown, Tennessee, TT 9
Morrow, Henry A., AP *30-31*
Morse, BL 25
Morse, Charles F., LE 108
Mortar boats, CO 57-58, *59*, 61, 64-67, *70*, 73, 157-158; at Island No. 10, SH *158-159*
Mortars, FO *104;* improvised, MI 136, *154*
Mortar schooners, MI 24, 162
Morton, John W., TE 97
Morton, Oliver, TE 24
Morton, Oliver P., AS 53
Morton's Light Artillery (Tennessee), TE 97
Mosby, John Singleton, AS 39, 115, FL 42, 43, *44-45*, 159, LE 98-99, SP 114, *117*, 120, 126; at Aldie, SP 121, *128-129;* background, SP 115; capture of, SP 116; and Confederate Army, SP 115-116; and Coquette (horse), SP *130-131;* and Gettysburg Campaign, SP 119, 122; portraits, SP *132-139;* and railroads, SP

122, 130-131; and Sheridan, FL 135-136; and Stoughton, SP 117-119; strategy and tactics of, SP 127-128; and supply train attack, FL 26, 104, *106-107;* wounding of, SP 131
Mosby's Confederacy, SP 2, 127
Moses, Franklin J., Jr., NA 66, 119
Mosher, CO *4*, 68
Motivation. *See* Morale and motivation
Mott, Gershom, KI 70-71, 80, 91-92, TR 50, 52, 97-98, 107
Mott, Lucretia, BR 67
Mott, Thaddeus, NA 154
Moulton, Albert, CO 42
Moultrieville, South Carolina, BR 121
Mound Battery, CO 158-159, *160-161*
Mound City, SH 59
Mound City naval station, SH *68-69*, 74
Mound City Sharp's Rifle Guards (Kansas), SP 144. *See also* Kansas troops, 7th Cavalry Regiment
Mountain House, BD 47, DE *8*
Mountain road, KI 118-119
Mount Crawford, Virginia, FL 42, 45
Mount Jackson, Virginia, DE 65, 82-83, 115, 157, 170, FL 28, 30, 39, *138*, 158
Mount Pleasant, Tennessee, SM 83
Mount Solon, Virginia, DE 114-115
Mouton, Jean Jacques Alexandre Alfred, FR 56, 57, 59
Mower, Joseph A., AP *54*, 75, FR 53, 54, 70, 71
Mowry, James, YA 66
Mudd, George, AS 111, 154
Mudd, John J., MI 62
Mudd, Samuel A., AS 21, 68, *109*, 114; arrest of, AS 110-111; imprisonment, AS 160-161; sets Booth's leg, AS 105-106; trial of, AS 145, 148, 154, *156*, 158
Mudd, Mrs. Samuel A., AS 106
Muddy River, Kentucky, SH 54
Mudge, Charles, GE *154*
Mud in camps, TT 45
"Mud march," RE 95, *96-97*
Muffly, Joseph, KI 148
Muggins, Pete, AS 10
Muldoon, Arthur, CO 167
Mules, OR 26, 29
Mule Shoe, KI 89-94, 96, 98, 101, 104-105, 125
Mullen, Bernard F., TE 153
Mulligan, James A., FL *91*
Mumford, William B., CO 75-76
Mumma (Samuel) farm, BD 67, 76, 80, 82-83, 93, 97, *102*, 103, *112-113*, 140-141
Munch's Battery, SH *130*
Mundy, Sue. *See* Clark, Marcellus
Munford, Thomas T., AP 87-88, 91, 118-120, BD 53, *54*, 55, DE 99, FL *141*, GE 27-28
Munfordville, Kentucky, TE 51, 55
Munson, John M., CH *75*
Munson's Hill, Virginia, FO 39
Murders, TT 65
Murfreesboro, Tennessee, CH *map* 2, 19,

AP Pursuit to Appomattox; AS The Assassination; AT Battles for Atlanta; BD The Bloodiest Day; BL The Blockade; BR Brother against Brother; CH The Fight for Chattanooga; CO The Coastal War; DE Decoying the Yanks; FI First Blood; FL The Shenandoah in Flames; FO Forward to Richmond; FR War on the Frontier; GE Gettysburg;

Lieutenant Guy V. Henry's battery of U.S. Artillery on Morris Island, South Carolina

22, 23, 25, 80, SH 98-99, SM 83, 125, TE 25, 26, *30-31,* 50, 83, 85, 88, *93, 111, 160;* conditions in after Stones River, TE 142; courthouse, TE *93;* Union army at, CH 18, 21
Murphy, Robert C., MI 36, 60-62
Murray, William H., GE *154*
Murrell, Thomas, SM *84*
Music, OR 52-54
Musical instruments, FO *54-61,* TT 67. *See also* Bugles; Drummers
Musicians, CO *43,* DE *41,* 70, *132,* FO *13, 54-55,* 57, 59, 99, MI *128-129,* TT *26,* 66, 128. *See also* Bands; Buglers; Drummers; Fifers
Muskets and rifles, FO *100-101;* ammunition improvised, SH 21; ammunition loads, FI 50, *52;* ammunition shortages, SH 51; effect on tactics, FI 48-50; Enfield rifle, OR 18, *64-65;* excessive loading, FI 52; loading and firing procedure, FI 48-50, *52-53;* models and modifications, FI *50-51;* models used, FI *70-71;* production and procurement, OR 17, 23; range and effectiveness, FI 50, 71. *See also* Carbines
Musters. *See* Recruitment
Mutinies, TT 85-86
Myer, Albert J., RE 42, *44-45,* SP 44, 45, 64, *68*
Myers, Abraham C., OR 25-26
Myrick, Andrew J., FR 77, *78*
Myrick, John D., SM 21

N

Nags Head, North Carolina, CO 21, 30
Nahant, BL *108-111,* CO 118
Nansemond River, BL 46
Nantucket, CO 118
Napoleon Bonaparte, influence on tactics, FI 48-50, 54
Napoleon cannon, GE *127,* OR 22, SM 130-132, TE *134-135,* 145
Napoleon III, BL 120, 125, 128, 155, FO 21, FR *38,* 40, 42, 44, 47. *See also* France
Nasby, Petroleum Vesuvius, AS 76
Nash, Charles, hat of, KI *57*
Nashville, BL *144-145,* CO 114
Nashville, Battle of, SM 126-144, *map* 131, TT 32; artillery bombardment at, SM 135; assault on Overton Hill, SM 135-136, 142; attack on Shy's Hill, SM 138-139, *140-141;* casualties at, SM 144; civilian spectators at, SM 128; Confederate flank breaks, SM 139-142; Confederate fortifications at, SM 125, 130, *132,* 137; Confederates regroup at end of first day's action, SM 133-134; Confederate withdrawal and rearguard action, SM 142-144; Lee rallies troops at,

SM 142; storming redoubts at, SM 130-*132,* 133; Thomas' plan of attack, SM 126, 134-135; Union rear-echelon troops at, SM *128 129;* winter storm before battle, SM 123-124
Nashville, Tennessee, AT 24, CH 168, NA 50, 121, SM *map* 2-3, 17, 34, 44, 82, 84, TE 21, *69-79,* TT *106;* armorer for western Confederacy, TE 88, 89; base for Federal operations, TE 81, 159; battle at, OR 158-160; capture by Union Army, TE 68; casualties removed to, after Stones River, TE 142-143; civil disorders in, SH 98-99; civil law and order, TE 81; Confederate evacuation, SH 97-98; convention, BR 43; living conditions in, TE 70; munitions produced at, OR 22; Rosecrans' headquarters, TE *70;* state capitol, SM *124;* State Capitol building, TE *70, 72-73;* steamboats at, TE 68-69, as supply base, TE 13, 15; strategic and political value of, SH 9, 53-54, 79, 84; supply base, SM 14; theater, TE 68; Union fortifications at, SM 120, *124;* Union occupation of, SH 98-99, *100-101,* 104, 140; Union supply base, CH 30, 97, 165; use of slave labor for Union fortifications, TE 72
Nashville & Chattanooga Railroad, CH 18, 29, 33, 97, 171, TE 25, 76
Nashville & Louisville Railroad, TE 91
Nashville *Daily Press,* TE 70
Nashville Pike, TE 92, 94, 98, 117, 124, 126, 127, 133, 145, 152, *162-163*
Nassau, as blockade-runners' port, BL 21, 86-88, 90, 93, 95-98, *99,* 100, 121
Nast, Thomas, BL 143, NA 110, *128,* 132, *138;* cartoons by, NA *128-139;* engravings by, SP 76-77; paintings by, AP *146,* SM *56-57*
Natchez, OR 106
Natchez, Mississippi, MI 18, OR *159*
Natchitoches, Louisiana, FR 54, 67
Nation, The, NA 73, 108, 127, 140, 156
National debt, YA 59
National Hotel, AS *22,* 24, 41, *42,* 53, 59, 67, 68, 72, 110
National Intelligencer, AS 71
National Republican, NA 155
National Road, BD *map* 23, 44, 47, 51
National Union Party, NA 54, YA 153, 159. *See also* Union Party
Nations, Reuben, SM *33*
Natural Bridge, DE *14-15*
Naugatuck, FO 128
Navajo Indians, FR 20, 118-*120, 121-*122
Naval Academy, United States, BL 22
Naval actions, FO 85, 93
Naval gunfire support. *See* Gunboats
Naval-gun production, OR 22
Navy, Confederate States. *See* Confederate Navy
Navy, United States. *See* United States Navy
Navy Yard, AS *23,* 136, *141*

Navy Yard Bridge, AS 20, 72, 104, *106-107,* 108
Neal, Ralph J., CH 134
Neal, W., SM *41*
Nebraska Territory Act, BR 71
Neeley, Temple, NA 36
Neese, George, BD 53, DE 48
Neff, Neal, SM 38-*39*
Negley, James Scott, CH *38,* 39, 42, 45, 46, 47, 49, 53, 55, 56, 63, 84, TE 21, 98, 99, 119, 122, 124, 127, 150, 154, *155*
Nelson, Lord, CO 24
Nelson, William (Bull), FL *15,* SH 116, 140-141, 144, TE 31, 32, 45, 47, 48, 54; shot by Davis, TE *56*
Nemaha, SM *155*
Neosho, FR 66-67
Neosho, Missouri, SH 33
Netherlands, the, immigrants from, YA 21
Neuse River, CO *33,* 34-36, 84-87, 91-94, 97
Newark *Evening Journal,* YA 29
New Bern, North Carolina, BL 21, 87, OR *50, 120;* armament and fortifications, CO 35; casualties, CO 37; ground operations, CO 36-37, 84-87, *88-89,* 90-92, *map* 93, 95-97; joint operations, CO 17, 19, *33,* 34-35, *36,* 37; naval operations, CO 87, 91-92, *map* 93, 94, 96-97; as staging area, CO 35
New Bridge, LE 24, 31, 36, 49
Newby, Dangerfield, BR 88
New Carthage, Louisiana, MI 84-86
New Cold Harbor, Virginia, LE 37
Newcomb, Edgar, BD 169
Newcomb, James P., OR 75
New England Freedman's Aid Society, OR 142
Newenham, William, TR *63*
New Era, SH 73
Newhall, Frederic C., AP 108, 122
New Hampshire: policy on blacks, YA 35; typical farm, YA 22
New Hampshire troops, TT 33; at Bull Run, FI 137, 155; 2nd Infantry Regiment, FI 137, LE 148-149, TT 22, 71; 3rd Infantry Regiment, BL 34, CO *40-45,* TR *28,* TT 52, 159; 5th Infantry Regiment, BD 105, 170, RE 79, 87, TT 55, 157; 6th Infantry Regiment, BD 124, KI 171; 11th Infantry Regiment, TR 46; 12th Infantry Regiment, KI 158, 164-167, TT 71; 13th Infantry Regiment, TT 85, 110, TT 33
New Hope Church, Battle of, AT 51-53; battlefield, AT *16, 17, 53*
New Inlet, BL 88, 94, 101, CO 158-159
New Ironsides, BL *19,* 51, CO 115, 118, 124, 139, 164, 169
New Jersey troops, CO 19, RE 144, *168-169,* TT 157; New Jersey Brigade, FO 21, LE 45-46, 132
  Artillery: 3rd Artillery, AP 37
  Cavalry: 1st Cavalry Regiment, DE *154,* 157, GE 19, 21, TR 26; 3rd Cavalry

Nashville's state house, fortified by its Federal occupiers with earthworks and 30-pounder Parrott Rifles

Major Samuel Duncan, 14th New Hampshire, who suffered four wounds at New Market Heights in 1864.

KI The Killing Ground; LE Lee Takes Command; MI War on the Mississippi; NA The Nation Reunited; OR Confederate Ordeal; RE Rebels Resurgent; SH The Road to Shiloh; SM Sherman's March; SP Spies, Scouts and Raiders; TE The Struggle for Tennessee; TR Death in the Trenches; TT Tenting Tonight; YA Twenty Million Yankees

91

Lieutenant William Starks, adjutant
of the 3rd New Jersey Cavalry

New Jersey troops (continued)
   Regiment, FL *108*
      Infantry: 2nd Infantry Regiment, FI
      114-115; 4th Infantry Regiment, BD 54;
      5th Infantry Regiment, FO 18-20; 7th
      Infantry Regiment, RE 145-146; 9th
      Infantry Regiment, CO 84; 11th Infantry
      Regiment, GE 145-146, *155,* KI 105;
      12th Infantry Regiment, GE *124,* TR 95;
      13th Infantry Regiment, BD *93;* 14th
      Infantry Regiment, FL 78, 81, *83;* 15th
      Infantry Regiment, RE 155; 23rd
      Infantry Regiment, RE 155; 24th
      Infantry Regiment, RE *76;* 28th Infantry
      Regiment, RE *76;* 33rd Infantry
      Regiment, AT 35; 33rd Infantry
      Regiment (Zouaves), SM *43;* 35th
      Infantry Regiment (Zouaves), SM *41*
New Kent Court House, Virginia, LE *85*
New Madrid, Missouri, LE 93, SH 32, 101,
   158-159, map 160, 164
Newman, Georgia, AT 138
New Market, Battle of, FL 2, 30-31, *map*
   32, 33-39, KI 130; cadet charge at, FL
   34, *35,* 37
New Market, Virginia, DE 84, 86, 115-116,
   120, 157, FL 17, 28, 30, 42, 45, 139, 158
New Market Heights, Battle of, TR 117,
   123-124, 138-145, *148*
New Market road, TR 70, 97, 139, 142,
   146, 148, 153
New Mexico Campaign, FR *map 2-3,* 16-37;
   Confederate retreat, FR 34-36, *37;*
   Glorieta, Battle of, FR 16, 31-32, 33;
   Peralta, Battle of, FR 34-35; Valverde,
   Battle of, FR 24-26
New Mexico statehood application, BR 43
New Mexico Territory, Indian conflicts, FR
   112-122
New Mexico troops: TT 31; state militia,
   FR 23; 1st Cavalry Regiment, FR 114,
   118; 1st Infantry Regiment, FR 16, 19,
   23-25, 29, 117; 2nd Infantry Regiment,
   FR 23, 25, 26, 27, 28, 115
New Orleans, Battle of (1815), TT 21
New Orleans, Louisiana: BL 21, 25, 87,
   CH 86, CO *map 62,* FR 46, 47, 50, SH
   101, TT 44; casualties, CO 69, 73; civil
   disorders, CO *72-73,* 74-75; cotton
   brokers, NA *122-123;* fortifications, CO
   54-55, 57, 73-74; forts seized by state, BR
   128; garrison strength, CO 73; industry,
   OR 63; legislature, NA *143;* martial law
   declared, CO 63, 74; money engraving,
   OR 69; money issue, OR *72;* munitions
   production, OR 21-22; naval operations,
   CO *map 2-3, 4,* 17, 55-59, 61, 72-75, 77,
   142; occupied by Union, CO 77, OR 96,
   114-115, SH 157; population, BR 14, CO
   54; as port, CO 54, *56-57;* port facilities,
   BR *8-9, 30;* racial violence in, NA 34, *35,*
   36, 131, 143; rams at, CO 69-72;
   security, fears for, CO 54, 63, 73;
   shipping trade, MI 16-17; strategic value,
   CO 77; surrender, CO *68-69, 72-73,*
74-77; Union assault and occupation, MI
   16-18, 24, 35, 73, 159; Union garrison,
   NA 61, 156-157
New Orleans *Bee,* OR 51
New Orleans *Crescent,* OR 51
New Orleans *Daily Crescent,* BR 24
New Orleans *Picayune,* NA 156, 157
New Orleans *Times,* NA 141
Newport, Indiana, BR *60-61*
Newport News, Virginia: BL 46, 54-55, 58,
   map 60, FI 77-78, 81
New River, DE 75, *78-79*
New River Bridge, attack at, FL 21, *22,* 23
Newspapers, MI *157,* TT 67; and
   Anderson, SP 159; cartoons on black
   enlistment in Confederate Army, AP *26;*
   on Charleston, CO 110, 115, 119;
   Congress criticized by, OR 49;
   contributions to, OR 48; criticism by, SH
   33; Davis criticized by, OR 49, 53;
   exaggerated reports by, SH *95;* freedom
   of expression, OR 49; government
   criticized by, OR 49, 53; McClellan
   criticized by, FO 14, 29, 52, 73-74,
   86-87; and military intelligence, SM 19,
   44; on Mobile Bay, CO 150; Northern
   cartoons, SM *53, 59, 135;* Northern
   concern for Sherman, SM 147;
   partisanship among, BR 84; pressure on
   Lincoln, FI 110; propaganda in, OR
   51-52; publication ceased, OR 48-49;
   raids on, YA 20, *22,* 27, 29, *30,* 108, 110;
   relations with Lincoln, YA 29-31, 40; and
   Scott's plans, FI 45; security breaches by,
   OR 49-51; Sherman, Northern criticism
   of, AP 159; Sherman and reporters, AT
   24; sources of military intelligence, SP
   46, 52; Southern reports on march, SM
   62, 68; suppression of, YA 29-31; and
   Trent Affair, BL 116-117; war reports by,
   OR *50. See also individual newspapers*
Newsprint substitutes, OR 48, *51*
Newton, John, AT 69, 71, 74, 92, 93, FO
   111, GE 74, 133, LE 95, RE 94, 96,
   153-154
Newton, Massachusetts, NA 91
Newton Station, Mississippi, MI 89-91
Newtown, Virginia, DE 71, 129, *131,* 156,
   FL 41
New Ulm, Minnesota, FR 72, 74, 80;
   attack on, FR 81, *82, 83, 86*
New Verdiersville, KI 60
New York Central Railroad, YA 65
New York City, BL *68-69, 132-139,* BR
   16-17, 114-115, FI *22-23,* TT *28-30,* YA
   4, *40-55,* 72, *90-91, 94-95,* 97, *104;* Boss
   Tweed, NA 109-110, *132-133,* 149; civil
   disorders, YA 40, 53, 103-105, *106-107,*
   108, *109,* 110; Confederate arson in, SP
   62; Confederate arson plot, AS 20, 37;
   disease and mortality rates, YA 23; draft
   riots, YA 103-105, *106-107,* 108, *109,*
   110; housing, YA 48, *50-51;* industrial
   expansion, YA 45; life styles, YA 23, 45;
   Lincoln funeral procession, AS *121-123;*
patriotic demonstrations in, FI 10, 23,
   32-33; population, BR 16, YA 40; port
   facilities, BR *31;* prostitution in, TT
   60-61; recreation, YA *52-55;* recruitment,
   YA 40, 45; relief work in, YA *134-135,*
   137-139; shantytowns, NA *89;* shipping
   industry, YA *42-43;* slums, YA *50-51;*
   South, trade with, YA 40, 43, 56
New York *Daily News,* YA 29
New York Evening Post, OR 129, YA 151
New York Fire Zouaves, FI *59,* 61, 64,
   141, *142,* 143-144, *153, 160-163*
New York Gold Room, NA *108*
New York *Herald,* AP 58, BL 136, CH 81,
   CO 115, FI 10, KI 22, NA 67, SM 45,
   SP 52, YA 70, 76-77, 144; front page,
   AS *101*
New York *Illustrated News,* TE 56, 100, TT
   67, YA 89, 92
New York *Post,* YA 87
New York State: civil disorders, YA 40, 53,
   103-110; industrial resources of, FI 46;
   population growth, YA 22; slavery
   abolished in, YA 40
New York Stock Exchange, NA 106, 125
New York *Sun,* YA 65
New York Times, The, BD 65, BL 115-116,
   CO 161, DE 153, FI 10, 153, MI 134,
   NA 110, 152, OR 16, SP 52, TR 139,
   YA 64, 72, 86-87, 105, 144, 146
New York *Tribune,* AS 150, BD 70, BR 18,
   78, 101, CO 30, 110, 115, FI 63-64, FO
   11, 62, 74, 87, FR 74, 148, MI 134, NA
   26, 34, 54, 63, 78, 85, 107, 111, 117,
   123, 134, 156, SH 78, SP 52, YA *35,* 37,
   57, 77, 98, 108; criticism of Scott's plans,
   FI 45
New York troops, AP 85, 90, CO 19, 170,
   GE 73; at Big Bethel, FI 80-82, *84-86;* at
   Bull Run, FI 116, 118, 120-121, 141,
   142, 143-145, *148, 153, 156-157, 160-163,*
   168-169; Excelsior Brigade, FO *165,*
   GE 104; German Brigade, DE 164;
   German units, TT 29; in invasion of
   Virginia, FI *59*-61, 64, *114-115;* prisoners
   lost, FI *154*
      Artillery: 1st Artillery, TR 152; Battery
      B, 1st Artillery (Rorty), GE 135, KI 64;
      Battery D, 1st Artillery (Winslow), RE
      124-125; Battery I, 1st Artillery
      (Wiedrich), GE 117; 1st Battery (Cowan),
      1st Artillery Regiment, GE *120-121,* 135,
      140, TR *46-47;* 1st Light Artillery
      Regiment, RE *117;* 2nd Heavy Artillery
      Regiment, KI 108, TT 81; 4th Battery
      (Smith), GE 81, 85-87; 4th Heavy
      Artillery, TR 43, 50; 5th Heavy Artillery,
      FL 47; 6th Artillery Battery (Bramhall),
      FO 109; 6th Battery (Martin), GE 22; 7th
      Heavy Artillery, KI *158-159,* 170, TR 45;
      8th Heavy Artillery, KI 161, 171; 9th
      Heavy Artillery, FL 74, *83;* 10th Heavy
      Artillery, FL *127;* 12th Battery, TR 109;
      13th Heavy Artillery, AP *111;* 14th
      Heavy Artillery, AP 36, TR 76

AP Pursuit to Appomattox; AS The Assassination; AT Battles for Atlanta; BD The Bloodiest Day; BL The Blockade; BR Brother against
Brother; CH The Fight for Chattanooga; CO The Coastal War; DE Decoying the Yanks; FI First Blood; FL The Shenandoah in Flames;
FO Forward to Richmond; FR War on the Frontier; GE Gettysburg;

Cavalry: 1st Cavalry Regiment, FL 27, 28, 29, 42, 46, SP 114; 4th Cavalry Regiment, RE 108; 8th Cavalry Regiment, BD 56, 58, GE 16; 10th Cavalry Regiment, AP 126; 12th Cavalry Regiment, AP 65, TT 119-120; 13th Cavalry Regiment, AS 110, SP *120-121;* 15th Cavalry Regiment, AP 135; 16th Cavalry Regiment, AS 132, 133, *134-135;* 24th Cavalry Regiment, TT 122, *125;* Independent Company Oneida Cavalry, AP *8-9*

Engineers: 15th Engineer Regiment, FO 20-21, RE 51, *166-167;* 50th Volunteer Engineer Regiment, AP *22, 23,* KI *138-139,* RE 35, 50-51, TT 68

Infantry: 1st Infantry Regiment, FI 80; 2nd Infantry Regiment, FI 80, *86,* YA *97;* 3rd Infantry Regiment, FI 80-82; 4th Infantry Regiment, RE 38, 72, 77; 5th Infantry Regiment (Duryee's Zouaves), BD 164, FI 80, *81, 82, 84-85,* FO 69, KI 170, LE 22, 37-39, 42, 75, 83, *85, 86, 87, 88-89,* 145, 153, 155, *158,* RE *31,* 54, 91, 95, 101, *120-121,* TR *106-107,* TT 60, 101; 6th Infantry Regiment, TT 63; 7th Militia (Infantry) Regiment, FI *22-23,* 26, *28,* 29, 55, 59, 80, YA *90-91,* *109,* 110; 9th Infantry Regiment (Zouaves), BD 49, *121, 132,* 133-138, CO 27, *28-29,* 30, 34, RE 41; 10th Infantry Regiment (Zouaves), FL 160, LE *150-151,* 153, 155; 11th Infantry Regiment (Fire Zouaves), FI 59, 61, 64, 141, *142, 143-144, 153, 160-163,* GE *124,* TT *114,* YA 108; 12th Infantry Regiment, RE *115;* 12th Militia (Infantry) Regiment, FI *42-43,* 118, 120-121; 14th Brooklyn Chasseurs (Infantry) Regiment, BD 74, FI 141, *142,* 143, *168-169,* GE 50, *155;* 14th Infantry Regiment, FO 133; 16th Infantry Regiment, LE 41, 45, *54-55;* 17th Infantry Regiment, AT 149, FO *36-37, 132-133;* 20th Infantry Regiment, RE 158; 20th State Militia Infantry, LE *145,* 153, 170; 21st Infantry Regiment, LE 142, 154; 22nd Militia Infantry Regiment, BD *34-35,* TT *18-19;* 23rd Infantry Regiment, FI *114-115;* 24th Infantry Regiment, LE 137, 154; 25th Infantry Regiment, FO 133; 28th Infantry Regiment, LE 105, 107, NA 168; 34th Infantry Regiment, BD *87,* 89, RE 101; 37th Infantry Regiment, FO *125;* 38th Infantry Regiment, FI 145, RE 95; 39th Infantry Regiment (Garibaldi Guards), DE *154,* FI *96-97;* 40th Infantry Regiment, FO 166; 41st Infantry Regiment, LE *130-131,* RE 130; 42nd Infantry (Tammany) Regiment, FO 44-45, 47-48, 50-51, GE *121,* 141, 142; 44th Infantry Regiment (Ellsworth's Avengers), FI 68, TR 51, TT 83, 94-95; 45th Infantry Regiment, RE 130; 46th

Infantry Regiment, CO 111; 48th Infantry Regiment, CO *52-53,* 127; 51st Infantry Regiment, BD 125-126, *127-129,* CO 27-30, LE 163; 52nd Infantry Regiment, BD *101,* TT 113, 115, 122; 53rd Infantry Regiment, TT *41;* 54th Infantry Regiment, RE 130; 55th Infantry Regiment, FO 140, TT 30; 57th Infantry Regiment, FO 159, KI 171, RE 100, TT *100-101;* 59th Infantry Regiment, AP 131, BD 90; 60th Infantry Regiment, GE *112-113,* LE 111, *121,* TT 147; 61st Infantry Regiment, BD 102, FO *94-95,* 161, 164, LE 71, TR 109-*111,* TT 162; 63rd Infantry Regiment, TT 110; 64th Infantry Regiment, BD 102, FO 161; 65th Infantry Regiment, FL *128;* 66th Infantry Regiment, GE *155,* KI 160; 68th Infantry Regiment, DE *155;* 69th Infantry Regiment, BD 100, FO *162-163,* RE 87, YA 96, *97;* 69th Militia (Infantry) Regiment (Irish), FI *60-61,* 108, TT *28-29, 146-147;* 71st Infantry Regiment, FI *156-157,* FO *165;* 76th Infantry Regiment, LE 141; 77th Infantry Regiment, KI 29, 153, RE 141; 79th Infantry Regiment (Highlanders), BD 131, CH 107-108, 113, *119,* DE 137, FI 116, *137,* 145, FO 16-17, LE 167, TT 30; 88th Infantry Regiment, FO 162-163, RE 74; 89th Infantry Regiment, RE 53; 93rd Infantry Regiment, BD *158-159;* 95th Infantry Regiment, GE 50; 97th Infantry Regiment, BD 70, GE 55; 102nd Infantry Regiment, BD 83, GE *112-113;* 103rd Infantry Regiment, BD 66; 104th Infantry Regiment, TT 71; 106th Infantry Regiment, FL 79, KI 170; 107th Infantry Regiment, SM 62, *63;* 108th Infantry Regiment, BD 97-99, KI 82; 112th Infantry Regiment, KI 171; 114th Infantry Regiment, FL *130;* 115th Infantry Regiment, BD 43, 59; 117th Infantry Regiment, TR *28;* 120th Infantry Regiment, GE 104; 121st Infantry Regiment, KI 91, RE 155; 123rd Infantry Regiment, AP 53-54, AT 52, 63, 92, RE 151; 124th Infantry Regiment, AP 41, 151, GE 85, *87,* KI 98, RE 142-143; 125th Infantry Regiment, BD 56, GE *154;* 126th Infantry Regiment, BD 42-43, GE 139; 127th Infantry Regiment, TT 147; 128th Infantry Regiment, TT 80; 136th Infantry Regiment, NA 64; 137th Infantry Regiment, SM *42;* 140th Infantry Regiment (Zouaves), GE 83-85, KI 63-65, 67; 141st Infantry Regiment, RE 162; 143rd Infantry Regiment, AT 96; 146th Infantry Regiment (Zouaves), KI 63-67, 170, RE 72; 147th Infantry Regiment, AP 30, GE 50; 149th Infantry Regiment, CH 93, 130, 131, GE *155;* 150th Infantry Regiment, NA 11; 151st Infantry Regiment, FL *129;* 154th

Infantry Regiment, AT *34,* GE 151, *155,* RE 133; 156th Infantry Regiment, FL 135; 160th Infantry Regiment, FL 147; 164th Infantry Regiment (Zouaves), KI 161, *164,* 171, SP *104,* TT *17, 61;* 165th Infantry Regiment (Zouaves), FL *130,* NA *164;* 169th Infantry Regiment, KI 171; 111th Infantry Regiment, GE *124,* KI 66, 171, TT 37, *41,* 122, 128; 170th Infantry Regiment, KI *136-137;* 185th Infantry Regiment, AP *141;* Irish Brigade, BD 63, 99-100, 170, FO *162-163,* 165, GE *100,* 101, 148
New York *World,* OR 157
Ney, Michel, FR *44-45*
Niagara, BL 24
Niagara, Pennsylvania, TT 150
Niagara Falls, BL *140*
Niblo's Garden, YA 53
Nichols, Charles H., AS 151
Nichols, G. W., FL 145
Nichols, George Ward, AP 52, 55, 58
Nicodemus (Jacob) farm, BD 68, 76
Nicodemus Heights, BD 88
Nicolay, John, FO 71, 85, YA 162
Nightingale, Florence, TT 98, YA 120
Nina (doll), SP *45*
Nine Mile Road, LE 31
Nisbet, James C., AT 71, 90, *106*
Niter production, OR 19-20
Nix, F. M., TE 24
Nix, Jacob, FR 81
No. 290, BL 120-121
Noe brothers, AT 149
Nolensville, Tennnessee, TE 97
Nolensville Pike, SM 121, 125, TE 93
Noncommissioned officers, TT 49
Norfolk, Virginia, BL 21, 46, CO 19, *96,* FO 81, 85, 89, 124-125, OR 131, TR 8. *See also* Gosport Navy Yard
Norfolk & Petersburg Railroad, TR 19, 35, 39, 41, 48, 50, 53
Norris, William, SP 46, *47,* 57; background, SP 47-50; as spymaster, SP 51, 52, 63
North: debt and inflation, NA 124-125; immigration in, NA 77, 78, 89, 91, 127; industry in, NA 25, 78, *79;* political divisions in, NA 16, 18; racial attitudes in, NA 70-72, 76, 156
North, James H., BL 125-126, 128
North Anna River, KI *138-147,* RE 33, 36, TR 21, 22, 69; action at, KI *map 2-3,* 133-137
North Anna River, Battle of, TR 16
North Atlantic Blockading Squadron, BL 24, 46
North Carolina: blockade running by, OR 76; educational system, OR 55; guerrillas in, OR 89, 91-92; and habeas corpus suspension, OR 154; joins Confederacy, BL 11, FI 10, 18; money issues, OR *72-73;* newspapers, OR 48; provisional government in, NA 32;

Colonel Noah Farnham, 11th New York Fire Zouaves, mortally wounded at First Bull Run

A mounted officer of the 12th New York (3 months) Regiment in camp near Washington, D.C., in 1861

KI The Killing Ground; LE Lee Takes Command; MI War on the Mississippi; NA The Nation Reunited; OR Confederate Ordeal; RE Rebels Resurgent; SH The Road to Shiloh; SM Sherman's March; SP Spies, Scouts and Raiders; TE The Struggle for Tennessee; TR Death in the Trenches; TT Tenting Tonight; YA Twenty Million Yankees

93

Lieutenant Alexander H. Shotwell of the 34th North Carolina, mortally wounded at Frazier's Farm, in 1862

Color Guard of the 43rd Ohio Volunteers, XVI Corps, Army of the Tennessee

North Carolina (continued)
railroads, OR 27; readmission to Union, NA 69; refugees in, OR 121; secession by, BR 3; slave emigration from, OR 131; subversion in, OR 154; textile industry, OR 25; Union control of, OR *map* 152-153, 167; Union operations in, AP 66-77, 155-160; Union settlers in, NA 64; violence in, NA 98; weapons procurement, OR 22
North Carolina troops, AP 36, 88, 125, 133, BD 39, 45, 81-82, CO 84, FL 150, FO 133, GE 53, 116, KI 32-34, 65, 100, 115, RE 145, TT 31, 156; Junior Reserves, AP 65, 66, *73;* militia, CO 90-91
   Artillery: 1st Battalion, AP *30,* 131; Starr's Battery, AP 75; Williams' Battery, AP 132
   Cavalry: 1st Cavalry Regiment, BD 17, KI 65; 2nd Cavalry Regiment, GE 22
   Infantry: 1st Infantry Battalion, CO 34; 1st Infantry Regiment, FI 79-80, KI 64; 2nd Infantry Battalion, CO 21; 2nd Infantry Regiment, BD 103; 3rd Infantry Regiment, KI 64; 4th Infantry Regiment, BD 101, RE 147; 5th Infantry Regiment, FO 113, TT 26-28; 10th Infantry Regiment, CO 169; 11th Infantry Regiment, KI 74; 12th Infantry Regiment, BD *46-47,* FL 82; 13th Infantry Regiment, BD 47, GE *154,* RE 144; 18th Infantry Regiment, LE *63,* RE 138; 20th Infantry Regiment, RE 41; 21st Infantry Regiment, GE 117; 23rd Infantry Regiment, BD *46-47,* 50, FL 74, *123,* GE 54-55; 24th Infantry Regiment, RE 73; 26th Infantry Regiment, CO 37, FO *57,* GE 61-62, TR 108; 27th Infantry Regiment, BD 103-104, 108; 28th Infantry Regiment, GE *150;* 30th Infantry Regiment, RE *106;* 31st Infantry Regiment, CO 92, 124; 32nd Infantry Regiment, CO 88; 33rd Infantry Regiment, CO 37, KI 74; 35th Infantry Regiment, BD 127, CO 37; 43rd Infantry Regiment, FL *123;* 44th Infantry Regiment, TR 108; 47th Infantry Regiment, TR 108; 49th Infantry Regiment, AP 35, 90; 51st Infantry Regiment, CO 124; 52nd Infantry Regiment, KI 156; 53rd Infantry Regiment, AT 93, 102, *103-107;* 55th Infantry Regiment, GE 49-50; 57th Infantry Regiment, AP 35, GE 117; 61st Infantry Regiment, TR 88; 64th Infantry Regiment, OR 88, 91
North Chickamauga Creek, CH 121
Northern Central Railroad, YA 73
Northern lights, RE 89
Northern Pacific Railroad, NA 125
Northern states: abolitionist movement in, BR 30, 34-35, 38-39, 40-41, 46-47, 62-69, 70-76; agricultural production, BR *20-21;*

and blacks' equality, BR *100;* disdain for, OR 10, 51, 58-59, 110, 112; and Dred Scott ruling, BR 105; economic dependence on, OR 17, 25-26, 29; economic dependence on South, BR 9, 32-33; economic and industrial capacity, BR 18-19, 29, 101; emigration from, BR *32,* 74-75; and Fort Sumter, BR 127-128, 135, 147; and fugitive slaves, BR 46-47; investments in South, BR 32-33; and John Brown, BR 78, 89, 109; militia musters by, BR 84; munitions supply from, OR 17; population, BR 16, 35; railroad-track mileage, OR 26; relations with South, BR 28-29; and secessionist movement, BR 27-28, 118; and slavery extension, BR 42-43, 71-76, 98, 101, 104-105, 110; Southern economic dependence on, BR 9, 32-33, 35-37; states remaining in Union, BR *map* 2-3. *See also* United States
North Fork of the Shenandoah, FL 17, 30, 141
North River, FL 42; operations around, DE 158-160, 165, *map* 169
Northrop, Lucius, AP 25
Northrup, Theodore F., AP *71*
North Star, The, BR 64
North Woods, BD 66-68
Norton, Ambrose D., AT 56
Norton, Edward, SP 56-57
Norton, Henry, BD 58
Norton, Oliver, TE 24, TT 49, 157
Norwich University Cadets, FI *102*
Nothey, John, AS 157
Nottoway River, TR 115
Noyes, George F., BD 150
Nugent, James H., FL *91*
Nullification doctrine, BR 37-38
Nuns as nurses, TT 98
Nurses, OR 60, TT 78, *93-95, 97,* 98, *106,* YA 116, 126-131, *132,* 133

O

Oakey, Daniel, SM 44, 45, 53
Oak Grove, Virginia, LE 31
Oak Hill, GE 44-45, 53
Oak Ridge, GE 44, 52-59
Oak Ridge Cemetery, AS *130*
Oates, William C., CH 65, 90, 91, 92, GE 68, 77, 80-81, *81,* 83-84, KI 165, 167, TR *98*
Oatley, William, TT *43*
O'Bannon, Mrs., SP 125
O'Beirne, James R., AS 114
O'Brien, Henry, YA *106,* 108
Occoquan Creek, RE 36
Occupation: area of Union control, OR 29, 51, 96, 98, 148, *map* 152-153, 167-168; behavior under, OR 111-112, *114-116,* 159; living conditions under, OR *120, 122. See also* Baton Rouge

Ocmulgee, BL 149, 152
Ocmulgee River, AT 138
Oconee River, BR *14-15,* SM 63
O'Connor, Edgar, LE *139*
O'Connor, John, YA 98
O'Connor, Michael P., BR 138
Octorara, CO 145
Officer candidates, TT 48-49
Officers: assaults on, TT 65; blacks commissioned, TT 33; disrespect toward, TT 65; election of, TT 22, 48; examinations for, TT 48-49; foreigners commissioned, TT 29; ineptness among, TT 53; joining Confederacy, TT 21; leadership by, TT 157; training programs, TT 52-53
Ogeechee River, CO 114, SM 63, 68, 146, 147, 148, 150, *154*
Oglesby, Richard, AS 76
Oglethorpe, Georgia, OR 59
Ohio: disloyalty in, YA 23-27, 29; and recruits for Union Army, SM 47; strategic value of, FI 16, 44-45, 76; volunteer response in, TE 25. *See also* Vallandigham, Clement L.
Ohio and Mississippi Railroad, FO 12
Ohio River, TE *36-37;* impressed steamboats for defense of, TE 32; strategic value of, SH 8, 11, *34-41,* 46, 54; as trade route, YA 24
Ohio State Journal, NA 155
Ohio State Penitentiary, TT 124
Ohio troops, AT 61, BD *32-33,* 42, 45, *46-47,* 122, 137, DE 170, FL 39, 81, FO 12, MI *92,* SM 129, TE *10-11, 156-157, 164-165,* TT 52; on Andrews' raid, SP 111; German units, TT 29; Guthrie Grays, FI 36-37; Ohio Brigade, LE 159; training program, FI 87; Union Light Guard, AS 12; in western Virginia operations, FI 85-93
   Artillery: 1st Artillery Regiment, RE 135; 1st Battery, BD 47; 1st Light Artillery, FI *54;* 2nd Heavy Artillery, CH *152;* 5th Light Artillery (Hickenlooper), SH *124-125,* 126, 135; 11th Battery, MI 37; 14th Battery, AT 99; 19th Battery, AT 64
   Cavalry: 5th Cavalry Regiment, SM *36;* 6th Cavalry Regiment, RE *110;* 11th Cavalry Regiment, FR 107, *111, 132*
   Infantry: 3rd Infantry Regiment, TE 12, 124, 144, TT 152; 4th Infantry Regiment, KI 154, RE *76;* 8th Infantry Regiment, BD 96, 103, GE 138, RE 54, 76; 9th Infantry Regiment, SH 56, TR 102; 12th Infantry Regiment, BD 47; 14th Infantry Regiment, AT *149;* 15th Infantry Regiment, AT *39,* 56; 17th Infantry Regiment, SM *36-37;* 19th Infantry Regiment, TE 153; 20th Infantry Regiment, MI 111, 129, SH 86, SM *41,* 71; 21st Infantry Regiment, CH 68, 74, *75,* TE 143; 23rd Infantry

AP Pursuit to Appomattox; AS The Assassination; AT Battles for Atlanta; BD The Bloodiest Day; BL The Blockade; BR Brother against Brother; CH The Fight for Chattanooga; CO The Coastal War; DE Decoying the Yanks; FI First Blood; FL The Shenandoah in Flames; FO Forward to Richmond; FR War on the Frontier; GE Gettysburg;

Roundhouse of the Orange & Alexandria
Railroad in Alexandria, Virginia

Regiment, BD 45-47, FL *22, 23, 127,*
TT *62,* 63; 27th Infantry Regiment, AT
100, MI 41, *42-43,* 58; 31st Infantry
Regiment, TE *86-87,* 163, *168-169;* 32nd
Infantry Regiment, BD 42; 33rd Infantry
Regiment, AT 42; 36th Infantry
Regiment, FL 56; 39th Infantry
Regiment, AT 100; 41st Infantry
Regiment, CH 64, TE 127; 42nd Infantry
Regiment, MI 63-66; 47th Infantry
Regiment, DE *74-75;* 48th Infantry
Regiment, FR 60, MI 130; 49th Infantry
Regiment, AT 56; 51st Infantry
Regiment, SH *100-101,* TE 153; 52nd
Infantry Regiment, AT 60, 72, 77; 53rd
Infantry Regiment, CH 81, SH 111,
114-116; 54th Infantry Regiment, SM
38-39; 55th Infantry Regiment, RE 129;
56th Infantry Regiment, MI 103; 57th
Infantry Regiment, AT *86-87;* 58th
Infantry Regiment, TE 57; 60th Infantry
Regiment, BD 59; 61st Infantry
Regiment, RE 132; 63rd Infantry
Regiment, AT *59,* MI 40-41, SM *40;*
64th Infantry Regiment, AT 70, SM 103;
65th Infantry Regiment, SM 105, TE
112; 66th Infantry Regiment, BD 82;
70th Infantry Regiment, SH 111; 73rd
Infantry Regiment, TT *34-35;* 74th
Infantry Regiment, TE 92; 75th Infantry
Regiment, RE 130-131; 80th Infantry
Regiment, MI *114-115,* SM *38-39;* 81st
Infantry Regiment, AT 45, *82-83,* 99,
100; 83rd Infantry Regiment, MI 68;
89th Infantry Regiment, CH 68; 91st
Infantry Regiment, FL 56, 60; 97th
Infantry Regiment, SM 122; 98th
Infantry Regiment, AT 72; 100th
Infantry Regiment, TE *34-35;* 104th
Infantry Regiment, CH 101, SM 105,
122; 105th Infantry Regiment, CH 30,
79, TE *160;* 110th Infantry Regiment,
AP *40,* FL 82, *83,* 152; 111th Infantry
Regiment, SM 94, *138;* 113th Infantry
Regiment, SM *37;* 115th Infantry
Regiment, CH 66; 116th Infantry
Regiment, AP 99, FL 61; 123rd
Infantry Regiment, AP 118, FL 30,
33; 125th Infantry Regiment, AT 93,
CH 148; 149th Infantry Regiment, FL
74; 157th National Guard Infantry
Regiment, TT 119; 192nd Infantry
Regiment, TT 28
Ohlenschlager, Dr. Emil, FL 135
Oil City, Pennsylvania, YA *80-81, 84-85*
Oil Creek, YA 67, 70, *80, 81, 82-83,* 85
Oil industry, YA 67-69, *70,* 71, 72, 78-
79, *80-85*
O'Keeffe, Joseph, FL 152
Okhotsk, Sea of, BL 159
Olathe, Kansas, SP 149
O'Laughlin, Michael, AS 20, 24, *25,* 29,
39, 40, 67-68; arrest and confinement of,
AS 110, *143;* imprisonment and
death of, AS 160; and plot to kidnap

Lincoln, AS 48-51; quits conspiracy, AS
53, 54; trial of, AS 145, 151-154, *156,*
158
Old Abe (eagle mascot), TT *151*
Old Bahama Channel, BL 116
Old Blandford Church, TR *9*
Old Capitol Prison, AS 110, 139, *144,* SP
31, 51, 54, 55, 116, TT 116, YA 32;
reporters at, NA *37*
Old Church crossroads, LE 27-28
Old Church Hotel, TR *20-21*
Old Cold Harbor, Virginia, LE 37, 41
Old Dominion Rifles (Virginia), FI *58*
Oldest soldier, TT 28
Old Guard of Richmond, NA *161*
Old Hagerstown Road, BD 51
Old men, enlistment of, TT 26-28
Old Penitentiary, AS 139, 141, *162-171;*
cell key, AS *151*
Old Richmond Road, RE 57, 62, 64, 71
Oldroyd, Osborne, MI 129
Olds, Edson, YA 32, 34
Olds, William W., MI 63-66
Old Sharpsburg Road, BD 45, 49, *50*
Old Tavern, Virginia, LE 31, 33
Oliver, William A., TR *99*
Olley's Creek, AT 75
Olmstead, Charles, CO 46-47
Olmsted, Frederick Law, YA 120, 122,
123
Olustee, Florida, CO 139
Omaha, Nebraska, NA 84
O'Meara, Timothy, FO 51
Omenhausser, John T., TT *136-143*
O'Neal, Edward A., GE 53-54, 127
Oneida, CO 69, 145, 150, MI 18-19
O'Neill, James, sketch by, FR *154*
Onondaga, AP 45, BL *19,* 70-71
Onondaga Salt Company, YA 72-73,
79
Oostanaula River, AT 13, 40, 44, 45,
48
Opdycke, Emerson, SM 89, 90, 98,
100-102, 112, *117;* counterattacks at
Franklin, SM 112-113
Opdyke, George, YA 109
Opelousas, Louisiana, NA 34, 142
Opequon Creek, TR 136
Opequon Creek, Battle of, FL 112-117, *map*
118, *119;* cavalry charge at, FL 119,
120-121
Opium, SM 106
Opothleyahola, FR 136, *139,* 148
Opp, Milton, KI *171*
Orange & Alexandria Railroad, DE *142,*
FI 61, 113, 117, 135, FO 72, 83, KI 28,
45, 57, LE 95-98, *117-119, 122-123,*
124-125, *126-127,* RE *map 8, 14, 16-17,*
33, 108, SP *93, 98-100, 104,* 119, 122,
128-130
Orange County, Virginia, OR 80
Orange Court House, Virginia, LE 99, 101,
KI 57
Orange Plank road, KI 58, 60-62, 68,

70-71, 77-78, 83
Orange Turnpike, KI 58, 60-61, 73
Ord, Edward O. C., AP 19, 26, 79, 97, 99,
114, 118, 127, 129-130, 135-139, 144,
145, *146-147,* DE 151, MI 34, 36, 40,
148, 153, NA 61, 70, TR 73, 80, 87,
139-140, 142-144
Ord, Mrs. Edward, AS 53
Order of the Heroes of America, OR
151-152
Ordnance Bureau. *See* Gorgas, Josiah
Oregon Trail, FR *map 2-3, 10-11,* 107,
128
Oregon troops: 1st Cavalry Regiment, FR
132
Ore resources, BR 9, 18
Oreto, BL 115, 120-121
Orleans, Virginia, LE 127
O'Rorke, Patrick H., GE 84-85
Orphan Brigade (1st Kentucky Infantry
Brigade), AT 57, 59, 146, 149, 150, 152,
CH 55, 149, TE 148, 149, 150, 153, 154,
155
Orr, Robert, AP 92
Osage Indians, FR 147
Osawatomie, Kansas, BR 79
Osbon, B. S., CO 65, 68
Osceola, Missouri, SP 142-143
Osliaba, BL 133, *140-141*
Ossabaw Sound, SM 150, 155
Ossipee, CO 145, 156
Osterhaus, Peter J., CH 118, 130, 131, 142,
FR 141, 142, 143, MI 102-103, 119-121,
SM 50, *51,* 60, 66, 71
Osterman, Jacob, BD 54
O'Sullivan, Timothy, LE 111, *113,* NA *95;*
photographs by, KI *126-129, 138-147,*
NA *94-95,* TR *120-121*
Otis, Elmer, TE 120
Ott, William B., FI *100*
Ottawa, Illinois, BR 106, SH *153*
Otter Island, BL *40-41*
Otterville, Illinois, NA 20
Otto (John) farm, BD 136-137
Our American Cousin, AS 59, 64, 68, 70, 71,
74, 79, 83; Ford's Theatre playbill for,
AS *73*
Outer Banks, CO 16-17, 21, 30
Overall Creek, TE 133
Overland Mail Company, FR 112
Overland Trail, FR *map 2-3,* 107, 117, 125,
128
Overseers of the Poor, NA 125
Overton, William, FI *103*
Overton Hill, SM 134, 135, *136,* 142
Owen, Joshua, RE 81
Owen, Richard, TT 119
Owen, Samuel W., LE *79*
Owen, William, BD 21
Owen, William M., AP *97, 113,* RE 76,
TR 137
Owl Creek, Tennessee, SH 105, 113,
139
Ox Ford, KI 132, 135
Oxford, Mississippi, MI 57

Infantry private from Ohio with rifle
and full accoutrements

Timothy O'Sullivan, one of the
War's best photographers, employed by
Mathew Brady's company

KI The Killing Ground; LE Lee Takes Command; MI War on the Mississippi; NA The Nation Reunited; OR Confederate Ordeal; RE Rebels
Resurgent; SH The Road to Shiloh; SM Sherman's March; SP Spies, Scouts and Raiders; TE The Struggle for Tennessee; TR Death in the
Trenches; TT Tenting Tonight; YA Twenty Million Yankees

95

Marsena Patrick (*seated, center*),
Provost Marshal General of the
Army of the Potomac, and his staff

An early wartime photograph of
Brigadier General William Nelson
Pendleton, Lee's Chief of Artillery

P

Padrick (pilot), CO 90
Paducah, Kentucky, SH 46, 53, SP 72
Page, Charles, SP 52
Page, Corporal, SH 91
Page, Richard L., CO 142, 150, 156
Paine, Charles J., CO 164, TR 139, 146-147
Paine, Lewis (Lewis Thornton Powell), AS 41, 44-48, 54, 56, 71, 99; arrest and confinement, AS 110, *111, 142;* assault on Seward, AS 95, *96, 97;* background, AS 39-40; execution of, AS 159-160, *161, 162-171;* knife of, AS *97;* noose used for, AS *133;* plot to kidnap Lincoln, AS 48-50, 53; plot to murder Grant, AS 68, 69; plot to murder Lincoln and Seward, AS 71-74; trial of, AS 144-145, 151, 154, 158
Painter, Hettie K., YA *132*
Paint Rock, Alabama, TE 12
Paiute Indians, FR 106, 112
Palace, NA 157
Palfrey, Francis W., BD 91, RE 29
Palfrey, John C., BR *144*
Palmer, Benjamin, OR 58
Palmer, Innis, AP 65, 66, 67
Palmer, John M., AT 39, CH 64, TE 96, 99, 122, 124, 127, 154
Palmer, Joseph B., TE 130, 144, 149
Palmer, Kennedy, FL *69*
Palmer, Oliver H., BD 97-99, RE 77
Palmerston, Henry, BD 159
Palmerston, Lord: Confederacy, policy on, BL *121,* 125-126; and *Trent* Affair, BL 117, 119; and warship construction, BL 121. *See also* United Kingdom
Palmetto, Georgia, SM 19
Palmetto Guard, BR 148, 156
Palmetto Guards, SP 14
Palmetto Sharpshooters, FO 145
Palmetto State, CO 113
Palmito Ranch, Battle of, AP 162
Palo Alto, Mississippi, MI *map* 90
Pamlico River, CO 88, 90
Pamlico Sound, CO 17, 21-22, 34, 37, 97
Pamunkey River, FO 129-130, *134-135,* TR 21, 26, 34, 35; operations around, LE 25, *82-84*
Panic, FO 109, 139-140, 165; in Confederate Army, MI 121; in Union Army, MI 111
Panic of 1873, NA 125-127, 148
Paper: industry, YA 67, 78; production, OR 62; shortages, OR 48, *51*
Parades and reviews, FO 24-25, *69,* TT 52, 55
Paris, Comte de, CH 146, FO 22-24, *115,* KI 96
Paris, Declaration of (1856), BL 12
Paris, Kentucky, TE *27*
Paris, Virginia, DE 39

Park, Robert E., FL 120
Parke, John G., AP 39, 92, CO *32,* MI 134, RE *28,* TR 99, 150, 152, 154; at Fort Macon, CO 39; at New Bern, CO 36-37; at Roanoke Island, CO 25, 32
Parker, Ely S., AP *146-147,* 149, 150
Parker, Joel, YA 144
Parker, John F., AS 76-79, 82-83
Parker, Richard, BR 91, *94-95*
Parker, Theodore, BR *64,* 84
Parker, William, TR *62*
Parker, William W., BD 129
Parker's Battery, BD 129
Parkersburg, West Virginia, FI 85
Parkersburg-Staunton road, DE 45, 101
Parker's Store, KI 61
Parkhurst, John G., TE 27, 30
Parkman, Francis, FR 10
Parole pass, AP *151*
Parole system, TT 111
Parrott, Robert, TE 134
Parrott, Robert P., CO 82, FI 51
Parrott guns, CO 135-136, *137,* FO 105, GE *84-85,* MI *164-165,* SM *21,* TE 134
Parsons, Charles C., TE 64
Parsons, Mosby M., FR 56, 63, 65
Parsons' Battery (4th U.S. Artillery), TE 64
Partisan politics, YA 142-144, 146, 149-152, 154-158. *See also* Congress; Radical Republicans
Partisan Ranger Act, SP 107-108, 110, 126
Partisans. *See* Guerrillas
Pasha, Ismail, NA 154, *155;* army of, NA 154
Pasquotank River, CO *31,* 32-33
Passaic, BL *19, 44,* CO *81,* 118
Passports. *See* Travel passes
Pastimes. *See* Recreation
Patapsco, CO 118
Pate, Henry Clay, KI 119
Patents and inventions, NA 79, *80-81, 107, 151*
Paterson, New Jersey, NA 79
Patrick, Marsena R., KI 167, LE 97, 138, 141-142, RE *28,* SP *31,* 80, 81, TR 94
Patrick, Robert, AT 62
Patrick Henry, FO *128*
Patriotic demonstrations, FI 10, *12-13,* 14, *16,* 18
Patriotic displays, TT 20, 24, YA *24-25,* 87, 96, *112-115, 121,* 159
Patrols. *See* Reconnaissances
Patrons of Husbandry, NA 90
Patterson, Lewis, BD 125-126
Patterson, Martha Johnson, AS 159
Patterson, Robert, DE 35-36, 38, 59, FI 58, SP 26; and Harpers Ferry seizure, FI 95; Scott, relations with, FI 95; in Shenandoah Valley operations, FI 95, 111, 122, 126
Patton, George S., FL 34, 36, 116, 122, *123*
Patton, John M., DE 165, 167
Paul, Gabriel R., FR 28
Paul, William, BD 71
Paulding, Hiram, BL 51-52

Pauli, Émilie, FR 82
Pawnee, BR 152, 156
Paxton, Elisha, RE 147
Pay: black soldiers', TT 33; military, OR 80; rates and regularity, TT 24, 63
Payne, Andrew S., SH 99
Payne, William H., FL 144, 151
Payne's farm, KI 29
Paytes, Simeon Chesterfield, RE *107*
Peabody, Everett, SH 111, 113, *114,* 117
Peabody, George, NA 58
Peabody, J. H., RE 132
Peace: initiatives, AP 20-25, 26; movement, YA 20-21, 23-31, 149, 151, 155; movement and negotiations, OR *149,* 151-152, 154-157, 160, 162-165
Peace and Constitutional Society, OR 151-152
Peace Democrats, YA 24, 26, 142, 151, 155
Peace River, DE 26
Peace Society, OR 151-152
Peach Orchard, GE 71, 75-78, 87, 98-101, *102-103,* 106, *map* 108, 126, 129, 168
Peach Orchard Hill. *See* Overton Hill
Peachtree Creek, AT 78, 91, 92
Peachtree Creek, Battle of, AT 92-95
Peaks of Otter, DE *12-13*
Peals, Thomas, AP 92
Pea Ridge, Arkansas, SH 101
Pea Ridge, Battle of, FR *cover,* 140-141, *map* 143, *144,* 145, SP 73
Pearl River, MI *map* 90, 91, *94,* 117
Pearson, Henry, KI *171*
Peck, John J., FO 110
Peck, Joseph, FL *126*
Peck, Lafayette, BR *143*
"Peckerwoods" (poor whites), OR 8
Peeble farm, Battle of, TR 150-151, *152-153*
Peekskill, New York, YA 87
Peer, John A., patent model of, NA *81*
Peffly, Alfred, AT *59*
Pegram, John, AP 17, *19,* 30, 31, 38, 90, 155, FI 87, 89-91, FL 122, 148, 149, 150, 157, OR 126, TE 99, 123, 150
Pegram, William Johnson, AP 90, LE 67, RE 147, TR 72, 107
Pegram's redan, TR 69, 75
Pegram's Richmond Battery, TR 67, 72, 75
Peirson, Charles, field glasses of, KI *92*
Pelham, John, RE *61,* 64-65, 109, 111; Bible of, SP *49*
Pember, Phoebe Yates, AP 108, OR 123, TT *97,* 98
Pemberton, John Clifford, CH 18, 19, CO 110-112, MI *62,* OR 88, SP 67, 75, 76, TE 85, TR 53, TT 86; at Baker's Creek, MI 116; and Big Black River, MI 111, 122-123; at Bovina, MI 123; at Champion's Hill, MI 116, 118-122; and Chickasaw Bluffs, MI 96-97; at Clinton, MI 116; distrusted, MI 62, 126; at Edwards Depot, MI 111, 113, 116; evacuation plans, MI 152; food requisitions by, MI 149-150; and Grand Gulf, MI 96-97; Grant, meeting with, MI

AP Pursuit to Appomattox; AS The Assassination; AT Battles for Atlanta; BD The Bloodiest Day; BL The Blockade; BR Brother against Brother; CH The Fight for Chattanooga; CO The Coastal War; DE Decoying the Yanks; FI First Blood; FL The Shenandoah in Flames; FO Forward to Richmond; FR War on the Frontier; GE Gettysburg;

Gunners of the Keystone Independent
Battery of Pennsylvania Light Artillery

153-156; at Grenada, MI 59; and
Grierson's Raid, MI 90-91, 96; and Holly
Springs, MI 60; at Raymond, MI 116;
surrender, MI 134, 152-156; tactical
plans, MI 60, 86, 109-111, 116, 122, 152;
troop strength, MI 84, 90, 116, 126; in
Vicksburg defense, MI 59-60, 75, 86, 90,
96-97, 109-111, 116, 122-123, 126, 131,
134, 140-142, 149-150, 152; and Yazoo
Pass project, MI 76
Pemberton, Patty, MI 62
Pencils, production of, OR 26
Pendel, Thomas, AS 77
Pender, William Dorsey, GE 113, RE 61,
139, 144, 160; at Cemetery Hill, GE map
63, 69; at Cemetery Ridge, GE 112-113;
at Gettysburg, GE 51, 59; in Pickett's
Charge, GE 128; at Seminary Ridge, GE
62
Pendergast, Harrison, SM 72
Pendergrast, Garrett J., BL 24
Pendleton, Alexander S. (Sandie), BD 76,
DE 93-94, FL 124, RE 139, 152
Pendleton, George H., YA 155
Pendleton, William, LE 67, OR 59
Pendleton, William Nelson, AP 135, 153,
BD 153, DE 36, FI 138, 141
Peninsula, the, FI 76, 78-79, 84
Peninsula Campaign, BL 125
Peninsular Campaign, CO 35, 38-39, 58,
DE 21, 45, 61, 83, 89, 114, 121-123, 135,
146-147, 151, 170, FO map 2-3, map
90-91, map 96, LE 23-31, YA 87;
amphibious phase, FO 91-92; artillery
actions, FO 92, 93-94, 99, 102, 105,
107-111, 122-123, 133, 139, 144, 154-155,
164; balloons in, FO 99, 105, 148;
cavalry actions, FO 107-108, 110;
command failures in, FO 167;
fortifications in, FO 94, 98-99, 108-109,
111; Navy in, FO 89-91, 93, 96, 124-125,
127-128, 129; night operations, FO 105;
panic in, FO 109; planning phase, FO
14, 63-64, 67-68, 73, 75, 84, 89-92,
96-97; railroads in, FO 130;
reconnaissances in, FO 94, 111; river
obstacles in, FO 92-94; road system, FO
89, 93, 108, 136-138; terrain features in,
FO 92-94, 109, 141; Union commanders
in, FO 86-87; weather, effect on
operations, FO 93, 107, 109, 133, 138,
155. See also Johnston, Joseph E.;
McClellan, George Brinton
Penitentiaries, industries in, OR 62
Penn, Pat J., LE 46
Pennington, William, BR 109
Pennsylvania elections, BR 118
Pennsylvania House, AS 98, 110
Pennsylvania Railroad, BD 18, SP 8, YA
65, 78
Pennsylvania troops, AP 38-39, 125, BD
67-70, 76-78, CH 139-140, CO 19, FO
18-19, GE 72, 85, KI 38, 63, 66, RE 113,
115, 132, TT 24, 41, 53, 122, YA 88,
159; Bucktail Brigade, GE 58, 158-

159; number furnished, FI 21;
Philadelphia Brigade, BD 90-91, GE 111,
NA 171; Reserve Division, GE 90-91,
105, LE 31, 35-36, 59; training program,
FI 24-25
    Artillery: Battery E, Light Artillery
(Knap), BD 94-95; Battery G, 1st
Artillery (Kerns), LE 158; Battery G, 1st
Artillery (Ricketts), GE 114, 115-116,
117; Battery H, 1st Light Artillery, FO
154-155; Knap's Independent Light
Artillery, NA 168; Ringgold Light
Artillery, FI 24-25
    Cavalry: 1st Cavalry Regiment, LE
107; 2nd Cavalry Regiment, GE 43; 3rd
Cavalry Regiment, FO 24, GE 132, LE
76-77, 79-81, TT 58; 4th Cavalry
Regiment, LE 78, TT 58; 5th Cavalry
Regiment, FO 116-117, TR 32; 6th
Cavalry Regiment, GE 18, 22, 36; 7th
Cavalry Regiment, TE 27; 8th Cavalry
Regiment, RE 133, 134; 9th Cavalry
Regiment, TE 22, 59; 11th Cavalry
Regiment, TR 32, 55; 12th Cavalry
Regiment, LE 129; 13th Cavalry
Regiment, GE 24-25, TR 114-115; 14th
Cavalry Regiment, FL 132; 16th Cavalry
Regiment, RE 108; 17th Cavalry
Regiment, FL 152; 18th Cavalry
Regiment, KI 8-9
    Infantry: 1st California Infantry
Regiment, FO 43-44, 46, 50; 4th
Reserves Infantry Regiment, LE 59; 5th
Reserves Infantry Regiment, KI 171; 8th
Infantry Regiment, DE 68-69; 9th
Reserves Infantry Regiment, BD 60; 10th
Reserves Infantry Regiment, BD 64, 68;
11th Infantry Regiment, LE 125, 137,
RE 52, 67, 68-69, 70; 13th Reserves
Infantry Regiment (Bucktails), BD 64,
65, 76, LE 163, DE 158, 160-163, KI
134; 26th Infantry Regiment, LE 169;
28th Infantry Regiment, BD 141, NA
168, SP 109; 31st Infantry Regiment, FO
28; 46th Infantry Regiment, LE 105;
48th Infantry Regiment, AP 92, 94-95,
LE 149, TR 65-68, 70-71, 75; 49th
Infantry Regiment, AP 123, 124, KI 91;
51st Infantry Regiment, BD 125,
126-129; 53rd Infantry Regiment, RE 89;
54th Infantry Regiment, AP 118, FL 33,
36, 37, 48, 126; 57th Infantry Regiment,
CO 165, GE 102; 61st Infantry Regiment,
AP 79, 92; 62nd Infantry Regiment, FO
133; 63rd Infantry Regiment, KI 71, LE
60; 69th Infantry Regiment, GE 131,
137, 140-142; 71st Infantry Regiment,
BD 91, GE 122-123, 131, 140-141; 72nd
Infantry Regiment, BD 89, GE 96-97,
132, 141-142; 73rd Infantry Regiment,
LE 168; 74th Infantry Regiment, LE
165; 76th Infantry Regiment (Keystone
Zouaves), TR 101; 76th Infantry
Regiment, CO 124, 127; 77th Infantry
Regiment, CH 28, 50, TT 124; 78th

Infantry Regiment, AT 55, TE 154-155,
158; 81st Infantry Regiment, BD 105,
FO 160-161, 164, KI 170; 83rd Infantry
Regiment, GE 69; TT 52, 157; 84th
Infantry Regiment, KI 171; 85th Infantry
Regiment, FO 124; 87th Infantry
Regiment, FL 78; 88th Infantry
Regiment, LE 42; 90th Infantry
Regiment, BD 71; 95th Infantry
Regiment (Zouaves), FL 128; 95th
Infantry Regiment, KI 105, TT 43; 96th
Infantry Regiment, FO 34-35, KI 91;
97th Infantry Regiment, CO 168; 102nd
Infantry Regiment, TT 150; 103rd
Infantry Regiment, FO 139; 104th
Infantry Regiment, FO 142-143; 105th
Infantry Regiment, LE 71, TT 52; 106th
Infantry Regiment, BD 151; 109th
Infantry Regiment, AT 98; 110th
Infantry Regiment, RE 112, TT 32;
111th Infantry Regiment, AT 91, CH 93;
114th Infantry Regiment (Zouaves), AP
11, 15, KI 126; 114th Infantry Regiment,
GE 102, TT 13; 116th Infantry
Regiment, GE 101; 118th Infantry (Corn
Exchange) Regiment, BD 154-155, 156;
125th Infantry Regiment, BD 83, 89;
132nd Infantry Regiment, BD 86, 93,
96-97, RE 75-76; 138th Infantry
Regiment, AP 95; 140th Infantry
Regiment, TR 35; 143rd Infantry
Regiment, GE 55; 147th Infantry
Regiment, NA 168; 148th Infantry
Regiment, GE 154, KI 148, RE 118;
149th Infantry Regiment, GE 56-57, 58,
155, TR 142-143; 150th Infantry
Regiment, GE 64; 153rd Infantry
Regiment, RE 129-130; 155th Infantry
Regiment (Zouaves), AP 141; 155th
Infantry Regiment (Zouaves), KI 66, 67;
203rd Infantry Regiment, CO 165, 168;
209th Infantry Regiment, GE 148
Pennypacker, Galusha, CO 168
Pensacola, CO 66-67, 69
Pensacola, Florida, BR 128, CO 8, 13-15,
74, FI 15, TT 36-37; as blockade target,
BL 21, 30-31; navy yard at, BL 22-23.
See also Fort Pickens
Pensacola Bay, BR 129, CO 8, map 9, 14-15
Pepper, George, SM 38-39
Pepper, George Whitefield, NA 78
Peralta, Battle of, FR 34-35
Perils of a Spy (Boyd), SP 48
Periodicals: contributions to, OR 48; war
reports by, OR 51. See also Literature
Periodicals. See Reading
Periscope, MI 136
Perkerson, Lizzie, SM 47
Perkins, George, CO 73, 74
Perley, Charles, SP 164
Perley, Thomas F., RE 101
Perrin, Abner, KI 102
Perry, BL 28
Perry, Agnes Land, AS 35
Perry, "Major," NA 28

Colonel Turner G. Morehead of the
106th Pennsylvania, photographed
on the battlefield of Antietam

KI The Killing Ground; LE Lee Takes Command; MI War on the Mississippi; NA The Nation Reunited; OR Confederate Ordeal; RE Rebels
Resurgent; SH The Road to Shiloh; SM Sherman's March; SP Spies, Scouts and Raiders; TE The Struggle for Tennessee; TR Death in the
Trenches; TT Tenting Tonight; YA Twenty Million Yankees

97

Color Sergeant David W. Young of the 139th Pennsylvania, decorated for gallantry at Petersburg

A period watercolor of Confederate Lieutenant General Leonidas Polk, a former Episcopal bishop

Perry, William, BL 13
Perryville, Battle of, TE *60-61*, 62-67, *map 63*, *64-65*, *102*
Peters, George B., CH 22
Peters, Jessie, CH 22, SM 93
Petersburg, siege of: and Crater, TR 75-87, *88-89*, *90-93;* explosion at, TR 75, *76-77*, *90-91;* tunneling at, TR 67-69, *71*, *72-73*, 75. *See also names of individual battles*
Petersburg, Virginia, AP *map 2-3*, 33, 34, 78, CO 91, 97, KI 169, NA 78, TR *map 2-3*, *8-15*, 18-19, 27, *30-31*, 36, 57, TT *13*, 67-68, *69*, 98, 104, 153, 157; artillery bombardment at, AP 92, 102; Confederate withdrawal, AP 97-99; cotton production, OR *24-25;* damage from artillery, TR *137;* entrenchments at, AP 18-19, 79, 97; fortifications at, TR 39, *map 40*, *42-43*, *60-61*, 65, 67, *73*, *map 96*, *120-121*, *126-135*, *144;* life in, TR 10-11, 137; rail hub, TR 8, 18-19; under siege, TR 53, 104; siege of, OR 148, 151; Union advance on, TR 28, 31-33, 39-43; Union attack at, AP 79, 92, *map 93*; Union occupation, AP 108
Petersen, William, AS 92
Petersen house, AS *23*, 92, 98, 100, *102*, *103*
Peticolas, Alfred B., FR 16, 36; sketches by, FR *36-37*
Petigru, Louis, BR 25, 27
Peto, S. Morton, YA 71
Petrel, BL *13*, 142
Pettigrew, James Johnston, CO 87, FO 156; at Cashtown, GE 35; at Gettysburg, GE 35, 45; at McPherson's Ridge, GE 61; in Pickett's Charge, GE *123*, 128, 136-138; in Potomac crossing, GE 157
Pettigrew, William, OR 74
Pettit-Smith, Francis, BL 47
Pettus, Edmund W., CH 133
Petty, Elijah P., FR 46, 56, 62
Pevey shell, SP *166*
Peyton, Randolph, AS 116
Pfeiffer, Albert H., FR 119
Phelan, James, OR 80
Phelps, S. L., SH 78
Philadelphia, Pennsylvania, BR *132*, FI 23, 33, YA 88; and drug production, SM 108; Lincoln funeral procession, AS *120-121;* relief work in, YA *119*, *126-127*, *136-137*, *139-140;* shipbuilding at, BL 22
Philadelphia, Wilmington & Baltimore Railroad, FI 23, SP 8, 11
Philadelphia & Erie Railroad, YA 78
Philadelphia Academy of Fine Arts, YA *121*
Philadelphia Brigade, BD 90-91, NA *171*
Philadelphia Female Anti-Slavery Society, BR 67
Philadelphia *Inquirer*, SP 52, YA 30
Philbrick, Charles, FO 40-41
Philippi, West Virginia, FI 85-86, 88, *89*
Philippoteaux, Paul, GE 120-122, *123*, 124-125
Phillips, Dinwiddie, BL 54

Phillips, John, FR 160
Phillips, P. J., SM 60, 61
Phillips, Wendell, BR 47, *68*, FI 13, NA 40, 52, 56, 156, YA 36; letter by, NA *49*
Phillips, William A., FR 148, 150, 152, 155
Phillips House, RE *90-91*
Phoenix Hotel, TE *48*
Photographs: for medical records, TT 81; popularity of, TT 38
Pickens, Francis, BR 126-127, 135, 161
Pickens, Francis W., CO 112
Pickerell, Sergeant, FR *171*
Picket, CO 21, 24
Pickets, TT 47, *158*
Pickett, George E., AP 79-80, 82, 84-85, *86-88*, 90, 95, 110, 125, 128, CO 91-94, FO 159, 164-165, GE *135*, KI 43, NA 170, 171, RE 33, 36, 104-105, TR 49, TT 158; at Chambersburg, GE 68; commands charge, GE *122*, 126, 128, 136, 138, 144; evaluated by Longstreet, GE 126; at Gettysburg, GE 126; as romantic, GE 126
Pickett, Mrs. George E., AP 101, 109
Pickett's Charge, GE *cover*, *8-9*, *96-97*, *120-125;* artillery actions, GE 129-138, 140-141; assault phase, GE *136-137*, *map* 138, 139, 140, 141, *142-143;* casualties, GE 136, 144, 150; troop strength, GE 128; withdrawal phase, GE 143-145, *147*
Pickett's Mill, AT 53, 54
Pickett's Mill, Battle of, AT 39, 54-59
Pickle, John, TT *42*
Piedmont, West Virginia, DE 39, SP 126; action at, FL 46-47, *48-49*
Piedmont region, DE 21
Piedmont Station, Virginia, FI 122
Pierce, Abial R., FR 161
Pierce, Byron R., TR 156
Pierce, Ebenezer, FI 80-82, 84
Pierce, Franklin: as Democratic nominee, BR 100, 102; and Kansas elections, BR 74-75
Pierce, George F., OR 59
Pierce, H. H., TR *134-135*
Pierpont, Francis H., FI 87
Pierson, Stephen, AT 35
Pigeon Hill, AT 66, 68, 69
Pigeon Mountain, CH 32, 36, 37, 38, 42
Pigeon's ranch, FR 31, 32, 33
Pike, Albert, FR 136, *138*, 139, 141-144, 146, 148-149
Pike, James Shepherd, NA 26, 117-118, 127
Pike, William, TE 123
Pike's Peakers. *See* Colorado troops, 1st Infantry
Pillaging, TT 63
Pillow, Gideon J., OR 80, SH *87*, TE 130, 149, 153, 154; at Belmont, SH 48; cartoon, SH *87;* escape from Fort Donelson, SH 93, 95; at Fort Donelson, SH 81, 84-86, 90-91, 93; Grant's evaluation of, SH 81, 95;

ineptness, SH 87
Pillsbury, Charles A., NA 83
Pima Indians, FR 118
Pinchback, Pinckney B. S., NA 69, 71
Pine Mountain, AT 60, 61
Pinkerton, Allan (alias E. J. Allen), FO 28-29, *131*, SP 8, 21-22; background, SP 11; in Baltimore, SP 14, 15; and Lincoln, SP 8, *9*, 16, 21; and McClellan, SP *22*, 33; military intelligence, SP 32-33; and Mrs. Greenhow, SP 23, 25, 27-29; postwar career, SP 89; and Webster, SP 34, 36-38, 41-43
Pinn, Robert A., TR *125*
Pinola, CO 64-65
Pioneer Brigade, TE 98, 119
Pipe Creek line, GE 44, 67
Piper (Henry) farm, BD 94, 99, 103, *104*, 105, *114-115*
Pistols. *See* Revolvers
Pittsburgh, SH 59, 83-84, *166-167*
Pittsburgh, Fort Wayne & Chicago Railroad, YA 78
Pittsburgh, Pennsylvania, BR *18-19*, NA 83
Pittsburgh *Dispatch*, YA 145
Pittsburg Landing, Tennessee, SH *142-143*, *145*, *146*, *148-149;* Union advance to, SH 104-106; Union flight to, SH 115-116, *118*, 137, *map* 138, 139, 141, 143
Place, George, KI 165
Plantations: economic decline, BR 36-37; land-expansion need, BR 31-32; organization and work force, BR *10-11*, 29; social activities, BR *12-13*, 14
Planter, OR 127
Planters: in Congress, OR 11; and cotton production, OR 29; family connections, OR 43; farm-tool shortages, OR 44, 149; hostility to, OR 74-75; life style, OR *31*, 42, 46, *52-53*, *56-57;* livestock losses, OR 149; loyalty oaths taken by, OR 136; migration by, OR 128; and military service, OR 42-43, 78, *81;* number and influence of, OR 8, 46; property losses, OR 110-112, 116, *130-131;* and railroad construction, OR 28; and slavery issue, OR 75; 20-Negro law, OR 80, 93. *See also* Agriculture; Farmers
Playing cards, commemorative, BL *61*
Plays, OR 54
Pleasant Hill, Battle of, FR 56, 60-62, *map 63*
Pleasant Hill, Missouri, SP 146
Pleasants, Henry, TR 67-68, *70*, 72, 75
Pleasant Valley, BD 39, 44, 55, 64, 108, 122, 151
Pleasonton, Alfred, BD 23, 45, FR 157, 160, GE *13*, RE *32;* at Blue Ridge gaps, GE 25, 27-28; at Brandy Station, GE 10, 16, 22; at Cemetery Ridge, GE 133, 144; at Upperville, GE 28
Plum, William R., SP 71
Plum Run, GE 76, *map 78*, 79, 85, *90-91*, 105-106, 108, *164-165;* Confederate dead near, GE 79

AP Pursuit to Appomattox; AS The Assassination; AT Battles for Atlanta; BD The Bloodiest Day; BL The Blockade; BR Brother against Brother; CH The Fight for Chattanooga; CO The Coastal War; DE Decoying the Yanks; FI First Blood; FL The Shenandoah in Flames; FO Forward to Richmond; FR War on the Frontier; GE Gettysburg;

Plunkett, Thomas, RE *73*
Plymouth, North Carolina, CO 84, *map* 93, 94-97
Poague, William, KI 70, 76-77
Poague's Battery, BD 86, DE 135
Pocahontas, BL 32, BR 152, 156
Pocahontas, Virginia, TR *15*
Pocotaligo, South Carolina, AP 54
Poe, Orlando M., AT 132, CH *116*, SM *21*, 45, 46
Poetry, OR 42, 46, *47*, 48-49. *See also* Literature
Poffenberger (Alfred) farm, BD 89-90
Poffenberger (Joseph) farm, BD 65-66, 68, 79, 127-129
Poffenberger (Samuel) farm, BD 66
Pohlé, C.R.M., FI *99*
Poilpot, Théophile, LE 156, SH 130-132
Poinsett, BL 143
Point Isabel, Texas, DE 25
Point Lookout, Maryland, FL 73, *85*, 86, KI 113, 166
Point Lookout, Tennessee, CH *151*, *152*, *153*
Point Lookout prison camp, TT 115, 119, *136-143*
Point of Rocks, Virginia, TR 121
Point Pleasant, Missouri, SH 166
Poison Spring, Arkansas, TT 35
Polignac, Camille Armand Jules Marie, Prince de, FR 52, 56, 59, 60, 61, 63, 67, TT 31
Polish immigrants, YA 21
Politicians in military service, OR 11
Polk, James K., BR 22
Polk, Leonidas, AT 31, 38, *40*, 49, CH 23, 28, 29, 34, 37, 38, 39, 85, SH *49*, *110*, SP 78, TE 50, *51*, 55, 57, 58, 91, 94, 99; baptizes Hood, AT 39; at Belmont, SH 48; at Chickamauga, CH 53, 54, 56, 65, 67, 72; at Columbus, SH 46, 48, 53-55, 59, 79-81, 101; commands in West, SH 19; Davis, relations with, SH 19; death of, AT 61, *63;* family as refugees, OR 117; on guerrillas, OR 93-95; at Island No. 10, SH 101; and Johnston, AT 39; military reputation, TE 51; at Morgan's wedding, TE 90; at Munfordville, TE 51; at Perryville, TE 60, 61, 62, 64, 66-67; promotion, TE 83; relations with Bragg, CH 83, 84, TE 82; at Resaca, AT 39, 40; at Shiloh, SH 106-110, 113, 120, 122, 143-144, 147; at Stones River, TE 118, 121, 123, 124, 127, 129, 130, 132, 144, 145, 150, 152, 157, 158, 159, 170-171
Polk, Lucius E., TE 117
Pollaky, Ignatius, BL 115-116
Pollard, Edward A., AP 101, 163, TT 26-28
Polley, Joseph B., TR 140, 154, 159
Pollocksville, North Carolina, CO 91
Pomeroy, Marcus Mills (Brick), YA 24, 29
Pomeroy, Samuel Clarke, YA 152
Pomeroy Circular, YA 152
Pond Spring, Georgia, CH 42
Pontoon boats, CH *91. See also* Bridges;

pontoon
Pook, Samuel, SH 74
Pool, John, NA 98
Poolesville, Maryland, FO 39-40
Poor whites, OR 8
Pope, John, AP 162, 163, BD 15, CO 77, FR 86, 90, 91, 93, 95, 99, 129, 130, 138, LE *92*, MI 47, NA 61, 70, SP 109, 110, 116, TT *38;* aggressiveness, SH 9; at Bristoe Station, LE 133-134; at Cedar Mountain, LE 103, 109, 111, 124; at Centreville, LE 144, 146, 164-165; at Culpeper, LE 101, 124; at Island No. 10, SH 155, 159-160, 166; and McClellan, LE 93-95, 124-126, 133, 151; proclamations by, LE 97-98; and Rappahannock operations, LE 125-126; at Second Bull Run, LE 126-127, 132-138, 143-167; tactical plans, LE 95-98, 101, 133-134, 138, 146, 151-152; in Western operations, LE 93
Pope house, AT 106
Pope Pius IX, gift to Jefferson Davis, NA 23
Pope's Creek, AS 27, SP 51
Pope's Run, TT *17*
Poplar Grove, Virginia, Union camp at, AP 22, *23*
Poplar Springs Church, TR 150, 154
Popular-sovereignty doctrine, BR 71-72, 106, 108, 113, 116
Population, OR 8; blacks, percentage of, YA 21; national, BR 9; national growth, YA 20-22, 62; Northern states, BR 16, 35; Southern states, BR 14; urban shift, YA 20, 22-23
Porcher, C. P., TR *29*
Port Conway, Virginia, AS *map* 113, 115, 132
Porter, Andrew, FI *128*, 130-131, 133, 135-137, FO 16, *86*
Porter, Benjamin H., CO 143
Porter, David Dixon, AP 45, 76-77, 109, AS *58*, BL 91, CO *58*, FR 51-*52*, 53-55, 59, 63, 66-68, 70, 71, MI *86;* Butler, relations with, CO 157-158, 162; Cadwallader's evaluation of, MI 78; Farragut, relations with, CO 60-61, 66-67; fleet strength of, CO 159; at Fort Fisher, CO 157-170; at Fort Hindman, MI 68; at Forts St. Philip and Jackson, CO 64-66, 73, 75, 76-77, 157-158; at Grand Gulf, MI 97-99, 100-101; Grant, relations with, MI 78, 86; and mortar boats, CO 57-58, 61, 64-66, 73, 157-158; at New Carthage, MI 84-86; reconnaissances by, MI 79-80; in Red River Campaign, CO 157; and Red River operations, MI 77-79; ruse by, MI 78, *79;* on shipping hazards, MI 76; Stanton, relations with, MI 78; at Steele's Bayou, MI 80-83; at Vicksburg, MI 4, 16, 18, 32, 57, 62, 79-80, 87, 96-97, 130, 136-137; Welles, relations with, CO 57; wounded, MI 32; and Yazoo Pass project,

MI 76; on Yazoo River, MI 28-29, 57, 63, 67, 79-80
Porter, Fitz-John, BD *162-163*, FO 87, 105, 130, 133, FR 52, LE *30*, 95, *151;* at Antietam, BD 64, 86-87, 108-109, 132, 139, 141, 152; at Aquia Landing, LE 125; at Bristoe Station, LE 144; at Centreville, LE 144; in Chickahominy operations, LE 25-33, 48; and Confederate retreat, BD 153, 156; at Second Bull Run, LE 133-134, 146, 150-155, 167; in Seven Days' Battles, LE 33-47, 52, 58, 72
Porter, G. T., YA 103
Porter, Horace, AP 76, 81, 85, 87-89, 91-92, 133, *146-147*, 150, CO 49, KI 56, 61, 81, 102-103, 156, 169, TR 35, 147
Porter, Hugh, TR *62*
Porter, John, BL 48, SH 65, 67
Porter, Peter A., KI *171*
Porter, Robert K., OR 58
Porter, William, FR 52
Porterfield, George A., FI 85-87
Porter house, TR *168-169*
Port Gibson, Mississippi, MI *map* 2-3, 101-102, *map* 103, 104-105
Port Hudson, Louisiana, CO 77, FR 46, 47, OR 106, 108-109, 149; land operations, MI 73, 90, 110, 140, 159, *map* 160, 161-163, 164, *166-169;* mine warfare, MI 168; naval operations, MI 161, *162-163;* surrender, MI 168; "Fort Desperate," MI *169*
Port Republic, Virginia, FL 17, 45, 46, 125, 135; actions at, DE 99-100, 157-168, *map* 169, 170
Port Royal, CO 145, FO 128
Port Royal, South Carolina, CO 17, 110, OR 33, SM 148, 155, 156, 158
Port Royal, Virginia, AS 116, 117, 132, KI 148, RE 39-40, 58, 61
Port Royal Sound, CO 17, *20*, 57; as blockade target, BL 29, 31, *32-33*, 34, *43*, 87
Portsmouth navy yard, BL 46
Port Tobacco, Maryland, AS 27, 39, 50, 51, 74, 111
Port Tobacco River, SP 51
Port Washington, Wisconsin, YA 92
Post, P. Sidney, TE 117
Post, Philip Sidney, SM 135, *136*
Postal service, OR 5, 48. *See also* Reagan, John H.
Potomac Creek bridge, RE 14, *15*
Potomac River, FL 17, 28, 69, *85*, *90*, 91, 106, FO 8, 17, 39-51, 63, 74, 81, 83-84, RE *18*, 30, 35-36, SP 50, YA *18-19;* contraband traffic on, SP 50, 51, 52; crossing of, GE 26, *map* 32, 34, 72, 156, *157;* operations around, DE *16-17*, 33-34, 44, *48-49*, 54, 61, *64-65*, 129, 135, 146-147, 151; operations on, BD 10, *12*, 13-15, *map* 22, *40-41*, 129, 151, 153, 154-155, 156, 166, 168, *169;* strategic value of, FI 76, 113, *114-115*

Colonel Horace Porter, aide to General U.S. Grant and author of *Campaigning with Grant*

KI The Killing Ground; LE Lee Takes Command; MI War on the Mississippi; NA The Nation Reunited; OR Confederate Ordeal; RE Rebels Resurgent; SH The Road to Shiloh; SM Sherman's March; SP Spies, Scouts and Raiders; TE The Struggle for Tennessee; TR Death in the Trenches; TT Tenting Tonight; YA Twenty Million Yankees

99

Major General Sterling Price of Missouri, prominent Confederate commander in the West

An example of harsh Civil War punishment: black soldiers "riding the wooden horse" at Vicksburg

Pottawatomie Creek, Kansas, SP 141
Pottawatomie Massacre, BR 70-71
Potter, Robert B., AP 39, 93, BD 125, *127*, KI 74, 103, TR 45-46, 67, 74, 78, 83, 87, 152
Potts, David, LE *169*
Powell, Daniel Lee, FL *13*
Powell, Eugene, BD 82
Powell, James E., SH 111, 113-114
Powell, Lewis Thornton. *See* Paine, Lewis
Powell, William H., FL 125, 136, 137, 140-141, 144, TR 75-76, 78
Powhatan, BL 146, BR 152, 156, CO 57
Prairie Grove, Battle of, FR 135, 151, TT 152
Prather, John, FL 56, 60
Pratt, Franklin A., RE *164-165*
Pratt, George J., kepi of, FL *41*
Pratt, George W., LE 168, *170*
Pratt, Harrison, FL 61
Prentiss, Benjamin M., SH 105, 111, 113, 118-122, *123*, 131, *135*, 136-139, 148
Prescott, Arizona Territory, NA *105*
Presidential election, and Union war effort, TR 16, 94, 157-158
Press freedom, OR 49. *See also* Newspapers
Presstman, Stephen W., SM 88
Preston, J.T.L., DE 44
Preston, John, FL *10*
Preston, John S., AP 20, OR 149
Preston, Noble D., AP 126
Preston, Samuel D., TR 78
Preston, William, CH 67, 69, TE 130, 149
Prevost, Charles E., BD 154-155
Price, James W., TR *29*
Price, Samuel W., TE 123, 150, 153
Price, Sterling (Pap), FR 52, 56, 60, 63-64, 136-138, 140-141, *144*, 145-146, 152, 154, 156-*157*, 158, 160, 161, 163, MI 34-37, SH 26, SP 142, 149, TE 42, 80; Blair, relations with, SH 16-17; at Boonville, SH *20;* commands Missouri troops, SH 16; at Lexington, SH 9, 33; Lyon, relations with, SH 16-17; in Missouri operations, SH 17-24, 26, 32, 48; sword of, SH *9;* training program, SH 21; at Wilson's Creek, SH 9, 24-29
Prince, Henry, CO 90
Princess, CO *56-57*
Princeton, BL 51
Prisoner of war camps, SH *96-97*
Prisoners: Confederate, DE 87, LE *116-117,* SH 56, *96,* 97, 166, *168-169;* Federal, DE 38, 128, 151, 170; Union, LE 28, 46-47, 52, 59-60, 72-73, 75, 167, SH 30, 33, 120, *131,* 134, 138-139, 141
Prisoners lost: Confederate Army, MI 44, 68, 95, 103-104, 123; Confederate Navy, MI 20; Union Army, MI 60, 94, 117, 123
Prisoners of war: rations, TT 113-115, 118, *132;* black soldiers, TT 111; camps for, TT 20, 113; clothing shortages among, TT *111,* 116, 129; Confederate, OR 60, TT *111-113,* 135, *168-169;* crafts by, TT 118, *120-121, 136-143;* crime and

disorders among, TT 122; deaths among, TT 118, 129, 131, *133,* 134-136; debilitation of, TT 128, *135;* diseases among, TT 117-118, 129; escaped prisoners and tracking dogs, SM 59; escapes by, TT 122-129; exchange of invalids, SM 145; exchanges, TT 110-111, 133; executions, TT 122; hardships of Southern camps, SM 68; living conditions and treatment of, TT 110, 113-122, 128-132, 136; medical services for, TT 118, 133; numbers confined, TT 135; paroles, TT 111, 133; recreational activities, TT 118, *120-121;* Regular Army losses, TT 110; religious services among, TT 118, *123;* and Sherman, SM 157; Union, OR *38-39,* TT 110-111, *114,* 135; used to clear torpedoes, SM 152, *153;* water supply, TT 115, 132-133, 136
Prisons: Confederate, SP 86, 87; Union, SP *17, 20,* 37, 39, 54, 56, 58-59, 86
Pritchard's Hill, DE 67
Privateers, BL 11, *12-13,* 24-25, 28, 31-33, CO 8
Privet Knob, SM 116
Prizes and prize money, BL 11, 28-29, 31, 91, 153
Profanity, prevalence of, TT 56
Profiteering, MI 151, OR 30, 83, 84, *85. See also* Graft
Prohibition laws enacted, OR 29
Promontory, Utah Territory, NA *84-85*
Propaganda, BR 47, 89, 108-109, 118 159, OR 42, 44, 51, *52,* 58-59, 149-150, YA *21, 28, 31, 33, 37-38,* 124; activities, BL 120, 122-123; on Virginia secession, BR 138
Property taxes, OR 83
Prospect Hill, RE 61
Prostitution, TT 60-61
Prostrate State, The, NA 117, 127
Providence, Rhode Island, FI *40-41*
Provost guard, action by, FO *13,* 16-17, 137
Pry (Philip) house, BD 65, 70, *76-77, 86-87*
Pry (Samuel) farm, BD 64
Pryor, Roger A., BD 114-115, FO 159, 166
Pryor, Sarah, OR 126
Publishing industry, OR 46-48
Puebla, Mexico, battle at, FR 38, 39, *40-41,* 42
Puffer, Richard, TT 33
Pugh, George, YA 150
Pugh, Isaac C., SH 104
Pughtown, Virginia, DE 50
Pulaski, Tennessee, NA 36, SM 83, 84, 85
Pulpit Battery, CO *168-169*
Pumphrey, James W., AS 68, 108
Pumphrey's livery, AS 71
Punch, BL 14, 67, *121*
Punch Bowl, KI 113
Punishments, TT *64,* 65-66, 153; military, OR 88. *See also* Executions
Pup tent, TT 45-46

Purdy, Andrew M., personal effects of, TR *35*
Pursell, Hiram W., FO 142-143
Putnam, Haldimand S., BR *145,* CO 125, 127
Putnam, Holden, CH 140
Putnam, Sallie, AP 17
Pyne, Henry, TR 26
Pyron, Charles L., FR 24, 28, 29, 30, 31, 32

Q

Quaker guns, FO 39, *85,* 86
Quantrill, William Clarke (alias Charley Hart): FR 153, 154, 157; Anderson, break with, SP 157; background, SP 147-148; at Baxter Springs, SP 154, 155, 158; death, SP 161; in Kentucky, SP 143; and Lane, SP 144; at Lawrence, SP 148, 152-153, *154;* tactics, SP 149; Todd, split with, SP 157-158
Quarles, William A., SM 113
Quarles Mill, KI *141*
Quartermaster's Department. *See* Myers, Abraham C.
Quattlebaum, Paul J., BR *142*
Queen of the West, MI 20, 28-29, 32, 77, *78,* 79
Quesenberry, Elizabeth, AS 114
Quincy, Illinois, BR 106, SH 22
Quinine, SM 106
Quinine Brigade, MI 88
Quintard, Charles T., CH 30, SM 88

R

R. E. Lee, BL *19, 100*
Raccoon Mountain, CH 32, 37, 89
Raccoon Roughs, FO 141
Race relations, YA 23, 86, 99-103
Radar, Adam, TT 56
Radford, R.C.W., FI 149
Radical Republicans, FO 65, 71, 87-89, 92, 97; and Cabinet changes, YA 146-147; and Chase's nomination, YA 152; Lincoln, relations with, YA 143, 151-154; war aims, YA 142-143, 151-152. *See also* Congress; Partisan politics
Ragged Dick, NA 88
Raguet, Henry W., FR 25, 31, 32
Railborne artillery, LE 50
Railroad operations: captured rolling stock, TE 11; damage by Confederates, TE 15, 31, 49; depot at Nashville, TE *78-79;* hijacking of *General*, TE 8; importance in war west of Appalachians, TE 10; supply routes disrupted by Confederates, TE 81; troop movement by Bragg, TE 42, 43; use in Tennessee by Union, TE 79
Railroad Redoubt, MI 130, 136

AP Pursuit to Appomattox; AS The Assassination; AT Battles for Atlanta; BD The Bloodiest Day; BL The Blockade; BR Brother against Brother; CH The Fight for Chattanooga; CO The Coastal War; DE Decoying the Yanks; FI First Blood; FL The Shenandoah in Flames; FO Forward to Richmond; FR War on the Frontier; GE Gettysburg;

Railroads, RE *map* 8; accidents on, OR 28; Anderson's attacks, SP 160; Andrews' raid, SP 111-113; assaults on, DE 34-36, 45-46, *64-65*, 123; at Atlanta, AT 21, 132; Baltimore & Ohio, DE *16-17*, 33-34, *36-37*, 43, 45-46, 61, *64-65*; bridges, AT *8-9*, *14*; in Bull Run campaign, FI 122, *123*; civilian travel ban, AT 24; clerks, RE *20*; Confederate attacks on, SM 19; Confederate demolition of, FO 63, 74, *118-119*; and Confederate supplies, TR 18-19, 53, 57, 99, 104; construction, MI 13, OR 27-28; construction and repair, RE 9, *10-17*, TT 26; control and coordination, RE 9, 20-21; Credit Mobilier Affair, NA 109, 110; damage by Confederate raiders, SP 90, *98-99*, *118-119*; damage by Confederate raids, CH 20, 25, 97; damage by Union cavalry, CH 29; deficiencies, OR 10, 25, *26*, 27-29; demolitions by Union Army, OR *156-157*; demolition by Union, MI 63, 115; election campaigns, NA 54; expansion, BR 18, 28, YA 47, 64-66; expansion by, NA 83-86, 123, 154; and farmers, NA 89-90; fortifications for, CH 29, *168-169*; government control of, OR 28-29; Haupt's wrecking manual, SP *90-103*; importance, MI 9, 16; influence on military operations, FI 2, 56; labor force, RE 10; Lincoln funeral trains, AS 118, *120-121*, *124*, *125*; Manassas Gap, DE 39, 86, 114, 121, RE *map* 8, *22-23*; McNeill's attacks, SP 126; Memphis & Charleston, MI 40; mileage and specifications, RE 9; Mississippi Central, MI 56, 83, 88; misuse, RE 21; Mobile & Ohio, MI 88, 96; monopolies, YA 78-79; Mosby's attacks, SP 122, 130-131; national system, FI 46, 57, 59; operations against, RE 14, *16*, *22-23*, 93, 108, 159; Orange & Alexandria, DE *142*, RE *map* 8, *14*, *16-17*, 33, 108; parlor car, NA *86-87*; in Peninsular Campaign, FO 130; protection for, SP 104; repair of, SP *100-103*, 104; repair work, CH 25, 97, 169; Richmond, Fredericksburg & Potomac, RE *map* 8, 50, 93; rolling stock types, RE *12-14*, *22-23*; routes, YA *map* 2-3; sabotaged, FI 29; sabotage on, FO 69; safeguarding, FI *28*, 29, *30*, 31, 85; security measures, TT *17*; South, destruction in, NA 26; Southern Mississippi, MI *13*, 16, 88-89, 122, 130; Stanton's control of, DE 146; in supply operations, RE 18, *20-21*; supply routes, CH 18, 25, 30, 78, 97, 136, 156, 168; track mileage, BR 9, OR 26; transcontinental routes, NA 78, 83, *84-85*, 154; transfer of Longstreet's troops, CH 42, *55*, 100, 101; transfer of Union troops, CH 83; in troop movements, DE 100-101; and Union attacks, TR *54-55*, 56-57, 101, 103-105; Union demolition of, AT 141-142, *168*, *169*, *170-171*, FO 133; Union destruction of, SM *46*, 62, *64-65*; Union raids on, MI 88-94, *95*; Union security, AT 9; and Union supplies, AT 22-24, 26, 37, 50, SM 14, 17, 19, 29, TR 136, *170-171*; and Union troop movements, SM 20-21; and Union troop transport, AT *50-51*; use in Confederate retreat, CH 150; Vicksburg, Shreveport & Texas, MI 16; Virginia & Tennessee, DE *12-13*, 21; Virginia Central, DE *8-9*, RE 93; wartime priorities, MI 17. *See also* Bridge construction; Haupt, Herman; *individual names*; Transportation system, deficiencies of

Rains, Gabriel J., FO 139, 141, SM *152*, SP 163

Rains, George Washington, OR *21*

Rains, James E., TE 115, *121*, 155

Raith, Julius, SH 145

Raleigh, BL 53

Raleigh, North Carolina, OR 49

Raleigh *Standard*, OR 154

Rams: Confederate, MI 20, 26-32, 80; Union, MI 20, *24-25*, 27-29, 32, 77-78

Ramsay, John A., BD 136

Ramseur, Nellie, FL 79

Ramseur, Stephen Dodson, FL 60, 74, 75, 79, 89-91, 109, 122, GE 54-55, 59, 119, KI 100, 126, RE 147; ability of, FL 68-69; at Cedar Creek, FL 144, 148-150, 157, *166*; on deathbed, FL *170*; at Opequon Creek, FL 112-114, 119, 122

Ramsey, Alexander, FR 72, 74, 79, 80, 84, 86, 90

Ramsey, H. A., BL 55

Ramsey, John, AP 96

Randall, George M., AP 36

Randall, James Ryder, OR *49*

Randol, Alanson M., LE 59, TR 26

Randolph, George E., RE 71

Randolph, George Washington, FO 103, RE 33; Davis evaluated by, OR 16; leaves Confederacy, OR 160; as Secretary of War, OR 16

Randolph, George Wythe, FI 80

Randol's battery, LE 59, *62*

Ranney, William, painting by, FR *8-9*, *12-13*

Ransbottom, Alfred, SM 122

Ransom, Floyd, SH 117

Ransom, Matthew W., AP 36, 88, 90, 125

Ransom, Robert, Jr., FL 69, LE 71, RE 33, 36-37, 73

Ransom, Thomas E. G., FR 57, SH *117*

Ransom bonding, BL 147-148, 152, 159

Rapidan River, FO 102, RE 33-34, 118, 120, 123; operations around, LE 99, 124-125

Rapidan Station, Virginia, LE 101

Rappahannock County, Virginia, OR 111

Rappahannock River, FO 63, 83, 89, 102, GE 2, 10, 13, *14-15*, 20, 22, OR *134-135*; operations around, LE *map* 2-3, 24-25, 93, 101, *110-111*, *118-119*, 125-126, 132,

RE *2-3*, 30-33, 35-36, 39-40, 50, *52-55*, 56-57, 72, 85, 91, 93, 95, 105-111, 118-119, 120-121, *map* 122, 123, 158, *159*, 160; railroad facilities, RE 8; strategic value of, FI 76, 111

Rappahannock Station, Battle of, KI *33*

Rath, Christian, AS 160, 162, *166-167*, *168-169*; noose made by, AS *133*

Rathbone, Henry Reed, AS 76, 77, 85, 86, 88

Rations, TT 20, 80, 82, *84*, 85-86, *87*, 113-115, 118, *132*, 156. *See also* Mess facilities

Raulston, William C., TT 122-124, *125*

Rawdon, Horace, painting by, CH *30-31*

Rawlins, John A., AP 144, *146*, KI 127, 151, *162*, MI *145*, 146-147, SH 48, 78, 87, SP 72, 73, TR *17*

Raymond, Henry J., OR 158, YA 20, 144

Raymond, Mississippi, MI 111-112

Read, Henry, rifle of, FL *17*

Read, Theodore, AP 118, 120

Read, Thomas Buchanan, FL 158

Reader, Samuel J., diary of, FR *162-171*

Reading, TT 9, 66-67

Ready, Mattie, TE 90, *92*

Ready house, TE *93*

Reagan, John H., KI 165, OR 14

Reams's Station, Battle of, TR 94, 107-110

Reams's Station, Virginia, TR 55-56, 104

Reaney, Henry, BL 46, 56

Rebel Queen, SP 58

Reconnaissances, FO 39-41, 50, 64, 94, 99, 102, 136, MI 73, 79-80; Confederate, DE 66, 70-71, 114, 129, 133, 149; Federal, DE 72, *74*, 76-77

Reconstruction: aftermath of, NA 157-158; black government during, NA 67-70; carpetbaggers, NA 63-64, 145; corruption in South, NA 66, 69, 117-119; election of 1876, NA 148-156; military districts in South, NA 61-63; Northern industrial interest in, NA 61; Panic of 1873, NA 127, 148; Republican plans for, NA 16-18, *30*, 41, 52, 56, 112; State constitutional conventions, NA 65, 67-69; Union troops, withdrawal of, NA 156-157; voting rights in South, NA 63, 65, 156

Reconstruction Acts, NA 56, 61, 63, 66, 70, 71, 75, 76

Recreation, OR 54, *56-57*, 126

Recreational activities, TT 9, *13-15*, 30, *60-61*, 62, 66-69, 70-71, 118, *120-121*, *166-167*. *See also* Crafts; Sports activities; Theatricals

Recruiting campaigns, OR *36*, 74, 78

Recruiting campaigns, Union, LE 93

Recruiting programs, FO 16, 18, 97, SH 11, 21, 54-55, *80*

Recruitment, YA 40, 45, 62, 86-87, 95-98; age requirements, TT 26; of blacks, TT 32-33, 35; bounty payments, YA 87, 89, *94-95*, 98; bounty system, TT 24; boys enlisted, TT 26; Confederate, TT *25*,

Confederate Major General Robert Ransom, Jr., who served in Virginia, Tennessee and South Carolina

Brigadier General John A. Rawlins, Grant's Chief of Staff, in camp with his wife and daughter

KI The Killing Ground; LE Lee Takes Command; MI War on the Mississippi; NA The Nation Reunited; OR Confederate Ordeal; RE Rebels Resurgent; SH The Road to Shiloh; SM Sherman's March; SP Spies, Scouts and Raiders; TE The Struggle for Tennessee; TR Death in the Trenches; TT Tenting Tonight; YA Twenty Million Yankees

Recruiting poster for the Washington Cavalry of Pennsylvania, raised in late summer of 1862

Two youthful Rhode Island soldiers and a friend, photographed in the first weeks of the War

Recruitment (continued)
35-37; enlistment period, TT 22; muster laws, TT 21; muster rolls, TT 20; old men enlisted, TT 26-28; of physically unfit, TT 37, 79-80; by states, TT 22-24, *25;* state troops inducted, TT 22-24; troops raised, YA 87-89, 92, 111; Union, TT 21, *25, 30,* 32-33. *See also* Draft

Recruits: metamorphosis into veterans, TT 44, 47, 52, 55; and romance of war, TT 20. *See also* Soldiers

Rector, John, SH 63, 67
Rectortown, Virginia, FL 136
Redans, at Petersburg, TR 39-42, 45, *46-47,* 48, 65, 67
Redfield, James, SM 24
Red Iron, FR 87, *90, 105*
Red River, FR 46-47, 51-52, 54-55, 63, *66-67,* 70, 146, 155; operations on and near, MI 16-17, 73, 77-79, 110, *map* 161

Red River Campaign, CO 157, FR *map 2-3,* 46, 51-57, *map 58, 58-59,* 60-71; Pleasant Hill, Battle of, FR 60-*62;* Union fleet and dams, FR *68-71*

Red River War, NA 96
Red Shirts, uniform, NA *141*
Redstone brothers, SP 171
Redwood, Allen C., LE 127, 129
Reed, Booker, AT 149
Reed, Charles W., GE 32; letter of, GE *33;* sketch by, FL *75*
Reed, Wallace, AT 153
Reeder, Andrew, BR 74-76
Reeder, Charles, AP 99
Reed's Bridge, CH 44, 45, *46,* 47
Reelfoot Lake, SH 166
Rees, Lucian G., TR *45*
Refugees, OR 3, 110, 112-115, *118-119,* 120; in Alabama, OR 121, 123; in Georgia, OR *112-113,* 121, 123; in Louisiana, OR 121; from Maryland, OR 123; in Mississippi, OR 117-119; slaves, MI *50-51,* 57-58; in South Carolina, OR 116, 121, 123; in Tennessee, OR 117, 121; in Texas, OR 121; treatment of, OR 121, 123, 126-128; at Vicksburg, MI 18, 26, 126; in Virginia, OR 34-35, *40-41,* 117, 121, 123-128. *See also* Migration

Regiments, histories of, TT 20. *See also* by state

Regiments. *See* names of commanders, units, or under states

Regular Army, Confederate, troop strength, TT 21

Regular Army, United States, BD 132, 153, FR 28, 35, 107, KI 63, 66, RE 51, 86-87, 89, 91; 1st Sharpshooters Regiment, BD 153, GE 76; 2nd Sharpshooters Regiment, BD 74-75, GE 80; 1st Volunteers, FR 99; Mortar Battery No. 14, TR 130; at Bull Run, FI 118, 141, *142,* 148-149, 157, 162-169; composition and leadership, TT 21; horse artillery, TR 26; officer assignments, FO 28; officers joining Confederacy, FI 27-28;

prisoners lost, TT 110; seniority system, FI 56; and state appointments, FI 56-57; Sykes's division, LE 36-37; troop strength, FI 20, TT 21

Artillery: 1st Artillery, AP *111;* Battery E, 1st Artillery (Graham), BD 108; Battery E, 1st Artillery (Randol), LE 59, *62;* Battery H, 1st Artillery (Webber), FO 109; Battery I, 1st Artillery (Ricketts), FI 137, 139, 141, *142,* 144, 160-161; Battery I, 1st Artillery (Ricketts and Kirby), FO *26-27,* 155; Battery I, 1st Artillery (Woodruff), GE 138-139; 1st Brigade Horse Artillery, KI *10;* 2nd Artillery, BD 150, RE *168-169;* Battery A, 2nd Artillery (Calef), GE 45; Battery F, 2nd Artillery, AT 104; Battery F, 2nd Artillery (Totten), SH 27; Battery C, 3rd Artillery (Gibson), LE *64-65;* Battery E, 3rd Artillery (Ayres), FI 118; Battery A, 4th Artillery (Cushing) GE *121,* 131, 140; Battery B, 4th Artillery (Campbell) BD 74-75, LE 137-139; Battery B, 4th Artillery (Stewart), GE 62, 161; Battery G, 4th Artillery (Wilkeson), GE *58;* 5th Artillery, FL 150, FO *4, 106-107;* Battery C, 5th Artillery, KI 102; Battery D, 5th Artillery (Griffin), FI 137, 139, 141, *142,* 144, 157, *160-161;* Battery D, 5th Artillery (Hazlett), GE *84-85,* LE 153; Battery I, 5th Artillery (Watson), GE 108

Cavalry: 1st Cavalry Regiment, FL 100, 103, 135, FR 23, 24, SH 29; 2nd Cavalry Regiment, FL 136, FR 19, GE 22, *36-37,* RE *32;* 3rd Cavalry Regiment, FI 162, FR 23, 24; 5th Cavalry Regiment, AP *14,* LE 27, *44-45,* 46; 7th Cavalry Regiment, NA 92, 93, 96, *101, 104-105;* 9th Cavalry Regiment, NA *100-101*

Infantry: 7th Infantry Regiment, FR 19, 23, 26; 10th Infantry Regiment, FR 23; 11th Infantry Regiment, FI 169, RE 89; 13th Infantry Regiment, MI 127, 136; 14th Infantry Regiment, TT *43;* 1st Veteran Infantry Regiment, FR 119; 3rd Infantry Regiment, NA 143, 156-157; 4th Infantry Regiment, BD 139-141, KI 114, TR 168-169; 5th Veteran Infantry Regiment, FR 23, 119

Reid, John C., NA 152
Reid, Whitelaw, NA 29, 34, 123
Reiley, Robert, RE 131
Reilly, James, CO 169
Relay House, Maryland, FI *30,* 31
Relief agencies. *See* United States Christian Commission; United States Sanitary Commission

Relief and welfare agencies, TT 108, 115-116, 147, *148*

Relief programs. *See* Welfare programs

Religion: influence of, BR 12, 20, *21;* revival movement, OR 59-60; tracts issued, OR 55. *See also* Churches; Clergymen

Religious prejudice, BR 100
Religious publications, TT 147, 148, *149*

Religious services, TT 62, 118, *123,* 144, *146-147,* 148-152. *See also* Chaplains

Relyea, Peter, AS 122
Remond, Charles Lenox, BR 67
Rennehan, F., SP 24
Reno, Jesse L., BD 45, 48-50, *51,* CO *32,* LE 133-134, 148-149, 152, 163-164; at New Bern, CO 36-37; at Roanoke Island, CO 25, 27-30, 32

Reno, Marcus A., BR 142
Renshaw, William B., FR 48, 49
Renty (slave), BR *49*
Renville Rangers, FR 80, 81, 87
Repetti, Alexander, DE *154*
Replacement of losses, TT 48
Reporters. *See* Correspondents
Representatives, Congressional. *See* Congress, Confederate States

Reprisals by Confederates, TT 65
Republican Party: carpetbaggers, NA 65; Chicago convention, BR 111-113; coalition in South, NA 66-67, *68,* 99; elephant symbol, NA 129, *139;* emergence and growth, BR 101, 103, 105, 109; factions in, NA 16-17; platform, BR 101, 103, 111, 116; Wide-Awake element, BR *114-115*

Requa battery gun, CO *129*
Requia battery, SP *169*
Requisitioning. *See* Impressment program
Resaca, Battle of, AT 40-48; battlefield, AT *12, 13. See also* Resaca, Georgia

Resaca, Georgia, AT 32, 36, 37, 38, 39, 40, 45, SM 28, 29

Research program, OR 22
Reveille, TT 49
Revels, Hiram Rhodes, NA 69, *70*
Revere, Joseph, RE 145
Revere, Paul Joseph, FO 52, GE 154, *155,* KI 92

Revere House (Cumberland), SP 127
Reviews. *See* Parades and reviews
Revival movements, TT 148
Revolutionary War tradition, TT 21, 26
Revolvers, OR *19, 65,* YA *69;* Adams, FI *75;* Colt, GE *41;* models used, FI *74-75;* Navy, MI *65*

Reynolds, Daniel H., SM 142
Reynolds, Francis, BD 63
Reynolds, George, AT 102
Reynolds, John F., GE 35, 45-47, *48, 51, 88-89,* LE 137-138, 143, 152-153, 162, RE 57-58, 60, 120, 135, 140, 158

Reynolds, John H., CH 25, 26, 35, 45, 46; at Chickamauga, CH 47, 48, 57, 64, 68
Reynolds, Thomas C., FR 156
Reynolds, Tom, SP 157
Reynolds' Plantation, SM 67
Rhett, Albert, AP 68, 69
Rhett, Robert Barnwell, BR 127, 130
Rhett, Robert Barnwell, Jr., OR *53*
Rhett, Thomas, FI 139
Rhind, Alexander C., CO 160
Rhode Island, BL 64
Rhode Island troops, AP 99, BD 42, 56,

Rapid-firing Spencer rifle, tinned to prevent corrosion, issued to Federal naval personnel

TT 116, 144; at Bull Run, FI 119, 130, *134, 156-157;* in Washington defense, FI 26

    Artillery: 1st Artillery (Brown), GE 127, 131-133, 135; 1st Light Artillery Regiment, RE 85; Battery A, 1st Artillery (Arnold), GE *124;* Battery A, 1st Artillery (Tompkins), BD *102;* 5th Heavy Artillery Regiment, CO 85

    Cavalry: 1st Cavalry Regiment, RE 108, *110;* Battery B, 1st Cavalry Regiment, GE 28; 7th Cavalry Squadron, BD 57

    Infantry: 1st Infantry Regiment, CO 16, FI *40-41, 134, 156-157,* RE 27; 2nd Infantry Regiment, AP *118,* 124, FI 119, 130, *156-157,* FO *32-33;* 4th Infantry Regiment, BD 136-137, CO 34, 37, TR 83; 5th Infantry Regiment, CO 90

Rhodes, Elisha H., AP *118*
Rice, Edmund, GE *155*
Rice, J. M., TE 126
Rice, James C., KI 65
Rice, Owen, RE 129
Rice production and marketing, BR *11*
Rice's Station, Virginia, AP 115, 117, 118, 120, 128
Richards, A. C., AS 85-86, 108
Richards, George, YA 36
Richardson, Albert, SH 59, 78, 82
Richardson, Beale, SP *18*
Richardson, Edmund, NA 124
Richardson, Hollon, AP 90
Richardson, Israel B., BD 87, 99-101, 104-106, *107,* 108-109, FI 117-122, 149, 155, FO 158-160, 164-165, LE 53, 59
Richardson, Nathaniel, TR 114-115
Richardson, Samuel, FR *134*
Richardson, William, NA 112, 114, 116, TE 29
Richmond, CO 66-67, 145, 150-151, TR 144
Richmond, Fredericksburg & Potomac Railroad, KI 82, 130-131, RE *map 8,* 50, 93, SP 84, 85, 86; destroyed bridge, KI *134*
Richmond, Kentucky, Battle of, TE 45-48
Richmond, Virginia, AP 33, 78, BD 8, 13, 164, 168, CH 18, CO 38-39, 86, 97, DE 2, 21, 114, 121-123, 146, 147, FI *map 3,* NA 26, 61, *114, OR 12, 20, 34-41,* TR 8, 16, *18,* 28, 36, 57, 64, TR life in, 137; alarm at, TR 145; arms production in, FI 46; becomes Confederate capital, FI 18; FO 8; black soldiers enlisted at, OR 167; civil disorders in, OR 30, 82, 85-86, *88,* 168; clothing production in, OR 25; Dahlgren's raid, KI 39, *40-41;* demoralization in, FO 127; destruction in, AP 101, 108, *164-171;* devastation in, OR 167, *168-169;* evacuation of, AP *100-101,* OR 167; food costs and shortages, OR 30, 85-86, 160; and food for troops, AP 16-17; fortifications at, TR *102,* 138; inflation in, KI 32; Lincoln's visit, AS 54, *58;* living conditions in, AP

17, 18; made capital, OR 35; medical services, OR *36-38,* 59; money-engraving plant, OR 68; munitions production, OR 17, 21-23, 64, 66; paroled Confederate soldiers at, AP *156;* plans for capturing, FI 44, 77; political importance of, SH 9; population, BR 14, FO 127; population expansion, OR *34-35, 40-41,* 123; prisoner camps, OR *38-39;* prostitution in, TT 61-62; as railroad center, OR 27; refugees in, OR 35, *40-41,* 123-128; security measures, FO 103, 127-129, 133, 138; Sheridan's raid, KI 122-123; as slave market, BR *50-53;* as troop-staging area, FI 18; Union approach to, FO 14, 63-64, 73, 84, 89-91, 93, 102, 124-127, 130; Union drive on, OR 13, 59, 148, 151, 160, 167-168; Union occupation, AP 108, *111;* Union threat to, LE *map 2-3,* 23-24, 31, *map 32,* 48, 90-91; Van Lew's activities in, SP 86-89. *See also* Peninsular Campaign
Richmond & Danville Railroad, AP 27, 78, 79, 97, *168,* TR 53, 55, 57
Richmond & Petersburg Railroad, AP *168,* TR 18, 27, 28, 44
Richmond & York River Railroad, FO 129, 136, LE 25, 28, 49, *86*
Richmond *Daily Enquirer,* FI 17
Richmond *Daily Examiner,* YA 56
Richmond *Dispatch,* OR *82,* 84, SP 107, YA 43
Richmond *Enquirer,* OR 83; theater bill, AP *18*
Richmond *Examiner,* BD 20, CO 30, KI 39, LE 22, 92, OR 13, 49, 166
Richmond Grays, AS 18
Richmond Howitzers (Virginia), AP *123,* FI 79-80, FO 48, TT 26
Richmond Laboratory, OR 64
Richmond *Sentinel,* MI 142-143
Richmond *Whig,* LE 22, 92, OR 13, 54, 82, 167, SP 86
Rich Mountain, FI 87-89, *90,* 91
Rich Mountain, Battle of, FO 12-13
Richter, Hartman, AS 110, *111*
Ricketts, James B., BD 67, 70-71, FI 137, 142-144, 155, FL 73, 75, 79, 81, 83, 89, KI 54, LE 101; at Cedar Creek, FL 149; at Cedar Mountain, LE 108; at Opequon Creek, FL 112, 115; at Second Bull Run, LE 152; at the Berryville road, FL *114;* at Thoroughfare Gap, LE 134-135, 143
Ricketts, R. Bruce, GE 114, *115-116,* 117
Ricketts' battery, FI 137, 139, 141, *142,* 143-144, *160-161,* FO 26-27
Riddle, Unus, OR 91
Rider, Godfrey, Jr., CH 95
Ridley, Bromfield L., AT 52
Ridley, Samuel J., MI 56, 118
Rifle and Light Infantry Tactics (Hardee), FI *51,* TT 52
Rifles, YA *68-69;* Spencer, MI *92. See also* Muskets and rifles
Riggin, John, MI 145

Ringgold, Georgia, AT *10,* 31, CH 39, 54, 55, 150
Ringgold Light Artillery (Pennsylvania), FI *24-25*
Rio Grande, FR 19, 23, 35, *36, 37,* 46, 47, 50, 51, 113
Riots. *See* Civil disorders
Ripley, Edward, BD 59
Ripley, Roswell, BD 97
Ripley, Roswell S., LE 36
Ripon, Wisconsin, BR 101
Rippetoe, William B., CH 19
Rise and Fall of the Confederate Government, NA 24
Risedorph, John, SM 38-39
Ritter, William L., SM 135
Ritterspaugh, Jacob, AS 151
River Defense Fleet, CO 63-73
River Queen, AP 24, 25, 41, 76, 77, AS 53, OR 163
River Road, LE 58, 65
Rivers, strategic value of, SH 8-9
Rives, Francis, TR 13
Rives, William C., OR 161-162
Rives's Salient, TR 50-51
Roach, Mahala, MI 17
Road construction, LE *38-39, 87;* repair, MI 129, TT 52
Road system, DE 45, 84-86, 118-119, 129, *map 130*
Roanoke Island, FO 74, 81; armament and fortifications, CO 21; artillery actions, CO 25; casualties, CO 27, 30; channel obstructions, CO 23-24; joint operations, CO 16-19, 22-25, *map 26, 27,* 28-29, 30-31, 35; reconnaissances, CO 24; terrain features, CO 25, 27-30; weather, effect on operations, CO 21-22, *23,* 24
Roanoke River, CO 94-95; operations in, BL *80-85*
Robber barons, NA 86-88
Robert, Henry M., BR *144*
Roberts, Benjamin S., FR 24, 25
Roberts, Derring, TT 92
Roberts, George, SH 163
Roberts, George W., TE 122
Roberts, Otis, KI 33
Roberts, Thomas L., FR 113
Robertson, Beverly H., CO 87, LE 91, 101
Robertson, Felix, TE 149
Robertson, Jerome B., GE 78, 80-81, 84-86, LE *170*
Robertson Hospital, OR 59
Robertson's Battery (Florida), TE 149
Robins, W. W., LE 28-29
Robinson, Augustus G., BR *145*
Robinson, Charles, BR 84, SP 144, 145
Robinson, Corporal, SH 91
Robinson, George F., AS 95, 96, 97
Robinson, Gilbert P., TR 76-78
Robinson, James, AT 43
Robinson, James S., AP 71, 72, 73
Robinson, John, KI 86, 87, RE *68*
Robinson, John C., GE 52-53, 59, 105, 112
Robinson, Martin, KI 36

Colonel George W. Roberts of the 42nd Illinois, killed while commanding a brigade at the battle of Stones River

Brigadier General Beverly H. Robertson, Confederate cavalry commander under Jeb Stuart

KI The Killing Ground; LE Lee Takes Command; MI War on the Mississippi; NA The Nation Reunited; OR Confederate Ordeal; RE Rebels Resurgent; SH The Road to Shiloh; SM Sherman's March; SP Spies, Scouts and Raiders; TE The Struggle for Tennessee; TR Death in the Trenches; TT Tenting Tonight; YA Twenty Million Yankees

Brigadier General Isaac P. Rodman, mortally wounded leading a division of IX Corps at Antietam

Federal soldiers entrenching under cover of huge wicker gabions or sap rollers

Robinson, Thomas B., DE 32
Robinson, William, paintings by, TR *8*, *14*
Robinson house, FI 137, 139, *158-159*
Roche, Thomas, AP 102; photographs by, AP *103-107*
Rocheport, Missouri, SP 159
Rochester, New York, BR 64
Rock, John, YA 102
Rockbridge Artillery, BD 86, DE 46, *115*, 130, 135, 161
Rock Creek, GE 74, 115, 128
Rockefeller, John Davison, NA 83, 86, 88, YA 71, *78*, 79
Rockets, use of, CO 64
Rocketts Landing, Virginia, OR *40-41*
Rockfish Gap, DE 8, FL 49, 57, 58, 59
Rock Island prison camp, TT 116
Rockville, Maryland, FL 84
Rockwell, William Harrison, LE *63*
Rocky Face Ridge, AT 30, 32, *34*, 35, *37*, 38, 39
Rocky Mount, Virginia, FL 53
Roddy, Robert R., FO 124
Rodes, Robert E., BD *106*, FL 68, 69, 74, 79, 84, 109, 112, 113, 115, *116*, 119, FO 139, 141, GE *54*, KI 62, 100-101, 103, 126, 149, RE 122, 130, 133-134, 138, 141-142, 146-148; at Antietam, BD 94, 101, 103, 106; at Carlisle, GE 31; at Cemetery Hill, GE 53, *map* 63; at Chambersburg, GE 26, 31; at Chancellorsville, GE 54; at Gettysburg, GE 26, 53-54, 59-60, 113, 118; at Oak Ridge, GE 54, 59; in Potomac crossings, GE 26, 156; at South Mountain, BD 51-52
Rodgers, George W., CO 130
Rodgers, John, FO 128, SH 70
Rodman, Isaac P., BD 122, 124, 126, 130-132, 136, CO 37
Rodman, Thomas J., CO 80
Rodman gun, YA *11*
Roe, Frances, NA *104*
Roebling, Washington A., TR 127
Roehrig, F.L.O., TT *41*
Roesler, John, lithographs by, DE *72-81*
Rogers, William P., MI 41, *42-43*, *44-45*
Rohrbach's Bridge. *See* Burnside Bridge
Rohrersville, road to, BD 121
Rolla, Missouri, SH 19, 21, *32*
Roll call, TT 49
Rolling Fork, MI 80
Rollins, Bettie, AS 115, 132
Rollins, Nathaniel, TT 120-121
Rollins, William, AS 115, 132
Romance of war, TT 20-21, 24
Romanticism, OR 8, 10-11, 46
Rome, Georgia, AT 48, CH 36, SM 20
Rome *Confederation*, OR 51
Romney, Virginia, DE 2, 44-46, 50, 52, *53*, 55-58, 99
Romney, West Virginia, SP 115, 122
Ronald, Charles, LE 103
Roos, Charles, FR 72
Roosevelt, Franklin D., NA 171

Root, Adrian, RE 67, 70
Root, Augustus I., AP 135
Root, George, TT 145
Rose, Thomas E., TT 124-128
Rose (John P.) farm, GE 99, 101, *166*
Rosecrans, William S., CH 2, 8, 18, *19*, 20, 25, 29, 34, *36*, 37, 42, *43*, 44, 54, 65, 66, 73, 104, DE 44, FI 88-93, FO 13, FR 156, MI *42*, SP 75, TE *83*, 85, 92, 95, 96, 98, 99, 100, *103*, 106, *109*, 142, 161; at Chickamauga, CH 45, 56, 52, 53, 56, 61, 63, 68; at Corinth, MI 38-40, 42-43; early service, TE 80; early success of, CH 19; Garesche's death and, TE 132; Grant, relations with, MI 44; at Iuka, MI 36-37; leadership, TE 98, 112; meeting with Grant, CH 88; at Nashville, MI 44, TE *70*, 84; outmaneuvers Bragg, CH 21, 22, 30, 32, 33, 35; overconfidence, CH 35, 39, 42; personal traits, MI 38; popularity, CH 19; in railroad defense, MI 34; relations with Halleck, CH 21, 32; ruses, use of, CH 23-24, 33-34, TE 99, 157; shaken by defeat at Chickamauga, CH 78, 83; at Stones River, TE 2, 118, 119, 123, 124, 126, 127, *128-129*, 130, *132*, 133, 134, 143, 144, 150, 152, 154, 155, 159; temperament, CH 19, 49, TE 81, 114
"Rosecrans' Victory March," CH *19*
Rosencrantz, Frederick, KI *10-11*
Rosenstock, J., BD 18-19
Ross, John, FR *139*, 148
Rosser, Thomas L., AP 80, 84, *86*, 87, 88, 118-120, FL 125, 138-139, *141*, 142, 144, 145, 147, 151, GE *27*, KI 86, TR 22, *24-25*, 114-115
Ross's Battery, TR 45
Rossville, Georgia, CH 49, 61, 64, 72
Rossville Gap, CH 117, 130, 136, 142
Rost, Pierre A., BL 16, 116
Roswell, Georgia, AT 77, 78
Roswell's Ferry, AT *81*
Rough and Ready, Georgia, AT 143, 147, SM 50
Roulette (William) farm, BD 93-94, 96, *map* 98, *99*, 150
Round Forest, TE 112, 124, 126, 127, 129, 130, 142, 143, 144, 145
Rouseville, Pennsylvania, YA *82*
Rousseau, Lovell H., NA 63, SH *150*, SM 125, TE 98, 120, 122, 123, 124, 126, 127, 163, *170-171*
Rowan, Stephen C.: at Elizabeth City, CO 31-33; at New Bern, CO 35-37; at Winton, CO 34
Rowe, Henry, TR 46
Rowett, Richard, SM 24
Rowley, William R., SH 118, 120
Royal Ape (play), OR 54
Royer, Samuel, GE *155*
Rubadou, Samuel, KI *104*
Rucker, Ed, SM 143-144
Rude's Hill, DE 83, 86-87, 157
Ruffin, Edmund, BR *156*, FI 149, OR 128;

in Fort Sumter bombardment, BR 137, 148-149, 156; on John Brown, BR 89; and Lincoln election, BR 98, 119; and secession, BR 24-25, 27; suicide, BR 156
Ruffin, Thomas, BD 47
Ruger, Thomas H., AP 65, 67, RE 144, SM 93, 95, 115
Rugg, Horace, TR 108
Ruggles, Daniel, SH 101, 136, *139*
Ruggles, David, SP 78
Ruggles, Gardner, TR *63*
Ruggles, George, LE 152
Ruggles, Mortimer B., AS 115, 116, 117
Rumsey, Israel P., SH *131*
Running Water Ravine, CH *170-171*
Rupert, Jessie, FL 30-31
Rural areas: educational system, OR 55; life style, OR 42-44. *See also* Farmers
Ruses, SH 157; by Grierson, MI 88-89, 91; by Porter, MI 78, 79
Rush County, Indiana, YA 99
Russell, Andrew J., RE 162-171, SP 90; photographs by, KI *30*
Russell, Charles, BD 43-44
Russell, Charles L., CO 27
Russell, David A., FL 112, 115, *117*, KI *33*
Russell, George, CO 77
Russell, Harry, RE *116*, 135
Russell, John: Confederacy, policy on, BL 16, 125-126; and *Trent* Affair, BL 118, *119;* and warship construction, BL 121, 126-128. *See also* United Kingdom
Russell, John, farmhouse of, TE 67
Russell, William Howard, FI 10, MI 9
Russia: Britain, relations with, BL 118; Confederacy, policy on, BL 16; fleet, visit by, BL *132-141*
Russian fleet, YA 23
Rust, John R., FL 143; brigade badge of, FL *143*
Ruth, Samuel, SP 85-86, 89
Rutledge, A. M., SH *107*
Rutledge Rifles, SH *107*
Ryan, Abram Joseph, OR 46
Ryan, George, BR *145*

Sabers, GE *40-41*, OR *64-65*
Sabers, Confederate, BD *24-25*, *39*
Sabers. *See* Swords and sabers
Sabine, George, TR *63*
Sabine Crossroads, Battle of, FR 56, *58*, 60, 62
Sabine Pass, Texas, FR 47, 50
Sackett, Delos B., BD 124
Sacramento, California, NA 84
Saddle, McClellan, GE *42*
Saddles, production of, OR 26
Safford, Henry, AS 92
Sagamon, AP *44*

AP Pursuit to Appomattox; AS The Assassination; AT Battles for Atlanta; BD The Bloodiest Day; BL The Blockade; BR Brother against Brother; CH The Fight for Chattanooga; CO The Coastal War; DE Decoying the Yanks; FI First Blood; FL The Shenandoah in Flames; FO Forward to Richmond; FR War on the Frontier; GE Gettysburg;

St. Albans, Vermont, SP *60*, 61
St. Cloud Hotel (Nashville), SM 126
Saint-Gaudens, Augustus, CO 126
Saint George, Bermuda, as blockade-runners' port, BL 21, 86-88, *89*, 90, 95-98, 100-101
Saint James's Church, GE 18, 22
St. John, Isaac M., AP 25, 26, 27, TR 57
St. Johnsbury, Vermont, FI *34-35*
St. Lawrence, BL *13*, 54
St. Louis, BL *151*, SH 59, *64*, *68-69*, 74, 83
St. Louis, Missouri, FR 138, 150, 156, 157; casualties in, SH 15-16; civil disorders in, SH *14-15*, 16; Confederate threat to, SH 101; patriotic displays in, SH 95; strategic value of, SH 8-9, 12, 32-33
St. Louis Arsenal, Missouri, SH 13-15
St. Louis *Evening News*, SH 33
St. Louis *Globe Democrat*, NA 115
St. Paul, Minnesota, FR *11*, 74, 80, 86, 99
St. Paul *Pioneer and Democrat*, BR *147*
St. Peter Frontier Avengers, FR 101
St. Peter's Church, LE *84*
St. Timothy's Hall, AS 18, 20
Sala, George Augustus, YA 119
Salacious pictures, TT *59*
Saldanha Bay, BL 152
Salem, Virginia, LE 127, SP 109
Salem Church, Virginia, RE 154, *map* 155, 156-158, 168, TT 161
Saline River, OR 120
Salisbury, North Carolina, NA 36
Sallie Robinson, OR 99
Salomon, Frederick, FR 148, 150
Saltillo, Mexico, LE 16
Salt industry, YA 72-73, 79
Salt Lake City, Utah Territory, FR *10*, 108, 112, 113, 128
Saltville, Virginia, FL 20, 21, TT 35
San Antonio, Texas, BR *131*, FR *18*, 22, 35, 37, OR 121
Sanborn, Franklin B., BR 85
Sanborn, John D., NA 112-114
Sanborn (spy), SP 75
Sand Creek Massacre, FR 106, 127-128, 129, *130-131*, NA 93
Sanders, George N., AS 144
Sanders, John C. C., TR 88
Sanders, Richard A., BD *151*
Sanders, William P., CH 106, 109
Sanders' Field, KI 62-65
Sandersville, Georgia, SM 71
Sandford, Charles, FI 59-61
Sand Mountain, CH 37
Sandusky, Ohio, TT 113
Sandy Ridge, DE *map* 66
Sanford, Edward, YA 108
Sanford, George, FL 100, 103, 135, 136, KI 9, RE 159
Sanford, Henry Shelton, BL 115, 122
San Francisco, BL 159
San Francisco, California, FR 107, 109, 128; population growth, YA 22

San Francisco Bay, shipbuilding at, BL 66-67
Sangster's Station, Virginia, TT *17*
Sangston, Lawrence, SP 17, *18*, 20; *The Bastiles of the North* (diary), SP 17
Sanitation: improvement of, YA 120-122; measures, TT 52, 80-82, 85, 94, 98
San Jacinto, BL 116
Santa Fe, New Mexico Territory, FR 19, 20, 23, 26-27, 33-34, 37, 113, 115, 118, 122
Santa Fe Trail, FR *map* 2-3, 120, 125
Santa Rosa Island, BL 31, BR 128-129, CO *map* 9
Sante Fe, New Mexico, NA *164*
Sap rollers, MI 136
Sassacus, BL *19*, *80-81*, CO 97
Satartia, Mississippi, MI 144
Saugus, AP *44-45*, AS 139, *142*
Savage's Station, Virginia, LE *map* 32, 50-52, *54-55*, 57, *86*, TT 104
Savannah, BL 28, SM 159
Savannah, Georgia, AP 19, 52, 53, CO 162, NA 59, 120, SM *map* 2-3, 15, 48, 52, 62, 66, 72, 144, 145, 155, TR 158; as blockade target, BL 21, 26, 29, 107; civilian life during Union occupation, SM *166-167*; Confederate defense of, SM 156-157; Confederate evacuation of, SM *158-159*; federal property seized, BR 128; fire in, SM *168-169*; fortifications at, SM *146-147*, 148, 152; newspapers, OR 51; patriotic demonstrations in, FI 14; population, BR 14; as railroad center, OR 27; refugees in, OR *112-113*, 123; surrender of, SM 160; Union capture of, OR 160; Union occupation of, SM 159, *160-163*; Union plans for capturing, FI 44; war atmosphere in, BR *129*; wharves at, SM *165*
Savannah, Tennessee, SH 104, 116, 147, 149
Savannah *Daily Morning News*, SM 68, *162-163*
Savannah *Press*, SM 30
Savannah prison camp, TT 128
Savannah *Republican*, OR 80
Savannah River, AP 53-54, CO 46-47, OR 113, SM *145*, 146, 147, 148, *158-159*, *164-165*
Savannah River Squadron, SM 145
Sayler's Creek, Battle of, AP *map* 119, AP 120-122, *123-124*, 125-128
Scalawags, NA 63, 65-66
Scales, Alfred M., KI 71
Scales, Cordelia Lewis, OR 111
Scammon, Eliakim, BD 45, 47
Scandinavian immigrants, YA 21
Scandinavians in Union Army, TT 30
Scannell, Mike, KI 160
Schenck, Robert C., DE 102-103, FI 127, 137, 145, LE *169*
Schenkl, John P., TE 140
Schimmelfennig, Alexander, GE 52, 60
Schofield, John M., AP 52-53, 61, 64, 65,

67, 70, 76, 78, AT 49, 76, 77, 140-142, FR 150, NA 61, 75, SH 27, SM 34, 83, 84, 89, 92-*94*, TT 157; as army commander, AT 31; background, AT 40; at Battle of Atlanta, AT 110, 111; Columbia, withdrawal from, SM 85-88; eludes Hood at Spring Hill, SM 93-95; at Franklin, SM 96, 97, 100, 112, 117, 118; and Hood, AT 91; at Kennesaw Mountain, AT 74-75; at Nashville, SM 120, 126, 133, 134, 137, 138; reputation of, SM 84; at Resaca, AT 42, 45; and Thomas, SM 84, 94, 122, 123; at Utoy Creek, AT 139
School system, OR 42, 54-55
Schoonmaker, James M., FL *120-121*
Schoonover, John, KI 105
Schroeder, Charles, FR *133*
Schurz, Carl, CH 93, 140, GE 52-53, 60, 74, 117, NA 26, 110, 111, 127, 144, 149, TT 29
Schwandt, Mary, FR 72, 74, 90
Schwendinger, Alexander, panorama, FR *88*, *89*
Scientific American, SP 170, YA 56, 59, 63
Scobell, John, SP *29*, 32
Scotsmen in Union Army, TT 30
Scott, Dred, BR 79-80, *81*, 98, 104-105, 108
Scott, George W., AP 132
Scott, Isaac, FR 60
Scott, John S., TE 44, 45, 48
Scott, Julian, LE 60; paintings by, AP *21*, FL *154-155*, KI *72*
Scott, Robert K., AT 102
Scott, T. B., MI 102
Scott, T. Parkin, SP *19*
Scott, Thomas A., FI 29-31, SP 23
Scott, Walter, FO 45, OR 46, TT 67
Scott, Winfield, BL *15*, CO 17, DE 25, 28-29, FI *47*, FO 8, 28-29, 53, 62, LE 16, RE 98-99, SM 16, SP 10, 16-21, 25; Anaconda Plan, FI 44-45, 48, 110, SH 8; as Army commander, FI 26-27; and blockade, FI 44-45; and Bull Run, FI 110-111, *112*, 155; Butler, relations with, FI 31, 77; and Fort Sumter relief, BR 121, 125-126, 133; Frémont relieved by, SH 33, 58; Greeley's criticism of, FI 45; and invasion of Virginia, FI 58-59, 77; Johnston evaluated by, SH 52; Lee, relations with, FI 27-28; loyalty to Union, BR 120, FI 28, *45*; and McClellan's strategic plans, FI 44; McClellan, relations with, FI 93; McClellan named Army commander by, FI 155; McDowell relieved by, FI 155; in Mexican War, FI 89, 111; and Missouri operations, SH 52; officer appointments by, FI 57-58, 95, 155; Patterson, relations with, FI 95; strategic plans, FI 44-45, 48, 110; and Washington defense, FI 29
Scott's Mill Ford, RE 156, 158
Scranton, Pennsylvania, NA 79
Scully, John, SP 42, 43

Lieutenant Colonel Emmett M. Morrison, 15th Virginia, who was captured at Sayler's Creek

KI The Killing Ground; LE Lee Takes Command; MI War on the Mississippi; NA The Nation Reunited; OR Confederate Ordeal; RE Rebels Resurgent; SH The Road to Shiloh; SM Sherman's March; SP Spies, Scouts and Raiders; TE The Struggle for Tennessee; TR Death in the Trenches; TT Tenting Tonight; YA Twenty Million Yankees

105

Confederate Admiral Raphael Semmes, renowned captain of the commerce raider C.S.S. *Alabama*

Colonel Robert Gould Shaw, killed leading the black soldiers of the 54th Massachusetts at Fort Wagner

Scurry, William, FR 24, *27*, 30-31, 32, 33, 37, 65
Sea Bird, CO 22, *31*, 32
Sea Bride, BL 153
Seabrook, John E., BL 36
Sea Islands, OR 124, *136-137*, *140-143*
Sea King, BL 159
Sears, Claudius W., SM 21, 24, 133
Seaton, John, SH 48-49
Secession from Confederacy. *See* Disloyalty; Secret societies
Secession from Union, opposition to, OR 75-77
Secessionist movement, BR 3, 24-25, *26-29*, 37, 43, 116-117, *118*, 119-121, 125, 128
Secessionville, South Carolina, CO 111
Secret Service Bureau, SP 46-47, 50, 57
Secret societies, OR 151-153, YA 28-29
Security measures: breaches of, OR 49-51; Confederate, DE 33, 65, 101; intelligence operations, OR *150*, 152; at railroads, TT *17*
Seddon, James A., AP 25, AT 29, MI 142, SP 126, TE 161, TR 153, TT 37; and impressment program, OR 83; leaves government, OR 161; on refugees, OR 123; as Secretary of War, OR 14-15; on subversive groups, OR 152
Sedgwick, John, BD 87-88, 90, 98, 122, DE 66, FO 155, GE 14, 16, 75, 105, 152, KI 29, 34, 68, 82, LE 59; at Chancellorsville, RE 140, 154, 162; death of, KI *88-89;* at Fredericksburg, RE 151-154; at Hamilton's Crossing, RE 123-124, 140; in Rappahannock operations, RE 120, *map* 122, 151, 156, 158, 167; at Salem Church, RE 154, *map* 155, 158; at Spotsylvania, KI 86-87; in the Wilderness, KI 56, 62, 73, 81; troop strength, RE 155-156
Seldon, Henry R., FR 24
Self-inflicted wounds, TT 52
Selfridge, Thomas A., Jr., CO 167
Selma, CO 143, 151
Selma, Alabama, CO 143; as railroad center, OR 27; refugees in, OR 121
Seminary Ridge, GE 44, 48-49, 50-51, 62, 65, *123*, *134*, 144-145, 147, *153*, *160*
Seminole, CO 145
Seminole Indians, FR 136, *139*, 146, 152
Seminole troops, TT 31
Semmes, Paul J., GE 99, 101, 108
Semmes, Raphael, BL *143*, *153;* as *Alabama* captain, BL 142-143, *148*, 149-155, 167, 170; and *Kearsarge* battle, BL 155-160; as *Sumter* captain, BL 24-25, 145-148; trial and release, BL 160
Senators. *See* Congress, Confederate States
Seneca Mills, Maryland, SP 122
Sentries. *See* Pickets
Sequatchie River, CH 78
Seven Days' Battles, BD 8, 15, 54, LE *map* 2-3, TT 149; beginnings, LE 31, *map* 32, 33; ending, LE 73. *See also individual battles*

Seven Pines, Battle of, DE 21, 151, LE 22-24, 31, 49, OR 36-37
Seven Pines, Virginia, FO *map* 2-3, 14, *map* 90-91, 130, 136-139, *map* 140, 141, *142-143*, 144-145, 150, 157-158, *map* 160, *165, 168-169. See also* Fair Oaks, Virginia
Sewall, Frederick D., FO *166*
Seward, Augustus, AS 95, 96, 97
Seward, Fanny, AS 95, 96, 99
Seward, Frederick, AS 66, 95, *96*, 97, SP 21
Seward, William Henry, AP 21, 24, 25, AS 10, 65-66, 72, *99*, 100, 145, BD 157, FO 62, 68, LE 93, NA 17, 31, 126, RE 94, SP 21, 23, YA *149;* assault on, AS 95-97; and blockade, BL 14, 26; Britain, relations with, BL 118; Chase, rivalry with, YA 146-147; and commerce raiders, BL 114; and Confederate commissioners, BR 133; on emancipation, YA 146; foreign war proposed by, BR 135; and Fort Sumter relief, BR 133-135, 137; France, relations with, BL 131; home, AS *22;* and intelligence operations, BL 115; and ironclad construction, BL 51; and John Brown's invasion plan, BR 85; and Kansas-Nebraska Act, BR 72-74; Lincoln, relations with, YA 146-147; and national security, YA 31; and peace negotiations, OR 162-165; as presidential candidate, BR 103, 111-113; removal sought, YA 146-147; and Russian fleet visit, BL 140; and slaveowners' reimbursement, OR 163-165; and *Trent* Affair, BL 118, *119. See also* United States
Seward, Mrs. William Henry, AS 99
Seward, William Henry, Jr., FL 83
Sewell's Point, Virginia: BL 46, 57-58, 64, FO 124
Sewing kits, TT 11
Sewing machine, YA 66, *139*
Sexton, James A., SM 94, 97, 103, 113
Seymour, Horatio, NA 61, 76; and draft, YA 103, 108-109; and emancipation, YA 144; as New York governor, YA 143-144
Seymour, Isaac G., LE 42
Seymour, Truman, AP 122, BD 68, 78, BR *148*, 149, 156, 159, CO 125, 128, 139, KI 81
Shackelford, James M., CH 103, 104
Shadburne, George, TR 110-111
Shaifer, A. K., MI 103
Shakespeare, William, TT 67
Shakespearean plays, OR 54
Shaler, Alexander, KI 81
Shanks, James, SP 59
Shanks, W.F.G., CH 81
Shannon, Alexander, SM *55*
Shannon, H., CH 139
Shannon, Wilson, BR 76
Shannon's Battery (Mississippi), CH 139
Shannon's Scouts (8th Texas Cavalry Regiment), SM *55*
Sharp, Jacob H., AT 107

Sharpe, George H., SP *80*, 82; and Chancellorsville Campaign, SP 81; and City Point explosion, SP 84; and Gettysburg Campaign, SP 81; postwar career, SP 89; and Ruth, SP 85, 86; and Van Lew, SP 87, 89
Sharpe, William, AT 46
Sharps & Hankins carbine, MI *64-65*
Sharp's Brigade, AT 107
Sharpsburg, Battle of. *See* Antietam, Battle of
Sharpsburg, Maryland, BD *map* 69, *map* 130, *134-135*, 157-159, *162-163*, FL 91, 104; Confederate advance to, BD *map* 2-3, 55, 59-60, 63, 65; operations at, BD 57, 86-87, 105, 120-121, 126, 129, 131, *132*, 135-137, 139-141, 152. *See also* Antietam, Battle of
Sharpshooters. *See* Snipers
Sharps model 1859 rifle, FI *70-71*
Sharps rifle, FO *101*
Shaw, Abner, TR 51
Shaw, Henry (alias E. C. Coleman), SP 79, 80
Shaw, Horace, TR 62
Shaw, James, TR 147
Shaw, Robert Gould, CO 125, *126*, 128
Shaw, William T., SH 122, *130*, 139
Shawneetown, Kansas, SP 149
"Shebangs," TT 46
Shedd, James N., TR 78
Sheehan, Timothy J., FR 81, *85*
Sheffee, John, FI 86-87
Shelby, Joseph O., FR 64, 150, 151, 153-155, 156, 157, *158*, 160, SH 17, 19; Iron Brigade, FR 151, 153-155
Shelbyville, Tennessee, CH 23, 24, 28, 30
Shellenberger, John, AT 70, SM 103
Shelton, David, OR 92
Shelton, W. H., KI 64-65
Shenandoah, AP 163, BL 143, *159*, 161
Shenandoah River, FL 17, 39, 109, 140; operations around, DE *16-17*, 33, 39, 83, 86-87, 99-100, 120, 123, *124-125*, 126, 156-157, *158-159*, 170
Shenandoah Valley, DE *map* 2-3, FI *map* 2-3, 57, FL *map* 2-3, FO 18, 36, 74-75, 83-94, 97, GE *map* 2-3, 25, *map* 32, OR 167, TR 18, 27, 57, 64, 95, 136; agricultural resources, DE 8-9, *12-13;* civilian sentiment in, FL 29, 134; and Confederate supplies, FL 17, 20; operations in, FI 93, 95, 111, 122, 126, LE 23-24, 30, 34, 97-98, RE 24, 26, 31, 33, 37; road system, DE 45, 84-86, *118-119*, 129, *map* 130; strategic value, DE 9, 21, 43, FI 31, 44, 76, 87; as supply source, DE 21; topography, DE 8-17, 101-102, 158; weather, effect on operations, DE 46, 50, *53*, 54-55, 83, 99-100, 151, 157; "the Burning," FL 19, 134, 137. *See also individual battle sites*
Shephard, Julia Adelaide, AS 83
Shepherd, Edward C., DE *111*
Shepherd, Oliver, TE 124, *125*

AP Pursuit to Appomattox; AS The Assassination; AT Battles for Atlanta; BD The Bloodiest Day; BL The Blockade; BR Brother against Brother; CH The Fight for Chattanooga; CO The Coastal War; DE Decoying the Yanks; FI First Blood; FL The Shenandoah in Flames; FO Forward to Richmond; FR War on the Frontier; GE Gettysburg;

Shepherdstown, Battle of, BD 61, 151, 153-156
Shepherdstown, road to, BD 151
Shepherdstown, West Virginia, FL 69, 106
Sheppard, Ella, NA *121*
Sheppard, William Ludwell, TT 53; paintings by, FL *29*, OR *60*, TR *151*
Sherfy, William H., AT 102
Sheridan, Philip H., AP 8, 78, 95, 110, 113-114, 117, 130, 133, 134, 162-163, CH 27, 42, *43*, 52, 64, FL 2, 52-53, 58, *102*, 105-106, 108, 113, 124-125, 144, 155, KI 38, 58, 85, 87, 115-118, 135, 148, NA 61, 63, 70, 72, *82*, *130-131*, 144, OR 167, SM 84, SP 127, 128, 131, TE *122*, TR *23*, 55, 73; at Appomattox, AP 135, 137-141, 143-145, *146-147;* assumes command in Valley, FL 101; background and temperament, FL 100-104; and Cedar Creek, FL 151-153, 156, 158, 159, *162*, *167*, *170-171;* at Chickamauga, CH 49, 57, 60, 61; at Cold Harbor, KI 151-152; and Deep Bottom raid, TR 69-70; and destruction in Valley, FL 134-135, 137; effect on troops, AP 88-90, FL 103, 109, 126, 152, *160-161;* and Five Forks, AP *80-82*, 84-92; and McNeill, SP 114; and Meade, KI 114; meeting in Washington, FL 140; at Missionary Ridge, CH 143, *146*, *147*, 149; and Mosby, FL 136; at Opequon Creek, FL 112-117, 119, 122; at Orchard Knob, CH 120; and partisans, SP 106; at Perryville, TE 60, 61, 66; promotion, TE 59, 122; pursuit of routed Confederates, CH 150, 155; ride to Cedar Creek, FL *cover*, *152;* and Sayler's Creek, AP 120-123, 125, 127-128; Shenandoah Valley, TR 95, 111, 136; at Stones River, TE 112, 113, 118, 119, 120, 121, 123, 124, 127; and Toms Brook, FL 139; and Trevilian Station raid, TR 19-21, 22, 24-27; at Winchester, FL 109; at Yellow Tavern, KI 119, 122-123
"Sheridan's Ride" (poem), FL 158
Sherman, (Dutch) Bill, BR 71
Sherman, (Dutch) Henry, BR 71
Sherman, Charles Robert, SM *8*
Sherman, Eleanor Mary, SM *12*
Sherman, Ellen Ewing, AT 50, 132, SM *12*
Sherman, Franklin O., FL *127*
Sherman, John, NA 77, 78, 97, SH 8, SM 8, 147, YA 37; on breakout of war, BR 146; as House Speaker candidate, BR 108-109
Sherman, Lizzie, AT 31
Sherman, Maria Boyle Ewing, SM *12*
Sherman, Mary Elizabeth, SM *12*
Sherman, Minnie, AP 62, AT 31
Sherman, Rachel Ewing, SM *12*
Sherman, Taylor, coat of arms of, SM *8*
Sherman, Thomas, CO 20
Sherman, Thomas Ewing, SM *13*

Sherman, Thomas W., BL 31
Sherman, William Tecumseh, AP 8, 19, 20, 26, 33, 41, AS 66, 67, 76, 145, AT *cover*, 3, *9, 11, 21, 23*, 59, 71, CH 120, 121, *122*, 130, 131, 132, 136, 149, 155, 160, 169, CO 141, 162, FR 51, 54, 67, 120, 157, KI 24-26, 42, 60, MI 66, NA *8-9*, 10, 76, *82*, *96-97*, 111, SH *113*, SM *9*, *12*, *13*, 17, *21*, 25, 29, *51*, 82, SP 24, 149; and Allatoona, SM 24; appearance, CH 122; under artillery fire, SM 145-146; and Atlanta's capture, SM 14; and Atlanta's destruction, AT 164-166, 170, SM 8, 45-46, 48; and Atlanta's evacuation, SM 15, 16; and Atlanta's fortifications, AT 116, 140; and Atlanta's occupation, AT 154-156; and Atlanta's railroads, AT 132, 139-142; at Atlanta, YA 158; at Battle of Atlanta, AT 97-98, 104, 109-110, 111; and Bentonville, AP 70, 73-75; and Bickerdyke, AT 24, 26, YA 130; at Big Black River, MI *127*, 142, 156; and blacks, SM *cover*, 58, 71, 73; Blair, relations with, SH 13; at Bull Run, FI 121-122, 126, 133, 135, 137, 145, 155; and canal project, MI 72-73; and Carolina plan, SM 156, 159; and Carolinas Campaign, AP *map 2-3*, 52-55, 57-58, 60-61, 66-69, 73, 78, 155; at Cassville, AT 48, 49; and casualties, AT 74; and cavalry, AT 136, 138-140; at Champion's Hill, MI 156; Charleston captured by, OR 166; at Chickasaw Bluffs, MI 57, 59, 63-67, *96-97*, 117, 144; and Cobb plantation, SM 60; and Columbia, AP 58, 60-62; commands Department of Ohio, SH 58-59, 104; commended by Halleck, SH 113; conciliatory actions in Savannah, SM 160-161, 166; correspondents, relations with, MI 86, 96; and Corse, SM 26; defensive measures by, SM 19-20, 28; disabled, MI 47; on draft, YA 111; on enemy cavalry, MI 93; evaluation of Wood, CH 56; and family life, SM 13; at First Bull Run, SH 104; flanking maneuvers, AT 15, 32, 50, 53, 60, 62, 75-78, 81; and flanking movements, SM 14; on food supplies, OR 29-30; and foraging, AP 57, 58, AT 26-27, SM 53-54, 71; foraging policy, OR 111; and Forrest, SM 88; and Fort Hindman, MI 68; and Fort McAllister's capture, SM 150; and Garrard, AT 80; and gift of Savannah, SM *135*, 159, *161;* at Grand Gulf, MI 109; and Grant, AT 20-22; Grant's evaluation of, SH 113; and Grant's resignation, MI 34; Grant's successor, CH 156; Grant, relations with, SH 104, 155-157; Grant evaluated by, MI 125, 134; Grierson evaluated by, MI 88; Halleck, relations with, SH 104; at Haynes' Bluff, MI 67; headquarters flag, SM *36;* and Hood, AT 91, SM 28, 32-33; and Hooker, AT 51, 64-65; and Howard,

AT 133, SM 50; at Jackson, MI 113-114, 116, 156; and Johnston's surrender, AP 157-160; Johnston evaluated by, SH 52; at Jonesboro, AT 148, 152, 153; at Kennesaw Mountain, AT 18, 19, 66, 74; in Kentucky operations, SH 141; and Kilpatrick, SM 50; and liberated slaves, AP 61-64; and march to the sea, SM 44, *46*, 48-49, 52, 62, 66, 144; march through Georgia, OR *map* 153, *156-157;* McClernand evaluated by, MI 58, 132, 147; and McDowell's plan, FI 155; and McPherson, AT 33, 39, 98, 102, 114-115; meeting with Lincoln and Grant, AP 76, *77;* at Memphis, MI 34; at Milledgeville, SM 62; at Milliken's Bend, MI 67, 86, 109; at Missionary Ridge, CH 118, 123; at New Carthage, MI 85-86; offensive plans, SM 2, 16, 32, 33-34, 35, 156, 159; opens offensive, AT 8, 32; and peace negotiations, OR 155; personal traits, SH 104; and Polk, AT 61, 62; in popular song, SM 157; at Port Gibson, MI 104; prewar career, SH 104, SM 10-*11;* and refugees, OR 112; relations with Grant, CH 122; relief of Burnside, CH 154; relief of Chattanooga, CH 83, 97, 100; and reporters, AT 24, SP 52; at Resaca, AT 40, 45; at Rocky Face Ridge, AT 32-33, 37, 39; and St. Louis hostilities, SH 15; at Savannah, SM 147, 156-159, *160-161;* Savannah captured by, OR 160; at Shiloh, SH 104-105, 111-120, 136, 138-143, 148, 151-152; sketches by, SM *10*, *13;* and Slocum, SM 49; and soldiers' vote, YA 158-159; at Steele's Bayou, MI 80-83; and Stoneman, AT 139; and subordinates, AP *54;* superseded by McClernand, MI 58, 68; and supplies, AT 22, 24, 26, 31; on supply operations, MI 108-109; survey of popular morale, SH 8; temperament, AT 102, CH 122, SM 8; and Thomas, AT 33; and torpedo use, response to, SM 152; on troop numbers required, SH 54; on troops' training, SH 106; troops, concern for, SM 36, 47; troop strength, MI 63, 80, 156; at Tunnel Hill, CH 136, 137, 139, 140, 141, 142; and U.S. Navy, link with, SM 149-150, 154, *155;* at Vicksburg, MI 57, 62, 68-69, 84, 87, 96, 123, 126-129, 131-132, 139, 147, 156; and war, nature of, SM 8, 15, 45-46; on weather, MI 72; wounded, SH 114; at Young's Point, MI 68, 87
Sherman, William Tecumseh, Jr., SM *12*
Sherrick (Joseph) farm, BD 131
Sherrill, Eliakim, BD 42-43
Sherwood, Isaac R., SM 128, *138*
Shields, James, DE *70*, 87, 99, 114, 147, FO 130; background, DE 65-66, 70; at Conrad's Store, DE 167-168; at Fredericksburg, DE 121-123; at Front Royal, DE 122, 149-151, 157; at

The C.S.S. *Shenandoah*, which escaped to England after the Confederate surrender

KI The Killing Ground; LE Lee Takes Command; MI War on the Mississippi; NA The Nation Reunited; OR Confederate Ordeal; RE Rebels Resurgent; SH The Road to Shiloh; SM Sherman's March; SP Spies, Scouts and Raiders; TE The Struggle for Tennessee; TR Death in the Trenches; TT Tenting Tonight; YA Twenty Million Yankees

107

1st Lieutenant Laurence Anderson
of Florida, killed at Shiloh

Major General Daniel E. Sickles (*left*),
who lost a leg at Gettysburg, visiting with
General Samuel Heintzelman

Shields, James (continued)
  Harrisonburg, DE 149; at Kernstown, DE 66-67, 71, 167-168; Lincoln, relations with, DE 65-66, 70; at Luray, DE 170; at Port Republic, DE 157-161, 165, 167-168, *map* 169, 170; at Strasburg, DE 65, at Winchester, DE 66
Shiloh, Battle of, DE 21, MI 33, 83, 144, OR 51, 77-78, SH *map* 112, *map* 122, *map* 138, *map* 144, TT 88-90, YA 87; artillery assaults, SH 114-115, 121-122, *124-125*, *130*, *132*, 136-139, 143-144, *145*, *150*; bayonet assaults, SH 116-117, 123-125; Beauregard's role in, SH 105-108, 110-113, 120-122, 128-129, 136, 144, 147-148, 151, 155; carnage described, SH 117, 119, 121-123, 126, 136-137; casualties, SH 9, 113, 116-117, 119, 125-126, 133-134, 137-138, *140-141*, 144-147, 151-152, *154*, 155; cavalry operations, SH 105, 111, 140, 148, 152; Confederate advance on, SH 107-110; Confederate assaults, SH 111-112, *map* 113, 114, *115*, 116, *117*, 120-123, *126*, 128-129, *130-133*, 134, *135*, 136-144, 150; Confederate command structure, SH 106, 120, 128; Confederate discipline deficiency, SH 110-111; Confederate troop strength, SH 106, 110; Confederate withdrawal, SH 144, 147, 150-152, 154; cyclorama of, SH *130-133;* Grant's role in, SH 105, 111, 116-120, 130, 135, 138-139, *140*, 143, 148, 150, 152, 155; gunboats at, SH *142-143*, 147; Halleck's role in, SH 104-105, 111; Johnston's role in, SH 111, 113, 116-121, 128, 136-137, 141-143; looting by Confederates, SH 119, 141; medical service at, SH 119, *131*, 144, 147-148, *154;* military and political results, SH 9; peach orchard, action at, SH *127*, 128-129; Sherman's role in, SH 104-105, 111-120, 136, 138-143, 148, 151-152; straggler crisis, SH *118*, 140-141, 143; terrain features, SH 114-115, 120; Union counterattacks, SH 126, 130, 138, 144, 146, 148, *150*, 151; Union defense measures, SH 105, 130, 139; Union intelligence failure, SH 111, 114; Union prisoners lost, SH 120, *131*, 134, 138-139, 141; Union strength and reinforcements, SH 106, 116, 139-141, *142-143*, 144, *146*, 150; weather, effect on operations, SH 108, 144-145, 152. *See also* Hornet's Nest; Pittsburg Landing, Tennessee; Sunken Road
Shiloh Branch, SH 114-115
Shiloh Church, SH 9, 105, 114, 115, 120, 147, *150*, 151
Ship Island, BR 128, CO 54-55, 61, TT 44; as blockade target, BL 29, 31
Shipp, Scott, FL 14, 16, 34, 37
Shipping industry, BR 8-9, 30-31
Shipping trade, MI 9, *12-13*, 16, *23*
Shoe industry, YA 57, 66, 76, 79
Shoes: cost, OR 33; production of, OR 25-26, 62, *66-67*
Sholes, Christopher, NA 82
Shorter, John G., OR 80
Shortest soldier, TT 28
Shoshone Falls, Idaho Territory, NA *94*
Shoshone Indians, FR 106, 108, 110-112
Shotwell, Randolph Abbot, FO 50
Shoup, Francis A., AT 76
Shoup, George L., FR 127
Shreveport, Louisiana, FR 46, 51-52, 54-56, 60, 62-63, 67, MI 16
Shubuta Rifles, SH 99
Shy, William M., SM 137, 139, *140*
Shy's Hill, SM 134, 137, 138, 139, *140-141*, 142
Sibley, Henry Hastings, FR 84-87, 90-*91*, 93, *105*, TT 45
Sibley, Henry Hopkins, FR 20, 22-23, *24*, 25-28, 33-35, 37, 70
Sibley tent, KI *12-13*, *110-111*, TT 45, *51*
Sick call, TT 52
Sickel, Horatio, AP 31
Sickles, Daniel E., FO *70*, 165, GE *105*, NA 61, 63, 70, *160*, RE 12, 71, 120-121, 126, 128, *129*, 133, 140-142, 148, 158, SP 81, TT 81; at Cemetery Hill, GE 67, 74; at Cemetery Ridge, GE 75; at Emmitsburg, GE 35; at Emmitsburg road, GE 74, 77, 98, 103-104; at Gettysburg, GE 65; and Little Round Top, GE 75; at Peach Orchard, GE 71, 75-76, 78, 81, 98, 101, *102-103*
Sigel, Franz, BD 15, FL 2, 20, 23, *24*, 27-30, 45, 69, 88, FR 140-141, 144-146, KI 26, 60, 130, LE 94, 101, *131*, OR 111, SP 122, TR 18, TT 29; background and political influence of, FL 24; at Cedar Mountain, LE 109; in Missouri operations, SH 19-20, *24-25;* at New Market, FL 31-33, 36-37, 39; at Second Bull Run, LE 131-134, 136, 138, 148, 163; soldiers' regard for, FL 25-26, 41; at Wilson's Creek, SH 24-29
Sigfried, Joshua K., TR 82, 121
Signal communications, SP 44-46, 50; codes and ciphers, use of, SP *64;* equipment, SP *64;* tower, SP *65*
Signal Hill, AT 74
Signal troops, FI 55-56
Sill, Joshua W., TE 55, 113, 118, *120*, 121
Silver Spring, Maryland, FL 84
Silver Wave, MI 82
Simmons, James F., YA 72
Simms, James P., AP 125
Simms, William Gilmore, OR 44
Simonson, Peter, AT 43
Simpson, Matthew, NA 75
Simpson, William, and son, paintings by, TR *8-15*
Sims, A., TE 115
Sims, Robert M., AP *142-143*
Sinclair, William, BR *145*
Singapore, BL 154
Singing, TT 67-68
Singleton, O. R., BR 109
Sinks. *See* Latrines
Sioux Indians, FR 11, 72, 74-75, 77, 78, *79*, 81-85, *86-87*, *88-89*, 90, 91, *92*, 93-95, *96-97*, *98-99*, *100-101*, *104-105*, 108, *124*, 125, 128-130, NA 92, 96, 102, 103
Sisson family, OR 89
Sisters of Charity, YA 127
Sitlington's Hill, DE *map* 101, 102-103
Sitting Bull's War, NA 96
Skaggs, Larkin, SP 153
Skinker's Neck, RE 39-40, 58, 61
Skinner, Frederick G., LE *169*
Skirmishers, role in assault, FI 50
Slater, Sarah, AS 53
Slaughter Pen, GE *162-165*
Slavery: abolitionist movement, BR 30-31, 34-35, 38-40, 44, 46-47, 62-69, 70-76, 89, 108-109; abolition legislation, YA 36; abolition movement, BD 156-161, 168; abolition as war aim, TT 24-26, 32; Confederate States' policy on, BR 130; defense of, OR 58; executions for trading in, YA 36; extension controversy, BR 35-36, 41-43, 45, 47, 71-80, 82, 98, 101, 104-106, 108, 110, 113, 116, 119; morality of debated, BR 30-31, 40, 47, 106, 108-109, 116; opposition to, OR 75; public opinion on, YA 34-36; states adhering to, BR *map* 2-3. *See also* Emancipation; Emancipation Proclamation
Slaves: in agricultural production, BR 10, *11*, 48; aid to Union by, CO 24; cash value, BR 32; caste system, BR *54-55;* colony for proposed, BR 38; Confederate employment of, MI 18, *23*, 148; as contrabands, OR 136; control of, OR *129*, 136; count in election ballot, BR 30; diet and living conditions, BR 48-49, *56-57;* displacement, OR 110, 128-129; education, OR *142-143;* emancipation proposed, BR 38, 62; enlistment, OR *146-147*, 166-167; escapes, OR 127, 129; escapes and recaptures, BR 40, 43, *44*, 45, *46*, 47, *59*, *60-61*, 64, 68, 75, 119; family life, BR *52-53;* freed by Frémont, SH 30-32; health and medical care, BR 49; importation banned, BR 130; impressment by government, OR 23; insurrections by, BR 40, 84-91; in labor force, OR 16, 23, 43; liberation of, OR 11, *124-125*, *132-141*, 146, 149, 158, 163, 166-167; looting by, OR *117;* loyalty to masters, OR 111, 128-129; migration, OR 125, 131, *134-135;* number, OR 133; number in Confederacy, TT 35; as officers' servants, OR 78, *81;* owners' reimbursement proposed, OR 163-165; ownership ratio, BR 47, OR 8; profit yield from, BR 11; punishments inflicted on, BR 49, *58-59*, 60; refugees, MI *50-51*, 57-58; sale process, BR *50-53;* service to planters, OR 42; treatment by Northerners, OR 129-131; 20-Negro law,

AP Pursuit to Appomattox; AS The Assassination; AT Battles for Atlanta; BD The Bloodiest Day; BL The Blockade; BR Brother against Brother; CH The Fight for Chattanooga; CO The Coastal War; DE Decoying the Yanks; FI First Blood; FL The Shenandoah in Flames; FO Forward to Richmond; FR War on the Frontier; GE Gettysburg;

OR 80, 93; and Underground Railroad, BR 40, 60-62, 67-68; uprisings by, OR 150; uprisings feared, OR 10, 23, 149-150; violence against, OR 150. *See also* Blacks

Slaymaker, Jack, SH 91

Slemmer, Adam, BR 128-129

Slidell, John, BL 116, *119*, 120, 122-123, 128

Slocomb's Creek, CO 35

Slocum, Henry W., AP 53, *54*, 59, 61-64, 67, 69-75, AT 153, 154, BD 53, CH 83, 91, LE 41, 45, 55, RE 120-121, 124-125, 140, 142, 158, SM 20, 28, 29, *51;* background, SM 49; at Cemetery Hill, GE 67; at Culp's Hill, GE 74, 114; at Gettysburg, GE 65, 119; Hooker, relations with, GE 16; and march to the sea, SM 48, 53, 59, 63, 67-68, 72, 150; at Savannah, SM 155

Slocum, John, FI 130

Slough, John P., FR 27, 28, *31*, 32, 34

Slums, YA *50-51*

Small, Abner R., KI 56, 73, 86, RE 67

Small arms. *See by type*

Small-arms fire, casualties from, TT 88

Smalley, George, BD 70

Smallpox, incidence of, YA 23

Smalls, Robert, OR *127*

Smart's Mill, Virginia, FO 51

Smeed, E. C., SP 94

Smith, A. B., BL 55

Smith, Alex, MI *93*

Smith, Algernon E., TR *28*

Smith, Andrew Jackson, FR 51, 53, 54, 55, 59, 60, 61, 62, 67, 70, 157, MI 116, SM 34, 121; at Nashville, SM 126, 128, 130, 132-134, 138-140

Smith, Ashbel, MI 130-131

Smith, Bush, SP 157

Smith, Caleb, KI *156*

Smith, Charles F.: at Fort Donelson, SH 81-85, 90-91, 94-95; at Fort Henry, SH 60-61, 63; at Shiloh, SH 105

Smith, Charles Henry (Bill Arp), AP 138, 139, OR 51, SM *30;* book by, SM *31*

Smith, Chauncey, uniform of, KI *66*

Smith, David L., LE 144

Smith, Edmund Kirby, FI 76, 123, 146-147, 164-165, OR 86, TE 2, 17, 21, 22, 25, 32, 34-35, 40, *43*, 44, 45, 47, 49, 51, 57, 58, 85; at Chattanooga, TE 41; hopes for recruits in Kentucky, TE 54, 55; Kentucky invasion, TE 42, 47, 48, 49; in Mexican War, TE 40; promotion, TE 83; relations with Bragg, TE 43, 82; resentment over assignment in West, TE 40; temperament, TE 40. *See also* Kirby Smith, Edmund

Smith, Francis, RE 161

Smith, Francis H., DE 29, FL *10*

Smith, George Washington, SM *117*

Smith, Gerrit, BR *63*, 84

Smith, Giles A., AT 95, 100, 104, 105, 111, 113, MI 127, 156

Smith, Gus, SM 94

Smith, Gustavus W., CO 85, FO 136, 145, 157, *158*, 159, 165, 167, SM 52, 60, 61, 148

Smith, Isaac, FL *131*

Smith, J. L. Kirby, BR *145*

Smith, James A., AT 95, 104, 105, CH 138, 139, 140, SM 136

Smith, James E., GE 81, 85-87

Smith, James Power, RE 138-139

Smith, John, AT 68

Smith, Joseph, BL 51-52

Smith, Joseph, Jr., BL 56

Smith, Julia, and mother, FR *104*

Smith, Martin Luther, KI 78, 105, MI 26, 63, 126, 152

Smith, Melancton, BL 80

Smith, Morgan L., AT 68, 69, 74, *86-87*, 106, 111

Smith, Philip, TT 24

Smith, Preston, CH *62*, TE 43, 47, 48, 57

Smith, Robert C., TT 118

Smith, Thomas B., SM 137

Smith, Truman, TT 134

Smith, Watson, MI 77, 82

Smith, William (Extra Billy), FI 141, FL 137, GE 30, KI *131*, TR 84

Smith, William F. (Baldy), BD 53, CH 89, *90*, 117, 123, FO *86*, 102, 109-110, *111*, KI 150-151, 153-154, 156, *163*-166, LE 53, *60-61*, RE 57-58, 60, 96, TR 35, 38-39, 41-45

Smith, William P., BR *142*

Smith, William W., BL 28

Smith (Otho) farm, BD *138-139*

Smith carbine, SM *86-87*

Smithfield, North Carolina, AP 64, 65, 69, 74, 75

Smith Island, BL 88

Smith's Creek, FL 28, 30, 33, 36, 39

Smith's Island, CO 158

Smithson, William T., SP 24

Smoke-screen use, BL 101

Smoketown Road, BD 66-68, 70, 82, 94, 97

Smuggling, YA 75; communications, SP *73;* devices used, SP *45;* in Maryland and Virginia, SP 51

Smyrna, Georgia, AT 76

Smyth, Thomas, KI 136

Smyth, Thomas A., AP 29, 30

Smyth Dragoons (Virginia) flag, FI *125*

Smythe, Thomas, AP 131

Snag boats, SH 72

Snake Creek, Tennessee, SH 105

Snake Creek Gap, AT 32, 36, 38-40, 44, SM 29

Snavely's Ford, BD 124, 126, *130*

Snead, Thomas, FR 138, SH 16, 26

Snell, James P., AT 145

Snicker's Gap, FL 89

Snipers, FO 45-46, 100, *101*, *116-117*, 128, 139; Confederate, CO 129, MI 136; Union, MI 149

Snively, J. M., MI *92*

Snodgrass Hill, CH 64, 66, 68, 69, 70-71, *124-125*

Snodgrass house, CH *72-73*

Snowball battles, TT 9, 68-71

Snyder, George W., BR *148*, 153

Soap, shortages of, OR 84

Soap Creek, AT 77, 78

Social changes, OR 10, 33, 42-44, 59-60

Social events, OR 126. *See also* Recreation

Sojourner Truth, BR 65

Soldiers: ages and social backgrounds, TT 26-28; battle, emotions during, TT 144, 156-161; behavior, YA 126; behavior in camp, TT 56-58; clothing, articles issued, TT 76-77; crime and disorders among, TT 56-58, 63; daily routine, TT *45;* desertions, TT 31, 37, 48, 153; fraternization among, TT *158;* metamorphosis into veterans, TT 44, 47, 52, 55, 157-159; morale and motivation, TT 20, 24, 150; multiple rifle and musket loadings by, TT 159; officers, relations with, TT 65; photographs, eagerness for, TT 38; physical characteristics, TT 28, 37; regional origins, TT 28-29; self-examination, TT 71; separated from families, YA *111;* vocational backgrounds, TT 26, 52; voting, YA 151, 158, *159*, 161. *See also* Black troops; Confederate Army; Officers; Union Army

Soldiers' Home, AS 10, *12-13*

Soldiers' welfare agencies. *See* United States Christian Commission; United States Sanitary Commission

Soles, Jacob J., AS 92

Solomon's Gap, BD 39

Somerset, BL 21

Songs, OR *49*, 52-54, TT 67-68, *145*

Songsheet, Confederate, TE *151*

Sons of Midnight, NA 36

Sorrel, G. Moxley, AP *33*, CH 54, 100, FO 154, GE 33, 126, 156, KI 78, LE 163

Soulé, Pierre, CO 74

South: convict leasing, NA 124; Democratic control, NA 148, 156; devastation in, NA 25-26; economic weakness of, NA 123; education, NA 120-123, 158; military districts and garrisons, NA *map 2-3*, 61-*62*, 63, 156-157; North, feeling against, NA 16, 18, 28; racial relations, NA 28, 64; secret organizations, NA 36, 76, 97-99, 120, 141, 142, *146-147*, 150; sharecropping, NA 42-44, 123-124

South Atlantic Blockading Squadron, BL 24, SM 155

South Carolina: cockade device, BR *25;* corruption in, NA 66, 117-119; cotton plantation, NA *44;* devastation in, NA 26; economic decline, BR 36-37; educational system, OR 54; education in, NA 120; and federal property, BR 25, 121-125, 133; former slaves educated in, OR *142-143;* and Fort Sumter reduction, BR 121-128, 132-141; guerrillas in, OR 89; land redistribution in, NA 29; militia mustered, BR 121, *122;* money issue, OR

A flag used by the Confederate Signal Corps

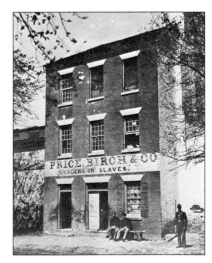

The former slave pen in Alexandria, Virginia, used as a military prison by occupying Federal troops

KI The Killing Ground; LE Lee Takes Command; MI War on the Mississippi; NA The Nation Reunited; OR Confederate Ordeal; RE Rebels Resurgent; SH The Road to Shiloh; SM Sherman's March; SP Spies, Scouts and Raiders; TE The Struggle for Tennessee; TR Death in the Trenches; TT Tenting Tonight; YA Twenty Million Yankees

109

Colonel Alfred Rhett of South Carolina, commander of Fort Sumter during the siege of Charleston

Oil painting of Major General John Sedgwick, popular commander of VI Corps, killed at Spotsylvania

South Carolina (continued)
73; Nullification Act, BR 38; Palmetto Guard, BR 148, 156; readmission to Union, NA 69; refugees in, OR 116, 121, 123; secedes, FI 27; secessionist movement in, BR 3, 24-25, 26-29, 37, 118, 119-121; slave emigration from, OR 125, 131, 136-137; slave uprisings in, OR 150; Union control of, OR 148, map 152-153, 167; Union hostility toward, AP 52-53, 55-56; Union operations in, AP 53-55, 56, 57-61; violence in, NA 98, 99, 149-150

South Carolina Railroad, AP 63

South Carolina troops, Confederate, AP 96, BD 131-132, 136-137, CO 111, 124, FI 112, 123, 129-130, 135, 137, 147-148, FL 105, 140, GE 99, KI 80, 133, 149, MI 114-115, TR 22, 67, 78, 104, 149, TT 115, 149; Charleston Battalion, CO 124; Gregg's brigade, LE 37, 39, 149; Hampton Legion, BD 76-78, FI 109, 123, 137, 139; Marion Artillery flag, FI 125; Palmetto Sharpshooters, FO 145; State militia, AP 53

Infantry: 1st Rifles Infantry Regiment (Orr's Rifles), AP 110, BD 137, KI 32, 59, 84, LE 39, 127, 149, 171, RE 37, 62, 67, TR 48, 99, 152, 159, TT 49; 2nd Infantry Regiment, FI 147, RE 89, 91; 3rd Infantry Regiment, FL 149, RE 106; 4th Infantry Regiment, FI 129-130, 149; 7th Infantry Regiment, BD 91; 10th Infantry Regiment, AT 106; 14th Infantry Regiment, LE 168, TR 152; 17th Infantry Regiment, LE 171, TR 75, 78, 81, 88; 18th Infantry Regiment, LE 169-170, TR 75; 19th Infantry Regiment, AT 106; 20th Infantry Regiment, KI 152; 21st Infantry Regiment, LE 129; 22nd Infantry Regiment, TR 75, 78; 23rd Infantry Regiment, TR 31; 24th Infantry Regiment, MI 114, SM 82; 26th Infantry Regiment, TR 81; 27th Infantry Regiment, TR 29

South Carolina troops, Union, 1st Volunteer Infantry Regiment, FL 41

South Carolinian, OR 51

Southeast Pass, MI 22

Southern Bank Note Company, OR 69

Southern Confederacy, SP 111

Southern Cultivator, NA 28

Southern Homestead Act of 1866, NA 36

Southern Illustrated News, SP 48, TT 67

Southern Literary Messenger, OR 48

Southern Mississippi Railroad, MI 13, 16, 88-89, 122, 130

Southern Pacific Railroad, NA 86

Southern states: abolitionist movement in, BR 39, 108-109; agrarian economy, BR 29; agricultural production, BR 10, 29, 31-32; and blacks' equality, BR 100; censorship in, BR 40; and cotton economy, BR 34; and Dred Scott ruling,

BR 104-105, 108; economic dependence on North, BR 9, 32-33, 35-37; economic and industrial capacity, BR 31-33, 36-37; Episcopalian influence, BR 12; federal property seized by, BR 25, 121-125, 128-130; and John Brown raid, BR 89; and morality of slavery, BR 30-31, 40, 106, 116; population, BR 14; and power loss in Congress, BR 35, 41; relations with North, BR 28-29; secessionist flags adopted by, BR 129; secessionist movement in, BR 24-25, 26-29, 37, 43, 116-117, 118, 119-121, 125, 128; and slavery extension and preservation, BR 35-36, 41-43, 47, 71-76, 104, 108, 110; states joining Confederacy, BR map 2-3. See also Confederate States; Plantations

Southern Telegraph Companies, telegram reporting Stanard's death, FL 36

Southfield, BL 78-79, CO 25, 95

South Fork of the Shenandoah, FL 17, 45

South Mountain, GE 33, 126, 147, 151, 153

South Mountain, Battle of, BD map 2-3, 18, 38-39, 44-45, 46-47, map 48, 49, 50, 52-53, 56, 81, 122, 156

South River, operations around, DE 158-159, 165, 167-168, map 169

Southside Railroad, AP 27, 78, 79, 93, 95, 96, 115, TR 19, 53, 54-55, 57, 139, 150, 154, 156-157

Southwick, Thomas, LE 22

Spach brothers, AP 30

Spangler, Edman (Ned), AS 21, 25, 29, 41, 68, 71-72, 79, 82; arrest and confinement, AS 108, 109, 143; imprisonment and death, AS 160-161; trial of, AS 145, 151, 154, 156, 158

Sparta, Louisiana, NA 140

Spaulding, Elbridge, YA 58

Spaulding, George, SM 143

Spaulding, Ira, RE 35-36, 50-51

Spears, James G., TE 157, 159

Special Orders No. 191. See Lost order

Specie. See Money

Speculators. See Profiteering

Speed, James, AS 140

Spencer, Christopher, CH 21, 74

Spencer, George E., SP 72

Spencer carbine, SM 86-87

Spencer repeating rifles, CH 21, 25, 26, 29, 74-75, SM 60, 137; operations of, CH 77

Spencer rifles, AT 145, MI 92

Sperryville, Virginia, DE 84, LE 101

Speth, Francis, SP 167

Sphinx, BL 128, 131

Spies, MI 115, TT 27; Confederate, DE 122, 149, FI 113; Union, SM 19

Spiller & Burr, OR 65

Spinola, Francis B., CO 90

Spooner, Horatio, TR 63

Sports activities, TT 71. See also Recreational activities

Spotsylvania, Battle of, KI map 2-3, 86-105,

map 93, map 99, 124-130, TT 93; bands at night, KI 105; Bloody Angle, KI cover, 100-101, 102-103, 105, 125; breastworks at, KI 51, 103; fighting at, KI 53; Mule Shoe, KI 89-94, 96, 98, 101, 104-105, 125

Spotsylvania, Virginia, KI 34, 82, TT 48, 49

Spotted Tail, FR 124, 125, 129

Sprague, Horatio J., BL 148

Sprague, John W., AT 102

Sprague, Mrs. William, AS 11

Sprague, William, IV, YA 150

Springer, Charles, TR 120

Springfield, Illinois, BR 117; Lincoln funeral procession, AS 128-129, 130, 131

Springfield, Massachusetts, BR 72

Springfield, Missouri, SH 19, 21, 25, 27, 29, 33

Springfield Pike, TE 57, 59, 60, 62, 66

Springfield Republican, NA 85

Springfield rifles, SM 85

Spring Hill, Tennessee: SM map 2-3, SM 88; action at, SM 89-92, map 91; Schofield eludes Hood at, SM 93-95

Spurlock, D. C., TE 142

Spy Company (Mexican War), SP 10

Squirrel Hunters (Ohio home guard), TE 32

Stabler, Brooke, AS 108

Stafford, F.E.P., SM 116

Stafford Heights, RE 36, 41, 120, 164-165

Staff organization, FO 17, 22-23

Stage plays, OR 54

Stagg, Peter, AP 122

Stahel, Julius, DE 152, 164, FL 31, 33, 34, 36, 41, 43, 46, 48-49, 51, 58

Stanard, Jaqueline B. (Jack), FL 36, 159

Stanardsville, Virginia, DE 84, 95

Standard Oil Company, NA 83, 108, YA 78

Standing Buffalo, FR 93

Stanford, Leland, NA 86

Stanley, David S., AT 42, 43, 57, 148, 152, CH 23, 30, MI 40, SM 34, 84, 89, 126, TE 93, 133; and Congressional Medal of Honor, SM 84; and Schofield, SM 84; and Spring Hill, SM 89-92, 95; wounded at Franklin, SM 112

Stanley, Timothy R., TE 154

Stanley, Wesley, TR 76

Stannard, George, KI 165

Stannard, George J., GE 139

Stannard, George S., TR 142, 148

Stansel, Martin, AP 85

Stanton, Edwin McMasters, AP 24, 26, 68, 113, 160, AS 11, 19, 54, 64, 75, 114, 123, 137, 142, 161, BD 168, BL 57, BR 123-125, CH 30, 83, 121, 154, CO 156, FL 100, 125, 140, 151, FO 70, KI 22, 38, LE 47, 92-93, 166, MI 27, 34, 56-57, 78, 105, NA 8, 17-18, 22, 32, 56, 70, 72-73, RE 9, 32, 93, 94, SM 106, 122, 123, 134, 155, SP 71, 131, 162, TE 14, TT 115-116; becomes Secretary of War, FO 70; Cabinet meeting, AS 66; commanders controlled by, FO 89; and

AP Pursuit to Appomattox; AS The Assassination; AT Battles for Atlanta; BD The Bloodiest Day; BL The Blockade; BR Brother against Brother; CH The Fight for Chattanooga; CO The Coastal War; DE Decoying the Yanks; FI First Blood; FL The Shenandoah in Flames; FO Forward to Richmond; FR War on the Frontier; GE Gettysburg;

draft evaders, YA 92; and draft riots, YA 110; at Lincoln's deathbed, AS 92-95, 100, *102;* and Lincoln's security, AS 43, 57, 76; Lincoln, relations with, FO 71; McClellan, animosity toward, FO 71, 74-75, 84, 87-89; McClellan, conferences with, FO 85; meeting with Grant, CH 88; and national security, YA 31; and newspaper suppression, YA 31; and Norfolk capture, FO 124; personal characteristics, FO 70-71; pursuit of Booth, AS 132, 134, 136; and Radical Republicans, FO 71-72; railroads controlled by, DE 146; reconstruction plans, AS 67; and recruiting, YA 87; recruiting deferred by, FO 97; and Sanitary Commission, YA 122; and Shenandoah Valley operations, FO 130-131; and Stone's arrest, FO 71-72; takes charge of government, AS 102-104; trial of conspirators, AS 139-141, 155; and Urbanna plan, FO 74-75; and Valley operations, DE 87, 89, 121; and Washington's security, DE 61, 64, 146, FO 97, 130-131

Stanton, Henry, FR 86, 93

Star Hotel, AS *115,* 117, 133

Starke, Alexander W., TR 146

Starke, William E., BD *75,* 148

Starkweather, John C., TE 60, 66, 96-97

Star of the West, BR 126-127

Starr, William, FL 37

State, Department of. *See* Benjamin, Judah P.; Hunter, Robert M. T.; Toombs, Robert

States: loyalty to, OR 10, 13, 75-76; money issues, OR *72-73;* recruiting programs of, TT 22; and secession from Confederacy, OR 155-157; welfare programs, OR 83

States' rights: applications of, OR 153-155; and central government, OR 75-76; doctrine, BR 33-34, 36-38, 130; safeguarding of, OR 10-11, 13, 27-28, 79

Statue of Liberty, torch, NA *150*

Staunton, Virginia, DE 21, 86, 95, 99, 101, 103, FL 16, 17, 20, 25, 27, 29, 41, 45, 46, *50-51,* 53, 68, 69, 134, 135, OR 26, TR 18, 20-21, 27

Staunton-Charlottesville road, DE *8-9*

Staunton-Parkersburg road, DE 45, 101

Staunton River, TR 55

Steamboats, CH *16-17, 94,* 95, 97, 136, *164-165,* 167

Stearns, Frazar, CO *34*

Stearns, George L., BR 85

Stearns, Joseph K., FL 42

Steck, Michael, FR 116, 120

Stedman, Charles, TR 108

Stedman, Charles Ellery, BL *102-113*

Stedman, Griffin, KI 164

Steedman, James B., CH 48, 66, 69, 125, SM 123, 126, 134, TE 66

Steel, Elijah, SM 113

Steele, "Coal Oil Johnny," YA 70

Steele, Frederick, FR 51, 52, 56, 63, *64,*

65, 152, 153

Steele, Joseph W., BL 92, 94

Steele's Bayou, MI *map* 72, 80-81, *82,* 83

Steel production, OR 19, 21

Steinacker, Henry Von. *See* Winkelstein, Hans Von

Steinwehr, Adolph von, CH 93, GE 52, 62-65

Stephens, Alexander Hamilton, AP 21, BR 43, 130, NA 34, 145, OR *90;* Congress, relations with, OR 13; Davis, relations with, OR 13, 90, 165; and habeas corpus suspension, OR 154; and peace negotiations, OR *149,* 151, 155, 157-158, 162-165; secession opposed by, OR 77; as Vice President, OR 11-13

Stephens, W. A., AT 48

Stephenson's Depot, FL 89, 109, 112, 113, 116

Stepney, Connecticut, civil disorder in, YA 20

Steuart, George H. (Maryland), DE 129, 165, GE 24, 26, 115-116, 127, *129,* KI 29, 64, 94-95, *98,* 102

Stevens, Charles A., LE 67

Stevens, George, TT 94-95

Stevens, George T., KI 29, 83, 88, 153

Stevens, Hazard, AP 16, 92, 93, FL 149

Stevens, Isaac, LE 133, 148, 167

Stevens, Joel S., TT *38*

Stevens, John, panorama by, FR *100-105*

Stevens, Simon, YA 73

Stevens, Thaddeus, NA 2, *33,* 40, *41,* 72, *73,* YA 151-152

Stevens, Thomas, CO 131-133

Stevens' Gap, CH 35, 39, 42

Stevenson, Alabama, CH 18, 33, 34, 78, 88, 97

Stevenson, Alexander F., TE 122

Stevenson, Carter L., AT 46, 63, 64, CH 101, 131, 137, 138, 139, 140, TE 41, 42, 44, 88, 92; at Big Black River, MI 122; at Champion's Hill, MI 116-118, 122; at Chickasaw Bluffs, MI 96-97; at Vicksburg, MI 152

Stevenson, James H., FL 29

Stevenson, Thomas G., CO 125, 128, KI 74

Stewart, Alexander P., AP 71, 72, *73,* AT 52, 90, 92, 143, 152, CH 47, 48, SH 57, SM 19, 83, 88, TE 65, YA 77; background, SM 83; at Ezra Church, AT 134-136; at Franklin, SM 98, 100, 113, 116; at Nashville, SM 125, 126, 128, 130, 133, 134, 142; at New Hope Church, AT 53; at Spring Hill, SM 93

Stewart, Joseph B., AS 86

Stewart, W. Scott, SM 114

Stewart, William H., AP 31, TR 64

Stibbs, John H., SM 130, 132, 133, 139

Stiles, Joseph Clay, TT 149-152

Stiles, Robert A., AP 101, 123-125, KI 91, 99, 135, FL 152, LE 52, TR 137

Stillwell, Leander, FR 65, NA 20-25, SH 117, TT 79

Stockade Redan, MI 127, 136

Stockbridge, Georgia, SM 50

Stock-market trading, YA *46,* 47, 65, 77-78

Stone, Augustus, SP 165

Stone, Charles P., FO 71, NA 154, *155,* SP 16-21; at Ball's Bluff, FO 39-42, 44, 48-50, 53, 68-71; imprisoned, FO 70-72; and Joint Committee, FO 68-70; prewar service, FO 40

Stone, Frederick, AS 145, 151

Stone, George A., AP 59

Stone, Henry, SM 85, 90, 103, 105, 138, 139

Stone, Kate, OR 60

Stone, Robert King, AS 98-99

Stone Bridge, FI 112-113, 122, 124, 127-129, 132, 135, 137, 145, *map* 146, 149, LE 137, 159, 162, 164, *165*

Stone fleet, BL 26-27

Stone House, LE 148, *162-163*

Stoneman, George, AT 39, 40, 138, *139,* 141, FO 108, RE 103, 118-120, *159*

Stoneman's Station, Virginia, RE *20-21*

Stones River, TE 4, 29, 112, 118, 127, 144, *156-157,* 158, *166-167*

Stones River, Battle of, TE *108-110,* 112-133, *map* 119, *map* 126, *128-129,* 142-160, *map* 152, *162-171,* TT 161; bayonet charge, TE *116;* Bragg's decision to retreat, TE 159; Breckinridge's attack routed, TE 154-155; effects on sympathizers in Kentucky and Tennessee, TE 159; Sheridan at, TE 118, 119, 120, 121, 122, 123, 124, 127, U.S. Regulars at, TE 125; Union counterattack, TE 154-155

Stonewall, BL *130,* 131

Stonewall Brigade, AP 153, FL 68, 82, 119, KI 31, 65, 98, TT 85-86

"Stonewall Jackson's Way" (song), OR 52

Stono, CO 113

Stono Inlet, CO 111

Stono River, BL *103,* CO 110-111, TT *16*

Stony Creek, DE 83-87

Stony Creek Depot, Virginia, TR 56

Stony Ridge, LE 132, 135, 138

Storey, Wilbur, YA 30-31

Stoughton, Edwin H., SP 117-119, *122*

Stowe, Harriet Beecher, BR 47, 65, 66, YA 39

Stragglers, SH *118,* 140-141, 143

Strahl, Otho F., SM 98, 116, *119*

Strasburg, Virginia, FL 17, 27, 42, 90, 122, 134, 137, 157; operations at, DE 43, 50, 65, 83-84, *88-89,* 114, 120-123, 128, *map* 130, 148-157

Strasburg-Front Royal road, DE 129

Stratford Hall, LE *11*

Stratton, Theophiles, TR *55*

Streight, Abel D., SM 135, TT 125

Stribling, Robert M., AP 36

Strickland, Francis, GE *155*

Strikes, YA 45, 78, 103

Stringham, Silas H., BL 26, 29, CO 16, 19

Lieutenant William H. Egan, 11th New Jersey, struck by a cannonball and killed at Spotsylvania

KI The Killing Ground; LE Lee Takes Command; MI War on the Mississippi; NA The Nation Reunited; OR Confederate Ordeal; RE Rebels Resurgent; SH The Road to Shiloh; SM Sherman's March; SP Spies, Scouts and Raiders; TE The Struggle for Tennessee; TR Death in the Trenches; TT Tenting Tonight; YA Twenty Million Yankees

111

"Sutler's Row" in Federal-occupied Chattanooga, Tennessee

Prewar photograph of J.E.B. Stuart *(standing, center)* with his brother *(seated, right)* and a friend

Colonel Thomas Sweeny, 52nd Illinois, who had lost an arm in the Mexican War

Strong, George C., BR *144*, CO 121, *124*, 125-127

Strong, George Templeton, CO 137-139, NA 40, 52, 110, 125; on Atlanta, YA 158; on draft, YA 86, 108; on draft riots, YA 103; on emancipation, YA 37; on habeas corpus suspension, YA 32; on Lincoln's reelection, YA 161; and Sanitary Commission, YA 120, 123; on war weariness, YA 146

Strong, Robert, SM *43*

Strong, Robert H., AP 58

Strong, William E., AT 99, 100, 101

Strother, David Hunter, FL 24, 31, 41, 42, 45, 46, 48-50, 53, 56-57, 59, 61, 87, 89, LE 134-135, 144, 152, 155, 162-163; sketches by, FL *54-55*

Strout, Richard, FR 84, 89

Stuart, David, SH 105, 121-122, 136-138

Stuart, Flora, KI 117, 123

Stuart, James Ewell Brown (Jeb), BD *24*, 103, BR *88*, DE 35-36, 38, FI 93, 140-141, 143, 149, 153, *160-161*, FL 45, 103, 139, FO 64, 110, GE *18*, KI 58, 86, 114-115, *116-117*, LE *25*, 91, NA 161, 163, RE *143*, SP 47, 54, 100, 116; at Antietam, BD 68, 76, 88, 91, 127; at Ashby's Gap, GE 25, 28; at Beverly Ford, GE 20; at Blue Ridge gaps, GE 27; at Brandy Station, GE 10, 16, *17*, 18, 21-22, 25; at Carlisle, GE 73; at Catlett's Station, LE 125-126; at Chancellorsville, RE 126, 139, 141, *map* 142, 146-147, *150-151;* commands corps, RE 139, 141; and Conrad, SP 57; criticized, GE 25; death of, KI 123; directive from Lee, GE 25-26; at Fredericksburg, RE 39, 50, 58, 61, 63-65; at Gettysburg, GE 71, 132; jacket and sash of, KI *115;* Jackson succeeded by, RE 139, 141; at Kelly's Ford, RE 109-110; in Lee's retreat, GE 151; Lee's tribute to, RE 143; at Middleburg, GE 26, 28; partisans, criticism of, SP 126; in Potomac crossing, GE 72; raids, Federal supply train, GE *72;* in Rappahannock operations, LE 125; reconnaissances by, BD 21, 44, 164, GE 25, RE 33, 121; review staged by, GE 10; ride around McClellan's army, BD 164, *166-167*, LE 25-27, *28-29;* at Salem, GE *map* 32, 72; screening operations, GE 25-26, *map* 32, 72-73; at Second Bull Run, LE 126, 145; in Seven Days' Battles, LE 49; tribute to Pelham, RE 111; troop strength, GE 14; at Turner's Gap, BD 44-45; at Upperville, GE 28-29; at Urbana, BD 17; at Yellow Tavern, KI 118-119, 122

Stuart, Richard, AS 114-115

Studebaker brothers, YA 79

Stults, Symmes H., FL *83*

Sturdivant, Nathaniel A., TR *46*

Sturdivant's Battery, TR 32

Sturgis, Samuel D., BD 50, 122, 124, 126-127, 129-131, LE 133, RE *29*, 81-85

Sturgis, William J., FR 80

Submarine, CO *138*, 139-141

Submersible vessels, production of, OR 22

Substitutes, policies on, TT 35

Subversive organizations. *See* Disloyalty; Secret societies

Sudley Church, FI *131*

Sudley Ford, FI 112, 122, 124, 126-130, *131*, 132, 144, *map* 146, 147, 149

Sudley road, LE 148, 152, 162

Suffolk, Virginia, CO 90

Sugar Creek, AT 99, 106, 110, 113

Sugar Loaf Mountain, BD *167*

Sugar Valley, AT 36, 39

Sulivane, Clement, AP 100, 101

Sullivan, Jeremiah, FL 41, 43, 46, 59, 60, 61, 89

Sullivan's Island, BL *97*, BR 137, 149-150, *151*, 152, CO *104-105*, 113, 118, 120, 133

Sully, Alfred, FR 91-95, 98, *99*, 129, 130, RE 81; painting by, FR *96-97*

Sultana, TT *134*

Summer White House (Corn Rigs), AS *12-13*, *23*

Sumner, Charles S., AS 12, 54, 99-100, BD *160*, BL 117, FI 44, NA 2, 33, 40, 106, 110, *134*, YA 151-152; assaulted by Preston Brooks, BR 76-77, *78;* and John Brown, BR 77; and Kansas-Nebraska Act, BR 72; opposition to slavery, BR 76

Sumner, Edwin Vose, FO 84, 93, 109-111, 130, 136, 155, 167, LE *58*, 95; at Alexandria, LE 151; at Antietam, BD 65, 87-93, 98-99, 109-111, 121-122; commands grand division, RE 30; death, RE 98; at Falmouth, RE 30-31; at Frederick, BD 22; at Fredericksburg, RE 34-35, 50, 58, 61, 71-74, 87, 89, 91, 154; McClellan's evaluation of, LE 58; personal traits, RE 29; and Rappahannock operations, RE 31-33, 39, 50, 53, 72; relieved, RE 98; in Seven Days' Battles, LE 50-52, 67-68, 72; at Warrenton, RE 30, 33

Sumner, Samuel, BD 93

Sumter, BL 145-146, *147*, 148-149

Sumter Light Guards (Georgia), FI *18-19*

Sunflower River, MI 80, 82-83

Sunken Road, BD 94-96, *map* 98, *99*, *110-115*, *118-119*, 120, 126, *149*, RE 73, *78*, 79-83, *84-85*, 86-91, 152-154, *170-171*, SH 120-122, 126, 128-129, *130*

Supply operations, FI 32-33, 40-41, 44-45, 54, TT *46-47;* Confederate, DE 50, 94, 146, 151, MI 16-17, 77, 149-150; Federal, DE 46, *118-119;* and system, OR 18, 23-26, 83; Union, LE 25, 29-30, 48-49, 58-62, *84*, *96-97*, *118-119*, 124-125, 144, 151, MI 56, 60, 62, 84, 89, 108-109, 129, 156, *165;* United States Navy, BL *38-39*, *112-113*. *See also* Foraging

Supreme Court, BR 79-80, 98, 104-105, 108, NA 39, 40

Supreme Court debated, OR 10, 13

Surgeons and surgery. *See* Medical services

Surgical instruments, OR *19*, TT *91*, 92

Surprise: applications of, SH 26, 33, 115; uses of, DE 41, 54, 87, *131*

Surratt, Anna, AS 25, *26*, 44, 110, 159

Surratt, Isaac, AS 25

Surratt, John Harrison, Jr., AS *25*, 29, 39, 40, 68, 105, 155, 157; background, AS 25-26; Booth, recruited by, AS 21-24; capture and trial, AS 159, 161; Confederate messenger, AS 26-27; escape to Canada, AS 109; plot to kidnap Lincoln, AS 43-44, 48-53; reward poster and search for, AS *93*, 108, 111

Surratt, Mary Elizabeth, AS 25-*26*, 40, 44, 50, 105; arrest and confinement, AS 110, 139, 144, *146-147;* Booth, delivers package for, AS 68-69; cell key, AS *151;* execution of, AS 159-*160*, *162-171;* Lincoln's death, reaction to, AS 109; trial of, AS 144, 148, 154-159

Surratt house, AS *23*, *26*, 40, 43-44, 51, 68, 108-109

Surrattsville, Maryland, AS 25, 74, 104-105, 155, 157

Surry Light Artillery, TR 137

Sussex Light Dragoons (Virginia), FI *104*

Sutlers, BD 57, TT *56-57*, 59, 115

Swain, Henry, KI 161

Swamp Angel (Parrott gun), CO 135-136, *137*, 139

Swank, James, NA 125

Swann, Oswell, AS 106

Swanwick, Francis, TE 122

Swayne, Wager, NA 70

Sweeny, Thomas, AT 44, 45, 48, 99, 100, *102-103*, 111

Sweet, Benjamin, SP *58*

Sweet, H.W.S., KI 64

Sweetwater, Tennessee, CH 100, 101

Sweet Water Branch, TT 132

Sweetwater Station, FR *111*

Swett's Battery, AT 132

Swift, Gustavus F., NA 83, 86

Swift Run Gap, DE 84, 86-87, 95, 99, 117

Swilling, Jack, FR *134*

"Sword of Robert E. Lee" (Ryan), OR 46

Swords, production of, OR 23

Swords and sabers, FI *72-73*

Sycamore Church, Virginia, TR 111, 114

Sykes, George, BD 141, 153, FI 148, GE 75, 77, 81, RE 86-87, 89, 91, 124-125; at Second Bull Run, LE 146, 162-164; in Seven Days' Battles, LE 36-37, 41-42

Sykes, Mrs., SM 120

Sylvan Grove, Georgia, SM 67

Syracuse, New York, BR *63*

T.B., Maryland (village), AS 105

Tabernacle Church, RE 124

Tabor, Iowa, BR 84-85

Tacony, BL 150

AP Pursuit to Appomattox; AS The Assassination; AT Battles for Atlanta; BD The Bloodiest Day; BL The Blockade; BR Brother against Brother; CH The Fight for Chattanooga; CO The Coastal War; DE Decoying the Yanks; FI First Blood; FL The Shenandoah in Flames; FO Forward to Richmond; FR War on the Frontier; GE Gettysburg;

Tactics: effect of weapons on, FI 48-50; Napoleonic influence on, FI 48-50, 54
Taft, Charles Sabin, AS 91, 98
Taft, Edward P., FL *83*
Taggart, Charles A., AP *121*
Taggart, John, BD 60
Tahlequah, Indian Territory, FR 148, 155
Talbot, Theodore, BR *148*
Taliaferro, R.C.M., TE 122
Taliaferro, William B., CO *124*, DE *51*, 92, RE 39, 58, 61, 67; at Cedar Mountain, LE 100, 103-105; Jackson, relations with, DE 103; at McDowell, DE 103; at Port Republic, DE 170; at Second Bull Run, LE 132, 138, 141-142; in Valley area, DE 48-50, 52, 58
Tallest soldier, TT 28
Talleysville, Virginia, LE 28-29
Tallmadge, James, BR 34
Tally, Spencer, TE 130
Taltavul's Star Saloon, AS *28-29*, 72, 82
Tammany Hall, YA *33*
Tammany Regiment, FO 44-45, 47-48, 50-51
Taney, Roger B., BR *80*, YA 33
Tanneries, OR 26
Taopi, FR 86, 87
Taos, New Mexico Territory, FR 16
Tappan, Henry, YA 24
Tariff controversy, BR 36-38
Tariff of Abominations, BR 36
Tar River, CO 87-88, *92*
Tattnall, Josiah, FR 125
Taxation, YA 56, 59, 72, 77
Tax programs, OR 10, 30, 33, 83, *84*
Taylor, Bayard, NA 77
Taylor, George W., LE 45-46, 132
Taylor, James E., FL 103, 104, 135, *161*; paintings by, FL *123*, *136*, *160-171*
Taylor, James E., paintings by, AT *102-103*
Taylor, Jesse, SH 61-67
Taylor, Joseph H., RE 41
Taylor, Nelson, RE 70
Taylor, Richard, AP 160, FR 50, 52, 54-*55*, 56-60, 62, 63, 66-67, 70-71, MI 110, NA 19; background, DE 117; at Cedarville, DE 129; as disciplinarian, DE 117; Ewell evaluated by, DE 95-98; at Front Royal, DE 123-126; Jackson evaluated by, DE 22, 114, 117-120, 146, 170; at Middletown, DE 130-131; at Port Republic, DE 168-170; at Strasburg, DE 156; at Winchester, DE 133-135
Taylor, Richard E., SM 11, 52, 148
Taylor, Thomas, BL 91-95
Taylor, Walter H., AP 140, CH 42, KI 60, LE 166, NA *57*
Taylor, Zachary, BR 42-43, DE 25, 40, TE *16*
Taylor Depot, TE *76-77*
Taylor's Branch, TR 46, 50

Tea, shortage of, OR 84
Teachers, shortage of, OR 42, 55, 60
Tecumseh, CO 143, 147, *148-149*
Teeple, Charles, TR *123*
Telegraph: codes, use of, SP 64, 68, 70; equipment, SP *68, 69;* industry, RE 42, 46, *48-49*, YA 78-79; services, FI 29, 56, 122
Telegraph road, KI 118-119
Tennessee, CO 143, *144-145*, *148-149*, 150-153, *154-155*, 156-157; anti-Klan laws in, NA 97; Beauregard's operations in, SH 61, 79-81, 97; Buell's operations in, SH 59, 97-98, 104; civilian atrocities, CH 31-32, 103; Confederate recruits, TE 22; Confederate sympathizers and supplies, SM 32, 128; Confederate territorial losses, SH 157; conscription evaded in, OR 80; corruption in, NA 119; difficulty of operations in mountainous country, CH 8, 32; divided loyalties in, SH 80; educational system, OR 55; Forrest's raids in, SM 19, 34, 82; guerrilla operations in, SH 80; guerrillas in, OR *92, 94;* Halleck's role in, SH 59-61, 67, 78, 84, 95; Hood's invasion, SM 82, 84; ideal for guerrilla operations, TE 18-19; Johnston's operations in, SH 58-59, 62, 67, 78-81, 84, 93, 97, 99; joins Confederacy, FI 18; leather production in, OR 26; and Lincoln, CH 18, 31; Lincoln on operations in, SH 59; loyalist government in, NA 30, 32; as mineral source, OR 20, 22; money issue, OR *73;* Murfreesboro, Forrest's attack on, SM 125; Nashville, Battle of, SM 126-144; operations in, MI 34, SH *map* 2-3, 9, 58-59, 61, 67, 78-81, 84, 95-98, *102-103*, 104; pro-Union sentiment, TE 10; railroad use by Union, TE 79; readmitted to Union, NA 54; refugees in, OR 117, 121; secession by, BR 3; slavery affected by Union occupation, TE 72, *107;* Spring Hill, action at, SM 89-92; Union control of, OR 148; Union foraging, CH 21, 156-157; Union informants in, SP 73; Union sentiment in, CH 31, 103, 155; Union settlements in, NA 64
Tennessee River, CH *8-9*, *14-15*, *16-17*, 18, 30, 32, 33, *36*, 37, 79, 80, 89, *91*, *94*, 95, 107, *110-111*, 117, 121, *128-129*, 130, 133, *151*, 155, *164-165*, 166-167, SM 32, 34, 44, 82, 144, TE *18-19*, 41, 50; avenue of supply, TE 15; not suited for supply vessels, CH 8, 78; operations on and about, SH *map* 2-3, 98, 101, 136, *142-143*; railroad bridge burned at, TE 14; strategic value of, SH 8-9, 11, 46, 54, 56-57, 59, 79
Tennessee troops, Confederate, AP 71, 73, GE 45, MI 31, *93*, 122, TE 20, 26, 30, 64, 65, 93, *102*, 118, 121, 124, 149, TT 31; Gano's Battalion, TE 24; Rutledge Rifles, SH *107*
  Artillery: Morton's Light Artillery, TE 97

  Cavalry: 12th Cavalry Regiment, SM 143-144
  Infantry: 1st Infantry Regiment, AT 28, 72, CH 19, 30, 150, SM 88, 142, TE 20, 50, 121; 2nd Infantry Regiment, TT 59; 3rd Infantry Regiment, AT 45, MI 111-112; 6th Infantry Regiment, SM *84;* 8th Infantry Regiment, TE 126; 13th Infantry Regiment, SH 85; 14th Infantry Regiment, FL *11*, RE 67; 16th Infantry Regiment, TE 126, 142; 17th Infantry Regiment, TE 81; 18th Infantry Regiment, TE 145, 154; 19th Infantry Regiment, TE 99; 20th Infantry Regiment, CH 134, TE 153; 23rd Infantry Regiment, SH 114-116; 26th Infantry Regiment, TE *158;* 27th Infantry Regiment, TE 65; 28th Infantry Regiment, MI 112, SH 91; 31st Infantry Regiment, TE *64-65;* 37th Infantry Regiment, SM 137, 139; 38th Infantry Regiment, TE 126; 41st Infantry Regiment, SM 102, 116; 44th Infantry Regiment, TR 45; 45th Infantry Regiment, CH 131; 51st Infantry Regiment, TE 126; 154th Infantry Regiment, TE 47
Tennessee troops, Union, AT 40-42, TE 157; 1st Cavalry Regiment, SP 73; 3rd Cavalry Regiment, TE 44, 45; 12th Cavalry Regiment, SM 143-144
Tents, FO *14*, *36-37*, TT 9, *10*, 13, 45-46, *50-51*
Tents, production of, OR 43
Tenure of Office Act, NA 56, 70, 72, 73
Tepe, "French Mary," RE *70*
Terceira Island, BL 121, 149
Terrett, George H., FI 61
Terrill, James, KI *153*, TE 58
Terrill, William Rufus, KI 153, TE *58*, 65
Terrorism. *See* Guerrillas, depredations by
Terry, Adrian, CO *163*
Terry, Alfred Howe, AP 18, CO *163*, 164-165, TR 154
Terry, B. Frank, TE 113
Terry, Theo P., SH 65
Terry, William, FL 79, 81, 82, 83
Terry's Texas Rangers, FR 22
Tew, Charles C., BD 103
Texas: animals supplied by, OR 29; compensation for cessions by, BR 44; in Confederate supply system, MI 16; federal property seized, BR 129-130; migration to, OR 121; money issue, OR *72;* Quantrill's winter quarters, SP 155; readmitted to Union, NA 69; secession by, BR 3, 128; seizure of Federal arms, FR 17, *18*, *21;* Union strategic interest in, FR 46
Texas & Pacific Railroad, NA 154
Texas (locomotive), SP *112*

Colonel Andrew Jackson, Jr., a West Point graduate, who commanded the 1st Tennessee Heavy Artillery

KI The Killing Ground; LE Lee Takes Command; MI War on the Mississippi; NA The Nation Reunited; OR Confederate Ordeal; RE Rebels Resurgent; SH The Road to Shiloh; SM Sherman's March; SP Spies, Scouts and Raiders; TE The Struggle for Tennessee; TR Death in the Trenches; TT Tenting Tonight; YA Twenty Million Yankees

Confederate army cartridge box manufactured in Texas

Texas Brigade, FO *80-81*, KI 77, TR *49*, 140, 146, 154-155
Texas troops, Confederate, AT 35, 54, CH 60, 140, 141, FR *18*, 22, 25, 26, 50, 57, 64, 71, 136, 141, 143, 146, 148-149, 152, 155, GE 78, 80, 162, MI 37, *146*, RE *104*, TE 47, 118, 121, TT 31, 35, *41*, 66, 86, 128; 1st Brigade, TT *12;* 4th Mounted Volunteers, FR 16, 24, 30, *135;* 5th Mounted Volunteers, FR 23-25, 28, 33-34, 70; Gano's Battalion, TE 24; Hood's Brigade, CH 48; Smith's Brigade, CH 138, 139, 140; Texas Brigade, AT 95, 104-105, 145, 150, 152, BD 76, FO *80-81*, KI 77, LE 40, 45, *47*, 155, *158*, 161, TR *49*, 140, 146, 154-155
   Artillery: Douglas' Battery, TE 47; Valverde Battery, FR 37
   Cavalry: 3rd Cavalry Regiment, FR *134;* 7th Cavalry Regiment, FR 30; 8th Cavalry Regiment, SM *55;* 8th Cavalry Regiment (Terry's Texas Rangers), FR *22*, TE 27, 29, 113; 10th Cavalry Regiment (Dismounted), TE 115; 14th Cavalry Regiment (Dismounted), SM 24, TE 142; 18th Cavalry Regiment, TT *42;* 18th Cavalry (Dismounted), AT 95; 24th Cavalry Regiment (Dismounted), AT 56, SM 120; 30th Cavalry Regiment, FR 155
   Infantry: 1st Infantry Regiment, BD 78, GE 87, LE 155; 2nd Infantry Regiment, MI 41, *42-43*, 130-131; 4th Infantry Regiment, GE 80, 83-87, LE 45-46, 155, TR 140; 5th Infantry Regiment, AP 16, GE 79-80, 83-86, LE 158, 161, 170-171; 6th Infantry Regiment, CH 52; 7th Infantry Regiment, MI 111-112; 9th Infantry Regiment, TE 121
Texas troops, Union, TT 31
Textile industry, OR *24-25*, 62, 66, YA 57, 66-67
Thayer, John M., FR 64, MI 66
Thayer, William Makepeace, DE 59
Theaters, OR 54
Theatricals, TT *15*, 67, 68
Thedford's Ford, CH 44
Theft, prevalence of, TT 63, 65
Thibodaux Sentinel, OR *51*
Thoburn, Joseph, FL 30, 46-48, 91, 117, 118, 141, 144-*146*, 158
Thomas, Edward L., RE 126, 144
Thomas, Ella Clanton, OR 75
Thomas, George Henry, AP 8, AT 54, 91, 141, 142, 154, CH 24, 28, 30, 33, 36, 37, 38, 39, 42, 45, 68, *70*, 87, 89, 98, 105, 117, 118, 132, 134, 142, 154, FI 28, FO 74, SH 55-56, SM 15, 32, 34, 94, 96, *127*, 155, 159, TE 50, 54, 93, 98; as army commander, AT 31; caution of, CH 35; at Chickamauga, CH 45, 46, 47, 48, 50, 53, 55, 56, 57, 61, 63, 64; and defense of Tennessee, SM 2, 19, 34, 44, 83-84; delays attack at Nashville, SM 121-123; headquarters, CH *159;* at Hoover's Gap,

CH 26, 30; at Jonesboro, AT 148; at Kennesaw Mountain, AT 69, 74; and Logan, AT 133; at Lookout Mountain, CH 133; at Missionary Ridge, CH 143, 145; at Nashville, SM 126, 133, 134, 137, 138, 139, 144; at Orchard Knob, CH 120, 121, *144-145;* at Peachtree Creek, AT 93, 94; at Pine Mountain, AT 61; pocket compass of, SM *127;* popularity of, CH 26; replaces Rosecrans, CH 88; reputation of, SM 125; at Rocky Face Ridge, AT 32-35; at Rossville, CH 72; and Schofield, SM 123; at Smyrna, AT 76; stand on Snodgrass Hill, CH 65, 66, 68, 69, *124-125;* at Stones River, TE 99, 112, 120, 125, 127, 130, 133, 144, 155
Thomas, Henry G., TR 82
Thomas, Lorenzo, BR 126, MI 105, NA 72, OR 159
Thomas, Minor T., FR 95, 98
Thomas, Stephen, FL 147, 153
Thomas farm, FL 75, 78, 81
Thomasville, Georgia, OR 149
Thompson, Charles R., SM 135
Thompson, David L., BD 49
Thompson, Denton L., GE *154*
Thompson, Frank, TT 27
Thompson, Henry Yates, CH 136
Thompson, Jacob, AS 75, 144, BR 123, 125-126, SP *59*
Thompson, James, RE *106*
Thompson, James (alias Richard Montgomery), AS 150
Thompson, James and George, BL 125-126, 128
Thompson, John B., SH *132*
Thompson, John R., LE 26
Thompson, M. Jeff, MI 20, 24, SH 32
Thompson, Michael (alias Colonel Empty), SP 24
Thompson, Richard, TR 95
Thompson, W. C., MI 102-103
Thompson, William C., SH 116, SM 114
Thompson's (Absolam) house, SM 93
Thompson's Station, Tennessee, CH 23, SM 93
Thomson, James W., TR 24
Thomson, T. P., BD 81
Thomson's Horse Artillery Battery, TR 24
Thoreau, Henry David, FR 8
Thornton's Gap, DE 84, 86, 121
Thornwell, James, OR 58
Thoroughfare Gap, operations around, LE *map 2-3*, 127, 132, 134-135, *136*, 143, 145
Thrasher, F. M., KI 82
Thruston, Gates, CH 61
Thumb, Tom, YA 52, 53
Tickfaw River, MI *map 90*, 94
Ticknor, Francis, OR 46
Tidball, John C., AP 39
Tigress, SH 116, *148-149*
Tilden, Samuel J., NA 149, 152, 153, 155, 156
Tilghman, Lloyd, MI 121, *125*, SH *65;* Foote, relations with, SH 65; at Fort

Henry, SH 57-58, 62, 67; surrender by, SH 65
Tillman, Ben, NA 149
Tillman, William, MI 10
Tilton Station, Georgia, AT 39
Timberlake, W. L., AP 122
Timber resources, BR 9
Timrod, Henry, OR 46
Tinker, Charles, SP 68
Tinsley, Howard, KI *65*
Tiptonville, Tennessee, SH 160, 166, *168-169*
Tishomingo Hotel, MI *46-47*
Titusville, Pennsylvania, NA 83, YA *70*
Tobacco, OR 29, 31
Tocqueville, Alexis de, YA 86
Tod, David, YA 32, 143
Todd, A. H., MI 35
Todd, David, MI 24
Todd, David H., SP 88
Todd, Elodie, OR 121
Todd, George, SP 148-149, *151*, 152-153, 159; death, SP 161; Quantrill, split with, SP 157-158
Todd, William, CH 107
Todd's Tavern, KI 61, 68, 84, 85
Toledo, Ohio, civil disorder in, YA 35
Tolles, Cornelius, FL 135
Tompkins, Charles H., AS *149*, FL 115
Tompkins, Sally, OR *59*, TT 98
Tompkins' Battery, BD *102*
Tompkinsville, Kentucky, TE 24
Toms Brook, Battle of, FL 139
Tom's Brook, Virginia, DE 83
Tonawanda, BL 152
Toombs, Robert A., BD *116-117*, 121-122, *125*, 126, 135-136, BL 16, OR 14, SM 52, SP *57;* as Confederate presidential candidate, BR 130; and Confederate States founding, BR 130; and Fort Sumter relief, BR 138; and Frémont candidacy, BR 104; and secessionist movement, BR 125; and slavery extension, BR 42
Torbert, Alfred T. A., BD 54, FL 101, 103, 106, 116, 124, 136, 139, 147, 158, KI 151-152, TR 21-22, *23*, 25-26
Torpedoes. *See* Mines; Mining operations
Torpedoes (land mines), SM 148, *152-153*
Totten's Battery, SH 27
Tourtellotte, John, SM 21, 24
Tower, Zealous B., LE 160, *171*
Towne, Laura M., NA 120, 123
Towns. *See* Rural areas
Townsend, Charles, KI *170*
Townsend, Edward D., AS *123*, 140
Townsend, Frederick, FI 82
Townsend, George Alfred, LE 83, TT 49
Townsend, M. W., TR 51
Toys, patriotic, YA 113, *114-115*
Trabue, R. P., TE 154
Tracie, T. C., AT 64
Tracy, Edward D., MI 104
Trade with enemy, YA 73-75
Trading Post, Kansas, SP 144

General George Custer saluting his foe, General Thomas Rosser, at the battle of Tom's Brook

AP Pursuit to Appomattox; AS The Assassination; AT Battles for Atlanta; BD The Bloodiest Day; BL The Blockade; BR Brother against Brother; CH The Fight for Chattanooga; CO The Coastal War; DE Decoying the Yanks; FI First Blood; FL The Shenandoah in Flames; FO Forward to Richmond; FR War on the Frontier; GE Gettysburg;

Training programs, DE 33, *42-43*, 136; Confederate, FI 52, 57, 93, SH 19, 21, 57, TT 9, *36-37*, 48, 53, 55; officers', TT 52-53; Union, FI *24-25, 34-35*, 49, 52, 54-55, 87, 110, MI 40, SH 19, *22-23, 40-41*, 45, 106, TT *18-19*, 22-24, *32*, 44, 48-53, *54-55*

Transatlantic cable, BR 28

Transportation systems, FI 33, 46; deficiencies of, OR 10, 25, *26-27*, 28-30. *See also* Railroads

Transports, SH *142-143, 146, 148-149*

Travel passes, OR 82, *119*, 129

Travis, William, TE *100*, 100-111

Travis, William D. T., painting by, CH *20, 36*

Treadwell, W. B., SP 167

Treason, OR 10, 13, 74-77, *87*, 88, *92*, 93-94, 110, 151-153

Treasury, Department of the. *See* Memminger, Christopher G.

Treasury Department, YA *12-13*, 14, 56. *See also* Chase, Salmon P.

Trecy, Patrick, TE *114*

Tredegar Iron Works, BL 48-49, OR *20*, TR *18;* munitions production, OR 17, 21-23, 65

Trego, William, LE 45

Tremain, Henry E., AP 125, RE 148

Trenches. *See* Fortifications

Trenholm, George Alfred, BL 98

Trent Affair, BL 116-118, *119*, 120, FO 64-65

Trenton, North Carolina, CO 91

Trent River, CO 37, 84, 92

Trent's Reach, Virginia, AP *44-45*

Trevilian Station, Virginia, TR 20-25

Trial of conspirators, AS 139-151, *152-153*, 154-159

Trice, John, TT 53

Trimble, Isaac R., DE 164-165, 168, GE 67, 128-129, 136, 138, 144, LE 103, 129, 141

Trimble, William H., BD 59

Trobriand, Philip de, AP 116, 131

Trobriand, Régis de, GE 99-100, RE 95, TT 29

Trollope, Anthony, YA 63

Trostle farm, GE 102, 105, *106-107*

Troup Hurt house, AT *82-83*

Trowbridge, John Townsend, NA 16, 26

Troy, New York, YA *97*, 110

Troy *Daily Times*, YA 110

True, B. H., NA 64

Truex, William S., AP 124, FL 73, 75, 78, 79

Trumbull, Lyman, NA 39, 40, YA 32-33, 142

Truth, Sojourner, BR *65*

Tubman, Harriet, BR *68*

Tucker, Beverly, AS 132, 144

Tucker, G. W., AP 95, 140, 145, 150

Tucker, John R., AP 111, 122, 127

Tucker, William F., CH 148

Tucson, New Mexico Territory, FR 19, 22-23, 35, 117

Tuerk, Julius G., AP 37

Tullahoma, Tennessee, CH *map* 2, 18, 22, 24, 28, 29, 30, 32, 33, 35, TE 85, 161

Tunnard, William, MI 151, 156-157

Tunnel Hill, AT 32, 37, CH 123, 136, 138, 141, 142, 150, SM 29

Tunnell, J. T., TE 142

Tunstall, Richard, FL *14*

Tunstall's Station, Virginia, LE *28-29*

Tupelo, Mississippi, AP 53, MI 34, TE 12, 17, 31, 40

Turchin, John Basil, CH 68, 89, 90, TE 14, 16, 17

Turner, Augustus J., DE *134*

Turner, Henry, NA 36

Turner, James, MI 112

Turner, John W., AP 99, TR 80, 83

Turner, Joseph A., OR 26

Turner, Mary Ann, AS 70

Turner, Nat, BR 40

Turner, Richard, TT 119

Turner's Gap, BD 44-45, 47, *map* 48, 49, *52-53*, 55-56

Tuscarora, BL 22, 121, 148

Tuscumbia, MI 100

Tuscumbia, Alabama, SM 33, 82, 83

Tuttle, James M., SH *130*, 138

Tutwiler, Edward, FL *14*

Twain, Mark, MI 140, OR 46, SH 8

Tweed, William Marcy (Boss), NA 109-110, 129, 149; Nast cartoon, NA *132-133*

20-Negro law, OR 80, 93

Twiggs, David E., BR 129-130, *131*, DE 28, FR 17, 18, *19*, 21, 22

Twining, William J., SM 94

Twitchell, Marshall Harvey, NA 140-142

Twombly, Corporal, SH 91, 95

Tybee Island, CO 46-47, 49

Tyler, MI 28-29, SH 70, *142*, 143

Tyler, Daniel, FI 117-121, 124, 126-127, 129, 135, 145

Tyler, Erastus B., DE 66, 168, 170, FL 71, 73, 74, 79, 83

Tyler, John, BR 119

Tyler, Robert O., KI 126, 160-161

Tyler, Texas, OR 121

Typhoid, incidence of, YA 23

Tyser, Mr. *See* Booth, John Wilkes

Tyson, Mr. *See* Booth, John Wilkes

U

U.S. Army Laboratory, SM *108*

U.S. Military Telegraph, SP 64, 71

U.S. Ordnance Department, SM 87

Uncle Tom's Cabin (Stowe), BR 46, 47

Underground Railroad, BR 40, 45, 60-62, 67-68

Underwood, Adin, SM 45

Underwriter, CO 93

Unemployment in North, TT 24

Unger's Store, Virginia, DE 52, 54-55

Uniforms, OR *19*, 25, 33, 43, *66-67*, *81;* Baker's Confederate, CH *40-41;* cavalry, GE *38-40;* Confederate, AP 75, DE 38, *117*, FI *58, 99-100, 103-104, 106, 109*, FO *59*, SH 106, TT *53, 73;* costs, OR 33; French influence on, FI 21, 63; Indians', TT 31; Longstreet's troops in blue, CH 43; misidentification of, SH 27; production and supply, OR 25, 43, *66-67;* 79th New York Highlanders, CH 119; 3rd New Jersey Cavalry, FL *108;* Union, FI 96-98, 101-102, 104, 107-108, 137, FO *60*, 63, 69, TT 72; Union forage cap, CH 79, 119; Veteran Reserve Corps, FL 76

Union Army: ambulance camp, KI *16-17;* ambulances, AT *84-85;* amphibious assaults, MI 69; amphibious operations, BL *map* 2-3, 26, 29-31, *32-35*, FO *map* 2-3, 14, 40-42, 44, 46, 67, 74, 84, 91-92, 105; animals, number used, FO 73, 91; areas controlled by, OR 29, 51, 96, 98, 148, *map* 152-153, 167-168; arms, FI 48-50, *52-53, 70-75;* artillery, CH *108-109, 110-111;* artillery actions, BD 47, 51, 64, 67-68, 70-71, 74-75, 78-79, 83, 91-92, *102*, 108, 125, 131, 153, *154-155*, CO 25, 32, 36, *38-39, 46-49*, 88, 94, *100-101*, 120-121, 124, 129-131, *132-133*, 134-135, *136-137*, 138-139, DE 67, 75, 130-131, 133, 151, 161, 164, 167-168, FO *40-41*, 46, 93-94, *102*, 105, 108-111, *122-123*, 133, 144, 154-155, 164, LE 31, *34-35*, 37, 41, 46, 50, 56, 58, *62*, 63, 67-68, 69, 70-71, 103, *140-141*, 148, 161, MI 35, *36*, 37, 40-41, 68, 71, 94, 102, 121, 130, 134, 136, 139, RE 51-53, 56, 64-65, 71, 85, 108, 133, 135, 144, 147, 149-150, TE 29, 93, *109*, 113, 127, 130, 145, 150, 152, 153, 154; artillery expansion, FO 17; artillery losses, BD 43, 59, CH 45-46, 50, 59, CO 96, 139, FO 110, LE 46, *47*, 59, MI 37, 102-103, RE 142; artillery lost, AT 104, 106, 107, SH 27, TE 113; artillery strength, FO 89, 91; artillery weapons, BD 42, 65, DE *136-137, 139-141;* Atlanta, entry into, SM 14; bakery, TR *166-167;* balloons, RE 40, *123;* balloons, use by, FO 99, 105, *146-153;* bands, AT *33*, CO *43*, 88, DE 132, RE 56, 63, 95, SH *22, 46*, 48; bayonet assaults, BD *72-73*, 131, 133-135, CO 124, 168, FO *45*, 164, LE 39, MI *42-43*, 114, 118, 123, *124-125*, 130, *146-147*, RE 74-75, 79-80, 86, 154; bayonet charge, AT 149, CH 69, 93, 95, SM 138; bayonet drill, FO *14*, 20; black people as servants, SH *88-89;* blacks employed by, MI 50-51, 58, *60-61*, 100; black servants in, LE *30;* blacks in, OR 144-147, 166-167, TT 31, *32-33*, 34-35; black soldiers, NA 47, *100-101;* black teamsters, KI *47;* black troops, AP *10*, *64*, 108, 139, FR 55, 64, *147*, 152, SM 113, 126, 135, 161, TR 27, 39, 43, 74,

Brigadier General Alfred T. A. Torbert, who led General Sheridan's cavalry in the Shenandoah Valley

French-born Philippe Régis de Trobriand, who attained the rank of Federal Brigadier General

KI The Killing Ground; LE Lee Takes Command; MI War on the Mississippi; NA The Nation Reunited; OR Confederate Ordeal; RE Rebels Resurgent; SH The Road to Shiloh; SM Sherman's March; SP Spies, Scouts and Raiders; TE The Struggle for Tennessee; TR Death in the Trenches; TT Tenting Tonight; YA Twenty Million Yankees

115

Shirt made for Private Edgar Yergason, 22nd Connecticut, by his mother

Union officers and their wives at their quarters in the defenses of Washington

Union Army (continued)

80, 82-83, 88, *116-125*, 139, 146; and Blockade Strategy Board, CO 16; bounty jumpers, TT 37; breastworks, use of, SH *30-31*, 157; bridge construction by, BD *30-31, 36-37*, DE 61, *64-65*, FO *20-21*, 74-75, 133, MI 84, 123, *127*, 128-129, RE 10, *12-17*, 30, *34*, 36, 50-53, *54-55*, 91, 120, 152, 156-158, *166-167*; bridge demolition by, DE 126; Bureau of Military Information, SP 80, 81; burial details, KI *120, 124*; Butternut Guerrillas, MI 89; camp, SP *32-33*; campaign equipment, TT *72, 74*; campaign life, KI *47, 53, 55, 145*; camp life, AP *8-9, 10, 11, 12, 13, 14-15, 22, 23*, CH 19, *82-83, 160-161*, CO *40-45, 122-123*, KI *8-21*, 32, *48-49, MI 47, 54-55, 98-99*, RE *31, 105, 114-115*; Canadians in, TT 30; casualties, AP 31, 39, 66, 67, 69, 99, 120, 130, *141*, 161, 162, AT 12, 25, 35-36, 42, 48, 52, 54, 56, 60, 64, 69, 71, 74, 75, 95, 114, 136, 139, 146, 152, 154, BD 47, 49, 51, 55, 64, 73, 76, 79, 83, 87, 89-91, 96, 99-100, 105, 108, *109*, 121-122, 126, 137-138, 150-151, *152*, 156, 159, CH 26, 28, 30, 44, 46, 48, 62, 66, 67, 69, 71, 73, 79, 91, 93, 109, 115, 119, 136, 139, 140, 141, 145, 150, 154, CO 27, 30, 37, 85, 111, 124, 128, 131, 134, 139, 162, 170, DE 69, 71, 103, DE 128, 135, FI 80, 82-85, *86*, 122, 152, FL 23, 29, 36, 39, 47, 48, 49, 61, 81, 83, 84, 87, 89, 122, 140, 147, 149, 158, *170*, FO 12, 16, 45, *51*, 52, 64, 102-103, 113, 133, 166-167, 168-169, FR 17, 19-20, 26, 30, 53, 57, 58, 60, 62, 64, 65, 70, 71, 79, 82, 83, 87, 89, 99, 112, 113, 128, 146, 151, 153, KI 4, 21, 31, 36, *52*, 65-66, 78, 81, 83, 89, 91, 104, 105, *120-121*, 125, 130, 133, 136-137, 140, 147, 149, 153, 161, 165, 169-170, LE 23, 31, 36, 41-42, 46-47, 54-55, 60, 72-73, 75, 107, *108*, 109, 142, 149, 158, 167-168, MI 20, 35, 37, 40-41, 43-44, 62, 67-68, 94, 96, 104, 112, 114-115, 119, 122-123, 127, 132, 146, 166, NA 25, OR 103, *109*, 151, RE 51, 53, 67, 71, 74, 77, 81, 83, 86-87, *88*, 111, 131, 133, 143, *145*, 160, SM 26, 55, 61, 67, 85, 103, 106, 118, 132, 144, 149, 150, SP 82, 121, 128, 153, 158, 161, TE 48, 83, TR 4, 16, 26, 28, 50, 52-53, 55, 62, 88-89, 99, 101, 103, 109, 111, 117, 119, 123, 142-144, 147, 149, 152, *155*, 157, TT 35, 78, 81, 83-85, 87-90, *93*, 98; casualties at Perryville, TE 67; casualties at Stones River, TE 117, 122, 125, 142, 159; cavalry, role of, AP 21; cavalry actions, BD 17, 45, 56-58, 152, CH 18, 24, 44, 79, 80, DE 87, 130, 160, FO 89, 108, *119*, LE 26-27, 29, 34, *44-45*, 46, 107, 134, MI 87-89, *map* 90, 91-93, *94*, 95-96, 97, RE *32*, 93, 105-109, *110*, 111, 118-119, 133, *134, 136-137, 159*; cavalry

corps activated, RE 118; Cavalry Corps emblem, FL *101*; cavalrymen, MI *92*; cavalry remount depots, FL *110-111*; cavalry weapons, SM *86-87*; chaplains, BD 91, 100, MI 58, RE 52, *83, 113*; character of, SM 36-43; at Chattanooga, CH 97; chief of staff, FO 17; civilian resistance to, OR 159; clothing, articles issued, TT *76*; color bearers, BD 71-73, 100, 133, 170, MI 119, 127, 130-131, *132-133*, RE 67, *68-69, 73*, 132, *156-157*; colors, BD *58, 87*, 100, *101, 127*, CO *85, 127*, RE *51, 82*; colors lost, FO 16-17; Columbia, destruction in, AP 59-*60*, 61; command and leadership deficiencies, FI 155; commanders, losses in, KI 169-170; command failures, FO 39, 50, 167; commanding generals, NA 77; communications system, BD 44, *71*, 86-87, *167*, FO 39, LE *70*, MI 62-63, 108, OR *107*, RE *42-49*, commutation policies, TT 37; and Confederate deserters, AP 20; and Confederate surrender at Appomattox, AP 151-152; conscription program, TT 35-37; corduroying roads, AP 55; corps activated, FO 84-85; corps badges, AT *21, 96, 98*, KI *57*; Corps emblems, AP *23*, 72; cotton traders in, MI 58; daily life in, TE 100, *101, 105*; demolitions by, CO 8, 85, 91-92, 96, LE 34, 49-50, *51*, 52, *53*, 86, 98, 165, MI 63, 78, 88-91, *94*, 95, 115; demoralization in, FO 8, 109; depredations by, MI *70*, 115; desertion, TE 81; desertions, RE 102, TT 31, 37, 48, 153; discipline, NA *105*, TE 16, 80; discipline breakdowns, FI 116-117, 136, 148-149, 157, 162-163, *169-170*; discipline in, FO 14, 16-17, 30; discipline and morale, LE 75, 132-133, 135; disease rates, FO 67; diseases in, MI 18, 35, 40, 47, 166; disparagement of enemy, FI 96, FO 155; dissension in, TR 94; draft animals, CH 78-79, 80, 81, 88, 97, 101, 105, *106, 107*, 111, 163; drill, CH 19; drummer boys, CH *23*, 65, KI *47*; drummers, MI 131; engineering operations, BD *30-31, 36-37*, CO 88, *128*, 129, *map* 130-131, 135-136, DE 61, *64-65*, LE *38-39*, 55, *120-121*, MI 26, 33, 69-74, 76, 84, 123, *127*, 128-129, 148, RE 10, *12*, 14, *15-17*, 30, 34, 36, 50-53, *54-55*, 91, 120, 152, 156-158, *166-167*; engineer operations, FO 8, 17-18, *20-21*, 74-75, 105, 133; engineers, AP *11*, 22, *23*, CH *170-171*; Englishmen in, TT 30; equipment discarded by, SH 81-82; equipment excavated from Crater, TR *90-93*; expired enlistments, TR 64; farm background of, SM 47; field-surgeon kit, SM *110*; flags, CH *127*, FI 25; food shortages, RE 101; foraging, AP 57-58, *59*, CH *20*, KI *150*, OR 149, SM 40, 53-56, 68-*70*; foreigners commissioned, TT 29; foreigners in, DE *152-155*;

fortifications, CH 29, 52, 56, 60, 64, 67, *86-87*, 91, 97, 106, 109, 110, 112, *114-115, 169*, LE 24; fortifications construction, FO 8, 17-18, 105, 139; in Fort Sumter defense, BR 121-128, 132-141, 146-157; fraternization by, MI 136; fraternization with enemy, AT 140, CH 99, 130-131, KI 32, RE *38*, 39, 41, TR 137, 159; Frenchmen in, TT 30; frontier life, FR 111, 119; furlough system, RE 102; garrison at Nashville, TE 72; Germans in, TT 29, *30*; Grand Review, NA *8-15*; Grant's evaluation of, CH 117, 120, 142, 143; and Grant, KI 85, 167-169; grenade assaults, MI *135*, 149; headgear, DE *57*; herd cattle for, SM *35*; and horses, SM 123; hospital steward, SM *111*; immigrants in, TT 24, 28-29, *30*; improvisations by, MI *135*, 136, *154*; Indian fighting and frontier garrisons, NA 93, *100-105*; Indians in, TT 31; intelligence operations, LE 48; intelligence reports, FO 28, 131, 151-153; intelligence service, DE 101; Irish in, TT 28-30; James River, crossing of, TR 34-36, *38*; and Jennison, SP 144-147; and Kansas violence, BR 79; and Lane, SP 142; language barriers in, TT 29; laundry service, FO *28*; lines of communication, FI 46; living conditions, RE 101-102; logistical staff work, TE 15; and looting, SM 45-46, 62; looting by, OR *104*, 111-112, *116*, RE 54-55, *56*, SH 48; mail for Sherman's troops, SM 156; mail wagon, KI *14*; mapping service, FO 93-94, *152*; marches, DE *150*; marching orders of, SM 48-49; mascots, SH *23*; matériel losses, SH 33, *53*; Medal of Honor awards, MI 131; medical officers, number in, TT 79; medical services, BD *109*, 136, *138-139*, 150, FO 17, 91, LE 52, *54-55, 106-107, 112-113*, 142, MI *46-47*, OR *108-109*, SH *88-89*, TT 78-79; *Merrimac-Virginia*, firing on, BL 55-57; mess facilities, CO *41*, TT *8-9*, 47; Mexican-Americans in, TT 31; Military Division of the Mississippi, AT 22; military garrisons in South, NA 28, 61, *62*, 63; morale, AP 8, 16, 30-31, 67, 91, 92, 133, AT 22, BD 100, 105, CH 64, 98, 134, 145, 147, 149, FI 33-34, KI 153, 156-157, MI 17, 40, 76-77, 129, RE 92, 95, 100, 102, 112, 140, SH 34, 49, SM 45, 47, SP 115, TE 81, 144, TR 34, 36, 94; morale restored, FO 14, 25; and Mosby, SP 120-121; motivation and morale, TT 20, 24, 37, 68; mule attack, CH 95; musicians, DE 132, FO *54-55*, 59, MI *128-129*; muster-outs, FO 16, 18; mutiny in, BD 131, FO 16, SH 45; Napoleonic influence on, FI 48-49, 56; and newspapers, SP 52; night operations, FO 105; officers, efficiency of, FI 56-57; officers, election of, FI 96; officer and soldier types, FI *96-98, 101-102, 104*,

AP Pursuit to Appomattox; AS The Assassination; AT Battles for Atlanta; BD The Bloodiest Day; BL The Blockade; BR Brother against Brother; CH The Fight for Chattanooga; CO The Coastal War; DE Decoying the Yanks; FI First Blood; FL The Shenandoah in Flames; FO Forward to Richmond; FR War on the Frontier; GE Gettysburg;

The Union Army Refreshment Saloon in Philadelphia, which served meals to troops bound for the front

107-108; officers remaining and resigning, BR 130, *142-145;* officer standards, FO 20-21, 39; panic in, BD 43, 90, 96-97, 137, 155, CH 44, 58, 60, FL 33, 151, FO 109, 139-140, MI 111, RE *132,* 133, 135, panic in, at Franklin, SM 105, TE 48, 115; parades and reviews, FO 24-25; physical conditioning of, SM 44; pontoon boats and bridges, KI *18, 49, 59, 142, 144, 147, 150;* prison camp survivors, NA 37; prisoners, KI 34, 36, 81, 105; prisoners captured by, DE 87; prisoners lost, AP 36-37, 39, 66, 67, 120, 130, 131, 150, AT 56, 80, 104, 114, 138, *141,* CH 23, 52, 69, 112, 113, 140, 154, CO 96, FI 149, *154,* FL 82, 107, *137,* 147, FO 51-52, FR 20, 50, 60, 160, *167-170,* OR *38-39,* SH 30, 33, 120, *131, 134,* 138-139, 141, SM 19, 29, 55, 67, 103, 118, SP 114, 116, 119, 121, 127, *128-129,* 130, TE 11, 24, 25, 26, 29, 30, 31, 48, 49, 51, 87, 91, 97, *98,* 117, 122, TR 24, 45, 56, 88, 103, 109, 114-115, 152, TT 110-111, *114,* 135; prisoners lost to Confederates, BD 59, MI 60, 94, 117, 123, RE 142; prisoners taken by Confederates, LE 28, 46-47, 52, 59-60, 72-73, 75, 167; property seized by South, BR 128-130; Provost Guard, AP *11,* FO 16; provost marshals, SP 31; Quartermaster Corps, CH *164,* TR *164-165;* racial relations, TR 121; Railroad Construction Corps, SP 90, 101, 104; railroad construction and repair, RE 9, *10-17;* railroads, demolition by, FO 133; railroad service, FO 130; railroad wrecking manual, SP *90-103;* rations, TT 85-87; reconnaissances by, CO 24, DE 72, *74, 76-77,* FO 39-41, 50, 64, 94, 99, 102, 111, MI 74, RE *32,* 40, 58, 103, *123,* 129, 153; recreation facilities, CO *52-53;* recruiting campaigns, LE 93; recruiting programs, CO 19, FO 16, 18, 97, SH *80,* TT 21, *25, 30,* 32-33, 78-79; reenlistment drives, KI 38-43; regard for Buell, TE 14; regard for Rosecrans, TE 81; regular officer assignments, FO 28; Regulars, TE *125;* reinforcements and draftees, TR 94, 136; reorganization, CH 88; reorganization by Grant, KI 37-38, 43; replacement system, TT 48; reprisals, SP 131, 153-154, 155; resentment at irregulars, SP 4, 107; returning veterans of, NA 20-25, 34, 78; Richmond, drive on, OR 13, 59, 148, 151, 160, 167-168; road construction, FO 105, LE *38-39, 87;* road construction and repair, MI 129; ruses, BD 52, 56-57, CO 87, FO 113, 136, FR 24, 32, MI 88-89, 91; sanitation measures, TT 80-81; sawmill, CH *162;* Scandinavians in, TT 30; Scotsmen in, TT 30; scouts, SP *30, 82-83;* security measures, FO *10-11,* 25; Sheridan's command in Valley, FL *126-133;* and Sherman, SM 47, 51; and Sherman, support for, AP *159;* ship transport of

troops, CH *102-103;* siege life, TR 65, 137, *140-141,* 158-159; Signal Corps, SP *64, 65;* signaling, SM 15, *22-23,* 24, *25,* 26-27; signal tower, TR *30-31;* signal troops, FO *18-19;* snipers, BD 127, 153, 156, FO 100, *101,* MI 149, RE 84; soldiers' civilian vocations, TT 26; soldier types, BL *44-45;* and South Carolina, feeling against, AP 52, 53, 55-56; and Southern women, SM 56; staff organization, FO 17, 22-23; state affiliation of units, FI 54-55; strategic plans, SH 8-9; strategy, CO *map 2-3;* substitutes, policies on, TT 35-37; supplies, AT 31, CH 21, TE 30-31, 76, 133, 143, 157; supply base at City Point, TR 136, *160-171;* supply depots, KI *106-113, 154-155;* supply lines, CH 18, 20, 33, 78, 79, 80-81, 90, 95, 97, 104-105; supply lines under attack, TE 40, *106;* supply operations, BD 27, *32-33,* 164, CO *88-89,* 90, *122-123,* 162, DE 46, *118-119,* FI 32-33, 40-41, 44-45, 54, FO 17, *22-23,* 130, LE 25, 29-30, 48-49, 58-62, *84, 96-97, 118-119,* 124-125, 144, 151, MI 56, 60, 62, 84, 89, 108-109, 129, 156, *165,* RE *18-21,* 30, 35-36, 41, 93, SH 21, 86; supply problems, CH 19, 30, 111, 136; supply trains, FL 26; supply wagons, CH *37,* 42, 79, 108, KI *16-17, 20-21, 46, 59,* NA *27, 102;* surprise, application of, SH 26, 33; and sutlers, KI 15, TR 167; tactics, DE 40, SH 20, 24-25; target practice, FO 20; teamsters, FL 55; tents, FO *14, 36-37;* and Thomas, SM 127; three-year troops in, FO 16, 18; topographical equipment, AT *78-79;* training, AT *28-29;* training programs, BD *34-35,* CO 19, DE *136-137,* FI 24-25, *34-35, 49,* 52, FI 54-55, 57, 87, 110, FO 18-20, 22, *26-27, 30-37,* 63, *76-77,* MI 40, RE 102, SH 19, *22-23, 40-41,* 45, 106, TT *18-19,* 22-24, *32,* 44, 48-53, *54-55;* transport service, FO 63, *88-89,* 91, *120-121,* 124, 130; troop strength, AP 18, 19, 53, 65, 69-71, 78-80, 92, 118, 122, 125, 160, 161, AT 22, 25, 31, 39, 40, 49, 52, 53, 54, 60, 64, 67, 68, 69, 99, 136, 138, 139, 141, 144, BD 8, 15, 44, 53, 63, 65, 67, 108, CH 19, 21, 24, 32, 33, 37, 39, 52, 64, 66, 67, 74, 81, 83, 89, 90, 95, 100, 106, 109, 130, 133, 136-137, 141, 143, 145-146, 156, DE 44, 61, 102, 114, 121-122, FL 20, 26, 27, 30, 34, 41, 45, 51, 71, 73, 85, 89, 90, 101, 141, 151, 153, FO 8, 24, 53, 64, 91, 105, 127, FR 14, 18-19, 23-24, 27-28, 31-32, 34, 44, 46-47, 50-52, 54-55, 57, 59, 64-65, 68, 70, 72, 78, 81, 85, 87, 91, 94, 108, 110, 113, 117-120, 126-127, 138, 140, 147, 150-153, 155-157, 160, KI 8, 20, 26, 28, 34, 36, 45, 58, 68, 70, 74, 78, 90, 95, 106, 114, 125, 130, 150, 157, LE 23, 45, 92, 103, 124, 126, MI 18, 24, 26, 84, 101, 110, 126, 134, 156, NA 25,

28, 61, 143, OR 148, RE 30, 39, 61, 118, 125, 140, 154, 156, SM 14, 20, 21, 34, 47, 60, 73, 83, 85, 91, 121, 126, 128, 144, 156, SP 12, 33, 58, 63, 106, 122, 142, 155, TE 8, 15, 17, 21, 24, 26, 31, 38, 41, 45, 47, 49, 51, 54, 61, 64, 70, 88, 92-93, 166, TR 18-19, 21, 27-28, 34, 36, 38-39, 42, 45, 49-50, 52, 55, 64-65, 80, 94-95, 97, 99, 101, 139, 145, 149, 153-154, 158, 159, YA 87; troop strength and reinforcements, SH 21, 25, 33, 54, 60, 78-79; uniforms, AT 96, FI *96-98, 101-102, 104, 107-108, 137,* FO 60, *63,* TR *60,* TT *72;* unit organization, FI 54-55; use of fugitive slaves, CH *25;* use of mounted infantry, CH 21, 28; use of pontoon boats, CH 89, 90, 123; veteran organizations and reunions, NA *159-171;* Veteran Reserve Corps, FL 76, NA 8-9; voting by, TR 157; wagon repair shop, KI *18-19;* wagon trains, SM 27, 47, 69, 94, 96, 97, *104-105;* weapons, improvised, SH *106;* women in, TT 27, XIV Corps officers, AT *22-23;* Zouave uniforms, KI *66-67;* Zouave units, BD *89, 121, 132,* 133-138, TE *143;* "assassination sympathizers," AS *158;* and "bummers," SM *70-71;* "seeing the elephant" origin, FI 156. *See also individual states;* Militia units; Regular Army, United States; McClellan, George Brinton; Soldiers

Union Church, Mississippi, MI *map* 90
Union Hospital No. 19 (Nashville), TE *74-75*
Union League, NA 67
Union Mills Ford, FI 113, 117, 122, 124, 149
Union Pacific Railroad, NA 83, *84-85,* 109
Union Party, NA 16, YA 149-151. *See also* National Union Party
Unions, development of, NA 89
Union Trust Company, NA 125
United Confederate Veterans, NA 160, *161;* badge, NA *161*
United Kingdom: and blockade, BL 14, 26, 95-96, 125; Confederacy, relations with, BL 14-17, 116, 119, *121,* 125-126; and cotton embargo, BL 14-16, 125; immigrants from, YA 21; ironclad construction, BL 47; and privateers, BL 12; and *Trent* Affair, BL 116-118, *119;* United States, relations with, BL 17, 116-119; warship construction in, BL 114-116, *117,* 120-121, 123-125, 126-128, *129,* 143, 149, 161
United States: agricultural resources, FI 46; arms sales to Southern states, FI 46; Britain, relations with, BL 17, 116-119; and Confederacy, recognition of, BL 116; division in 1861, BR *map* 2-3; Eastern theater, FI *map* 2-3; industrial resources, FI 45-46; intelligence operations, BL 114-116, 131; manpower resources, FI

A Union Infantryman clad in the regulation issue Federal Army overcoat

KI The Killing Ground; LE Lee Takes Command; MI War on the Mississippi; NA The Nation Reunited; OR Confederate Ordeal; RE Rebels Resurgent; SH The Road to Shiloh; SM Sherman's March; SP Spies, Scouts and Raiders; TE The Struggle for Tennessee; TR Death in the Trenches; TT Tenting Tonight; YA Twenty Million Yankees

117

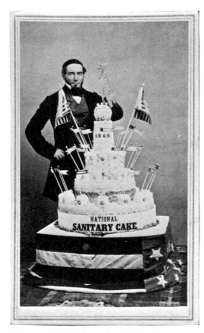

A huge cake baked as a fund-raiser for the U.S. Sanitary Commission fair

United States (continued)
45-48; mobilization, FI 11, 13-14, 21, 24, 32-33; officers loyal to, FI 28; patriotic demonstrations, FI 13, *16*, 20, 32-33; propaganda activities, BL 122-123; railroad systems, FI 46; transportation systems, FI 33. *See also* Lincoln, Abraham; Seward, William H.

United States. *See* Northern states

United States Army. *See* Militia units; Regular Army, United States; Union Army

United States Christian Commission, TT 147, *148*, YA *17;* medical services, YA *130-131*

United States Colored Infantry, AP *10*

United States Colored Light Artillery, FR *147*

United States Colored Troops, TR 74, 139; 1st Brigade, SM 126, TR 121; 2nd Brigade, SM 126, 135; 4th Infantry Regiment, TR *123;* 5th Infantry Regiment, TR *124-125*, 147; 6th Infantry Regiment, TR 140; 7th Infantry Regiment, TR *122-123*, 147; 9th Infantry Regiment, TR 147; 12th Infantry Regiment, SM 113, 126, 135; 13th Infantry Regiment, SM 135-136; 22nd Infantry Regiment, TR *116-117;* 23rd Infantry Regiment, TR *118-119;* 29th Infantry Regiment, TR *119;* 30th Infantry Regiment, TR 83; 36th Infantry Regiment, TR *125;* 38th Infantry Regiment, TR *124;* 107th Infantry Regiment, TR *120. See also* Black troops

United States Ford, RE 32, 118, 120-121, 135, 140, 159

United States government. *See* Lincoln, Abraham; Seward, William

United States Marine Corps, BR 87-89, 91, FI 141, 143-144, 162. *See also* Marine Corps, United States

United States Military Academy, LE *18*

United States Military Railroads. *See* Haupt, Herman; Railroads

United States Military Railroads Construction Corps, AT 14, 50, 146, CH *169, KI 106, TR 171*

United States Navy, BD 14, BR 133-135, 147, 152-153, 156-157, 160-161, FR 46, 53, *68-71*, LE 48, 52, 58, 63, 66, *70*, *88*, 91, SM 48, 144, 147, 149-150, *154*, TT blacks in, TT 32-33; amphibious operations, BL *map 2-3*, 26, 29-31, *32-35;* on Arkansas River, MI 17, *22, 69;* arms and equipment, MI *57, 64-65;* auxiliary vessels, use of, AP 48; at Baton Rouge, MI 18, *34-35*, OR 103; black sailors in, BL 24; blockade by, OR 17, 22, 29, 31, 33, 82-83, 148; and Blockade Strategy Board, CO 16; boarding operations, CO 32-33; camouflage used by, CO 64, 66; casualties, CO 69, 73, 118, 133, 147-150, 154, 156, 167, 170, MI 26, 32, 100, 139, 162, SH 65-67; at Chickasaw Bluffs, MI *70*, 96; command structure, BL 24; communications systems, BL *40-41*, 89, *90*, CO 67; demolitions by, CO 8; duty routine and recreation, BL 90-91, *102-113;* expansion and construction programs, BL 10-11, 17, 20-22, 33, 46, 48-53, 65, *66-73*, 75; expenditures, wartime, BL 20; fire-direction system, CO 65-66; fleet acquisitions and strength, CO 35, 61, 115, 143, 145, 159; at Fort Donelson, SH 78, 82-84, *85*, 87, 90; at Fort Henry, SH 58, 60-63, *64*, 65-67; at Fort Hindman, MI 68, *69, 71;* at Fort Pemberton, MI 77; at Fort Pillow, MI 20; frauds against, YA 73; at Grand Gulf, MI 97-99, *100-101*, 109; gunboats on Virginia rivers, AP 42; insignia, MI *17;* in invasion of Virginia, FI 61; ironclad construction, BL 46, 48-53, 65, *66-73;* ironclads, CO 112-115, *116-117*, 118, *119*, 124-125, 130-131, 133-135, 143-145, 147, *148-149*, 150-156, 159, 164, 169; at Island No. 10, SH 155, *158-159*, 160, 163, *164-167;* James River flotilla, AP 45; in James River operations, FO 124-125, 127-128, *129;* landing parties, AP *49*, CO 143, 165, *166-167;* maintenance and repair, BL *42-43, 75, 100*, 107, *110-111;* Marine Brigade, FR 52; medical services, BL *113;* at Memphis, MI 20; at Milliken's Bend, MI 146; mining operations, BL *82-83;* on Mississippi River, OR *98;* at Mobile, OR 148; mortar boats, CO 57-58, *59*, 61, 64, 67, *70*, 73, 157-158; mortar schooners, MI 24, 162; at Natchez, MI 18; at New Carthage, MI 84-86; at New Orleans, MI 16-18, 24, SH 157; and Norfolk capture, FO 124; officers joining Confederacy, BL 10, FI 27; Pacific Squadron, FR *14;* pay and prize money, BL 11, 28-29, 31, 91, 107; in Peninsular Campaign, FO 89-91, 93, *96;* personnel procurement, BL 22-24, *29*, 53, 67; personnel strength, BL 10, 20, 33; plans for Vicksburg, MI 3, 17; at Port Hudson, MI 161, *162-163;* rams, MI 20, *24-25*, 27-29, 32, 77-78; reconnaissances, MI 79-80; on Red River, MI 77-79; religious services, BL *44;* in riverine operations, SH 8, 48; ruse by, MI 78, *79;* searches and seizures by, BL 93, 116-118, *119*, 120; at Shiloh, SH *142-143*, 147; shipboard life, AP *44*, 46, *47;* shipping hazards, MI 76, 80-81, *82*, 83; ships captured and destroyed by, BL *13*, 28, 60, 65, *84-85, 108-109*, 117, *151*, 158-160, 164-171; squadron organization, BL 24, 33; steam and propeller adoption, BL 47, 51; in Steele's Bayou, MI 80-81, *82*, 83; and stone fleet, BL *26-27;* strategic plans for, FI 45; strategy, CO *map 2-3;* supply operations, BL *38-39, 112-113*, CO 20; tactics, BL 29-31; training programs, BL 10, 24, CO *80;* and *Trent* affair, FO 64-65; unpreparedness, BL 10; at Vicksburg, MI *map 2-3*, 4, 18-26, 28-29, *30-31*, 32-33, 57, 77, *78-79*, 84-86, *87*, 96, 130, 136-137; volunteers in, BL 22-24; warship losses, BL *54*, 55-57, *58-59, map 60, 64, 78-79*, 142, 152; warships, number in, BL 10, 20, 33, 87, 152; warships, types and armament, BL *18-19, 22, 25*, 47; warships damaged and lost, CO 22-23, *66*, 67, 69, 71, 73, 93-95, 97, 113, 118-120, 139, 141, 147, 150, 152, 154-156, MI 18, 26, 29, 31-32, 77-78, *80-81*, 85-86, 100, 139, *162-163;* water supply, BL *42-43;* at Yazoo Pass, MI 77, 79-80; on Yazoo River, MI 28-29, 57, 63, 67, *71*, 79-80, 109. *See also* Blockade; Gunboats; Warships; Welles, Gideon

United States Patent Office, NA 81

United States Regular Army. *See* Regular Army, United States

United States Sanitary Commission, KI *14-15*, 111, *120*, NA 78, TT 115-116, 151; auctions for, YA 116, 136; clothing provided by, YA *122-123*, 131, 133; fairs held by, YA 133-135, *136-141;* food provided by, YA 117, 119, 124-125, *126-127*, 130, 131; fund-raising, YA 117, 123-124, 133-136; instituted, YA 116-117, 120; lodging provided by, YA 125; medical services, YA 124; transportation system, YA 124

United States Secret Service, SP 22

United States Topographical Engineers, TR 102

United States Treasury Guards, regimental banner, AS *78*, *88*

United States troops: TE *125;* Parson's Battery, TE 64

United States Veteran Reserve Corps, AS *107*, 144; 6th Infantry Regiment, AS *162-163*

United States Volunteers. *See* Union Army; *names of commanders and under states*

United States Zouave Cadets, FI *63*

Unit histories. *See* Regiments, histories of

Unity of command, OR 15, 162

"Unknown Dead" (Timrod), OR 48

Upham, Charles, AP 65, 66

Upham, William, BR 43

Upper Agency, Minnesota, FR 77, 82, 87

Upperville, Virginia, GE 28-29

Ups and Downs of Wife Hunting, OR 52

Upson, Theodore, SM 44, 45, 47, 61, 147, 156, 158

Upson, Theodore F., AP 60

Upton, Emory, BD 150, FL 115, *117*, 119, KI 33, 89-92, *94*, 101-102, 153, 167

Upton, John C., LE *171*

Urbanna plan, FO 63, 67, 74-75, 84-85, 89, 91

Utah Territory, Indian conflicts, FR 107-112

AP Pursuit to Appomattox; AS The Assassination; AT Battles for Atlanta; BD The Bloodiest Day; BL The Blockade; BR Brother against Brother; CH The Fight for Chattanooga; CO The Coastal War; DE Decoying the Yanks; FI First Blood; FL The Shenandoah in Flames; FO Forward to Richmond; FR War on the Frontier; GE Gettysburg;

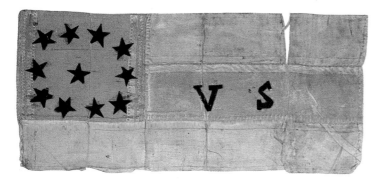

Personal flag of Captain Thomas J. Hanes of the Vicksburg, Mississippi, "Volunteer Southrons"

Ute Indians, FR 106, 108, 112, 120
Utica, New York, FI 63
Utoy Creek, AT 141
Utoy Creek, Battle of, AT 139

V

"Vacant Chair" (song), FO 39
Vaill, Theodore F., FL 115
Vallandigham, Clement L., NA 110, YA 26-27; and Burnside, YA 26; candidate for governor, YA 149; and emancipation, YA 36, 150; and Lincoln, YA 24-26, 30; in peace movement, YA 24-27, 155
Valley City, CO 32
Valley Turnpike, DE 67, 84, 116, 120, 129, map 130, 131, 133, 146, 151, FL 26, 30, 33, 42, 45, 91, 109, 116, 117, 122, 124, 137, 140, 141, 146, 149, 153, 164-165
Valverde, Battle of, FR 24-25, 26-27, 36
Valverde, New Mexico Territory, FR 23, 24
Van Brunt, Henry, BL 46, 56
Van Buskirk, David, TT 28
Van Camp, Aaron, SP 24
Vance, Zebulon Baird, CH 43, OR 79; on civilian morale, OR 77; conscription opposed by, OR 78; and educational system, OR 55; and guerrillas, OR 89, 91; and impressment program, OR 83; and peace movement, OR 154; and railroad construction, OR 28; and states' rights, OR 76, 79; supplies withheld by, OR 155
Van Cleve, Horatio P., CH 47, 48, 49, TE 99, 118, 120, 123, 126, 127, 143
Van Den Corput, Max, AT 46
Van Den Corput's Battery, AT 46
Vanderbilt, Cornelius, NA 86, 106
Vandever, William, SM 30
Van Dorn, Earl, CH 20, 22, 23, FR 18-19, 138, 140, 141, 144, 145, 146, 149, MI 43, SM 93, SP 73, TE 42, 43, 80, YA 75; in Arkansas operations, SH 101, 107; Bowen's charges against, MI 44; at Corinth, MI 38-40, 42-43, SH 157; at Holly Springs, MI 36, 60-62; and Missouri invasion, SH 101; at Pea Ridge, SH 101; at Vicksburg, MI 38, 44
Vanity Fair, Lincoln caricature in, AS 10
Van Lew, Elizabeth (Crazy Bet), SP 73, 87; background, SP 86-87; cipher, use of, SP 87-88; and Grant, SP 88-89; and Sharpe, SP 89
Van Ness, John Peter, SP 55
Van Pelt, George, CH 45
Van Valkenburg, J. D., FL 81
Variag, BL 136
Varina road, TR 139-140, 143, 146
Varuna, CO 66, 69
Vaughan, A. J., TE 118, 121, 123

Vaughan, Alfred, AT 70, 73
Vaughan's Brigade, AT 70
Vaughn, George L., grave marker of, TR 65
Vaughn, John C., FL 45, 46, 47, 48, 49, 50, 58, MI 122
Veale, George W., FR 164
Veatch, James C., SH 137
Venable, Charles S., AP 95, 135, 140, KI 71, 165
Venable, Reid, KI 118-119, 122
Venereal diseases, TT 62
Vera Cruz, Mexico, DE 25, LE 16-17
Verdi, Tullio, AS 95
Verdict of the People (Bingham), BR 22-23
Vermont, Confederate raid on St. Albans, SP 60, 61
Vermont Brigade, AP 92, FL 150, 154-155, FO 102, 105, KI 101, LE 60-61
Vermont troops: BD 54, FL 87, FO 66-67, KI 71, LE 60-61, RE 156-157, TT 24, 42-43, 56; at Big Bethel, FI 80-82; at Bull Run, FI 145-147, 164-165; Norwich University Cadets, FI 102; training program, FI 34-35; Vermont Brigade, FL 150, 154-155, FO 102, 105, KI 101, LE 60-61; 1st Cavalry Regiment, DE 130; 1st Infantry Regiment, FI 80-82; 2nd Infantry Regiment, BD 110, FI 164; 3rd Infantry Regiment, FO 102, 103; 4th Infantry Regiment, FL 128, FO 54-55, 102, NA 140; 5th Infantry Regiment, AP 93; 6th Infantry Regiment, FO 102, KI 171; 7th Infantry Regiment, OR 100-101; 8th Infantry Regiment, FL 118, 119, 134, 147, 150, 153, 157; 9th Infantry Regiment, BD 59; 10th Infantry Regiment, FL 72, 73, 74, 79, 81, 82, 114; 11th Infantry Regiment, FL 109, 112; 13th, 14th and 16th Infantry Regiments, GE 139; 19th Infantry Regiment, YA 159,
Veteran Reserve Corps, FL 76, NA 8-9
Veterans: effect of war on, NA 25; reunions and organizations, NA 158, 159-171
Vicksburg, Mississippi, CH 18, 19, 21, 32, 83, 85, 86, 88, CO 77, 134, 142, FR 46, 52, 150, 152, MI 8-15, NA 115, 145, SP 75-76, TE 17, 85; amphibious assaults at, MI 69; artillery strength, MI 18-19; canal project, MI 33, 69-71, map 72, 74-75; civilian casualties, MI 26, 140; commercial activities, MI 9, 10-13, 16; cultural activities, MI 9; engineering operations, MI 26, 33, fall of, OR 22, 48, 51, 128, 153; food shortages, MI 149-151; fortifications, MI 17, 59, 126, 128-129, 136; fraternization at, MI 136; garrison strength, MI 17-19, 26; land operations, MI 57, 68, 122-123, 126-127, 128-129, 130-131, 132-133, 134, 135, map 137, 138, 139-142, 143, 144-145, 146-147, 148-149, 150, 152, 153, 154-155; living

conditions in, MI 125-126, 139, 140, 141, 149-152; mine warfare, MI 136, 148-149; morale in, MI 151-152; naval operations, MI map 2-3, 4, 18-20, 24-26, 28-29, 30-31, 32-33, 57, 77, 78-79, 80, 84-86, 87, FO 96, 130, 136-137; plans for, MI 3, 17-18, 56-57, 62-63, 69, map 72, 73-75, 79-80, 83-84, 86, 96, 100-101, 108, 123; population, MI 9; profiteering in, MI 151; Railroad Redoubt, MI 130, 136; railroad service, Vicksburg, Shreveport & Texas Railroad, MI 16, MI 9, 13, 16; refugees from, MI 17, 26; shipping trade, MI 9, 12-13, 16, 23; siege operations, MI map 2-3, 134-156; Stockade Redan, MI 127, 136; strategic importance, MI map 2-3, 9, 16-17; surrender, MI 134, 152-157, 158-159, 168; topography, MI 9, 17, 26; Union loyalists in, MI 18, 126, 152; Union occupation, MI 158-159; Union threat to, SH 157; Union victory at, CH 30; water shortage, MI 151
Vicksburg campaign, BL 123, TT 86, 104, 158
Vicksburg Daily Citizen, MI 157, OR 48
Vidette, TT 67
Vienna, Virginia, FO 116-117
Villanow, Georgia, AT 32, 36
Vincent, Strong, GE 78, 81-84, 148, 162
Viniard's farm, CH 51
Vining's Station, Georgia, AT 76, 77, 78
Violence. See Civil disorders; Guerrillas, depredations by
Virginia, FO 85, 89, 93, 124-125, SP map 2-3; area under Union control, OR map 152-153, 167-168; civil disorders in, OR 30, 82, 85-86, 88, 168; Confederate intelligence operations in, SP 51-53; corruption in, NA 119; defensive plans for, FI 57; deserters in, OR 89; educational system, OR 55; industries, OR 62; invaded by Union, FI 58-61, 64, 77; Johnston supported by, OR 161; joins Confederacy, BL 11; FI 15, 28, 58; loyalist government in, NA 30, 32; minor actions in, FI 76, 78-93; money issue, OR 72-73; newspapers, OR 48-49; partisan activity in, SP 106-110, 114-131; partisans, recruitment of, SP 107; provisional Union government in, FI 85; railroads, OR 27; railroad system, FI 59; readmission to Union, NA 69; refugees in, OR 35, 40-41, 117, 123-128; secession by, BR 3; secession referendum, FI 76-77, OR 75, 76; slave emigration from, OR 131; subversion in, OR 152; topography, FI 76; Union Army reprisals, SP 131; Union intelligence operations in, SP 40-43, 57, 85-89; vulnerability, FI 76-77; waterways, FI 76. See also Western Virginia

Sergeant Stephen P. White of company C, 6th Vermont Infantry, VI Corps, Army of the Potomac

KI The Killing Ground; LE Lee Takes Command; MI War on the Mississippi; NA The Nation Reunited; OR Confederate Ordeal; RE Rebels Resurgent; SH The Road to Shiloh; SM Sherman's March; SP Spies, Scouts and Raiders; TE The Struggle for Tennessee; TR Death in the Trenches; TT Tenting Tonight; YA Twenty Million Yankees

119

Superintendent's residence, Virginia Military Institute, burned by General Hunter's Federals in 1864

Correspondent Frank Vizetelly of the *Illustrated London News*, who traveled with Jeb Stuart's headquarters

Virginia, conversion from *Merrimack*, FI 17. See also *Merrimac-Virginia*

Virginia & Tennessee Railroad, DE *12-13*, 21, FL 17, 20, 21

Virginia Central Railroad, DE *8-9*, 100, FL 17, 20, 45, 53, 134, 140, FO 133, KI 82, 115, 131, 148, LE 98, 124, RE 93, SP 85, 128, TR 18-22, 27, 53, 69

Virginia City, Montana Territory, YA 71-72

Virginia City, Nevada, NA 158

Virginia City, Nevada Territory, YA 71, 116

Virginia Military Institute, DE *30-31*, FI 76, *103*, FL *8-9*, *10-11*, 16, *56*, 159, RE *161*; cadet equipment, FL *33*; cadet register, FL *11*; cadets, FL *11*, 12, *13*, *14-15*, 16, 29-34, *36*, 37, 56, 59, 159; destruction of, FL 56-57; student life and instructional material, FL *12*, *13*

"Virginians of the Valley" (Ticknor), OR 46

Virginia troops, AP *84*, 85, BD 132, FL *29*, 72, 79, 81, FO 161, GE *52*, TR 82, 87; 1st (Stonewall) Brigade, DE 18, 35-36, 38-39, 43-44, 46, 52, 55, 67-70, 89, 133, 149-151, 156-157, 165, 167-169; 19th Militia, FL *13*; 35th Battalion (Partisan Rangers), FL 142; 43rd Battalion of Partisan Rangers, SP *117*, 122; at Big Bethel, FI 79-80; Black Horse Troop, FI 153; brigade flags, FI *125*; at Bull Run, FI 120-122, 124, 137-140, *map 141*, 143-145, 149, 152-153, 158-*161*; Carter's Battery, FO 139; Davidson's Battery, TR 78; Echols' Brigade, FL *123*; Funk's Consolidated Regiment, FL 82; Graham's Petersburg Battery, TR 32, 150; Highland County Company, FI 86-87; Home Guards, AP 119; Laurel Brigade, FL 139, 142; Local Defense Brigade, KI 35, 36; Local Defense Force, TR 145; militia, DE 46-50, *51*, 54-55; mobilization, FI *14*; Old Dominion Rifles, FI *58*; Richmond Grays, AS 18; Richmond Howitzers, AP *123*, FI 79-80, FO 48, TT 26; Richmond Locals, AP 111, 122; in Shenandoah Valley operations, FI 93; Smyth Dragoons flag, FI *125*; State militia, AP 101, TR 31-32, 55; Stonewall Brigade, AP 153, FL 68, 82, 119, GE 127, KI 31, 65, 98, LE 103-107, 154, TT 85-86; Sussex Light Dragoons, FI 104; Union quota allotted, FI 15; Virginia Military Institute, FI 76, *103*; Washington Mounted Rifles, FL 43; in western Virginia operations, FI 85-93

Artillery: 10th Heavy Artillery, TR 145; Albemarle Battery, TR *46*; Heavy Artillery, AP 101, 123, 125; Henry's Battery, RE 64; Kemper's battery, FI 149; Lunenburg Heavy Artillery, TR 143-144; Massie's Battery, FL 75-78; Parker's Battery, GE *154*; Pegram's Richmond Battery, TR 67, 72, 75; Poague's Battery, DE 135; Purcell Battery (Pegram), LE 67; Rockbridge Artillery, BD 86, DE 46, *115*, 130, 135, 161; Sturdivant's Battery, TR 32; Surry Light Artillery, TR 137; Thomson's Horse Artillery, TR 24; Virginia Light Artillery, RE *107*; Wright's Battery, TR 78, 82

Cavalry: 1st Cavalry Regiment, FI 93, 140-141, 143, 149, 153, *160-161*, FL 45, GE 132, KI 119-122, RE 108-109, SP 116, TT 94; 2nd Cavalry Regiment, BD 54, RE 108-109; 3rd Cavalry Regiment, AP 90, RE 108-109, SP 54; 4th Cavalry Regiment, FI 153, RE 108-109, *110*; 5th Cavalry Regiment, GE *27-29*, KI 119, RE 108-109; 6th Cavalry Regiment, AP 120, GE 16; 7th Cavalry Regiment, DE *106*, *113*, FL 142; 8th Cavalry Regiment (Smyth Dragoons), FI *125*; 9th Cavalry Regiment, AS 115, GE 22, LE 27, RE *107*, TR *99*; 10th Cavalry Regiment, GE 22; 11th Cavalry Regiment, FL 142; 12th Cavalry Regiment, AP 139, FL 142, 143; 18th Cavalry Regiment, FL 28, 30, 31, 41, 46; 22nd Cavalry Regiment, FL 30, 34; 23rd Cavalry Regiment, FL 28, 30, 34; 26th Cavalry Regiment, FL 36, 37; 30th Cavalry Regiment, FI 149; 35th Cavalry Battalion, GE 22; 35th Cavalry Regiment, AP 120; 43rd Cavalry (Partisan Rangers), FL 26

Infantry: 1st Infantry Battalion, GE *154*; 1st Infantry Regiment, BD 135, FI *99*, 121, LE 169, TT *23*; 2nd Brigade, DE 103; 2nd Infantry Regiment, AS 144, DE *111*, 156, 168, GE 155; 3rd Infantry Regiment, FI 79; 4th Infantry Regiment, DE 168, FI *100*, GE *154*; 5th Infantry Regiment, DE 36, 67, 70, 104, *108-109*, 132, FI 145, NA 168, RE 146; 8th Infantry Regiment, BD 11, FO 43, 50, GE 155; 11th Infantry Regiment, FI 120, TR *29*, TT 22; 12th Infantry Regiment, BD 11, 54, FO 164, KI 131, LE 69, TR 82, *84-85*, TT *39*, 45, 53, 56, 71, 81, 82, 85, 149; 13th Infantry Regiment, DE *105*, FL 69, KI 153; 14th Infantry Regiment, FO 164, GE 140-141; 15th Infantry Regiment, LE 71; 17th Infantry Regiment, AP *127*, BD 11, 133, 135, CH 29, FI 121, FO 144, LE 161, TT 98; 18th Infantry Regiment, GE 140; 19th Infantry Regiment, BD 52, GE 137, RE *107*; 21st Infantry Regiment, DE *110*, LE 105-106, 126, 144, 154, TT 148; 22nd Infantry Regiment, OR 152; 23rd Infantry Regiment, BD 75, KI 29; 24th Infantry Regiment, FO 113, GE 140; 27th Infantry (Irish) Regiment, DE 48; 30th Infantry Regiment, BD 92; 33rd Infantry Regiment, FL 138, 141, 143-144, *162-163*, KI 83, 98; 34th Infantry Regiment, TR 78; 37th Infantry Regiment, DE 131-132, 161; 40th Infantry Regiment, RE *62*; 41st Infantry Regiment, FO 164, TR 83; 44th Infantry Regiment, DE 169; 46th Infantry Regiment, CO 30, TR 31, TT 136; 47th Infantry Regiment, LE 59, RE *106*; 49th Infantry Regiment, AP 36, 38, FI 141, KI 156, LE 170; 51st Infantry Regiment, FL 34, 36, 37, RE *106*, TT 63; 53rd Infantry Regiment, FO 164; 54th Infantry Regiment, AT 146, OR 152; 55th Infantry Regiment, LE 59, 62, 127, *154*; 58th Infantry Regiment, DE 169; 59th Infantry Regiment, CO 99, TR 78; 60th Infantry Regiment, LE 59, *62*; 61st Infantry Regiment, AP 31, TR 64; 62nd Infantry Regiment, FL 30, 34

Vitiaz, BL 132

Vizetelly, Frank, CO 28; sketch by, TR *49*

Volck, A. J., sketch by, SP *50*

Volunteers. *See* Confederate Army; Union Army

Volunteer units. *See* Confederate Army; Union Army; names of commanders, or under states

Von Bachelle, Werner, TT 151

Von Borcke, Heros, RE 58

Von Gilsa, Leopold, RE 129

Von Kleiser's Battery, FL 33, 34, 35, 37

Voorhees, Daniel, YA 24

Voters, restrictions on, YA 144, 159

Vredenburgh, Peter, FL 78

W

Wabash, BL *19*, CO 20, *82*, *114*, *152*

Wabasha, FR 86, 87

Wabash River, as trade route, YA 24

Wachusett, BL 150, *151*

Waco, Texas, OR 121

Waddell, James Iredell, BL 143, *158*, 159, 161, TT 157

Wade, Benjamin Franklin, FO 65, 68, 76, NA 16, 30, YA 154

Wade, Jennie, GE *65*

Wade-Davis Bill, NA 30

Wadsworth, James A., GE 46-47, 50, 74, 115, KI 62, 65, 71, 73-74, 76-77, 78

Wadsworth, James S., FO 97, YA 144

Wage rates, YA 77-78

Wagner, George D., SM 89, 90, 97, 100, 102, *103*, 112, 118

Wagner, Orlando, FO 92

Wagons, OR *27*, 29, 43

Wainwright, Charles S., AP 82, BD 164, 170, FO 109, KI 37, 85, 134, 167, TR 103, 136, 150-152, 168

Wainwright, W. P., LE 141

Wakarusa River, BR 76

Walcott, Charles, CO 28, LE 135, 163

Walcutt, Charles C., AT 105, CH 139, 140, 141, SM 60, 61

Walden's Ridge, CH 32, 78, 81, 89

Walke, Henry, MI 28; Foote evaluated by, SH 60; at Fort Donelson, SH 82-84; at

120

AP Pursuit to Appomattox; AS The Assassination; AT Battles for Atlanta; BD The Bloodiest Day; BL The Blockade; BR Brother against Brother; CH The Fight for Chattanooga; CO The Coastal War; DE Decoying the Yanks; FI First Blood; FL The Shenandoah in Flames; FO Forward to Richmond; FR War on the Frontier; GE Gettysburg;

Battery Rodgers, a Federal earth-work on the Potomac River, part of the Washington, D.C., defenses

Fort Henry, SH 61, 65; at Island No. 10, SH 163-164
Walker, Aldace F., FL 87, 109, 112, 113, 115, 117, 153
Walker, Charles J., BR *144*
Walker, David N., TR 78
Walker, Francis A., NA 97
Walker, H. J. and L. J., GE *154*
Walker, Henry, KI 87
Walker, James, CH *125;* combat artist, CH 124; paintings by, CH *124-125, 126-127, 128-129*
Walker, James A., BD 68-70, DE 29, 98-99, GE 24, 127, KI 31, 98
Walker, John C., TE 29
Walker, John G., BD 18, 21, FR 50, 52, 56, 59, 60, 61, 63, 65-66; at Antietam, BD 63, 70, 86, 89, 92, 98, 121, 152; at Harpers Ferry, BD 18-22; at Loudoun Heights, BD 43, 56
Walker, John Stewart, LE 71
Walker, Jonathan, BR *43*
Walker, Joseph, FR 116, 117
Walker, Leroy Pope, BR 138, 140, FI 10, OR 14
Walker, Morgan, SP 148
Walker, Moses, TE 168, 169
Walker, Norman, LE 71
Walker, Robert J., BR 82
Walker, Robert Lindsay, AP 135, 136, RE 62, 65
Walker, William H. T., AT 45, 48, 68, 90, 92, 100, 104, 111, CH 37, 44, 45, 46, 50, 53, 56, MI 113, SP 24; death of, AT 99
Walker Among Sacred Stones, FR 83
Walker's Texas Division, FR 46, 50, 52, 56, 59-61, 63, 65-66
Wallace, Ann, SH 147, *153*
Wallace, Lew, AS *149*, 150, FL 71-73, *74*, 75, 78-79, 83-84, MI 145, NA 152, SH *151*, TE 32, 33, 49; at Corinth, SH 157; at Fort Donelson, SH 78, 81-82, 86-90, 95; at Shiloh, SH 105, 116, *131*, 139-140, 144, 151; sketches by, AS *156*
Wallace, William H. L., AP 126, AS 131; death of, SH 138, 145, 153; memorial to, SH *153;* at Shiloh, SH 105, 113, 116, 120-122, 137-138
Wallach House (Brandy Station), KI *10-11*
Walling, William H., CO 161
Wallis, Severn Teackle, SP *19*
Wall tent, TT *10, 13, 50-51*
Walthall, Edward C., AT 136, CH 131, 133, SM 113, 115, 130, 133, 139
Walton, Simeon T., KI 29
Wangelin, Hugo, AT 113
War: romantic appeal, TT 20-21, 24; tedium of, TT 20, 52, 56. *See also* Soldiers
Ward, J. H. Hobart, FO 164, 166, GE 78, 85, 86, 87
Ward, William T., AT 46, 47, 93, 94
War Democrats, YA 149-151. *See also*

Partisan politics
Wardensville, Virginia, DE 151
War Department, AS *22;* frauds against, YA 73, 76; and national security, YA 31-32; reward poster issued by, AS *93. See also* Benjamin, Judah P.; Randolph, George Washington; Seddon, James A.; Stanton, Edwin M.; Walker, Leroy
War financing, YA 56-59
War industries: organization, OR 13; production and procurement, OR 17; women in, OR 10
Warley, A. F., CO 69-72
Warmoth, Henry Clay, NA 117
Warm Spring Mountain, DE 52-54
Warm Springs, Virginia, DE *10-11*
Warne, Kate, SP 8
Warner, Adoniram Judson, BD 68
Warner, Edward R., BR *145*
Warner, Willard, AT *86-87*
War of 1812, tradition, TT 21
Warren, Gouverneur Kemble, AP 27, 30, 79-82, 85-87, 90, *91*, GE 77, *80*, 81, 84, KI 29, 35, 68, 82, 114, *132*, 148, 150, LE 153, 155, 162, NA 162, RE 92, TR 35-36, 49-50, 53, 99, 101, 103-*105*, 137, 154-155; at Cold Harbor, KI 154, 165, 169; and Crater, TR 73, 80, 87; at Mine Run, KI 31; at North Anna, KI 133, 135; and Peeble farm, TR 150-152; at Spotsylvania, KI 86-87, 89-*90*, 93, 104, 124-125; in the Wilderness, KI 56, 61, 62, 73
Warren County Courthouse, MI *10*
Warrenton, Virginia, BD 168, *170-171*, RE 26, 30, *31*, 33, TT 113
Warrenton Junction, Virginia, LE 95, 101, *121*, 132-133
Warrenton Turnpike, FI 111-112, 127, 135-137, 141, 149, *158-159*, LE 137, *140-141*, 145-152, 159-164
Warrior, BL 47
Warships: armament, CO 22, 54-55, 61, 63, 71, 94, 114-115; characteristics, CO 19-21, 55, 143; Confederate, damaged and lost, MI 20, *24-25*, 27, 32, *33*, 77-78; Confederate construction, MI 26-28; Confederate losses, CO 25, *31*, 32-33, 68-69, 72, 74, 76, 96-97, 141, 151, 156; mortar schooners, MI 24, 162; rams, MI 20, *24-25*, 26-29, 32, 77-78, 80; shipping hazards, MI 76, 80-81, *82*, 83; types, CO *70-71;* Union, AP *43-50;* Union, damaged and lost, MI 18, 26, 29, 31-32, 77-78, *80-81*, 85, 100, 139, *162-163;* Union losses, CO 22-23, *66*, 67, 69, 71, 73, 93-95, 97, 113, 118-120, 139, 141, 147, 150, 152, 154-156. *See also* Ironclads; Privateers, Confederate
Warships, characteristics and armament of, BL *18-19*, 22, 25, 47-49, *52-53*, 54, 62, 65, 67, 70-71, *72-73*, 76-77, 108, 125
Warships, construction of: in Britain,

BL 114-116, 120-121, *123-125*, 126-128, *129*, 143, 149, 161; in Confederacy, BL 10, 17, 20, 33, 46-48, 53, 65, 78, 114-116, *117*, 120-121, *123-125*, 126-128, 129-130, 131, 149, 160; in France, BL 47, 53, 126, 128, 130; in United States, BL 10-11, 17, 20-22, 33, 46, 48-53, 65, *66-73*, 75
Warships, losses of: Confederate, BL 60, *63*, 65, 84-85, *108-109*, 117, *151*, 158-160, *164-171;* United States, BL *54*, 55-57, *map* 60, 64, 78-79, 142, 153
Wartrace, Tennessee, CH 23, 24
Warwick River, FO 92, 94, 97, 99, 102, 105, 106-107
Washburn, Cadwallader, YA 76-77
Washburn, Francis, AP 118, 119, 120
Washburn, Israel, YA 36
Washburn, W. A., SM 115
Washburne, Elihu B., KI 59, 92, SH 45
Washington: Confederate threat to, FO 11, 17; defenses of, DE *136-145;* demoralization in, FO 8; discipline restored in, FO 16; fortifications system, FO 8, 17-18; prohibition in, FO 16; provost guard action in, FO *13*, 16-17; security measures in, FO *10-11*, 73-74, 84, 91, 96-97; threats to, DE 2, 43, 61, 64, 71, 136, 146
Washington, Booker T., NA 48, *50*, OR 133
Washington, D.C., AS *map* 22-23, BR *135*, FI *8-9, 24-25, 114-115*, FL 19, 52, NA 51, RE 8-9, 30, TR 58, 69, 94; Capitol, NA *12;* civilian guard, YA *8-9, 14-15;* Confederate intelligence operations in, SP 25-27, 55; Confederate threat to, BD 10, 13-15, 18; defeated troops' arrival in, FI 150-152; defenselessness, FI 18-20; defensive works at, FL *map* 62, 63, 84; disease and mortality rates, YA 23; Early's raid on, FL 68-88; financial crisis and raid, FL 87-88; fortifications, BD 8; FI 25, 61; government buildings, YA *8-13, 15;* hospitals, YA 8, *16-17;* hospitals in, TT 95,; Lincoln's assassination, reaction to, AS 92; Lincoln's funeral services, AS *118-119;* as military depot, YA 8, *10-13;* panic in, BD 14; population, FI 18, YA 8; safeguarding, FI 24, 27, 29, 31; slavery abolished in, YA 36, 39; troop units' arrivals in, FI 21-29, 40-41, *42-43;* victory celebrations, AS 55, *94-95. See also* District of Columbia troops
Washington, George, OR 11, *12*, SP 10
Washington, George, (Caddo Indian), TT *31*
Washington, Lewis, BR 87
Washington, Martha Custis, LE 51
Washington, North Carolina, CO 84-85, 87-90, *92, map* 93, 96-97
Washington, William D., LE 26
Washington Arsenal, AS *23*, 145, 159, NA 38, YA *10-11*

Major Charles S. Wainwright with fellow field and staff officers of the 1st New York Artillery

KI The Killing Ground; LE Lee Takes Command; MI War on the Mississippi; NA The Nation Reunited; OR Confederate Ordeal; RE Rebels Resurgent; SH The Road to Shiloh; SM Sherman's March; SP Spies, Scouts and Raiders; TE The Struggle for Tennessee; TR Death in the Trenches; TT Tenting Tonight; YA Twenty Million Yankees

121

Hardee pattern battle flag of the 5th Company, Washington Artillery of New Orleans

Washington Artillery, AP 97, 113, 131, TR *29*, 137
Washington College, FL *8-9*, NA *58-59*, *60*
Washington *Evening Star*, FI 61
Washington Light Artillery, BD 104-105
Washington Light Artillery (5th Company Louisiana), TE *144-145*
Washington Monument, YA *14*
Washington *Morning Chronicle*, AS 60
Washington peace conference, BR 119
Washington *Star*, AS 54
Washington *Sunday Times*, YA 111
Wasley, Frank, LE 148-149
Wassaw Sound, BL *108-109*
Waterhouse, A. C., SH 115
Waterloo, Virginia, operations at, RE *32*
Waterloo Bridge, LE 125
Water supply, MI 46-47, 136, 151, TT 52, 80, 82, 115, 132-133, 136
Watertown, Massachusetts, YA *67*
Waterways resources, BR 9
Watie, Stand, FR *139*, 142-143, 146, 148-150, 152, 155-156, 161
Watkins, Sam, AT 28, 29, 72-74, CH 19, 99, 150, TE 20, 50, 67, 94, 121
Watson, Alonzo, LE 141
Watson, Peter, YA 32
Watson, William, FR 142, TT 44, 55, 157
Watson farmhouse, AP 119
Watson's Landing, Missouri, SH *166-167*
Watterson, Henry, NA 112
Watt House, LE 43
Watts, Thomas, OR 155
Waud, Alfred R., FI 153, KI *37*, SP *53;* sketches by, AP *142-143*, BD *88*, FO *168-169*, KI *37*, *70*, TR *30-31*, *140-141*
Waud, William, BR 139, YA 159
Waugh, Henry H., TT *40*
Wauhatchie, Tennessee, CH 89, 92, 93, 100, 130, 170
Waverly Magazine, TT 67
Wayne, Harry, SM 61, 62, 63
Waynesboro, Battle of, SM 66, 67
Waynesboro, Virginia, FL 45, 46, 49, 50, 57, 134, 137, 159
Wead, Frederick F., KI *171*
Wealth, pursuit of, YA 72-79
Weapons: artillery, SM *21*, 130-132, *151;* captured, OR 19; carbines, SM 85, *86-87;* and guerrillas, SP 128, *148*, 149; Henry repeating rifles, SM 24; interchangeable parts, BR 18; production and procurement, OR 17-19, 21, *22*, 23-25, *64-65;* rifle muskets, KI *96-97;* shortages, SH 21, 25-26, 50, 54, 56, *106;* Spencer repeating rifles, SM 60, 137; Springfield rifles, SM 85; torpedoes (land mines), SM 148, *152-153;* unconventional designs, SP 162-171. *See also by type*
Wearn, Richard, AP *62*, photographs by,

AP *62-63*
Weather, effect on operations, DE 46, 50, *53*, 54-55, *76-77*, 83, 99, 151, 157, MI 67, 72-73, 84, 115, RE 31, *32*, 35-37, 88-89, 91, 95, *96-97*, 118-119, 128, 159, at Fort Donelson, SH 81-82, 85, 94; at Island No. 10, SH 163-164; at Shiloh, SH 108, 144-145, 152
Weaver, Corporal, SH 91
Webb, Alexander, GE *140;* at Cemetery Ridge, GE 111-112, *121*, 131-132, 138, *141*, 142; Medal of Honor, GE 140
Webb, John, FL *14*
Webb, Lysander, MI 130
Webb, Mary, and family, BR *46*
Webber's Battery, FO 109
Weber, Max, BD 96, *107*
Webster, Amos, AP 145
Webster, Daniel, BR *34;* legacy of, BR 47; as Union protagonist, BR 33, 45
Webster, Fletcher, LE 168, *170*
Webster, Joseph D., SH *88-89*, 139
Webster, Timothy, SP 32, *34-41*, 42, *43*, 56
Wedge tent, TT 45, *51*
Weed, Stephen H., GE 78, 83, 84-85, 162
Weed, Thurlow, BR 103, 111, YA 154
Weehawken, BL *108-109*, CO 115, 118
Weekly New Mexican, FR 122
Weeks, George H., BR *144*
Weer, William, FR 147, 148, 149, 150
Wehner, William, AT 88
Weichmann, Louis J., AS 24, 40, *43*, 44, 51-53, 68, 69; arrest of conspirators, AS 108-109; testimony at trial, AS 155-157
Weir, Robert, LE 19
Weisiger, Davis A., TR 82, *83*
Weitzel, Godfrey, AP 108, 109, 118, AS 59, CO 161, MI 110, TR 149
Welch, Norval, TR *152-153*
Weld, Lewis, FR 27
Weld, Stephen M., TR 34
Weldon Railroad, AP 18, 25, 27, 79, TR 19, 53, 55-56, 99, 101, 103-105, *106-107*, 110, 138
Welfare agencies. *See* Relief and welfare agencies; United States Christian Commission; United States Sanitary Commission
Welfare programs, OR *58*, 60, 83, *122*
Welles, Gideon, AS 92-95, 98, 99, *102*, 140, BL *20*, FR 109, KI 24, MI 26, 32, NA *8-9*, 17, 20, 31, 41, *55*, 110, SH 60, YA 142, 152; and blockade, BL 10, 12, 14, 21, 29; Butler, relations with, CO 58-59; and Charleston, CO 110, 112, 114-115, 119-120, 134; Farragut, relations with, CO 59, 61; and Fort Fisher, CO 156-157; and Fort McAllister, CO 115; on Gillmore, CO 121; and Hatteras Inlet, CO 16; and ironclad construction, BL 49-52, 65; and *Merrimac* threat, BL 57; on monitors, CO 112; and New Orleans, CO 54, 57-58; Porter, relations with, CO 57; and *Trent* Affair, BL 117; and

warship construction, BL 17, 20-22. *See also* United States Navy
Wellford, Charles, RE 126
Wells, David A., NA 88
Wells, Ebenezer, CH 50
Wells, Edward, TR 21-22
Wells, George D., FI 118, FL 36, 51, *126*, 140
Wells, James Madison, OR 75
Wells, William, AP 110
Wert, J. Howard, GE 148
Wesselhoeft, Reinhold, FO *50*
Wessells, Henry Walton, CO 94-96
West: cattle drives, NA 91-92; Confederate and Union interest in, FR 16; emigration to, FR 10, 106, 123; frontier life, FR *8-15;* government survey expeditions, NA 94-95; mining in, NA 92; opening of, NA 77, 83-85, 90-91; railroads, NA 78, 83, *84-85*, 91; settlement by veterans, NA 25, 78, 91, 93; sod houses and homesteaders, NA *90;* Southern sympathizers in, FR 17, 19, 23; troops in, FR 18, 106; Union supplies for, NA 27
West, Joseph R., FR 115, 116
West, William E., LE 13
West Chickamauga Creek, CH 12
Western & Atlantic Railroad, AT 8, 21, 27, 31, 32, 36, 60, 126, 132, 146-147, CH 18, 33, SM 19, 20, 28, SP 111, TE 8, 10, 11, 12
Western Bar Channel, CO 158
Western Flotilla. *See* Gunboats
Western Railroad, YA 79
Western states' economic resources, BR 101
Western theater, SH *map* 2-3; character of combat in, SH 9; loss to Confederacy, SH 157; weapons shortages in, SH 21, 50, 54, 56
Western Union Telegraph Company, YA 78
Western Virginia, FI *map* 2-3; admitted as state, FI 93; loyalists in, FI 76, 77, 84, *92;* operations in, DE 44-45, *72-81*, 95, FI 85-93
Western Virginia troops: in local operations, FI 87; number in Union service, FI 92
Westfield, FR 48, *49*
Weston, James A., KI 74
Weston, Missouri, SH *22-23*
West Point, Missouri, SP 146
West Point, Virginia, FO 92-93, 109, 111, 125, 129
Westport, Battle of, FR 160, *161*
West Virginia: racial violence in, NA 120; statehood proclaimed, OR 75, 76
West Virginia troops: FL 89; 1st Cavalry Regiment, FL *133;* 1st Infantry Regiment, FL 36; 3rd Infantry Regiment, LE 163; 12th Infantry Regiment, AP 99, FL 33; 14th Infantry Regiment, FL 23
West Woods, BD 67, 74-80, 83, 86-93, 96, 98, 108, *110-111*, 121-122, 127, 141, *144*

Wever, Clark R., SM 29
Weyer's Cave, DE *14*, 170
Weygant, Charles H., AP 41, 151, KI 98, RE 142-143
Whalers, as targets, BL 159
Whaling industry, BR *19*
Wharton, Gabriel, FL 20, 30-31, 33-34, 36, 109, 112-113, 117, 147, 149, 150, 157
Wharton, John A., CH 79, 80, FR 67, 70, TE 26, 27, 93, 99, 115, 118, 124, 150
Wheat, Chatham Roberdeau, DE *116*, 117, *123*, FI 129, 131-132, 143, LE 42
Wheat Field, GE 98-101, 103, 105, *map* 108
Wheaton, Frank, AP 30, 122, FL 87
Wheat's Tigers (Louisiana): flag of, FI *125*; at Bull Run, FI 120-132, 143
Wheeler, George, NA 94
Wheeler, H. S., FL *130*
Wheeler, Joseph (Fighting Joe), AP 53, 61; AT 29, 63, 95, 97, CH 20, 34, *81*, 100, 106, FR 18, SM 14, TE 59, 62, 66, *96*, 159; captures McCook's supply wagons, TE 97; commands Bragg's cavalry, TE 92; at Decatur, AT 102; delays Rosecrans, TE 93, 96, 97; and foragers, SM 56; and march to the sea, opposition to, SM 50-52, 53, 63, 71, 72, 144; plundering by cavalry, AP 58-59; on raid, CH 79, *80;* and raids on enemy, AT 138; at Resaca, AT 48; at Rocky Face Ridge, AT 39; and Union supply lines, AT 140, 143; at Waynesboro, SM 66, 67
Wheeling, Virginia, FI 85
Wheeling, West Virginia, FL 57, OR 76
Wheeling convention, FI 84-85
Wheeling *Intelligencer*, FI 84, 87
Wheelock, Julia S., YA *129*
Wheelwright, Joseph C., FL 159
"When Sherman Marched down to the Sea" (song), manuscript of, SM *157*
"When This Cruel War Is Over" (song), OR 46
Whig Party: decline of, BR 100-101; renamed, BR 110
Whipple, Henry B., FR 90
Whiskey ration, TT 59
Whiskey Ring, NA 115-116
Whitaker, Walter C., CH 130
White, Captain, SP 72-73
White, Elijah V. (Lige), FL 142, SP 106, *109*, 131; and Antietam Campaign, SP 110; background, SP 108-109; and Second Bull Run Campaign, SP 109; transfer to Confederate Army, SP 122-124
White, George L., NA 121
White, J. Rudhall, BD 155
White, Julius, BD 59
Whitehall, North Carolina, CO 84
White House (Virginia), FO 129-130, LE *51*, *82-83*, TR 26, 34, 35
White House (Washington, D.C.), AS *22*, FO 147, YA *8-9*, *12-13*
White House Landing, Virginia, FO 130,

134-135, KI 148, *154-155*, 166, LE 25, 28-29, 48-49, *82-84*, YA *129*
White League, NA 142-144
White Liners, NA 145, 147
White Oak Bridge, LE 52
White Oak Swamp, FO 136, 139, LE 24, 49-50, 52-55, 59, *60-61*, 62, TR *100*
White River, MI 17
Whites, in labor force, OR 16
White's Ford, BD *12*, 13-14, FL 88, *90*
Whiteside, Charles, OR 142
Whitestone Hill, battle at, FR 94, *96-97*
White Sulphur Springs, West Virginia, Confederate dignitaries at, NA *58*
Whiting, William H. C., CO 164, 167-169, FO 136, 138, 140, 145, *154-155*, 157-158, 165; in Chickahominy operations, LE 24, 30; in Seven Days' Battles, LE 40, 45, 65, 67-68, 72
Whitlow, William, mortar and pestle of, SM *106*
Whitlow, William P., TR 29
Whitman, George Washington, BD 125-126, CO 27-30
Whitman, Walt, FI 10, 150, TT *95*, YA 8; on medical services, TT 78
Whitney, Eli, BR 29
Whitney, J. H., CO 28
Whitney Navy revolver, FI *74*
Whittier, Charles A., AP 141, KI *88-89*
Whittier, John Greenleaf, BD 20, BR 62, 69, CO 126
Wiatt, William E., TT 152
Wickham, William C., KI 115, 119, TR *24-25*
Wide-Awakes, BR *114-115*
Widow Parker's farm, AT 97
Widows, relief for, YA 135
Widow Tapp farm, KI 70, 74, 81
Wigfall, Louis T., BR 126, 157-159, OR 23
Wiggin, Captain, CO *44*
Wight, Levi, FR 61, 71
Wilcox, Cadmus Marcellus, AP 95, 96, 97, FO 159, 166, GE *101*, KI 70-71, 73-74, 133-134, 154, LE 91, RE 154-155, TR 97, 107-108, 150, 152; at Cemetery Ridge, GE 109, 110-111; at Emmitsburg road, GE 104; in Pickett's Charge, GE 136; at Pitzer's Woods, GE 76
Wilcox, Nelson O., FL *128*
Wilcox's Landing, TR 34, 36
Wilder, John T., CH 21, 23, 24, 25, 26, *28*, 29, 30, 33, 44, 48, 57, 61, 74, 75, 99, NA 64, TE 51
Wilderness, RE 120-121, 124-125, 159
Wilderness, CO 160
Wilderness, Battle of, KI *map 2-3*, 62-81, *map 69, map 75;* fighting at, KI *50, 76, 80;* fires at, KI 64, *70;* skeletons at, KI *63;* skirmishers at, KI *72;* twisted ramrods from, KI *71*
Wilderness Campaign, KI *map 2-3*, TT 93-95
Wilderness Chapel, RE 128

Wilderness Tavern, KI 60-62, RE 139
Wilder's Lightning Brigade, NA 64
Wildes, Thomas, AP 99
Wildman, Charles B., FO 48
Wildrick, Abram C., BR *144*
Wilds, John Q., FL *131*
Wiley, Calvin H., OR 55
Wilkenson Pike, TE 94, 98, 112, 119, 123, 126
Wilkes, Charles, BL 116-117, 119
Wilkeson, Bayard, GE *58-59*
Wilkeson, Frank, TT 37, YA 99
Wilkins, Fred, BR 46
Wilkinson, Allen, BR 71, 78
Wilkinson, John, BL 100-101
Wilks, Lot, SP 165
Willard, George L., GE 108, *154*
Willard's Hotel, AS *22*, 57, 68, 71, 108, KI 22
Willcox, Charles, MI 102
Willcox, Orlando B., AP 39, FI 61, 137, KI 74, 103, RE *29*, TR 46, 50, 74, 78, 88, 109-110, TT *69;* at Antietam, BD 127, 130-132, 135, 137; at South Mountain, BD 49
Willey, Waitman T., NA 75
William R. Smith (locomotive), SP 112
Williams, Alpheus S., AT 43, 52, 63, 64, BD 80-81, 83, 87, DE *62-63*, 66, 71, GE 109, 127, LE 103, SM 49, *51*
Williams, Arthur B., AP 132
Williams, Charley, OR 131
Williams, George, TR 29
Williams, J. M., GE 112, 115-116
Williams, L. J., TT 80
Williams, Lizzie, AS 83
Williams, Seth, AP *146-147*, 148
Williams, Steele and Walter, LE *137*
Williams, Thomas, MI 19, 26, 33, *34*, 35
Williams, Watson D., AP 16
Williams' Battery, AP 132
Williamsburg, FO 90, 107, *108*, 109-111
Williamsburg Road, LE 31, 49
Williamson, Thomas, FR 79
Williamson, William, BL 48
Williamsport, Maryland, DE 35, *48-49*, 135, GE 26, 147, 150-152, 156
Willich, August, CH 24, 28, 145, TE 113-114, 115, 118, 120
Willis, William, KI *65*
Willis Church Road, LE 52, 55, 58, 62, 65, 69
Willis's Hill, RE 87
Willoughby Run, GE 44-46, 47, 48-49, 73
Wills, Charles, SM 61
Wills, George W., FL 122, *123*
Wilmington, Delaware, YA 87
Wilmington, North Carolina, AP 18, 25, 52, 53, 61, 64; as blockade-runners' port, BL 86-88, 93, 95-96, 100-101, 161; and blockade running, OR 76; as blockade target, BL 21; industry, OR 21; joint operations, CO 83-84, 91; as port, CO 142, 156, 158, 162; Union capture of, OR 167

Sketch artist **Alfred R. Waud,** who submitted artwork to *Harper's Weekly,* at Gettysburg

Elijah V. White, Lieutenant Colonel of the 35th Virginia Cavalry Battalion

KI The Killing Ground; LE Lee Takes Command; MI War on the Mississippi; NA The Nation Reunited; OR Confederate Ordeal; RE Rebels Resurgent; SH The Road to Shiloh; SM Sherman's March; SP Spies, Scouts and Raiders; TE The Struggle for Tennessee; TR Death in the Trenches; TT Tenting Tonight; YA Twenty Million Yankees

123

Colors of the 2nd Massachusetts Cavalry, veterans of the battle of Winchester

Drummer Griff J. Thomas of the 1st Wisconsin Heavy Artillery

Wilmington & Weldon Railroad, CO 35, 84, *map* 93, 97
Wilmot, David, BR 42, 119
Wilson, H., SM *41*
Wilson, Henry, BR 85, SP 23-24, 29, YA 93, 128
Wilson, Jacob P., FO *116-117*
Wilson, James, KI 86, 114, 119, 123, 167-169
Wilson, James H., AP 160, *161*, BD 63, FL 103, 104, 105, 112, 116, 117, 137, MI 75-76, 147-148, SM 83, 85, 88, *89*, 121, TR 21, *23*, 35-36, 38, *52-53*, 55-57; at Franklin, SM 97, 100, 117; at Nashville, SM 123, 126, 128, 133, 134, 137-139, 142; reorganizes Thomas' cavalry, SM 87; and Thomas, SM 124, 144
Wilson, John, CH 136
Wilson, Peter, TT 80, 161
Wilson, William L., AP 139
Wilson's Bayou, Missouri, SH 160, *161*
Wilson's Creek, Battle of, FR 137, SH 24, 26, *map 27, 28*, 29, SP 142, TT 111, 157; artillery assaults, SH 26-27, 29; casualties, SH 29
Winans, Elias, CO 84-85
Winchester, Battle of, DE *map* 130, 133-135
Winchester, Battle of (Third). *See* Opequon Creek, Battle of
Winchester, Oliver, AT 112
Winchester, Virginia, BD 156, 164, FI 93-95, 122, FL 25, 53, 91, 108, 109, 112, 113, 119, 120, 151, 152, FO 74-75, 83-84, GE 2-3, 22, 25-26, LE 93, 98, OR 141, SP 125; operations around, DE 35, 38, 43-44, 46, 48, 55, 58, 64-66, 121, 129, 146-147, 149-151, 156; as training site, GE *42-43*, 44
Winchester-Front Royal road, DE 129, 133
Winder, Charles Sidney, LE 91, *107;* at Cedar Mountain, LE 100, 103-106; at Culpeper, LE 99-101; at Harpers Ferry, DE 149-150, 156; Jackson, relations with, DE 89-90, 92; at Port Republic, DE 165-169; at Strasburg, DE 157; at Winchester, DE 133
Winder, John Henry, SP *56*, 87, TT 111,

113, 129, 133, 135
Winkelstein, Hans Von (alias Henry Von Steinacker), AS 149-150
Winnebago, CO 143
Winnebago Indians, FR 72, 91
Winona, CO 71, MI 32
Winslow, Cleveland, KI *170,* YA *108,* 109-110
Winslow, Gordon, YA *131*
Winslow, John A., BL 155-160, *162,* 164, *168*
Winstead Hill, SM 96, 97, 98, 100, 116
Winston's Gap, CH 35
Winter, John G., OR 75
Winter Garden, AS *36-37*
Winter quarters, TT 9, *12,* 46
Winthrop, Frederic, AP 85, 90
Winthrop, Frederick, TR *106-107*
Winton, North Carolina, CO 34
Wirz, Henry, NA *37-39,* TT 131-132, 135
Wisconsin: immigrants in, YA 62; troops enlisted, YA 62
Wisconsin troops, CH 140, DE 135, FR 147, 152, MI 123, SM 90, SP 143, TT 147, 149; Black Hat (Iron) Brigade, BD 51, 73-76, 79
  Artillery: 1st Battery, Light Artillery, MI *153;* 1st Heavy Artillery, CH *160-161;* 3rd Artillery, TE 145; 12th Battery, SM 26
  Cavalry: 1st Cavalry Regiment, CH 80; 2nd Cavalry Regiment, MI *92;* 3rd Cavalry Regiment, SP 155
  Infantry: 2nd Infantry Regiment, BD 31, *56,* 66, 74, FI 135, 145, GE 48-49, LE 137, *139,* 142, NA 64, TT 120-121; 5th Infantry Regiment, KI 33, RE 154, TT 53; 6th Infantry Regiment, BD 51, 68, 74-76, GE 44, 50, *154,* LE 137-142, 161-162, TT 151; 7th Infantry Regiment, AP 90, BD 74, LE 137, 140-142, TT 62; 8th Infantry Regiment, MI 36, 60, TT *151;* 9th Infantry Regiment, FR 148, TT 29; 12th Infantry Regiment, SH *22-23,* TT 150; 15th Infantry Regiment, CH *50-51,* TT 30; 16th Infantry Regiment, SH *22;* 21st Infantry Regiment, TE *60-61, 170-171,* TT 122; 24th Infantry

Regiment, CH 148; 25th Infantry Regiment, AT 140; 36th Infantry Regiment, KI 171
Wise, Henry A., AP 19, 126, 128, BR 93, CO 21-22, TR 8, 31-32, *33,* 39, 41-42, 44
Wise, John S., AP 18, 19, 20, FL 8, 9, 14, 16
Wise, O. Jennings, CO 30
Wise (Daniel) farm, BD 47, *50*
Wistar, Isaac, BD 91, FO 46
Witcher, B. H., BD 82
Witcher, William, KI 95
Withers, Jones M., TE 94, 118, 157, 158
Withers, William, Jr., AS 86
Witherspoon, Thomas, TT 147
Wivern, BL 129
Woerner, Christian, AP 37
Wofford, William T., BD 76, CH *113,* GE 101, 103
Wolf, Abraham, TT 119
Wolford, Aaron, SM 61
Wolford, Daniel, AP 95
Women: in abolitionist movement, BR *65-69;* in arms industry, YA 67; behavior under occupation, OR 111-112, *114-116;* Butler's order concerning, OR *114;* in civil disorders, OR 30, 82, 85-86, *88,* 149; and education, OR 54-55; in farm production, YA 62; fund-raising by, OR *58;* in labor force, OR 10, 25, 60, 67, 128; in medical services, OR 30, *36-37, 59, 60;* in military service, OR 59, TT *27,* 61, 79; as nurses, TT 78, *93-95,* 97, 98, *106,* YA 116, 126-131, *132;* patriotism of, YA 119; and politics, BR 114; in relief work, YA 117, *118,* 119-120, 123, 125-126, *129, 132, 134-135;* responsibilities undertaken by, OR 42-43, *44-45, 47, 60;* as smugglers, YA 75; in stock-market trading, YA 77; as teachers, OR 60; wage rates of, YA 77-78; welfare programs carried out by, OR *58, 60*
Wood, Benjamin, YA 29
Wood, Charles, AS 67
Wood, John Taylor, BL 49, 54-57, 60, CO 91-93
Wood, Mr. *See* Paine, Lewis

AP Pursuit to Appomattox; AS The Assassination; AT Battles for Atlanta; BD The Bloodiest Day; BL The Blockade; BR Brother against Brother; CH The Fight for Chattanooga; CO The Coastal War; DE Decoying the Yanks; FI First Blood; FL The Shenandoah in Flames; FO Forward to Richmond; FR War on the Frontier; GE Gettysburg;

Wood, Orlando, YA 43
Wood, Sterling Alexander Martin (Sam), SH 112-113, 151, TE 59, *66*, 117
Wood, Thomas J., AT 53, 54, 56, CH 39, 48, 49, *56*, 57, 58, 64, 120, 121, 143, SM 84, 97, 126, 128, TE 96, 99, 118, 120, 126, 127; at Nashville, SM 133, 134, 135, 137, 142
Woodbury, Daniel P., RE 35-36
Woodbury, Tennessee, TE 26
Woodford, TT 105
Wood Lake, Battle of, FR 87
Woodruff, William E., TE 118, 120
Woods, Charles R., AT 109, 110, 111
Woods, Joe, OR 92
Woodstock, Virginia, DE *41*, FL 26, 28, 29, 30, 42, 124-125
Woodstock Races. *See* Toms Brook, Battle of
Wool, John, LE *16*
Wool, John E., FO 124-125
Wool, production and marketing of, OR 25
Woolfolk, John, OR 80
Woolsey, Georgeanna, YA 130-133
Woolsey, Jane Stuart, YA 119, 131
Worden, John, BL 53, *57*, 58, 63-64
Work, Henry C., SM 75
Work details, TT 52
Work details, Confederate, FO *80-81*
Work force. *See* Labor force
World Anti-Slavery Convention, BR 67
Wormley House Conference, NA 155-156
Worsham, John, LE 126, 131, 144-145, 154, TT 148
Worsham, W. J., TE 99
Worthington farm, FL 75, 78, 81
Wright, Abel, LE *76-77*
Wright, Ambrose R., GE 104, 111-112, LE 68, TR 82-83, 87
Wright, Frederick E., GE *155*
Wright, George, FR 110
Wright, Horatio G., AP 41, 82, 92, 93, 97, 99, 113, 114, 121, 123, 125, FL *63*, 86, 87, 89, 90, 101, 109, 126, KI 62, 65, 73, 88, 148, TE 54, TR 35-36, 38, 44, 55-56; at Cedar Creek, FL 141, 146, 147, 149,

152, *162;* at Cold Harbor, KI 151-152, 154, 156, 161-*162*, 165; at North Anna, KI 133, 135; at Opequon Creek, FL 113; at Spotsylvania, KI 89, 92, 93, 101, 103, 125
Wright, Rebecca, FL *113*
Wright, S. T., TR 78
Wright, William W., AT 50, RE *171*
Wrightman, W., TT *81*
Wright's Battery, TR 78, 82
Wyeth, N. C., mural by, FR *161*
Wylie, Alexander, AS 159
Wyman, Peter, AT 107-108
Wyndham, Percy, DE *154*, 157-158, GE 20-22, *38*, SP *116*, *117*
Wynkoop, Edward, FR 125, *126*, 127
Wynkoop, John E., FL 48
Wytheville, Virginia, FL 20, 21

Y

Yalobusha River, MI 76-77
Yancey, William Lowndes, BL 16, 116, BR 110, 131; on dissension in Congress, OR 11; and Supreme Court debate, OR 13
Yandell, D. W., SH 129
Yates, Richard, AS 76, MI 105, SH 45
Yavapai Indians, FR 117
Yazoo City, Mississippi, MI 26, NA 64
Yazoo Pass project, MI *map* 72, 74-77, 80
Yazoo River, operations on and near, MI 26-29, 57, 63, 67, *71*, *map* 72, 75, 79-80, 109
Yellow Bayou, FR 53, 70
Yellow Tavern, Virginia, KI 119
Yerby House, RE 39, 58, 122
Yonah (locomotive), SP 112
York, Pennsylvania, GE 30-31, 73
York, Zebulon, FL 78, 81
York Peninsula, FI 76, 78-79, 84
York River, FO 89, 93, *96*, 103, 105, 109, 111, *126-127;* strategic value of, FI 76-77
Yorktown, Virginia, FO 91, 93, *94-95*, *96*,

97, *98-99*, 100-103, *104*, 105-108, *122-123*, 124, *126-127;* defense of, LE 23; Union advance on, FI 78-79
Young, Bennett, SP 60, *61*
Young, Brigham, FR 108, 112, 113
Young, George, AS 145, AT *96*
Young, J. K., CH 47
Young, John, SM 129
Young, Pierce Manning Butler, SM *67*, TR 22
Young, William H., TE 121
Young America, BR 110
Younger, Cole, SP *141*, *150*
Younger, Jim, SP *150*
Young Men's Christian Association, TT 147, 149
Young's (William H.) Brigade, SM 21, 24
Young's Branch, FI 132, 134-135, 137-138, 143, 145, 147, LE 155, 158
Young's Point, Louisiana, MI 68, 78, 87
Youngstown, Ohio, NA 79

Z

Zacharias, Daniel, BD 17
Zanesville, Ohio, NA 27
Zekiah Swamp, AS 106, 111, 114
Ziegler's Grove, GE *124*, 131, *136-137*, 138
Zigler, Bill, SP *36*, 37
Zollicoffer, Felix, SH 54-55, *58*
Zook, Samuel K., RE 77, 87
Zouave, BL 46, 55-56
Zouaves, SP *104*
Zouaves (French), FR 39
Zouave units, AP *11*, 15, 85, *141*, BD 89, *121*, *132*, 133-138, CO 27, *28-29*, 30, 34, DE *117*, FI 59, 61, *63*, 64, 68, 80, *81*, 82, *84-85*, *101*, 141-144, *153*, *160-161*, FL 55, *128*, *130*, 160, FO 63, 69, *122*, KI 63-66, *126*, 161, *164*, MI 117, NA *14-15*, *162*, *164*, SM 41, *43*, TE *143*, TR *101*, TT 36-37, *43*, 114, *166-167*

Federal 10-inch mortars shell Yorktown, in an oil painting by veteran Julian Scott

Tintype of a private in the 146th New York Zouaves, V Corps

KI The Killing Ground; LE Lee Takes Command; MI War on the Mississippi; NA The Nation Reunited; OR Confederate Ordeal; RE Rebels Resurgent; SH The Road to Shiloh; SM Sherman's March; SP Spies, Scouts and Raiders; TE The Struggle for Tennessee; TR Death in the Trenches; TT Tenting Tonight; YA Twenty Million Yankees

125

Treasured Images of the Unknown

No relic or memento of the War was more treasured by the citizen soldiers of both sides than a photograph of themselves in uniform. Although paper *cartes de visite* were the cheapest, most popular way of preserving their proudest hour as patriotic fighting men, those who could afford it preferred pictures of better quality. They chose one-of-a-kind am-

brotypes and tintypes in which their images were printed on glass or japanned iron. Encased in decorative gilt frames such as those shown on these pages, the photographs have survived long after the vicissitudes of time caused the identities of the men in the pictures to be lost.

In 1900, an old Confederate reflecting on the forgotten thousands of his genera-

tion, who, like these men, had gone off to war, nostalgically wrote: "No herald ever blew his trumpet in the market-place or on the housetops and told the story of their deeds to an assembled people, their statues do not stand in any national Valhalla, crowned with laurel — they were born, they lived, they fought, they died — that was all."

MEMBERS OF THE 7TH TENNESSEE CAVALRY AND THEIR SLAVES

FEDERAL CAVALRYMEN PLAYING CARDS

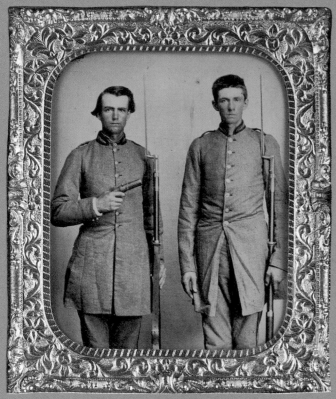

CONFEDERATE INFANTRY PRIVATES FROM TENNESSEE

CONFEDERATE PRIVATE, THE STONEWALL BRIGADE

MEMBER OF THE 14TH BROOKLYN "REDLEGS"

FEDERAL INFANTRYMAN

FEDERAL INFANTRYMAN

2ND LIEUTENANT OF THE VIRGINIA EIGHTH STAR BATTERY

CONFEDERATE INFANTRYMAN FROM GEORGIA

CORPORAL, FEDERAL ARTILLERY

FEDERAL CAVALRYMAN

INFANTRY OFFICER, ARMY OF NORTHERN VIRGINIA

CONFEDERATE SOLDIER FROM AUGUSTA COUNTY, VIRGINIA

CAVALRY LIEUTENANT, ARMY OF NORTHERN VIRGINIA

CORPORAL, 1ST GEORGIA INFANTRY

FEDERAL SAILOR

CONFEDERATE INFANTRYMEN

FEDERAL INFANTRYMAN FROM A WESTERN REGIMENT

MEMBER OF COMPANY B, CRAIG RIFLES, 28TH VIRGINIA

MEMBER OF THE 73RD NEW YORK (THE EXCELSIOR ZOUAVES)

MEMBER OF THE PENNSYLVANIA BUCKTAILS

CONFEDERATE 2ND LIEUTENANT, THE STONEWALL BRIGADE

SERGEANT OF THE CRESCENT REGIMENT, 24TH LOUISIANA

FEDERAL SAILOR

FEDERAL INFANTRYMAN

CONFEDERATE ARTILLERYMAN

CONFEDERATE MAJOR FROM ALABAMA, MEDICAL CORPS

FEDERAL ARTILLERYMAN

FEDERAL ZOUAVE

VIRGINIA ARTILLERYMAN

CONFEDERATE INFANTRYMEN, ARMY OF TENNESSEE

APPENDIX

Statistics kept for the Federal forces during the Civil War recorded only the total number of enlistments. Since many men enlisted more than once during the course of the War, it is difficult to arrive at the total number of men who served. The total number of enlistments in the Union forces between 1861 and 1865 was *2,778,304*.

The number of enlistments in the U.S. Army was *2,672,341* (including *2,489,836* whites; *178,975* blacks; *3,530* Indians).

The number of enlistments in the U.S. Navy and Marines was *105,963*. Taking the multiple enlistments into account, it is probable that about two million individuals served in the Federal ranks.

Owing to missing and destroyed records, Confederate statistics are difficult to compile. Estimates of total Confederate enlistments range from *750,000* to *1,227,890*.

STRENGTH OF THE ARMIES

Comparison of Federal and Confederate forces. (These numbers reflect men present for duty on the day given.)

	USA	CSA
January 1, 1861	14,663 (REG.)	----------
July 1, 1861	186,751	112,040
January 1, 1862	527,204	258,680
March 31, 1862	533,984	----------
June 30, 1862	----------	224,146
January 1, 1863	698,802	304,015
January 1, 1864	611,250	277,970
June 30, 1864	----------	194,764
January 1, 1865	620,924	196,764
March 31, 1865	657,747	----------
May 1, 1865	1,000,516	----------

Federal Army and Navy

Average age at time of enlistment: 25.8 years.
Average height at time of enlistment: 5'8''
Average weight at time of enlistment: 143½ lbs.
Civilian occupations:

FARMERS--------------------48%
MECHANICS----------------24%
LABORERS -----------------16%
COMMERCIAL --------------5%
PROFESSIONAL ------------3%
MISCELLANEOUS----------4%

Nationality:

NATIVE AMERICANS ----------------------75%
FOREIGN BORN----------------------------25%

The half million foreign-born troops came from:
Germany, 175,000; Ireland, 150,000;
England, 50,000; Canada, 50,000; Others, 75,000.

Confederate Army and Navy

No complete statistics exist for Confederate volunteers. In one study of 11,000 men enlisting in 1861-62 from eleven states, the age range was 18-35 years.

A second study of 9,000 men listed in 107 muster rolls from seven states (including the city of New Orleans) shows the following civilian occupations:

FARMERS--------------------69%
LABORERS -----------------5.3%
TRADE & MECHANICS ---9%
COMMERCIAL --------------5%
STUDENTS-------------------8%
PROFESSIONAL -----------2.1%
OTHER-----------------------1.6%

The Regiment as called for by Confederate and Federal regulations.

Field and Staff

1 Colonel
1 Lieutenant Colonel
1 Major
1 Adjutant
1 Quartermaster
1 Surgeon
2 Assistant Surgeons
1 Chaplain (none in Confederate
  regulations)
1 Sergeant Major
1 Quartermaster Sergeant
1 Commissary Sergeant
1 Hospital Steward
2 Principal Musicians

Company

1 Captain
1 First Lieutenant
1 Second Lieutenant
1 First Sergeant
4 Sergeants
8 Corporals
2 Musicians

1 Wagoner
82 Privates

10 Companies -----------------845 to 1,010 officers and men
Field and staff ------15 officers and noncommissioned officers.

Heavy Artillery Regiments (U.S.) 12 Companies-1,800 officers and men.

Organization of an Army

2 Battalions = 1 Regiment
3- 4 Regiments = 1 Brigade
3 Brigades = 1 Division
3 Divisions = 1 Corps

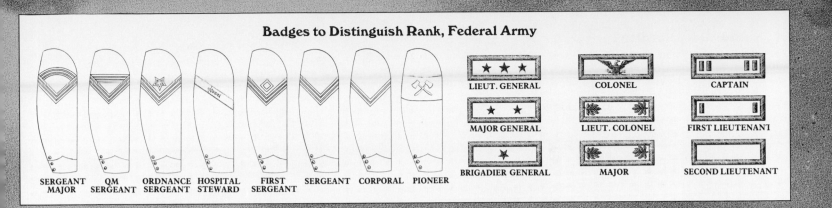

Badges to Distinguish Rank, Federal Army

SERGEANT MAJOR | QM SERGEANT | ORDNANCE SERGEANT | HOSPITAL STEWARD | FIRST SERGEANT | SERGEANT | CORPORAL | PIONEER

LIEUT. GENERAL | COLONEL | CAPTAIN
MAJOR GENERAL | LIEUT. COLONEL | FIRST LIEUTENANT
BRIGADIER GENERAL | MAJOR | SECOND LIEUTENANT

Badges to Distinguish Rank, Confederate Army

SERGEANT MAJOR | QM SERGEANT | ORDNANCE SERGEANT | FIRST SERGEANT | SERGEANT | CORPORAL

GENERAL
COLONEL | CAPTAIN
LIEUTENANT COLONEL | FIRST LIEUTENANT
MAJOR | SECOND LIEUTENANT

Federal Casualties

Federal Army

Killed in action or mortally wounded ----------------------------------110,100   67,088 KIA
43,012 MW

Died of disease ---------------------224,580
Died as prisoners of war -------------30,192
Nonbattle deaths ---------------------4,114 accident
4,944 drowned
520 murdered
104 killed after capture
391 suicide
267 executed by
Federal authorities
64 executed by the enemy
313 sunstroke
2,043 other causes
12,121 cause not stated
Total nonbattle deaths ----------------24,881
Wounded in action --------------------275,175

Federal Navy

Killed in action or mortally wounded ---1,804
Died of disease or accident ----------------3,000
Wounded in action ------------------------2,226

Total casualties, 1861 to 1865 ------------642,427

Confederate Casualties
(statistics incomplete)

Confederate Army

Killed in action or mortally wounded ---94,000
Died of disease -------------------------164,000
Died as prisoners of war--------------------31,000
Wounded in action ------------------------194,026
Total casualties, 1861 to 1865 ------------483,026

Confederate Navy No statistics available

Federal General Officers killed or mortally wounded in battle

Army Commanders

Maj. Gen. James B. McPherson ------Atlanta

Corps Commanders

Maj. Gen. Joseph K. Mansfield -------Antietam
Maj. Gen. John F. Reynolds ----------Gettysburg
Maj. Gen. John Sedgwick -------------Spotsylvania

Division Commanders

Maj. Gen. Isaac I. Stevens -------------Chantilly
Maj. Gen. Philip Kearny ---------------Chantilly
Maj. Gen. Jesse L. Reno ---------------South Mountain
Maj. Gen. Israel B. Richardson -------Antietam
Maj. Gen. Amiel W. Whipple ---------Chancellorsville
Maj. Gen. Hiram G. Berry -------------Chancellorsville
Maj. Gen. James S. Wadsworth ------Wilderness
Maj. Gen. David A. Russell ----------Opequon (1864)
Brig. Gen. William H. Wallace -------Shiloh
Brig. Gen. Thomas Williams ----------Baton Rouge
Brig. Gen. James S. Jackson-----------Chaplin Hills
Brig. Gen. Isaac P. Rodman -----------Antietam
Brig. Gen. Thomas G. Stevenson-----Spotsylvania
Brig. Gen. (Brevet) James A.
    Mulligan -------------------------------Winchester (1863)

Brigade Commanders

32 Brigadier Generals, 35 Colonels serving as brigade commanders. Total: 67

Confederate Generals killed or mortally wounded in battle

Army Commanders

Gen. Albert Sidney Johnston ----------Shiloh

Corps Commanders

Lieut. Gen. Thomas J. Jackson -------Chancellorsville
Lieut. Gen. Leonidas Polk-------------Pine Mountain
Lieut. Gen. Ambrose P. Hill ---------Petersburg

Division Commanders

Maj. Gen. William D. Pender ---------Gettysburg
Maj. Gen. J.E.B. Stuart ----------------Yellow Tavern
Maj. Gen. William H. Walker --------Atlanta
Maj. Gen. Robert E. Rodes-----------Opequon (1864)
Maj. Gen. Stephen D. Ramseur ------Cedar Creek
Maj. Gen. Patrick R. Cleburne -------Franklin
Brig. Gen. John Pegram----------------Hatcher's Run

62 Brigade Commanders

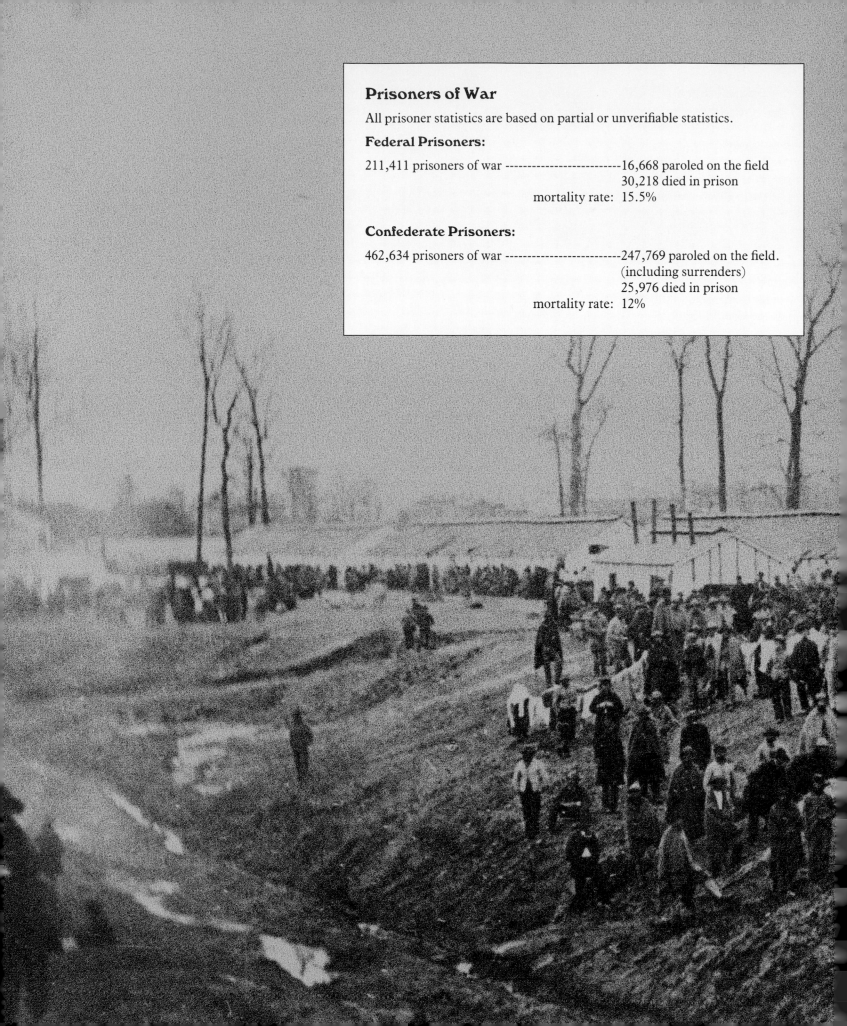

Prisoners of War

All prisoner statistics are based on partial or unverifiable statistics.

Federal Prisoners:

211,411 prisoners of war ------------------------16,668 paroled on the field
                                          30,218 died in prison
                        mortality rate: 15.5%

Confederate Prisoners:

462,634 prisoners of war ------------------------247,769 paroled on the field.
                                          (including surrenders)
                                          25,976 died in prison
                        mortality rate: 12%

The Bloodiest Battles
Total casualties

Gettysburg
Federal 23,053 -------- Confederate 28,063

Seven Days Battles
Federal 15,849 -------- Confederate 20,614

Chickamauga
Federal 16,170 -------- Confederate 18,454

**Chancellorsville/
Second Fredericksburg**
Federal 16,845 -------- Confederate 12,764

Antietam
Federal 12,410 -------- Confederate 10,316

Second Manassas/Chantilly
Federal 16,054 -------- Confederate 9,286

Shiloh
Federal 13,047 -------- Confederate 10,694

Fredericksburg
Federal 12,653 -------- Confederate 5,309

Regimental Losses

Federal

Most men killed or died of wounds during term of service.
1st Maine Heavy Artillery* ---------------- 23 officers, 400 men
5th New Hampshire Infantry ------------ 18 officers, 277 men
Most men killed or died of wounds in a single battle.
1st Maine Heavy Artillery ---------------- *Petersburg, June 18, 1864
                                                                                210 killed
5th New York Infantry -------------------- 2nd Bull Run, August 30, 1862
                                                                      117 killed

*Heavy Artillery regiments had greater numerical
strength than infantry and took greater casualties.

Confederate

Most casualties suffered during a single battle.

26th North Carolina ------ Gettysburg ----------------- 86 killed 588 wounded
6th Alabama ---------------- Seven Pines ---------------- 91 killed 277 wounded
4th North Carolina ------- Seven Pines ---------------- 77 killed 286 wounded
44th Georgia ---------------- Mechanicsville ------------ 71 killed 264 wounded
1st South Carolina Rifles Gaines Mill ---------------- 81 killed 140 wounded

Due to incomplete or missing records, no accurate losses can be determined
after July 1863.

A Gallery of Distinguished Postbellum Careers

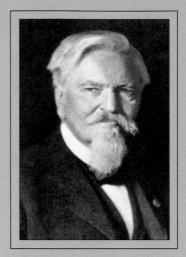

GEN. SIMON B. BUCKNER, C.S.A. (1823-1914), editor, Louisville *Courier;* Governor of Kentucky, 1887-1890; vice presidential nominee, 1896.

GEN. LEWIS "LEW" WALLACE, U.S.A. (1827-1905), Governor of New Mexico Territory, 1878-1881; Minister to Turkey, 1881-1885; author of *Ben Hur.*

GEN. JOSHUA L. CHAMBERLAIN, U.S.A. (1828-1914), Governor of Maine, 1866-1870; President of Bowdoin College, 1871-1883; Maj. Gen., Maine Militia.

GEN. WILLIAM MAHONE, C.S.A. (1826-1895), President, Norfolk & Petersburg Railroad; Republican leader in Virginia; U.S. Senate, 1880-1882.

GEN. NELSON A. MILES, U.S.A. (1839-1925), Col., 5th Infantry, 1866-1880; Indian campaigns, 1869-1891; General in Chief, U.S. Army, 1895-1903.

CAPT. OLIVER WENDELL HOLMES, U.S.A. (1841-1935), Massachusetts Supreme Court, 1883-1902; Associate Justice, U.S. Supreme Court, 1902-1932.

COL. JOHN S. MOSBY, C.S.A. (1833-1916), Consul to Hong Kong, 1878-1885; land agent in Colorado and assistant attorney, Dept. of Justice, 1904-1910.

GEN. FITZHUGH LEE, C.S.A. (1835-1905), Governor of Virginia, 1885-1889; Consul General to Havana, 1896-1898; Corps commander in Cuba, 1898.

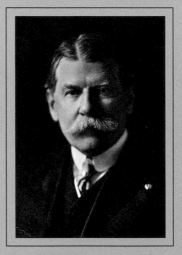

COL. HORACE PORTER, U.S.A. (1837-1921), military secretary to Grant, 1865-1872; Ambassador to France, 1897-1905; delegate to The Hague Conference, 1907.

GEN. JOSEPH WHEELER, C.S.A. (1836-1906), U.S. Congress, 1883-1900; commanded a division in Cuba, 1898, and a brigade in the Philippines, 1900.

William McKinley, former captain in the 23rd Ohio, takes the oath of office as 24th President of the United States in 1897.

Artistry with a Camera

Federal General Robert Tyler (*standing, second from right*) and his staff pose on a hillside near Culpeper, Virginia, in 1863, for photographer Timothy O'Sullivan.

This bulky sliding-box wooden camera was the Civil War photographer's basic equipment. The inner box, with its 8-by-10-inch glass negative, slides forward and back to sharpen the image; the knob on the front moves the lens for finer focusing.

The American Civil War was the first conflict to be widely photographed, and the results shocked the home fronts on both sides with the realities of warfare. At the same time, the War transformed the infant science of photography into a full-fledged industry, as new methods of mass production met the rising demand for pictures. *Carte de visite* soldier portraits and battlefield views sold by the millions, newspapers snapped up photographs from which to engrave their illustrations, and the combination catapulted a few photographers to fame.

The most renowned among them was Mathew Brady, who in fact took only a few of the combat-zone pictures he sold under his name. In 1861, Brady was a noted portraitist with thriving studios in Washington and New York — and failing eyesight; his genius during the War lay in financing and fielding a number of so-called operatives to bring back the images he sought. Though Brady denied his agents credit at the time, recognition eventually came to many, including Timothy O'Sullivan, who photographed the scene opposite.

The Civil War photographer's task was arduous, his equipment bulky and fragile, and his mission — to carry out a delicate chemical process in primitive conditions — sometimes brought him under enemy fire. He began every photograph by first preparing a so-called wet-plate glass negative, using two chemical baths in his elaborate mobile darkroom. He then had about 15 minutes in which to slide the plate into the camera, expose it and develop it before it dried. Light, dust or water could ruin the plate; long exposure times — 15 to 30 seconds on sunny days — limited him to motionless subjects. Yet the quantity and quality of the photographs created by these enterprising artists of the camera was astounding, as the representative works on these pages demonstrate.

Attended by a crowd of well-wishers in Detroit, the 1st Michigan Infantry receives its colors in May of 1861. Photographer Jex Bardwell's image of the ceremony is marred by a crack across the glass negative.

Captain Guy V. Henry's Battery B of the 1st U.S. Artillery awaits inspection under the summer sun on Morris Island, South Carolina, during the 1863 seige of

Charleston. The photograph is one of more than 40 views of the unsuccessful campaign made by the photographic team of Haas and Peale.

The regimental band of the 114th Pennsylvania assembles under the trees at Brandy Station, Virginia, in April of 1864. The portrait is one of many winter camp scenes taken by Timothy O'Sullivan during the Army of the Potomac's five-month respite before the Wilderness Campaign.

Men of Company A, 4th Vermont Infantry, lounge in camp near the Virginia front. The photographer, G. H. Houghton of Brattleboro, Vermont, traveled to the war zone in 1862 and again in 1863 to photograph his home state's regiments; nearly 100 of his images of army life have survived.

Newly recruited members of Company A, 5th Georgia Volunteers, with their black servant, gather before their tent in May of 1861. The *CR* on their tent identifies them as the Clinch Rifles. The photographer's name, like that of most Confederate photographers, has been lost.

Men of Company M, 3rd Rhode Island Heavy Artillery, put two 100-pounder Parrot rifles into action, firing on Fort Sumter from Battery Rosecrans on Morris

Island, in the autumn of 1863. An empty gun carriage at right in this photograph by Haas and Peale had held a third 100-pounder, until it burst.

Federal II Corps commissary wagons line up in shallow water to receive provisions from incoming barges at Belle Plain, Virginia, which served as Grant's supply and

communication center for two weeks in May 1864. James Gardner photographed the operation while the fighting raged at nearby Spotsylvania Court House.

Townspeople of Paris, Illinois, congregate in the spring of 1862 to see their local volunteers off to the front, in this ambrotype by an anonymous photographer. The wagons, loaded with the soldiers' gear, are bound for the railroad station, and in the background stands the Edgar County Courthouse, where lawyer Abraham Lincoln once argued cases.

Men of South Carolina's Palmetto Battalion of Light Artillery stage a mock drill for the anonymous photographer at their emplacement on the Stono River near Charleston, in 1861. Their guidon identifies the unit as Company F.

Federal soldiers watch from the ramparts of Nashville's Fort Negley in this study of the fort and terrain made by photographer George M. Barnard for Sherman's

engineers in March of 1864. When Barnard later published his war photographs, *Harper's Weekly* praised their "delicacy, scope and fidelity."

Sailors and marines crowding the deck of the U.S. gunboat *Mendota* use checkers and a banjo to pass their idle time in March 1865. The *Mendota* was on picket duty at the mouth of the James River when an unnamed photographer working for Mathew Brady photographed her racially mixed crew.

Two Federal supply ships lie peacefully alongside a wharf at the captured Confederate landing below Drewry's Bluff, Virginia, in April of 1865. The ships are en route down the James River with Federal artillery withdrawn from Petersburg after Richmond's surrender. The photograph is probably by Andrew J. Russell.

Black Union soldiers excavate a canal devised by General Benjamin Butler as a short cut at Dutch Gap, a horseshoe bend in the James River, in this 1864 Russell photograph. The sand-and-timber bombproof *(center)* protected the men against shells from nearby Fort Darling. When, after 20 weeks of digging, the last earth was blasted away, the canal proved too shallow for navigation.

A IX Corps wagon train trundles out of Petersburg on April 10, 1865, carrying rations and other supplies for Federal troops around the fallen city. The photograph

was taken by John Reekie, a former Brady assistant then working for Alexander Gardner.

Visitors to the Union works at Petersburg in May of
1865 examine the warren of bombproofs in which
Federal officers and men had lived during the six-
month seige; the barrels, lined with mud, served as
chimneys. When Alexander Gardner published this
picture in his *Photographic Sketchbook*, he took
care to credit it, "Negative by T. O'Sullivan; Posi-
tive by A. Gardner."

This carefree, unbloodied squad of the well-to-do Washington Artillery, one of Louisiana's oldest militia units, includes one fellow (*right*) wearing a mess tin on his head. Before the eager volunteers set off for the War in 1861, with a French restaurant chef to serve them, New Orleans photographer J. W. Petty visited their mustering-in camp.

Captured Confederate artillery pieces — field and seige guns, caissons, limbers and *(foreground)* a traveling field forge — fill a Richmond landing in May 1865,

awaiting shipment North. The photograph was made by Andrew J. Russell, a Union captain and the only military photographer on either side during the War.

In a canalboat full of furniture, blacks recently freed by Lee's surrender to Grant at Appomattox wait for the mules that will tow them out of the occupied city of

Richmond. This April 1865 view of the fallen Confederate capital is one of a series by Alexander Gardner.

ACKNOWLEDGMENTS

The editors wish to thank the following individuals and institutions for their valuable assistance in the preparation of this volume:

California: Vista — Kean E. Wilcox.

Michigan: Detroit — Dr. William Phenix, Historic Fort Wayne.

Pennsylvania: Carlisle — Randy Hackenburg, Michael J. Winey, U.S. Army Military History Institute.

Virginia: Alexandria — Sue Farr, Marilyn Burke, Lee-Fendall House. Richmond — David Hahn, Museum of the Confederacy. Waynesboro — Tom Farish.

Washington, D.C.: Eveline Nave, Library of Congress.

PICTURE CREDITS

Credits from left to right are separated by semicolons; from top to bottom by dashes.

Cover: Civil War memorabilia photographed at Lee-Fendall House, Alexandria, Virginia, by Michael Latil. 2-5: Maps by Peter McGinn. 10, 11: Painting by William T. Trego, courtesy The Pennsylvania Academy of Fine Arts, Philadelphia, gift of Fairman Rogers. 12: Painting by William Ludwell Sheppard, Museum of the Confederacy, Richmond, Va., photographed by Katherine Wetzel. 13: Painting by G. Grato, courtesy N. S. Meyer, Inc., photographed by Herbert Orth. 14, 15: Painting by Julian Scott, Smithsonian Institution No. CT-80-1290. 16, 17: Painting by Winslow Homer, The Metropolitan Museum of Art, gift of Mrs. William F. Milton, 1923. 18, 19: Painting by Julian Scott, West Point Museum Collections, U.S. Military Academy, photographed by Henry Groskinsky. 20, 21: Painting by Charles Hoffbauer, Virginia Historical Society, Richmond, Va., photographed by Henry Groskinsky. 22, 23: Painting by Edward Arnold, Anglo-American Art Museum, Louisiana State University. 24, 25: Painting by Peter F. Rothermel, Collections of the State Museum of Pennsylvania, Historical and Museum Commission, photographed by Henry Groskinsky. 26, 27: Painting by Edwin Forbes, Library of Congress. 28, 29: Painting by Conrad Wise Chapman, Museum of the Confederacy, Richmond, Va., photographed by Larry Sherer. 30, 31: Painting by James Walker, courtesy of Chickamauga-Chattanooga NMP and Eastern National Park & Monument Association, Fort Oglethorpe, Georgia. 32, 33: Painting by Edward Lamson Henry, The Corcoran Gallery of Art, gift of The American Art Association, 1900. 34, 35: Painting by Thure de Thulstrup, courtesy Seventh Regiment Fund, Inc., New York, photographed by Al Freni. 36: Painting by Thomas Waterman Wood, West Point Museum Collections, U.S. Military Academy. 37: Painting by Gilbert Gaul, Birmingham Museum of Art, Birmingham, Alabama, gift of John E. Meyer, photographed by George Flemming. 38: The Western Reserve Historical Society, Cleveland, Ohio — Library of Congress. 39: Massachusetts Commandery of the Military Order of the Loyal Legion of the United States and the U.S. Army Military History Institute (MASS-MOLLUS/USAMHI), copied by A. Pierce Bounds — Old State House, Little Rock, Arkansas. 40: The Western Reserve Historical Society, Cleveland, Ohio — Library of Congress. 41: National Archives Neg. No. 111-B-4405 — courtesy Don Troiani, photographed by Al Freni. 42: Andrew D. Lytle Collections, LLMVC, Louisiana State University Libraries — Collection of State Historical Museum, Mississippi Department of Archives and History, Jackson, Mississippi, photographed by Gib Ford. 43: Museum of the Confederacy, Richmond, Va. — painting by Conrad Wise Chapman, Valentine Museum, Richmond, Va. 44: From *The Navies*, Vol. 6, *The Photographic History of the Civil War*, edited by Francis Trevelyan Miller, The Review of Reviews Co., New York, 1912 — South Caroliniana Library, University of South Carolina. 45: Library of Congress. 46: Courtesy The Mariners' Museum, Newport News, Virginia — Indiana Historical Society. 47: U.S. Army Military History Institute (USAMHI), copied by A. Pierce Bounds — painting by James Lincoln, Rhode Island Historical Preservation Commission, photographed by Henry Groskinsky. 48: Albert Shaw Collection, Review of Reviews *Photographic History of the Civil War*, copied by Larry Sherer — Museum of the Confederacy, Richmond, Va., photographed by Larry Sherer — Library of Congress. 49: Valentine Museum, Richmond, Va. — The Western Reserve Historical Society, Cleveland, Ohio. 50: Museum of the Confederacy, Richmond, Va., photographed by Larry Sherer — Library of Congress. 51: Alonzo M. Keeler Collection, Michigan Historical Collections, Bentley Historical Library, University of Michigan — Library of Congress — courtesy Chris Nelson, copied by Larry Sherer. 52: Museum of the Confederacy, Richmond, Va., copied by Larry Sherer — Museum of the Confederacy, Richmond, Va., photographed by Katherine Wetzel. 53: Museum of the Confederacy, Richmond, Va., photographed by Larry Sherer — courtesy Tom Farish, photographed by Michael Latil. 54: Museum of the Confederacy, Richmond, Va., photographed by Larry Sherer. 55: Courtesy Tom Farish, photographed by Michael Latil — National Archives Neg. No. 111-B-3475. 56: Library of Congress — National Archives Neg. No. 111-B-5032. 57: Painting by Robert Hinckley, U.S. Naval Academy Museum, photographed by Erin Monroney — Valentine Museum, Richmond, Va. 58: Courtesy Nick Picerno — Library of Congress. 59: Painting by John Ross Key, Museum of the Confederacy, Richmond, Va., photographed by Katherine Wetzel — from *Even More Confederate Faces*, by William A. Turner, Moss Publications, Orange, Virginia, 1983 — courtesy Kean E. Wilcox. 60: Museum of the Confederacy, Richmond, Va. — courtesy Don Troiani, photographed by Al Freni. 61: U.S. Army Engineer Museum, Ft. Belvoir, Virginia — Museum of the Confederacy, Richmond, Va. 62, 63: Library of Congress. 64: Drawing by Adalbert Johann Volck, M. and M. Karolik Collection, courtesy Museum of Fine Arts, Boston — Library of Congress. 65: Museum of the Confederacy, Richmond, Va., photographed by Katherine Wetzei — Valentine Museum, Richmond, Virginia — Museum of the Confederacy, Richmond, Virginia. 66: Courtesy Samuel P. Higginbotham II, photographed by Larry Sherer. 67: South Caroliniana Library, University of South Carolina — courtesy Richard F. Carlile and Karl Rommel, copied by Erin Monroney. 68: Courtesy D. Mark Katz — Library of Congress. 69: National Numismatic Collections, Smithsonian Institution — National Archives Neg. No. 111-B-21. 70: Courtesy Roger D. Hunt — courtesy Don Troiani, photographed by Al Freni. 71: Courtesy Roger D. Hunt — National Archives Neg. No. 111-B-3544. 72: The Western Reserve Historical Society, Cleveland, Ohio — Library of Congress (2). 73: Valentine Museum, Richmond, Virginia — Historical Collection, Galena Public Library. 74: National Archives Neg. No. 111-B-292 — courtesy Michael J. McAfee. 75: Old Court House Museum, Vicksburg, Mississippi — from *From Sumter to Shiloh; Battles and Leaders of the Civil War*, Castle Books, New York 1956. 76: Painting by H. Durand Brager, courtesy The Union League Club of New York, photographed by Paulus Leeser — Lee-Fendall House, Alexandria, Virginia, copied by Michael Latil — Follett House Museum, Sandusky, Ohio, photographed by Andy Cifranic. 77: Museum of the Confederacy, Richmond, Va.—MASS-MOLLUS/USAMHI, copied by A. Pierce Bounds. 78: Museum of the Confederacy, Richmond, Virginia, copied by Larry Sherer. 79: Courtesy William A. Turner — painting by Ernest L. Ipsen, West Point Museum Collections, U.S. Military Academy. 80: Library of Congress. 81: Kean Archives, Philadelphia, Pennsylvania — Library of Congress. 82: MASS-MOLLUS/USAMHI, copied by A. Pierce Bounds — courtesy T. Scott Sanders. 83: Museum of the Confederacy, Richmond, Va.— drawing by Alfred R. Waud, Library of Congress. 84: Painting by William H. Powell, Collection of the City of New York, City Hall, New York, photographed by Al Freni — Valentine Museum, Richmond, Va. 85: Courtesy Roger D. Hunt — courtesy Chris Nelson, copied by Michael Latil. 86: Courtesy Chris Nelson, photographed by Michael Latil — courtesy Norman Flayderman, photographed by Henry Groskinsky. 87: Hall of Flags, State House, Boston, photographed by Jack Leonard — (Orlando Poe Collection) Special Collections, U.S. Military Academy Library, copied by Jeremy Ross — City of Alexandria, Fort Ward Museum, photographed by Henry Beville. 88: Courtesy Ronn Palm — Museum of the Confederacy, Richmond, Va. 89: Museum of the Confederacy, Richmond, Va. 90: Painting by Charles Hoffbauer, Virginia Historical Society, Richmond, Va., photographed by Henry Groskinsky. 91: Library of Congress — The Western Reserve Historical Society, Cleveland, Ohio — courtesy Roger D. Hunt. 92: MASS-MOLLUS/USAMHI, copied by A. Pierce Bounds. 93: Painting by J. Harrison Mills, courtesy Seventh Regiment Fund Inc., photographed by Al Freni — The Western Reserve Historical Society, Cleveland, Ohio. 94: Courtesy Jan P. Reifenberg — L. M. Strayer Collection, copied by Brian Blauser. 95: National Archives Neg. No. 111-B-5046 — James C. Frasca Collection — courtesy Larry J. West. 96: Library of Congress — Ellinor Gadsden Papers, Special Collections, The University Library, Washington and Lee University, Lexington, Virginia. 97: Kean Archives, Philadelphia, Pennsylvania — Library of Congress. 98: Courtesy Soldier's and Sailor's Memorial Hall, Pittsburgh — watercolor by J. Ricon, Alabama Department of Archives and History, photographed by John E. Scott, Jr. 99: MASS-MOLLUS/USAMHI, copied by A. Pierce Bounds. 100: State Historical Society of Missouri — Library of Congress. 101: USAMHI, copied by A. Pierce Bounds — Library of Congress. 102: Courtesy Norman Flayderman, photographed by Henry Groskinsky — courtesy Kean E. Wilcox. 103: U.S. Marine Corps Museum, photographed by Larry Sherer — USAMHI, copied by A. Pierce Bounds — Valentine Museum, Richmond, Va. 104: Library of Congress — painting by Alfred R. Waud, American Heritage Picture Collection. 105: Drawing by Private Newman, Museum of the Confederacy, Richmond, Virginia, photographed by Katherine Wetzel. 106: Valentine Museum, Richmond, Virginia — courtesy William Gladstone Collection. 107: From *History of the Confederate States Navy,* by J. Thomas Scharf, A.M., LL.D. The Fairfax Press, 1977, used by permission of Crown Publishers Inc. 108: From *Even More Confederate Faces,* by William A. Turner, Moss Publications, Orange, Virginia, 1983 — National Archives Neg. No. 111-B-258. 109: Washington Light Infantry 1807, Charleston, S.C., photographed by Harold H. Norvell — National Archives Neg. No. 111-B-4687. 110: Courtesy William A. Turner — painting by Peter H. Balling, West Point Museum Collections, U.S. Military Academy, photographed by Henry Groskinsky. 111: Courtesy Chris Nelson. 112: Library of Congress — Museum of the Confederacy, Richmond, Va.— courtesy Roger D. Hunt. 113: Courtesy William A. Turner. 114: Courtesy Russ A. Pritchard, photographed by Larry Sherer — drawing by Alfred R. Waud, Library of Congress. 115: Library of Congress — National Archives Neg. No. 111-B-3839. 116: Courtesy Don Troiani, photographed by Henry Groskinsky — The Western Reserve Historical Society, Cleveland, Ohio. 117: Kean Archives, Philadelphia, Pennsylvania — USAMHI, copied by A. Pierce Bounds. 118: Courtesy Lloyd Ostendorf Collection, Dayton, Ohio. 119: Old Court House Museum, Vicksburg, Mississippi, photographed by John R. Miller — courtesy Wendell W. Lang Jr., Collection, copied by A. Pierce Bounds. 120: Virginia Military Institute Museum, Lexington, Virginia, photographed by Michael Latil — Library of Congress. 121: Library of Congress. 122: Confederate Memorial Hall, New Orleans, Louisiana, photographed by John R. Miller. 123: Library of Congress — Lee-Fendall House, copied by Michael Latil. 124: Courtesy California State Capitol Museum, Sacramento, California, photographed by Robert DiFranco — G.A.R. Memorial Hall Museum, Madison, Wisconsin. 125. Painting by William T. Trego, West Point Museum Collections, U.S. Military Academy, photographed by Henry Groskinsky — courtesy Daniel Miller, copied by Nemo Warr. 126: Courtesy Tom Farish, photographed by Michael Latil. 127: Courtesy Kean E. Wilcox. 128: Courtesy Tom Farish, photographed by Michael Latil — courtesy Kean E. Wilcox. 129: Courtesy Kean E. Wilcox; courtesy Tom Farish, photographed by Michael Latil — courtesy Tom Farish, photographed by Michael Latil; courtesy Kean E. Wilcox. 130: Courtesy Tom Farish, photographed by Michael Latil except top left courtesy Kean E. Wilcox. 131: Courtesy Tom Farish, photographed by Michael Latil; courtesy Paul DeHaan — courtesy Tom Farish, photographed by Michael Latil; courtesy Kean E. Wilcox. 132: Courtesy Tom Farish, photographed by Michael Latil; courtesy Kean E. Wilcox — courtesy Kean E. Wilcox; courtesy Tom Farish, photographed by Michael Latil. 133: Courtesy Tom Farish, photographed by Michael Latil, courtesy Kean E. Wilcox — courtesy Kean E. Wilcox; courtesy Tom Farish, photographed by Michael Latil. 134: Courtesy Tom Farish, photographed by Michael Latil, courtesy Ken E. Wilcox — courtesy Kean E. Wilcox; courtesy Tom Farish, photographed by Michael Latil. 135: Courtesy Tom Farish, photographed by Michael Latil. 136, 137: Photograph of the 2nd Michigan Infantry at Fort Wayne, Indiana, courtesy of the Burton Historical Collection of the Detroit Public Library, copied by Nemo Warr. 138, 139: Insignia from *Civil War Atlas* Plate 172, courtesy Frank & Marie-T. Wood Print Collections, Alexandria, Virginia — photograph of unidentified Union Artillery Battery at Morris Island, South Carolina, courtesy Library of Congress. 140, 141: Photograph of the United States National Military Cemetery, Alexandria, Virginia, courtesy The Western Reserve Historical Society, Cleveland, Ohio. 142, 143: Photograph of Confederate prisoners at Camp Morton, Indiana, courtesy The Western Reserve Historical Society, Cleveland, Ohio. 144: From *Simon Bolivar Buckner: Borderland Knight,* by Arndt M. Stickles. © 1940 The University of North Carolina Press. Reprinted by permission of the publisher; Library of Congress (8); National Archives Neg. No. SC-90118. 145, 146: Library of Congress. 147: George Eastman House, Rochester, New York, photographed by Vincent Rotella. 148, 149: Courtesy of the Burton Historical Collection of the Detroit Public Library, copied by Nemo Warr. 150, 151: Library of Congress. 152, 153: Library of Congress — courtesy Vermont Historical Society; Albert Shaw Collection, Review of Reviews, *Photographic History of the Civil War,* copied by Larry Sherer. 158, 159: Courtesy Lloyd Ostendorf Collection, Dayton, Ohio; Library of Congress. 160, 161: (Orlando Poe Collection) Special Collections, U.S. Military Academy Library, copied by Henry Groskinsky. 162, 163: Photri Inc., Alexandria, Virginia. 164, 165: Library of Congress; State Historical Society of Wisconsin. 166, 167: Library of Congress. 168, 169: Special Collections, Van Pelt Library, University of Pennsylvania; USAMHI, copied by A. Pierce Bounds. 170-173: Library of Congress.